DISABILITY RIGHTS LAW AND POLICY

International and National Perspectives

Editors: Mary Lou Breslin and Silvia Yee
Afterword: Arlene B. Mayerson

Papers Conceived and Commissioned by the Disability Rights Education and Defense Fund (DREDF)

Transnational Publishers

Published and distributed by *Transnational Publishers, Inc.*
Ardsley Park
Science and Technology Center
410 Saw Mill River Road
Ardsley, NY 10502

Phone: 914-693-5100
Fax: 914-693-4430
E-mail: info@transnationalpubs.com
Web: www.transnationalpubs.com

Library of Congress Cataloging-in-Publication Data

Disability rights law and policy : international and national perspectives / edited by Silvia Yee ; foreword and introduction by Mary Lou Breslin ; after-word by Arlene
Mayerson ; the Disability Rights Education and Defense Fund.
p. cm.
Includes bibliographical references.
ISBN 1-57105-239-9 (hardcover)—ISBN 1-57105-240-2 (pbk.)
1. People with disabilities—Legal status, laws, etc. 2. People with disabilities—Legal status, laws, etc.—United States. I. Yee, Silvia. II. Disability Rights Education and Defense Fund.

K637.D577 2002
342'.087—dc21
2002027102

The article by Arlene B. Mayerson & Silvia Yee, "The ADA and Models of Equality," was originally published in 62 *Ohio St. L.J.* 535 (2001).

The opinions expressed by the authors in these collected papers are those of the individual authors, and do not necessarily reflect the views of the Disability Rights and Education Defense Fund, the sponsors of the *Principles to Practice* Symposium, or those of the editors.

Cover photo by Tom Olin.

Manufactured in the United States of America

Disability community advocates around the globe during the past quarter century have been working to challenge widespread discrimination, exclusion and segregation of people with disabilities by asserting their human and individual rights. The impact of their advocacy resonates from the United Nations to the constitutions of emerging nations, from laws enacted at the country level to local policies that recognize the rights of children and adults with disabilities to be treated equally and with dignity.

This book, which owes its inspiration to the strength of their commitment and to the promise their victories hold for the future, is dedicated to these heroes.

Acknowledgments

Many thanks to DREDF for making this book, an outcome of the *Principles to Practice* Symposium, a reality. Special thanks goes to my dear friends Arlene Mayerson and Pat Wright, without whose brains, chutzpah and commitment to the disability rights movement none of this would have been possible.

Mary Lou Breslin

I would like to give special thanks to Mary Lou Breslin and DREDF for the opportunity to edit this volume of articles. Their trust and high level of dedication challenges me never to settle for easy answers. I would also like to thank my parents, Gam and Jean Yee, who have shaped me simply by always being there.

Silvia Yee

Contents

Disability Rights Education and Defense Fund (DREDF)

Founded in 1979 by a unique alliance of people with disabilities and parents of children with disabilities, the Disability Rights Education and Defense Fund (DREDF) is the leading national law and policy center in the United States dedicated to protecting and advancing the civil rights of people with all disabilities. With offices in Berkeley, California and Washington, D.C., DREDF carries out its mission within the United States through strategies that include law and policy reform, litigation, advocacy, technical assistance, and education and training of attorneys, advocates, people with disabilities, and parents of children with disabilities. DREDF is also committed to building alliances with the broad civil rights community, and has maintained an uninterrupted 22 year service on the executive committee of the national Leadership Conference on Civil Rights (LCCR), a coalition of over 180 organizations promoting the civil rights of disenfranchised groups.

DREDF has worked successfully with both U.S. political parties to ensure and extend the civil rights of people with disabilities. Playing a pivotal role, DREDF attorneys and policy advocates have worked with the United States Congress on key civil rights legislation affecting people with disabilities, including the Civil Rights Restoration Act, the Handicapped Children's Protection Act, the Individuals with Disabilities Education Act (IDEA), and the Fair Housing Amendments Act. DREDF has been widely recognized, honored and credited for playing a key leadership role in the passage of the landmark 1990 Americans with Disabilities Act (ADA). In the area of litigation, DREDF represents clients, serves as co-counsel, and files *amicus curiae* briefs in the appellate courts and the U.S. Supreme Court. The organization has also authored, co-authored or coordinated *amicus* briefs on behalf of plaintiffs, the disability community and members of Congress in most of the disability rights cases heard by the U.S. Supreme Court; DREDF's leading edge law reform work has educated the Court about key disability rights issues for over two decades. DREDF handles an average of 25 litigation matters at any given time.

DREDF maintains close ties with the disability community nationwide. Hundreds of calls are received monthly from individuals seeking information about their legal rights, and the organization annually provides technical assistance, training and advocacy assistance to over 8000 people with disabilities and parents of children with disabilities on matters of disability law. Since 1990, DREDF has provided training on the ADA to over 50,000 people from virtually all 50 states. Combined with the highest level of policy and legal skills, this familiarity with the real issues adults and children with disabilities face day-to-day makes DREDF uniquely credible and influential in shaping law and policy reform. For over a decade DREDF staff have invested in the next generation of disability civil rights advocates and attorneys by operating a disability rights legal clinic in collaboration with San Francisco Bay Area law schools, and teaching a disability rights course at the University of California Boalt Hall School of Law.

DREDF welcomes the opportunity to offer its considerable advocacy experience to the world-wide disability community, and is eager to continue collaborative efforts with other disability organizations and groups in Europe, Asia, Africa, and Central America in fostering the international community's recognition of disability as an area of human rights concern.

Preface

CONCEIVING *FROM PRINCIPLES TO PRACTICE*

The idea to convene a group of international disability rights attorneys and advocates sharpened into focus during a conversation among a small group of us in 1999 as we sat around the conference table at the Berkeley, California office of the U.S.-based Disability Rights Education and Defense Fund (DREDF). While our work in the disability rights movement during the previous two decades had focused primarily on supporting and advancing domestic disability rights law and policy, throughout the 1990s we had also been meeting with delegation after delegation of international disability rights advocates visiting the United States. Most wanted to learn how the disability rights movement had come about, and how it had led to the enactment of the landmark 1990 Americans with Disabilities Act (ADA). Spurred by DREDF's role in the process leading to the enactment of the ADA, Pat Wright, DREDF's Governmental Affairs Director, Marilyn Golden, the organization's Policy Analyst, and I (one of DREDF's founders, serving as its Executive Director in the late 1980s, and working since then in a Jill-of-all-trades policy and advisory capacity) had also visited a total of 17 countries at the invitation of disability groups and organizations. We had participated in meetings and conferences focused on promoting a rights-based disability policy model, and we had consulted with people with disabilities and disability rights attorneys. In some countries we met with community groups and worked with them to develop ways to strengthen their institutional capacity for community organizing, organizational development and public relations. In other cases our colleagues also asked us to join them in meetings with political and government leaders whose support for anti-discrimination legislation they hoped to enlist or reinforce.

Through these experiences we learned first hand that people with disabilities, working city by city, country by country, region by region, were changing the way their governments and their societies responded to disability. They had built tremendous momentum toward the goal of establishing disability as a recognized individual and human rights issue in country-based laws, constitutions and legal instruments. Indeed, in many countries some form of disability rights law was in the pipeline or had already been enacted. Those of us who have had the privilege of meeting and working with advocates from abroad have come to appreciate the extraordinary tenacity and commitment of the disability community in so many countries. Furthermore, we also understood first hand some of the challenges they were facing as they struggled to turn their visions into reality because we had faced and continue to face similar ones in the United States.

Thus, our conversation turned to how we could draw on our expertise to support and contribute to this global phenomenon. We had learned from many of our international colleagues that they had had few opportunities to meet one another and to collaborate and exchange ideas specifically about disability anti-discrimination reforms. Apparently a meeting or conference focusing exclusively on country-based anti-discrimination law reform had never been convened, though the need for it had been discussed among many legal activists. Such an opportunity, we thought, would promote a much-needed discussion of basic theoretical and practical matters that legal advocates in every country were confronting. These included the role of prejudice in disability discrimination, theoretical underpinnings to the rule of law, how disability should be defined or redefined in a non-discrimination model, practical implementation issues related to accommodation, barrier removal, enforcement, and due process, the role of litigation, community organizing tactics, and education strategies. Such a gathering would also afford participants the opportunity to exchange information about their particular challenges, goals, strategies, and experiences, including failures as well as successes. Furthermore, we envisioned that it would foster a network through which everyone could exchange information and resources, seek feedback and support during the process of developing legislation and policies, and discuss evolving case law.

Organizationally, DREDF has helped shape most federal disability rights laws enacted in the United States during the previous two decades. We have also litigated cutting-edge disability rights education and access cases, and been called on by members of Congress, the disability community, and plaintiffs to write and consult on *amicus curiae* briefs in cases heard by the U.S. Supreme Court. Throughout, we have provided legal technical assistance, advocacy support and legal rights training to people with disabilities and parents of children with disabilities. This day-to-day contact has been essential for our understanding and development of adequate policy responses to real, everyday experiences. What we had to offer an international group of disability rights attorneys and advocates concerned lessons we had learned from the disability community, as well as insight from an ongoing analysis of the legislative, administrative and judicial history of the major U.S. disability rights laws and policies. We also had long-standing ties with other U.S. non-governmental organizations (NGOs), as well as government representatives and individuals working in the disability civil rights field, who could contribute important viewpoints. We recognized, however, that the U.S. experience represented only one perspective. Many nations had achieved important gains since 1990 and their experiences were equally vital to the dialogue. We had much to learn from one another. Our colleagues internationally, therefore, would become essential partners in the process of making the meeting both a reality and a success. They would be enlisted not only to help identify countries that had enacted disability anti-discrimination laws, but also to identify attorneys and advocates, and especially individuals with disabilities who would be interested in attending. Finally, they would be called on to help shape the meeting agenda so that it would address our collective needs.

While our concept percolated, we set about presenting it to friends and colleagues, exploring various options for funding. At the same time that we were envisioning the meeting, the U.S. Social Security Administration (SSA) was exploring ways to celebrate the tenth anniversary of the ADA scheduled for 2000. Thanks to the leadership and vision of two exceptional individuals within SSA, Marie Strahan and Susan Daniels, then the Deputy Commissioner, Office of Disability and Income Security Programs, SSA championed the idea of such a meeting as an exciting and effective way to celebrate the ADA's tenth birthday, and at the same time create an opportunity to support and facilitate the work of disability rights advocates working internationally.

SSA provided significant sponsorship for the meeting, later entitled "From Principles to Practice—An International Disability Rights Symposium," and they brought eight additional federal agencies on board as sponsor-partners: the Presidential Task Force on Employment of Adults with Disabilities, the President's Committee on Employment of People with Disabilities, The Department of State, the Center for Mental Health Services, the National Council on Disability, the U.S. Agency for International Development, the U.S. Information Agency, and the Office of Special Education and Rehabilitative Services. Private support was also provided by the Ethyl Louise Armstrong Foundation and the Interchurch Organization for Development Cooperation (ICCO).

PLANNING THE SYMPOSIUM

From the outset we envisioned the Symposium as a forum that would afford participants an opportunity to share strategies and solutions, build and strengthen regional networks, discuss complex and cutting-edge legal theories and questions, and share case law developments. However, the process of molding that broad concept into a real plan for action required the best efforts of a stellar ensemble.

DREDF's directing attorney, Arlene Mayerson had the initial broad vision for the Symposium's legal content. Pat Wright, who first raised the idea for a meeting, urged that practical concerns of non-lawyer advocates such as community organizing and coalition building be given appropriate attention and time on the agenda. Pat also served as DREDF's liaison with the Social Security Administration. Marilyn Golden added her expertise from the perspective of a seasoned and experienced substantive disability rights trainer and policy expert. We decided early in the process to commission papers that would present in-depth examinations of central themes that concerned everyone working for anti-discrimination reforms. It was serendipitous that Theresia Degener, a renowned expert in international disability anti-discrimination law and an attorney and professor of law in Germany, happened to be a visiting professor at the University of California, Berkeley's Boalt School of Law while the Symposium was being planned. She provided invaluable consultation, guidance and advice throughout the process, and also co-drafted with Gerard Quinn, Lecturer in Law, National University of Ireland, the seminal paper "A Survey of International, Comparative and Regional Disability Law Reform" for the Symposium.

As the planning process gained momentum Jenny Kern, an attorney and former director of Whirlwind Women, an international wheelchair building project of women with disabilities, joined the team to assist with outreach and planning. Deborah Doctor managed logistics and helped with development, and Silvia Yee, a Canadian attorney-consultant, undertook essential legal research and assisted DREDF to obtain the laws of the various countries, facilitated translations, and commissioned and supervised the creation of English summaries. Jane West, a Washington, DC-based education consultant and longtime friend and supporter, consulted, advised, encouraged, and facilitated throughout the process.

THE SYMPOSIUM

Approximately one hundred-fifty invited participants from 57 countries, including sponsor-observers, attended the *Principles to Practice* Symposium held in Washington, DC in October 2000. Attorneys representing diverse disability groups, including people with psychiatric and developmental disabilities and people with AIDS, participated as did faculty from various law schools, governmental representatives, policy experts, and researchers who focus their efforts on issues related to disability discrimination. Many who attended were also individuals with disabilities or parents whose children have disabilities.

The broad goals of the four-day Symposium were:

- To launch an international working group of attorneys, policy and legislative experts, and individuals with disabilities who are working or wish to work for disability laws and policies in their respective countries;
- To share ideas about laws and policies, enforcement mechanisms and approaches to reforms;
- To discuss basic conceptual and legal principles that serve as the foundation for disability law and policy;
- To identify specific strategies and tactics that will help advance legal reforms; and
- To encourage ongoing communication that will enhance organizing capacity and establish closer ties between community and law reform advocates and lawyers.

Susan Daniels from SSA welcomed the participants. Justin Dart, Jr., a longtime national disability rights champion, also extended greetings as did Jonathan Young, then Associate Director for Disability for The White House, who welcomed the participants on behalf of President Bill Clinton, DREDF's Pat Wright and myself. The opening plenary session—simultaneously translated into four languages, as was the entire Symposium—set the stage for the days to follow with a presentation and discussion of the nature of prejudice as an underlying explanation of disability discrimination. Panelists from Kenya, Peru and the United States served as respondents.

The first full day of the Symposium opened with presentations describing the state of disability law globally. In other sessions, models of equality were considered by panelists from Costa Rica, South Africa and the United States, and the definition of disability as it relates to disability rights protections was discussed by panelists from The Netherlands and the United States. Additional plenary topics included the challenge of reconciling the dissonance between medical and social policy models in anti-discrimination legislation, and the emerging right under international and U.S. law to community integration for people with disabilities living in institutions. Case law from the Organization of American States, the European Commission and the United States served as examples in the latter presentation. Effective community advocacy strategies were illustrated by case studies featuring India, Germany and the United States. The challenge of meaningful enforcement of anti-discrimination laws and policies were presented from the viewpoints of practitioners from South Africa, Hungary and the United States.

The Symposium also offered concurrent working groups on architectural accessibility, international development and civil society, transportation, employment under various social and economic circumstances, setting the goal of a UN convention on the rights of people with disabilities, and grassroots organizing and coalition building, and included "Open Space" sessions where participants could identify and discuss other topics of interest. Participants from Latin American, African, Pacific Rim and European Union countries used this opportunity to meet and strategize; others organized themselves around such topics as women's concerns and enforcement.

During the last day of the Symposium, participants met in regional groups to identify future needs and issues as well as ideas for collaboration. These recommendations, taken together with the outcomes of a written survey that asked participants to rank the relative importance of various issues for the future, informed the Symposium's final recommendations. Key recommendations fall into two categories: actions that the U.S. government should undertake and actions NGOs, other governments and the disability community should undertake.

Participants recommended that the U.S. government:

- Provide leadership and commit resources to an international effort aimed at advancing disability law and policy;
- Require that disability be recognized and specifically included in all internationally funded programs and initiatives but especially in those involving civil society, rule of law, citizen participation in government, and research concerned with human rights and equality;
- Ensure compliance with disability non-discrimination principles and policies in all international operations and programs;
- Encourage and participate in inter-governmental partnerships that support the local and regional law and policy reform initiatives of the disability community;
- Develop materials and provide training for law and policy advocates and community activists in the areas of self-determination, strategies for initiating and participating in public debate, community organizing, and public education. These activities could be carried out in the context of current U.S.-supported international programs that do not presently include disability, or as new initiatives.

Other general recommendations aimed at NGOs, other governments and the disability community included:

- Support for topical and general regional law and policy meetings, building on the network that began at the Symposium;
- Establishment of an Internet-based information clearinghouse that would support attorneys and community members by providing disability laws, policies, guidelines, standards,

sample judicial decisions, training materials, legal analysis, articles, enforcement models, disability discrimination-related research, links to affiliated sites, and related information;

- Increased fellowship and exchange opportunities for attorneys, policy analysts and community advocates who wish to study the legislative and policy models, enforcement approaches, community education strategies, and successes of other countries;
- Increased funds for targeted research that identifies obstacles to the advancement of laws and policies that challenge disability discrimination and that elucidate the need for such reforms.

AFTER THE SYMPOSIUM

While much was already taking place internationally at the time the Symposium was held, it contributed to the momentum by spurring alliance building in a variety of locales. In Costa Rica, Dr. Federico Montero brought back ideas and inspiration that has led to the formation of Costa Rica's first umbrella coalition of cross-disability organizations (El Foro por los Derechos Humanos de las Personas con Discapacidad). In turn, El Foro is reaching out to and building ties with Symposium participants from other Central American countries. Ireland hosted a one-day symposium on international disability issues in the spring of 2002 that was attended by Symposium participants from the United States and Asia. Several of the Symposium participants are now members of a new pan-European network of legal experts, recently formed under the European Commission's Social Action Programme to address disability discrimination.

DREDF staff continue to consult and work with advocates internationally, and we are building our web site with resources that the Symposium participants identified as important. Disability rights laws from over 45 countries are posted on the site. Short summaries in English are attached to each of the French and Spanish laws that we have listed in the Country Laws Index when a full English translation is not available. A list of Symposium participants and their contact information is also posted on the site as well as the papers that appear in this volume. In January 2002 DREDF established an international legal fellows program.

CONCLUSION

The articles in this volume, and the symposium for which they were produced, would not have been possible without the efforts of many committed, talented individuals. Marie Strahan and Susan Daniels, thank you for your whole hearted enthusiasm and your persistent efforts to raise the funds to ensure that the meeting was successful. Special thanks goes to the DREDF ensemble of staff, consultants and friends who have the highest standards of excellence and who always come through with an exceptional product—Arlene Mayerson, Pat Wright, Marilyn Golden and Jenny Kern for focusing us on substance and process; Silvia Yee for meeting the challenge of collecting the country-based disability rights laws and for meticulously editing the articles in this volume; Deborah Doctor for working with SSA's logistics contractors, and Susan Henderson for staying calm and managing a thousand details before, during and after the Symposium. Thanks too to Anna Bergman who managed the process of confirming participants, Cara Galbraith who, in consultation with Ken Stein collected vast amounts of materials in various languages for the gathering, and Wiltrud Harms, the librarian in charge of the United Nations Collection at Boalt Law School who contributed her expertise in the intricacies of UN documentation. Thanks also to Jane West, who worked with the authors of the articles prior to the Symposium, facilitated the plenary sessions, and kept us all on track. Recognition is incomplete without thanking the authors of the articles themselves, without whose effort, expertise and commitment there would be no book. Thank you! Last but certainly not least, many thanks to John Berger from Transnational Publishers who saw value in this unusual volume and who remained patient and committed as deadlines came and went. It has been a pleasure and an honor working with all of you.

Degener and Quinn conclude the first portion of their paper with the observation that "This global overview of discrimination laws for persons with disabilities gives rise to both hope and concern. The concern is that not every instance of anti-discrimination language in legislation may actually achieve or even aim at equal rights for disabled persons. National and international disability organisations need to act as watch dogs to ensure that their legislators do not use anti-discrimination language as a pretext while fundamentally adhering to a medical model of disability policy. But there is also clear evidence that anti-discrimination legislation for disabled persons is on the rise all over the world. With that fact, persons with disabilities can have real hope that disability policy will finally achieve the ideals of human rights and structural equality."

We hope that this book will affirm the extraordinary accomplishments of disability anti-discrimination advocates, attorneys and others working for equality for people with disabilities around the globe. We also hope that it will inspire future activists and become a useful tool as they face the challenges ahead.

Mary Lou Breslin
Disability Rights Education and Defense Fund (DREDF)
Berkeley, California, U.S.A.
April 2002

Introduction

BACKGROUND

Numbering six hundred million, people with disabilities represent almost one in ten of the world's population, and form one of its largest minorities. According to Mary Robinson, United Nations High Commissioner for Human Rights, "We know that persons with disabilities frequently live in deplorable conditions, and face physical and social barriers, which prevent their integration and full participation in the community. As a result, millions of adults and children throughout the world are segregated, deprived of virtually all their rights, and sometimes lead wretched and marginalized lives."[1] Former United Nations Secretary-General Javier Perez de Cuellar, in a 1998 report to the UN, echoed this observation. He said, "Equality of opportunity simply does not exist where a disabled child cannot go to school, where a disabled mother has no health care, where a disabled man cannot get training or a job, or where disabled people cannot move freely on the streets."[2]

HISTORICAL PERSPECTIVE

Historically, organized society has persecuted, segregated, and marginalized people with disabilities. Especially onerous examples during the early 20th century include pseudo-scientific rationales that spawned eugenics and sterilization policies, legitimized institutionalization, and led to the extermination of thousands of people with disabilities in Germany prior to World War II. While these policies and practices later gave way to a growing emphasis on charity, medical treatment and rehabilitation, they left behind bricks and mortar institutions where people

---

1 Mary Robinson, United Nations High Commissioner for Human Rights, Video Message to the International Seminar on Human Rights and Disability, Almåsa Conference Centre, Stockholm, Sweden (Nov. 5, 2000).

2 World Disability Report (Geneva, International Disability Foundation, 1999).

with disabilities continue to be warehoused today, and a legacy of prejudice and paternalism that remains deeply embedded in the social consciousness.

Spurred by the civil rights movements of the 1950s and 1960s, people with disabilities in the United States began to recognize and interpret the artificial restrictions placed on their lives as forms of oppression. Using advocacy, protest, law reform and group identity as primary tools, disability activists built a new political movement that sought equality and social justice. In doing so they called upon society itself to take responsibility for policies, barriers and stereotypes that isolated and excluded people with disabilities from community life.

The disability rights movement in the United States undeniably has served as a beacon for the international community by recognizing early in the process the role of discrimination and prejudice in shaping choices and opportunities. Following in a long civil rights tradition, the first Federal disability rights law, Section 504 of the 1973 Rehabilitation Act, set the stage for a new era by adopting the social model of disability policy. Not only did the law establish an anti-discrimination standard for covered entities, it also established all-important judicial remedies to discrimination. Equally as significant, Section 504 also empowered disability activists to examine their own experiences by using a rights-based analysis, thus sparking a grassroots political movement that built and sustained the community momentum that was required to enact the landmark 1990 Americans with Disabilities Act (ADA).

Equality of opportunity, accommodation and inclusion comprise the core principles of the ADA, a law that prohibits disability discrimination by private employers, state and local governments, public accommodations, and by public and private transportation and telecommunications. Since its enactment, over forty-five countries have also passed some form of disability anti-discrimination legislation or included disability specifically in the country's constitution. Meaningful implementation and enforcement of these new laws, however, remain a persistent challenge to governments and disability communities in most countries. Irrespective of these complications the very existence of the laws signifies a profound shift toward social awareness of disability discrimination.

The international community first recognized the social model of disability policy during the United Nations Decade of Disabled Persons (1983-1992). Leading up to the decade, the UN had passed various resolutions that led to the *World Programme of Action Concerning Disabled Persons*. It presents a comprehensive statement of both the goals of treatment and rehabilitation, and equal social and economic opportunity, justice and citizenship for people with disabilities, and even includes strategies countries are encouraged to employ to make its promise a reality. In 1993 the UN adopted the *Standard Rules on the Equalization of Opportunities for Persons with Disabilities*, which sets forth critical steps countries should take to fulfill the promise of equality established in the *World Programme of Action*. While the *Standard Rules* and the *World Programme of Action* are non-binding, they have established a blueprint for action.

Responding to increasing pressure from the international disability community, the UN General Assembly, on December 19, 2001, adopted a resolution to create an Ad Hoc Committee "to consider proposals for a comprehensive and integral international convention to protect and promote the rights and dignity of persons with disabilities"—a resolution that was first passed by the General Assembly's Third Committee on November 28, 2001.[3] Momentum towards achieving a convention continues to build this year, with the passage of a *Resolution on a comprehensive and integral international convention to promote and protect the rights and dignity of persons with disabilities* by the Commission for Social Development.[4] The Resolution recommends the adoption of the convention by the UN's high-level Economic and Social Council, including the convention's requirement for ECOSOC to remain apprised of the matter.

---

3 G.A. Res., 56th Sess. [on the report of the 3rd Committee on the draft resolution concerning a comprehensive and integral international convention to promote and protect the rights and dignity of persons with disabilities (A/56/583/Add.2)], U.N. Doc. A/RES/56/168 (2001).

4 Agenda item 3(b)(ii), adopted at the 40th Sess. of the Committee for Social Development (Feb. 11-27, 2002) available at <http://www.un.org/esa/socdev/csd/2002disabilityres(B).htm>.

Advocates have maintained that while existing UN human rights treaties, which now have been interpreted to recognize disability, offer significant potential to advance the rights of individuals with disabilities, they have been widely underutilized. Unquestionably the process of recasting disability policy internationally from the charity or medical model to the social model would accelerate if human rights instruments were employed more frequently on behalf of people with disabilities. The proposed Disability Convention, however, would unequivocally establish and elevate disability to its rightful place as an internationally recognized and enforceable human rights concern.

At the regional level, the Organization of American States (OAS) has enacted disability anti-discrimination legislation. The OAS is the first intergovernmental organization to adopt a binding human rights treaty on disability. In 1999 the OAS adopted the Inter-American Convention on the Elimination of All Forms of Discrimination Against Persons with Disabilities. It is the first regional treaty to define disability-based discrimination, though it does not provide for individual rights of enforcement.

By enacting the 1990 ADA the United States embarked on an historic journey. It sent the message to its own citizens as well as to the international community that it is both practical and socially beneficial to take steps to challenge disability-based discrimination. While the U.S. Supreme Court in a recent series of misguided decisions has redefined who is entitled to protection under the ADA, and somewhat narrowed the obligation of states to comply with it, practically speaking the ADA has permanently and dramatically altered the architectural and attitudinal landscape of the nation. Now that the principles of accessibility and accommodation are embedded in the public's consciousness, it will seem to future generations that it has always been so.

As Degener and Quinn so eloquently stated in their paper *A Survey of International, Comparative and Regional Disability Law Reform*, "[t]he UN Standard Rules of 1993 undoubtedly provided the key moral imperative for change on a worldwide basis, but there equally can be no doubt that the enactment of the Americans with Disabilities Act (ADA) showed that change was both possible and practicable."

THE PAPERS—*FROM PRINCIPLES TO PRACTICE*

Against this backdrop, topics were identified that reflected key historical, theoretical and practical issues and problems facing disability rights advocates and law reformers everywhere. Leading experts were invited to prepare papers and lead plenary discussions on their respective topics at the Symposium.

The dynamic nature of disability rights law and policy in the world today means that changes have inevitably taken place in national, regional and international laws since October, 2000. A number of the papers have been revised since the *Principles to Practice* Symposium took place, and all of the articles presented here have been edited and updated to reflect the state of the law through the end of the year 2000. A few articles incorporate legal developments, enactments and literature up to the spring of 2002. Because currency varies somewhat from article to article all of our authors have included their contact information (also available on the DREDF web site at http://www.dredf.org), and welcome reader inquiries concerning specific laws, jurisprudence or organizations that may have been amended since a given article's final submission for publication.

The articles, presented in this volume, are grouped into four thematic sections.

Part I—Disability Anti-Discrimination Law—The State of the World

While many countries have enacted some form of anti-discrimination legislation or included disability in the constitution, when the Symposium was being planned we did not know how many countries had taken such steps, and these important laws and amendments had not been collected in one place or analyzed to determine which disability model each had adopted. For the first time a comprehensive assessment has been undertaken and the results presented in a seminal article entitled *A Survey of International, Comparative and Regional Disability Law Reform* authored by Theresia Degener and Gerard Quinn. This work identifies and categorizes disability anti-discrimination law and policy, including instruments adopted by the United Nations, legislation and constitutional reforms at the level of individual countries, and recent regional reforms. An exceptional and much-needed contribution to the body of knowledge about disability anti-discrimination law, this article affirms that the disability rights movement has had a substantial impact worldwide, and inspires and motivates all those who care about advancing human and individual rights for people with disabilities globally. It also provided the contextual framework for the Symposium. Theresia Degener is Professor of Law, Administration and Organization, University of Applied Sciences Rheinland-Westfalen-Lippe, Bochum, Germany. Gerard Quinn is Lecturer in Law, National University of Ireland (Galway Campus).

Part II—Foundational Issues in the Use of Anti-Discrimination Law

This section contains three articles on the complex topics of disability prejudice, defining disability, and the dissonance between the welfare model and the civil rights model for disability law.

Observed broadly, prejudice is the irrational belief that another—or "other"—is different in a way that makes them inherently less worthy than ourselves and merits unequal treatment. Disability literature is just beginning to theoretically explore disability prejudice's complex history and the factors that root prejudice and fear so deeply in the human psyche in relation to disability. Since the social welfare model is so pervasive in disability public policy, we thought it important to start the conference with a discussion of prejudice as a common denominator for adopting a civil rights approach.

Two articles presented here explore the topic. Silvia Yee, International Law and Policy Fellow at DREDF, has authored *Where Prejudice, Disability and "Disablism" Meet*, which appears in this section. Yee examines how the burgeoning field of disability studies has responded to the notion of prejudice and how fields of study that explore prejudice as a psychological, social and cultural phenomenon can inform this examination, but for the most part have failed to do so. She also focuses on some of the factors that make disability prejudice so difficult to examine and evaluate and suggests future possibilities and implications. *What Is Prejudice as it Relates to Disability Anti-Discrimination Law?* appears in Part IV. Authored by David Ruebain, a British attorney and noted education and disability law expert, the article presents examples of the impact of prejudice on children and adults with disabilities and the role anti-discrimination law plays in reversing negative practices and policies, including examples from Ruebain's personal life. The article also discusses the relationship of disability discrimination to the evolving field of bioethics.

Historic definitions of disability in social welfare, social supports and health policies are rooted in functional limitation models that pay little heed to the impact of prejudicial social norms. The legacy of these definitions resonates throughout the world. In an article entitled *Different Definitions—Same Problems—One Way Out?*, Aart C. Hendriks explores the definitional dilemma from historical, social, political, and legal perspectives, and suggests alternatives for consideration.

Recent developments in ADA case law make this discussion even more crucial. The ADA defines disability by requiring that people with disabilities show they possess an impairment that qualifies them for protection from prohibited discrimination. They must possess either a physical or mental impairment that substantially limits a major life activity, or a record of such an impairment. It also prohibits discrimination based on perception of impairment, whether or not the individual actually possesses one. This hybrid definition combines a restrictive impairment model with a prohibition against discrimination based on perception alone, which acknowledges and builds on the social model. These conflicting principles in the ADA definition of disability have created confusion for the courts, and recently resulted in the narrowing of the definition by the U.S. Supreme Court.

By combining a medical definition of disability with one rooted in the social model the ADA typifies the dissonance that advocates confront everywhere as they grapple with creating effective anti-discrimination initiatives that afford broad protection from discrimination for people with disabilities. As anti-discrimination legislation and policies evolve, a more appropriate definition of disability must also evolve or perhaps give way altogether to the recognition that the discriminatory actions of others should be the focal point rather than whether the victum of discriminaton fits some defined notion of "disability." Definitional questions present a tremendous challenge both practically and theoretically and will be the subject of continuing explortion and debate as the civil rights paradigm matures. Aart C. Hendriks is Secretary of the Programme on Health Law Evaluation of the Health Research and Development Council (ZON), The Hague, The Netherlands.

In an article entitled *Tensions and Coherence in Disability Policy: The Uneasy Relationship Between Social Welfare and Civil Rights Models of Disability in American, European and International Employment Law*, authors Lisa Waddington and Matthew Diller examine the relationship between the social welfare and civil rights models of disability policy and consider whether or not the dissonance between the two can be resolved or reduced, to what extent the tension is a problem, and whether or not a new disability policy model is needed. While disability advocates internationally have gained substantial recognition for the social model of disability policy, its predecessor is still deeply entrenched in most societies, though often co-existing with the social model in an uneasy and paradoxical truce.

While medical and technological advances have dramatically improved the probability that people with disabilities who have access to such care will survive illness or injury, medical intervention will not heal discrimination. Such a person-centered model, furthermore, fails to recognize or account for the impact of social stigma and prejudice, which exists outside the boundaries of the body. Likewise, social welfare historically has aimed to provide important, even essential services or support to the individual, but has not responded to the impact of external social norms that include pity and prejudice. The unfortunate legacy of the medical model is offending assumptions and stereotypes about disability. The problems that flow from these fundamental conceptual conflicts raise important questions about the direction of future reforms and call for consideration of alternative models that harmonize their underlying principles. Lisa Waddington is Senior Lecturer in Law at Maastricht University, The Netherlands and Matthew Diller is Professor of Law at Fordham University School of Law, New York.

Part III—Focus on the Operation of Laws

This section contains two articles that look at foundational issues concerning the underpinnings of law—how they are drafted and interpreted in accord with society's basic idea of fairness.

In an article entitled *The ADA and Models of Equality*, Arlene B. Mayerson and Silvia Yee discuss formal versus substantive equality as they are regarded in U.S. and Canadian law.

The ADA intended to achieve equal opportunity by calling for affirmative steps to remove barriers and provide accommodations. However, the goals of the ADA have been undermined by Supreme Court decisions, which adopt an equal treatment or formal equality approach to the 14th Amendment equal protection guarantee in the U.S. constitution. The authors examine the alternative material equality model that is widely found in international disability anti-discrimination law. They also analyze Canadian equality theory found in the constitution and in jurisprudence. Arlene B. Mayerson is Directing Attorney with DREDF and lecturer in disability rights at University of California Boalt Hall School of Law, and Silvia Yee is the International Law and Policy Fellow with DREDF.

People with disabilities have been institutionalized in virtually every country around the globe. The disability rights movement considers incarceration of people with disabilities in institutions to be the most onerous form of disability discrimination. In a proactive attempt to garner attention to this inhumane practice that violates basic human rights, disability rights attorneys and activists have turned to international law. In an article entitled *The Right to Community Integration for People with Disabilities Under United States and International Law*, Eric Rosenthal and Arlene Kanter examine how the right of people with disabilities, especially those with mental disabilities, to community integration has been carved out of existing general international laws. They observe that while the right exists more explicitly under the ADA, judicial interpretation has been required to spur any meaningful action that actually remedies the widespread practice, and furthermore, at this writing, the right remains conditional. Eric Rosenthal is Executive Director, Mental Disability Rights International and Arlene Kanter is Professor of Law at Syracuse University College of Law.

Part IV—Real Life—Needing, Getting and Living with Disability Anti-Discrimination Law

This section presents three articles that discuss surviving prejudice, enacting the ADA, and the effect of the ADA from the viewpoint of people with disabilities.

David Ruebain's paper entitled *What Is Prejudice as it Relates to Disability Anti-Discrimination Law*, previously described, is presented here.

In an article entitled *When to Hold 'Em and When to Fold 'Em: Lessons Learned From Enacting The Americans with Disabilities Act*, Jane West and Pat Wright collaborate to examine the political process that led to the passage of the ADA. Wright and West introduce the human dynamics that surrounded the legislative process leading to the law's enactment. In light of the worldwide call by the disability community for anti-discrimination laws, we hope that others can draw upon some of the lessons learned and the tactics used during the passage of the ADA. As the article's title suggests, some of these have universal appeal and likely will become essential tools in a successful legislative campaign. Jane West is an education consultant working in Washington, DC and Pat Wright is DREDF's Governmental Affairs Director.

In *Achieving Accessibility: How the Americans with Disabilities Act Is Changing the Face and Mind of a Nation*, Silvia Yee and Marilyn Golden present testimonials "from the trenches," and discuss how through litigation, settlements and voluntary compliance the ADA is functioning as an effective tool against disability discrimination. This article is especially relevant as an affirmation that while imperfect, the ADA has indeed profoundly changed and improved the lives of people with disabilities. Silvia Yee is the International Law and Policy Fellow with DREDF, and Marilyn Golden is a Policy Analyst with DREDF.

Mary Lou Breslin
Disability Rights Education and Defense Fund (DREDF)
Berkeley, Califronia, U.S.A.
April 2002

Part I:
Disability Anti-Discrimination Law—The State of the World

A Survey of International, Comparative and Regional Disability Law Reform

Theresia Degener and Gerard Quinn***

Introduction

The purpose of this article is to survey the rise and influence of the rights-based approach to disability throughout the world. We take the equal opportunities model with its particular emphasis on non-discrimination as our key departure point.

The equal opportunities model has grown in status and authority at the international level and in the United Nations system. We examine the process of reform currently underway in many countries throughout the world. Although this process of reform is, by necessity, varied and complex, it does tend to gravitate more and more towards the equal opportunities/non-discrimination model, and this has been especially the case since the early 1990s. The UN Standard Rules of 1993 undoubtedly provided the key moral imperative for change on a worldwide basis, but there equally can be no doubt that the enactment of the Americans with Disabilities Act (ADA) showed that change was both possible and practicable.

This article takes as a case study the steady move towards the eventual enactment of an equivalent to the ADA in the European region—we call this possibility a "Europeans with Disabilities Act." The first tentative steps in that direction are currently being taken, and we note how regional organizations such as the Council of Europe and the European Union can play a significant role as catalysts in the process of change, both at a regional level and also within individual member states.

---

* Theresia Degener is Professor of Law, Administration and Organization, University of Applied Sciences, Rheinland-Westfalen-Lippe, Bochum, Germany.

** Gerard Quinn is Lecturer in Law, National University of Ireland (Galway Campus).

We present this article in three parts:

Part 1[1] deals with the underlying philosophical assumptions that are driving the process of change and the paradigm shift from welfare to rights. It traces the growing influence of non-discrimination values and principles at the level of the United Nations. It also takes a close look at the variety of strategies used by many countries to implement and place this paradigm shift into national operation, both in non-discrimination laws and in other ways.

Part 2[2] focuses on how one particular region in the world is beginning to take note of this paradigm shift, and initiating a corresponding process of change in law and policy. Our analysis demonstrates the importance of regional organizations as a driving force behind the process of change at both a regional level, and also within the relevant member states.

Part 3 draws together some tentative conclusions about the nature of the reform process, its effective stimulation, and the space it leaves for new agendas, including the development of social rights policies that will underpin (and not undermine) the positive accomplishments of the non-discrimination ideal in the disability field.

---

[1] Theresia Degener wishes to thank Susan Dennehy, Arlene Kanter (Professor of Law and Director of Clinical Legal Education, Syracuse University), Debby Kearney, Jenny Kern, Martin Ladstaedter, Silvia Yee, Rodrigo Jiménez and Yoshiko Osawa.

[2] Gerard Quinn wishes to thank Thorsten Afflerbach of the Council of Europe and André Gubbels of the European Commission.

Part 1
The Paradigm Shift in International and Comparative Law

A. THE BASIS OF THE SHIFT: PEOPLE WITH DISABILITIES AS SUBJECTS AND NOT OBJECTS

Disability law has not been a field of legal research and teaching at many universities in the United States, nor has it been widely acknowledged in other countries around the world. In North America and most European countries, disability as an issue of law has commonly been addressed as an aspect of social security and welfare legislation, health law or guardianship. Thus, disabled persons were depicted not as subjects with legal rights but as objects of welfare, health and charity programs. The underlying social policy behind such a legal response has been one that segregates and excludes people with disabilities from mainstream society, sometimes providing them with special schools, sheltered workshops, and separate housing and transportation. This policy was justified by the pervasive belief that disabled persons were incapable of coping with either society at large or all or most major life activities.

Fortunately, when some countries eventually made attempts to take a more integrative and inclusive approach to disability policy, major legal reforms resulted. Attempts to open up employment, education, housing, and goods and services for persons regardless of their disabilities have accompanied the growing understanding that disability issues belong in a social and not a medical category. A key element of this new concept is the recognition that exclusion and segregation of people with disabilities do not logically follow from the fact of impairment, but rather result from political choices based on false assumptions about disability. Inaccessibility problems are not inevitably raised by mobility, visual or hearing impairments, but instead are a corollary of political decisions to build steps but not ramps, to provide information in printed letter version only, or to forgo sign language or other forms of communication. Instead of viewing disability as an individual problem, the focus finally has shifted to how the environment and society as a whole fails to consider human differences.

1. The Significance of Viewing Disability as a Human Right Issue

With the paradigm shift from the medical to the social model of disability,[3] disability was reclassified as a human rights issue under international law. Reforms in this area were intended to provide equal opportunities for disabled people and to expose their segregation, institutionalization and exclusion as typical forms of disability-based discrimination. With the evolution of such civil rights legislation for disabled persons as the Americans with Disabilities Act (ADA), national legal paradigms shifted even further, from welfare law towards civil rights law. This new dimension of disability law has been welcomed as a major milestone on the path toward eventual recognition of the human rights of disabled people, a path which more and more governments seem to be willing to take.[4]

What remains unclear, however, is the scope of change. If the now undermined assumption that disability is a medical problem anchored much of the older welfare disability laws, should governments replace these laws with what we now call civil rights legislation? Do we still need benefits that traditionally had been given as compensation for social exclusion? What are the legal consequences of replacing the medical model of disability with the social model? Of course, these questions raise the delicate issue of how to distribute resources in society.

---

[3] There is a large body of literature on this subject. *See, e.g.*, Victor Finkelstein, *Attitudes and Disabled People: Issues for Discussion* (New York, World Rehabilitation Fund, 1980); Michael Oliver, *The Politics of Disablement: A Sociological Approach* (London, St. Martin's, 1990); Michael Oliver, *Understanding Disability: From Theory to Practice* (New York, St. Martin's, 1996); Jenny Morris, *Pride Against Prejudice: Transforming Attitudes to Disability* (Philadelphia, New Society, 1991).

[4] *See* United Nations, General Assembly, *Implementation of the World Programme of Action Concerning Disabled Persons; Report of the Secretary-General*, U.N. Doc. A/54/388/Add.1 (1999).

Then, too, these questions are closely connected with another issue that affects the outcome of law reform in disability law: the principle of equality. This principle, one of the most fundamental human rights, is relational: equality for disabled people raises additional questions, such as equal compared to whom, to what extent, and under which circumstances? Is it enough to open the doors to education, employment and political participation, or do we need to help everyone get inside? Have we helped everyone get inside if schools, job premises and public buildings are accessible but public transportation is not? Is it enough to prohibit invidious disability discrimination in employment, or do we need to ensure that more subtle or even "good will" forms of discrimination are also covered?[5] Is it enough to allow some disabled people to live outside institutions, or do we need to ensure that everyone gets out?[6] Have we achieved equality if disabled workers receive the same salary as non-disabled co-workers, but have to spend 60 percent of their salary on personal assistance services that non-disabled employees do not need?

2. The Rich Diversity of Equality Concepts

While there is consensus about the fundamental nature of the equality principle in domestic as well as in international law, the interpretation of this principle varies. The three main ways of understanding equality are as (1) formal or juridical equality, (2) equality of results, and (3) equal opportunity or structural equality.[7]

---

5 For example, should relegation to sheltered employment be considered a form of discrimination?

6 *See, e.g.*, Olmstead v. L.C. *ex rel* Zimring, 527 U.S. 581 (1999).

7 *See* Gerard Quinn, "The Human Rights of People with Disabilities Under EU Law," *in The EU and Human Rights* 281, 290 (Philip Alston ed., Oxford, New York, Oxford University Press, 1999). Other equality concepts with respect to disability law have been described by Aart Hendriks, "The Significance of Equality and Non-Discrimination for the Protection of the Rights and Dignity of Disabled Persons," *in Human Rights and Disabled Persons: Essays and Relevant Human Rights Instruments* 40–62 (Theresia Degener & Yolan Koster–Dreese eds., Dordrecht, Boston, London, Martinus Nijhoff Publishers, 1995); and Lisa Waddington, *Disability, Employment and the European Community* 53–66 (Antwerp, Maklu *et al.* [under the auspices of METRO—Institute for Transnational Legal Research at the University of Limburg, Maastricht], 1995).

Juridical equality prohibits direct discrimination and aims at shifting the focus of a potential discriminator away from such characteristics as race, gender, disability, or sexual orientation. Since legitimizing unequal treatment on the basis of such characteristics is deemed to be arbitrary, juridical equality requires society to ignore the differences. This concept meets the demands of disability rights activists who try to overcome the medical model of disability, and it underlines the notion that disability is not the source of the problem. To achieve equality, however, disability does have to be taken into account when providing accessibility requires such changes as architectural modification or program adjustments. Granting equal access to all members of societies requires acknowledging the differences that exist among these members. Martha Minow has pointed out the moral policy dilemma of dealing with human differences such as disabilities.[8] Ignoring differences helps prevent stereotypes and stigmatization but at the price of failing to do justice to the reality of difference. Taking difference into account does justice to the reality of difference but potentially perpetuates false assumptions about the nature of difference.

Equality of results essentially examines disability through an outcome-analysis. Thus, according to equality of results, disabled workers who receive equal pay but bear an unequal cost-of-living burden with regard to their personal needs are discriminated against. The human rights theory that all human beings have equal value and dignity stands at the core of this way of understanding equality. As there can be no justification for inherently equal beings to own common resources unequally, this theory legitimises the demand for equal allocation of resources.

Equality of results poses some thorny problems, however. The principle must first tackle the question of responsibility. Who is responsible for meeting these needs? Is it the state or the private sector? Second, equality of results might require a strong welfare state, which may interfere with the ideology of a free market system. At the same time, equality of results itself could perpetuate injustice, because its focus is on results rather than treatment. Segregated education for disabled students, for example, might be deemed legitimate if special schools for disabled

---

[8] *See* Martha Minow, *Making All the Difference: Inclusion, Exclusion and American Law* 19–79 (Ithaca, NY, Cornell University Press, 1990).

students provide the same educational opportunities and degrees as regular schools. To put it bluntly, if we accept equality of results as the sole way of understanding equality, the mainstreaming of disabled students into regular schools could be viewed as an illegitimate goal.

The third way in which to view equality, equal opportunity, is less rigid than the other two concepts in that it seeks to provide equal chances without ensuring equal results. In this regard, equal opportunity is more compatible with the market economy. It looks at the history of group discriminations, and identifies traditional or classic forms of discrimination. The equal opportunity paradigm recognises both stereotypes and structural barriers as obstacles to inclusion: if stereotypes are the basis for discrimination then the fact of disability must be ignored, but disability must be taken into account where environmental or social norms act as the bars to genuine access and inclusion. This latter aspect of equal opportunity is encapsulated in the term "reasonable accommodation," which was developed in the United States in the 1970s.[9] Since then the idea has been adopted around the world, though often rephrased in other countries.[10]

The concept of equal opportunity is currently the most frequently applied equality concept in modern disability legislation. One reason for this might be the fact that this equality concept is compatible with the long-term goals of the free market economy, which is now the global economic model. Since civil rights legislation provides equal opportunities to underrepresented groups or minorities, it opens the gates for those who have not been able to participate meaningfully in the market, and thereby increases the pool of both consumers and producers. Nonetheless, in the absence of non-discrimination legislation there will always be instances in which the operation of purely self-interested individuals in the free market will produce unsatisfactory results for per-

---

9 *See* U.S. Commission on Civil Rights, *Accommodating the Spectrum of Individual Abilities* (Washington, DC, Clearinghouse Publication 81, 1983); Gerard Quinn, Maeve McDonagh & Cliona Kimber, *Disability Discrimination Law in the United States, Australia and Canada* (Dublin, Oaktree Press, 1993).

10 For instance, the term "adjustments" instead of "accommodations" is used in U.K. law. *See* Brian J. Doyle, *Disability Discrimination: The New Law* (London, Jordans, 1996).

sons with disabilities, either individually or as a group. Even though the concept of equal opportunity for all works within the ambit of the free market, it also has the potential for gradually changing the notion of the capitalist market. This latter possibility might explain why those who have not been beneficiaries of the market economy in the past support this intermediate model of equality.

3. A Multi-Layered Reform Process: International, Regional and National Developments

The reform process in disability law has been going on in all parts of the world. The United States and Canada were the first countries to adopt anti-discrimination laws and other human rights legislation for persons with disabilities, starting with scattered equality provisions in various areas of the law in the 1970s and following with more comprehensive laws in the 1990s.[11] The 1990s in particular was a banner decade for disability law; more than 40 nations enacted disability discrimination laws during this period. New equality laws for disabled persons emerged at the national as well as at the supranational and international level. Today we have binding and non-binding international human rights instruments adopted by the General Assembly of the United Nations that explicitly protect the rights of disabled persons. At the regional level, the Organization of American States (OAS) and the European Union (EU) have passed strong equality legislation on disability. The OAS is the first intergovernmental organization to have a binding human rights treaty on disability. In 1999, the *Inter-American Convention on the Elimination of All Forms of Discrimination Against Persons with Disabilities* (IACPWD)[12] was adopted. While it does not

---

[11] The landmark law being the ADA of the United States. *See Americans with Disabilities Act*, Pub. L. No. 101-336, 104 Stat. 327 (July 26, 1990) [42 U.S.C. § 12101 *et seq.*]. In Canada the 1982 *Canadian Charter of Rights and Freedoms* and the 1985 *Canadian Human Rights Act* contain anti-discrimination provisions for disabled persons. *See* Can. Const. (Constitution Act, 1982) pt. I (Canadian Charter of Rights and Freedoms); The *Canadian Human Rights Act*, R.S.C. ch. H-6, § 1 (1998) (Can.).

[12] *Inter-American Convention on the Elimination of All Forms of Discrimination Against Persons with Disabilities*, A.G. Res. 1608, 29th Sess., O.E.A. Doc.

contain individual rights, it is the first regional treaty to define disability-based discrimination.

National disability rights movements, which seem to have been able to learn quickly from each other as well as cooperate among themselves at the international level, have been a major driving force behind the above legal changes.

B. INTERNATIONAL HUMAN RIGHTS AND DISABILITY: DEVELOPMENTS WITHIN THE UNITED NATIONS HUMAN RIGHTS MACHINERY

1. Soft Law Policy Developments

Despite being one of the largest minority groups in the world, encompassing 600 million persons (of which two out of three live in developing countries), disabled people had been rather ignored during the first three decades of the United Nations' existence. The drafters of the International Bill of Human Rights did not include disabled persons as a distinct group vulnerable to human rights violations. None of the equality clauses of any of the three instruments comprising this Bill (the *Universal Declaration of Human Rights* (1948), the *International Covenant on Civil and Political Rights* (1966) (ICCPR), and the *International Covenant on Economic, Social and Cultural Rights* (1966) (ICESCR)) mention disability as a protected category.[13] If disability is raised as an issue in these documents, it is only in connection with social security and preventive health policy.[14]

OEA/Ser. P AG/doc.3826/99 (1999). For the period prior to the new treaty, *see* Rodrigo Jiménez, *Los Derechos Humanos de la Personas con Discapacidad* (San José, Costa Rica, INAUD, Programa Mujer, Justicia y Género, Instituto Interamericano de Derechos Humanos, Disabled People International, 1996).

[13] *See Universal Declaration of Human Rights*, G.A. Res. 217 A(III), U.N. Doc. A/810, at 71 (1948) [The *Universal Declaration of Human Rights* may also be viewed *at* http://www.unhcrh.ch/udhr/index.htm, where it is available in most major world languages]; *International Covenant on Economic, Social and Cultural Rights*, 16 Dec. 1966, 993 U.N.T.S. 3; *International Covenant on Civil and Political Rights*, 17 Dec. 1966, 999 & 1057 U.N.T.S. 171 & 407 respectively.

[14] *See Universal Declaration of Human Rights, id.* art. 25; *International Covenant on Economic, Social and Cultural Rights, id.* art. 12.

Only in the 1970s, with the promulgation of the *Declaration on the Rights of Mentally Retarded Persons* (1971)[15] and the *Declaration on the Rights of Disabled Persons* (1975),[16] did persons with disabilities become explicit subjects of human rights declarations. Even so, these early instruments still reflect a notion of disability that falls within the medical model, according to which disabled persons are primarily seen as individuals with medical problems, dependent on social security and welfare, and in need of segregated services and institutions. It was also during this time that the General Assembly clearly affirmed that disabled persons were covered by the "other status" category listed in the equality provisions found in the International Bill of Human Rights.[17]

Throughout the 1970s and the 1980s the General Assembly of the United Nations passed a number of resolutions that eventually led to the 1982 *World Programme of Action Concerning Disabled Persons* (WPA), the guiding instrument for the United Nations Decade of Disabled Persons 1983–1992.[18] The first two goals of the WPA, prevention and rehabilitation, reflected a more traditional approach to disability law and policy, but the third goal, equalization of opportunities, set the scene for change at the international level. "Equalization of opportunities" was defined as:

> the process through which the general system of society, such as the physical and cultural environment, housing and transportation, social and health services, educational and work opportunities, cultural and social life, including sports and recreational facilities, are made accessible to all.[19]

---

[15] G.A. Res. 2856, U.N. GAOR, 26th Sess., Supp. No. 29, at 93, U.N. Doc. A/8429 (1972).

[16] G.A. Res. 3447, U.N. GAOR, 30th Sess., Supp. No. 34, at 88, U.N. Doc. A/10034 (1976).

[17] For a more comprehensive analysis see Hendriks, *supra* note 7.

[18] G.A. Res. 37/52, U.N. GAOR, 37th Sess., Supp. No. 51, at 185, U.N. Doc. A/37/51 (1983).

[19] United Nations, General Assembly, *World Programme of Action Concerning Disabled Persons; Report of the Secretary-General: Addendum*, at 21, U.N. Doc. A/37/351/Add.1 (1982).

Throughout the decade, the equal rights component of disability policy and law became the main target of the emerging international disability rights movement.

Other major influences that helped to shift the paradigm from the medical to the human rights model of disability were two thematic reports, one on human rights in the field of mental health and one on human rights violations with regard to disabled persons; both prepared by the United Nations Commission on Human Rights.[20] These reports were the first to recognise disability as a thematic subject within the human rights division of the United Nations, which in turn helped disabled persons to be regarded not only as recipients of charity measures but as subjects of human rights (violations). While one report resulted in a non-binding international human rights instrument aimed at the protection of disabled persons in institutions,[21] the outcome of the other has been rather poor. No significant follow-up activities were taken under the auspices of the United Nations Commission of Human Rights. Other significant guidelines and standards were adopted during the decade,[22] but proposals for a binding treaty on the human rights protection of disabled persons did not find majority support within the 3rd Committee of the General Assembly in either 1987 or 1989, years in which Italy and Sweden respectively raised the possibility of such a convention.

As a compensatory alternative, the General Assembly eventually adopted the non-binding UN *Standard Rules on the Equalization of*

---

20 *See* U.N. Sub-Commission on Prevention of Discrimination and Protection of Minorities, *Principles, Guidelines and Guarantees for the Protection of Persons Detained on Grounds of Mental Ill-Health or Suffering from Mental Disorder; Report by the Special Rapporteur: Erica-Irene A. Daes*, U.N. Doc. E/CN.4/Sub.2/1983/17/Rev.1, U.N. Sales No. E.85.XIV.9 (1997); U.N. Sub-Commission on Prevention of Discrimination and Protection of Minorities, *Human Rights and Disability: Report by Special Rapporteur: Leandro Despouy*, U.N. Doc. E/CN.4/Sub.2/1991/31, U.N. Sales No. E92.XIV.4 (1993).

21 *See The Protection of Persons with Mental Illness and the Improvement of Mental Health Care*, G.A. Res. 46/199, U.N. GAOR, 46th Sess., Supp. No. 49, at 188, U.N. Doc. A/46/49 (1992).

22 *See*, for example, the *Tallinn Guidelines for Action on Human Resources Development in the Field of Disability*, G.A. Res. 44/70, U.N. GAOR, 44th Sess., Supp. No. 49, Annex at 196, U.N. Doc. A/44/49 (1990).

Opportunities for Persons with Disabilities (Standard Rules) in 1993.[23] The Standard Rules firmly build on the WPA and clearly accentuate equality, now defined as follows:

> The principle of equal rights implies that the needs of each and every individual are of equal importance, that those needs must be made the basis for the planning of societies and that all resources must be employed in such a way as to ensure that every individual has equal opportunity for participation. Persons with disabilities are members of society and have the right to remain within their local communities. They should receive the support they need within the ordinary structures of education, health, employment and social services.[24]

In contrast with other non-binding international disability instruments, the Standard Rules have a Special Rapporteur and a panel of experts who have been given the mandate to promote and monitor the implementation of the rules. The panel of experts consists of ten representatives from six major international non-governmental organizations in the disability field.[25] Their reports reflect a clear human rights orientation towards monitoring, although the monitoring body was placed under the auspices of the United Nations Commission for Social Development instead of the Commission on Human Rights.[26]

---

[23] *See Standard Rules on the Equalization of Opportunities for Persons with Disabilities*, G.A. Res. 48/96, U.N. GAOR, 48th Sess., Supp. No. 49, Annex at 202-11, U.N. Doc. A/Res/48/49 (1994) [hereinafter *Standard Rules*]. For comment, see Theresia Degener, "Disabled Persons and Human Rights: The Legal Framework," *in Human Rights and Disabled Persons*, *supra* note 7, 9–39, and Bengt Lindqvist, "Standard Rules in the Disability Field—A New United Nations Instrument," *in Human Rights and Disabled Persons*, *supra* note 7, 63–68.

[24] *Standard Rules, id.* at 204, ¶¶ 25–26.

[25] The organizations were as follows: Disabled Peoples' International, Inclusion International, Rehabilitation International, World Blind Union, World Federation of the Deaf, and World Federation of Psychiatric Survivors and Users.

[26] *See* United Nations, General Assembly, *Report of the Special Rapporteur of the Commission for Social Development on Monitoring the Implementation of the Standard Rules on the Equalization of Opportunities for Persons with Disabilities*,

2. Hard Law Developments: Protection Under General Human Rights Instruments

Non-governmental organizations which focus on disability have had an increasing impact on how traditional human rights norms are interpreted and implemented, as well as on how modern human rights instruments are being designed.[27] While disability was a forgotten category when the ICCPR and the ICESCR were drafted, these treaties are currently interpreted in a way that supports the human rights approach to disability. General Comment No. 18 to the ICCPR, which deals with the right to equality (ICCPR, Art. 25), clearly rejects the concept of formal equality in the human rights context. The Comment affirms that equal treatment does not always mean identical treatment, and that states have a duty to take steps to eliminate conditions that perpetuate discrimination.[28]

U.N. Doc. A/50/374, Annex at 4 (1995) [first report]; United Nations, General Assembly, *Final Report of the Special Rapporteur of the Commission for Social Development on Monitoring the Implementation of the Standard Rules on the Equalization of Opportunities for Persons with Disabilities*, U.N. Doc. A/52/56, Annex at 3 (1996) [second report]; United Nations, Economic and Social Council, *Final Report of the Special Rapporteur of the Commission for Social Development on Monitoring the Implementation of the Standard Rules on the Equalization of Opportunities for Persons with Disabilities on His Second Missions*, 1997–2000, U.N. Doc. E/CN.5/2000/3 (1999) [third report]; *see also* Dimitris Michailakis, "The Standard Rules: A Weak Instrument and a Strong Commitment," *in Disability, Divers-Ability and Legal Change* 117–30 (M. Jones & L.A. Basser Marks eds., Hague, Boston, London, Martinus Nijhoff Publishers, 1999).

27 While we focus here on the human rights division of the UN, it should be mentioned that specialized international agencies such as WHO, ILO and UNESCO have also taken an equal opportunity approach to disability in recent years. As a strong binding instrument, ILO Convention No. 159, Convention Concerning Vocational Rehabilitation and Employment (Disabled Persons), 1983 is worth mentioning. *See* "Convention No. 159: Convention Concerning Vocational Rehabilitation and Employment (Disabled Persons)," *in International Labour Organization, 2 International Labour Conventions and Recommendations* 1919–1991 (1992). For an overview of the specialized agencies *see* Theresia Degener, "Disabled Persons and Human Rights: The Legal Framework," *supra* note 23, at 20–33.

28 *See General Comment No. 18, Report of the Human Rights Committee*, U.N. GAOR, 45th Sess., Supp. No. 40, at 175, U.N. Doc. A/45/40 (1990).

The Committee on Economic, Social and Cultural Rights went even further and adopted a General Comment on how to interpret and implement the ICESCR with respect to persons with disabilities.[29] General Comment No. 5, which the committee adopted in 1994, is the only legal United Nations document to date that broadly defines disability-based discrimination:

> Both de jure and de facto discrimination against persons with disabilities have a long history and take various forms. They range from invidious discrimination, such as the denial of educational opportunities, to more "subtle" forms of discrimination such as segregation and isolation achieved through the imposition of physical and social barriers. For the purposes of the Covenant, "disability-based discrimination" may be defined as including any distinction, exclusion, restriction or preference, or denial of reasonable accommodation based on disability which has the effect of nullifying or impairing the recognition, enjoyment or exercise of economic, social or cultural rights.[30]

The Comment also emphasises the human rights approach to disability by including a clear demand for anti-discrimination legislation:

> In order to remedy past and present discrimination, and to deter future discrimination, comprehensive anti-discrimination legislation in relation to disability would seem to be indispensable in virtually all States parties.[31]

In a similar vein, the Committee on the Elimination of Discrimination Against Women has adopted General Recommendations that ask

---

[29] *See* Philip Alston, "Disability and the International Covenant on Economic, Social and Cultural Rights," *in Human Rights and Disabled Persons*, *supra* note 7, 94–105.

[30] *General Comment No. 5 (1994) on Persons with Disabilities, Report on the Tenth and Eleventh Sessions*, U.N. ESCOR 1995, Supp. No. 2 [according to U.N. Doc. E/1995/22/Corr.1-E/C.12/1994/20/Corr.1], at 102, ¶ 15, U.N. Doc. E/1995/22-E/C.12/1994/20 (1995).

[31] *Id.* ¶ 16.

state parties to include specific information in their reports on the status of disabled women,[32] and has addressed the issue of disability in other thematic recommendations.[33]

More recent human rights treaties, such as the International Convention on the Rights of the Child, also include specific provisions concerning persons with disabilities that reflect a strong human rights approach.[34]

3. The New Agenda: Towards a New International Treaty on Disability?

The lack of binding human rights law for persons with disabilities at the global level has prompted disability rights activists and scholars to press for the adoption of a new convention on the elimination of discrimination against disabled persons.

Advocates of this idea recognise that states are reluctant to adopt yet another special human rights treaty. They appreciate the concern that an abundance of current human rights treaty obligations has created "treaty fatigue" in member states that are already burdened by and unable to fulfill their existing reporting obligations.[35]

However, at least six principal arguments can be marshaled in favor of a new treaty on disability rights. First, a new treaty would be a significant advance in the creation of binding law and the ability to take

---

[32] *See General Recommendation No. 18, Report of the Committee on the Elimination of Discrimination Against Women*, U.N. GAOR, 46th Sess., Supp. No. 38, at 3, U.N. Doc. A/46/38 (1992).

[33] *See*, for example, *General Recommendation No. 24, Report of the Committee on the Elimination of Discrimination Against Women*, U.N. GAOR, 54th Sess., Supp. No. 38, at 6, ¶ 25, U.N. Doc. A/54/38/Rev.1 (1999).

[34] For a discussion of article 23 of the United Nations Convention on the Rights of the Child, *see* Thomas Hammarberg, "The Rights of Disabled Children—The UN Convention on the Rights of the Child," *in Human Rights and Disabled Persons*, *supra* note 7, 147–155.

[35] For more on this problematic aspect of human rights implementation, *see* Henry Steiner & Philip Alston, *International Human Rights in Context* at 559 (Oxford, Clarendon Press, 1996).

action to prevent disability discrimination. In contrast, the current international standards represent a regime that is little more than a "toothless tiger" when it comes to actual human rights advocacy. Second, a new treaty would legitimise claims for additional attention and resources from the human rights division of the United Nations, governments, and other organizations. Third, a treaty on disability rights would provide an opportunity to both add specific content to the human rights of persons with disabilities and address hitherto unexplored areas, such as the right to be different. In light of recent developments in the area of bioethics and biomedicine concerning the detection and appropriate "treatment" of physiological differences, the right to be different might be as fundamental as the right to equality for persons with disabilities.[36] Fourth, a treaty would give disability rights organizations a specific tool for promoting human rights for persons with disabilities in domestic contexts and to their own governments. Fifth, a treaty would be a catalyst for empowering and mobilizing the global disability rights movement. Finally, the adoption of a disability treaty would place the disability agenda squarely within the United Nations human rights program. Thus, this step would underscore the fact that disability was primarily a human rights rather than a social welfare issue.

For these reasons, the United Nations, its member states, and disability rights organizations should initiate the process for the adoption of an international treaty dealing specifically with the human rights of disabled persons. A resolution on the rights of persons with disabilities is traditionally tabled at meetings of the United Nations Human Rights Commission in Geneva. Ireland has taken over the role of main sponsor of that resolution from the Philippines for the past few years. During the Commission's 56th session in March-April of 2000, Ireland tabled a resolution that, *inter alia*, called for the drafting of an international convention. The relevant part read:

> 30. Considers that the next logical step forward in advancing the effective enjoyment of the rights of persons with disabilities requires that the Commission for Social Development

---

[36] For more on this issue, *see* Theresia Degener, "Disabled Persons and Human Rights: The Legal Framework," *supra* note 23, at 36; Katarina Tomasevski, "The Right to Health for People with Disabilities," *in Human Rights and Disabled Persons*, *supra* note 7, 131–46.

> should, as a matter or urgency, examine the desirability of an international convention on the rights of people with disabilities, and the form and content of such an instrument, and solicit input and proposals from interested parties, including particularly the panel of experts [set up to assist the UN Rapporteur under the UN Standard Rules].

Ireland received considerable support at the session, but not enough to secure passage of the resolution with paragraph 30 intact. In the evening, a resolution was adopted that was silent on the issue of a convention. However, the resolution will be tabled again in 2002 and Ireland has signaled its intention of trying again to get the question of a convention raised and agreed to.

C. THE REFORM PROCESS IN COMPARATIVE LAW

At the domestic level, disability law in many countries underwent significant changes during the last decades. More than 40 out of 189 United Nations member states have now adopted some kind of anti-discrimination law for persons with disabilities.[37] To compare and analyze these laws globally is a difficult enterprise for a number of reasons. First not only do these countries have different historic, economic and political backgrounds, they also adhere to different legal systems, notably common law or civil law. Since the common law tradition is based on case law and precedent, the judiciary plays a different role than the one that it assumes in the civil law tradition. Secondly, disability law as a branch of legal research is a fairly recent development in most countries. Thus, both legal literature on disability law and comparative studies on disability laws are still rather rare.[38] Most of the comparative legal literature that is published is focussed on European countries.

---

37 We have found anti-discrimination laws in the following countries: Australia, Austria, Bolivia, Brazil, Canada, Chile, China, Costa Rica, Ethiopia, Finland, Fiji, France, Gambia, Germany, Ghana, Greece, Guatemala, Hong Kong (SAR), Hungary, India, Ireland, Israel, Korea, Luxembourg, Madagascar, Malawi, Mauritius, Namibia, New Zealand, Nicaragua, Nigeria, Philippines, South Africa, Spain, Sri Lanka, Sweden, Switzerland, Uganda, United Kingdom, United States, Zambia, and Zimbabwe. *See Annex I* for the names of the laws.

38 Lisa Waddington, "Legislating to Employ People with Disabilities: The

1. The Template: Using the ADA and Standard Rules as Model Laws Globally

With these reservations in mind, some observations still can be made with respect to anti-discrimination laws for disabled persons around the world. Most of these anti-discrimination laws were enacted during the last decade, with some countries enacting laws in the 80s. The United States was exceptionally early in adopting the Rehabilitation Act of 1973 as one of its first pieces of anti-discrimination legislation for disabled persons. U.S. law has subsequently been instrumental for the evolution of disability discrimination law in many countries. The Americans with Disabilities Act (ADA) of 1990, in particular, has had such an enormous impact on foreign legal development that one is tempted to say that the international impact of this law is larger than its domestic effect.[39] Another incentive to enact disability discrimination legislation came from the UN *Standard Rules for the Equalization of Opportunities of 1993* (Standard Rules) which states in Rule 15:

> States have a responsibility to create the legal bases for measures to achieve the objectives of full participation and equal-

---

European and American Way," 1(4) *Maastricht J. Eur. & Comp. L.* 367 (1994); Quinn *et al.*, *supra* note 9; M. Jones & L.A. Basser Marks, *supra* note 26; Marge Hauritz, Charles Sampford & Sophie Blencowe, *Justice for People with Disabilities: Legal and Institutional Issues* (Sydney, Federation Press,1998); Marcia H. Rioux, "The Place of Judgement in a World of Facts," 41(2) *J. Intell. Disability Res.* 102 (1997); Patricia Thornton & Neil Lunt, *Employment Policies for Disabled People in Eighteen Countries—A Review* (York, University of York, Social Policy Research Unit, 1997), *at* http://www.gladnet.org/ref/employment/18-count.htm (visited June 14, 2000); Mark Carley, "International Equality at Work: Disability, Employment and the Law in Europe—Part One," Dec. *Eur. Indus. Rel. Rev.* 251 (1994), *at* http://www.gladnet.org/ref/legislation/europe_d.htm" (visited June 14, 2000); Eric Besner, "Employment Legislation for Disabled Individuals: What Can France Learn from the Americans with Disabilities Act?", 16 *Comp. Lab. L.J.* 399 (1995); Bernard Gutow, "Survey of Rights of Workers with Disabilities: Comparison of the United States with the European Community," 11 (2) *N.Y. Int'l L. Rev.* 101 (1998).

[39] Within the U.S. legal literature there is today no consensus on whether the ADA has been successful. *See* the ADA Symposium Issue: "Backlash Against the ADA," 21 *Berkeley J. Employment Lab. L.* (2000).

> ity for persons with disabilities. . . . States must ensure that organizations of persons with disabilities are involved in the development of national legislation concerning the rights of persons with disabilities, as well as in the ongoing evaluation of that legislation. . . . Any discriminatory provisions against persons with disabilities must be eliminated. National legislation should provide for appropriate sanctions in case of violations of the principles of non-discrimination. . . .[40]

The history of disability discrimination law in a number of countries reveals that either the ADA and/or the Standard Rules served as the model law for the development of domestic legislation. With respect to the legal character of the Standard Rules, this finding is an interesting example of the kind of impact a soft law can have internationally if taken seriously by governments. The fact that governments took disability seriously as a discrimination issue is a testament to the work of the disability movement in each country. Anti-discrimination laws for disabled persons are the result of determined effort by a social movement of organised persons with disabilities and disability advocates around the world. Disabled persons demanded human rights instead of pity laws, thereby acting as the impetus behind, as well as a living reflection of, the paradigm shift in national and international disability policy.

2. Excursion: Disability Law as Pity Law in Europe

Disability law before the anti-discrimination era often helped construct and perpetuate the medical model of disability. The history of European domestic disability law is illustrative in this matter. In Europe we can distinguish three periods of modern disability law at the domestic level.[41]

The first period starts after World War I, when welfare legislation for disabled war veterans was introduced in most European countries. These welfare laws reflected society's obligation to compensate war vet-

---

40 *Supra* note 23.

41 For a comprehensive overview, *see* Waddington, *supra* note 7.

erans through disability pensions, rehabilitation benefits and employment quotas.

The second period of disability law began in the 60s, and extended welfare legislation to cover all disabled persons, with some countries focussing on disabled children in particular. These welfare laws brought charity for a broader group of people with disabilities. While disabled veterans were still (and continue to be) privileged, this second period of disability law paid less attention to the origin of impairment. The goal now was to rehabilitate persons with disabilities no matter what the cause of impairment. Laws were enacted in such areas as special education, medical and vocational rehabilitation benefits, employment quotas, and institutionalised care services.

Both the first and the second period of disability law in Europe reflected the medical model of disability. Disabled persons received welfare benefits because disability was seen as a medical problem that left an individual unable to cope with society at large and all or most major life activities. Disabled children received a right to education, but in separate schools for the disabled. Disabled persons received medical and vocational rehabilitation, administered under the control of medical rehabilitation experts. Thus, while disabled persons were elevated from the status of being objects without rights to being subjects of welfare rights, these rights were given at the price of exclusion and the loss of self-determination. Even laws that had the explicit textual purpose of integrating disabled persons into the open labour market were based on the medical model. Employment quotas that obligated employers to hire a certain percentage of disabled employees were introduced because disabled individuals were seen as incapable of competing for jobs on their merits. These traditional quota schemes are not based on equality theory as we now know it, nor on the understanding of systemic discrimination that animates affirmative action programs within a contemporary race or gender context.

Thus, the first two periods of disability law helped to construct and perpetuate the medical model of disability. Legally disabled persons were denied the status of citizens through their relegation to the realm of pity law. A case from Germany elucidates this process. In 1992 the local court of Flensburg decided that non-disabled tourists are entitled to a reduction of their travel price if they are confronted by disabled tourists in their hotel.[42] A couple with two children booked a full board holiday package with a German travel agency, and then filed a law suit against the travel agency because ten disabled tourists had spent their holidays at the same hotel with the family. The court's statement of facts elucidates the court's perception of disabled persons as "the other":

> For a week, the hotel was occupied by a group of ten severely disabled persons, some of which were wheelchair-bound. These disabled persons participated in common meals in the dining-hall of the hotel. Most of them could not eat the food in a normal way, it ran from their mouths onto bibs that were tied around their necks. They were fed using instruments, among others one that was similar to a syringe. This scene was disgusting and impaired the well-being of the plaintiffs and their children. They could not avoid it because of the common mealtimes and the small physical dimensions of the dining-hall.

The court then makes the following legal finding:

> The plaintiffs are entitled to reduce the travel price. . . . The service that was carried out by the defendant was inadequate. Its suitability for an unencumbered vacation was impaired. The plaintiffs and their small children could not enjoy their meals in the hotel in an untroubled manner. The inescapable sight of disabled persons in a small place, at each mealtime, caused disgust and constantly reminded them of the potentials of human suffering in a haunting way. Typically, these experiences do not belong in the expected course of a vacation. If it were possible, the average holiday-maker would avoid these experiences. A holiday-maker does not necessarily have to be selfless or have high ethical standards. In particular, unimpaired meals in a hotel are an integral part of a relaxing experience during a vacation. Advertisements of most tour organizers correspond to this.

---

42 AG Flensburg, decision of Aug. 27, 1992–63 C 265/92 (case-No), *Neue Juristische Wochenschrift* 272 (1993).

While this decision has been highly criticised in Germany, it is not exceptional for German case law. Disabled persons are not perceived as citizens but as objects. They are put in the same category as broken toilets and dirty beaches—phenomena that can ground breach of warranty claims in German travel law. Non-disabled citizens have a right not to be confronted by disabled persons. Germany's history, in which disabled persons were excluded and eliminated under the regime of National Socialism, might have some impact on the formation of this legal perception. The legal construction of disability as a welfare and pity issue helps to avoid the human rights issues involved in this case. With regard to the human rights of the disabled persons in the *Flensburg* decision, the Court states:

> Contrary to the defendant's point of view, the human dignity of the disabled persons, causing this reduction, is not violated by the granting of a warranty claim. Moreover, there is no exclusion of the disabled persons. The disabled persons are neither directly nor indirectly affected by these proceedings. This case is not about their rights, but about the question of which party has to bear the risk of the circumstances which lead to the unavoidable impairment of the plaintiff's vacation. A dismissal of the action would not undo the unpleasant encounter with the disabled persons, but instead only burden the plaintiff.

The denial of citizen's status to disabled persons does not necessarily follow from welfare legislation, but the themes of inherent disadvantage and segregation which underlie welfare policy easily lead to the further belief that disabled persons are somehow unequal and less worthy as human beings and members of society. Even in states as rich as Germany, which have the economic means to support a broadly justified social welfare system, the welfare approach can have a lingering and inhibiting influence on the development of a rights-based perspective in disability policy.

The third period of disability law started in the 90s when some European countries adopted anti-discrimination legislation for disabled persons. With these new laws, disabled persons finally gained the status of full citizens, because the paradigm shifted from a focus on individual impairment to the recognition of societal exclusion. A key element of disability discrimination legislation is the understanding that the exclusion and segregation of people with disabilities does not logically follow from the fact of impairments, but rather results from political choices based on false assumptions about disability. With the introduction of these laws, discrimination was finally recognised as a major obstacle in the lives of disabled persons. These laws are also the first disability laws which have been enacted because disabled persons campaigned and lobbied for their own rights, and not because rehabilitation experts decided what was best for "the handicapped."

Disability discrimination laws in Europe did not come over night. Rather, they had precursors in what may be called integration laws. During the 80s—the era of the United Nations Decade of the Disabled—many countries adopted integration, mainstreaming and de-institutionalization laws. The Scandinavian countries were outstanding with respect to integrating disabled children in education. Italy took the lead in the European de-institutionalization movement with the enactment of the *Psychiatric Reform Act*[43] as early as 1978. These laws were important for they helped to condemn the segregation and exclusion of disabled persons from society, but these laws did not identify discrimination as the main reason for exclusion and marginalization.

3. A Comparison of Anti-Discrimination Laws Globally

The laws that we analyse come from 42 countries, and vary widely with respect to scope, concept of discrimination and equality, who is protected, enforcement method, etc. Some laws define disability based discrimination and clearly prohibit such acts of discrimination, while others leave the question of what constitutes discrimination to the courts or other monitoring bodies. Some laws purport to uphold the principle of equality, but provide no clear picture of what needs to be changed in society in order to reach this goal. While such questions are often dealt with in separate regulations enacted under the act, the language and structure of the statute may still reveal legislative intent. Some laws give the overall impression that even though they contain some anti-

---

[43] Law 180 of 13 May 1978, *cited* in Thornton & Lunt, *supra* note 38.

discrimination language, they are essentially social welfare laws, fostering programs that are not necessarily aimed at complete social equality and integration for persons with disabilities.[44] However, it is important to remember that disability anti-discrimination law is truly a new development in disability policy around the world. These laws manifest a very recent shift in paradigm from the medical model to the social model of disability. The mere legal acknowledgment of disability as a discrimination category carries the recognition that persons with disabilities are persons with rights not problems.[45] Some of these anti-discrimination laws are strong, others appear to be "toothless tigers." Often domestic disability groups fought very hard for equality laws, and were not fully or perhaps even partially satisfied with the act that was finally passed by their legislators.[46] If the history of U.S. anti-discrimination law informs us of only one thing, it is that the legislative battle for equality is long, and more than one statute needs to be enacted before we can reach the goal of comprehensive protection against discrimination. From the first attempts to include disability in the Civil Rights Acts of 1964 until the passage of the ADA in 1990, several decades went by in which at least five federal disability anti-discrimination acts[47] were passed by Congress.

---

44 The Korean laws for example. Each statute's prohibition on discrimination takes place in a kind of vacuum. There is no bestowal of individual rights or any mechanism that allows persons with disabilities to enforce the prohibition or report violations of the law. While the laws contain the potential for actual reform, the main legal emphasis is on discretionary and welfare-oriented disability programs that have led to exclusion in the past.

45 Quinn, *supra* note 7, at 290.

46 In the United Kingdom, disability groups had fought for decades to achieve anti-discrimination legislation. They had prepared their own draft legislation which was rejected by the parliament. When the Disability Discrimination Act was passed in 1995 many disability rights activists were disappointed. *See* Doyle, *supra* note 10; Caroline Gooding, *Blackstone's Guide to the Disability Discrimination Act* 1995 (London, Blackstone Press, 1996).

47 The Architectural Barrier Act of 1968, Pub. L. No. 90-480, 82 Stat. 718 (codified as amended at 42 U.S.C.A. §§ 4151–4157 (2000)); the Rehabilitation Act of 1973, Pub. L. No. 93-112, 87 Stat. 390 (codified as amended at 29 U.S.C.A. §§ 791, 793, 794 (2000)); the Individuals With Disabilities Education Act (IDEA), Pub. L. 91-230, Title VI (codified as amended at 20 U.S.C.A. §§ 1400–1485 (2000))

a. A Wide Diversity of Different Legal Approaches

Those states that currently have some kind of disability anti-discrimination law have chosen different legal approaches. Four different legal approaches to the enactment of anti-discrimination provisions for the protection of disabled persons can be distinguished: (i) criminal law; (ii) constitutional law; (iii) civil law; and (iv) social welfare laws.

i. Using the Criminal Law

France,[48] Finland,[49] Spain,[50] and Luxembourg[51] prohibit discrimination against disabled persons in their criminal laws. The Spanish law prohibits disability-based discrimination in employee recruitment or in the course of employment if a disabled worker is capable of doing the job. Luxembourg and France outlaw disability-based discrimination in employment, business activities, and in the provision of goods and services to the public. The punishment is a maximum of two years imprisonment or a fine. The Finish Penal Code punishes employment-related discrimination, and discrimination with respect to goods and services for the general public. Some other states that generally have adopted a civil or social law approach to prohibit disability discrimination nonetheless make provision for the imposition of sanctions that have a broad penal or administrative aspect. For instance, the Australian discrimination statute characterises the incitement of unlawful discrimination or harassment as an offense punishable with six months imprisonment or a fine. The victimization of a person who exercises his or her rights

---

which was enacted under another name (Education For All Handicapped Children Act) in 1975; the Voting Accessibility for the Elderly and Handicapped Act, Pub. L. No. 98-435, 98 Stat. 1678 (codified as amended at 42 U.S.C.A. §§ 1973ee–1 to 1973ee-6 (2000)); the Fair Housing Act Amendments Act of 1988, Pub. L. No. 100-430, 102 Stat. 1619 (codified as amended at 42 U.S.C.A. §§ 3610–3614, 3614a (2000)).

48 Loi 90-602 de 12 Juliet 1990.

49 Penal Code as of 1995, Chapter 11, § 9 and Chapter 47, § 3.

50 Law on Infringements and Penalties of a Social Nature, 1988.

51 Penal Code of 1997, §§ 444 & 453–457.

under the act is similarly declared an offense.[52] The Hong Kong *Discrimination Ordinance* also carries like provisions: a person who incites hatred towards, serious contempt for, or severe ridicule of persons with disabilities commits a serious offense of vilification and is liable to a fine or up to two years imprisonment.[53] The law of Mauritius imposes imprisonment or an administrative fine for certain violations of that country's anti-discrimination rules.[54] The same holds true for the anti-discrimination acts of Israel,[55] the Philippines,[56] Zambia,[57] and Zimbabwe,[58] respectively.

While Finland and Spain also have anti-discrimination provisions in other fields of their legal system, France and Luxembourg stand out in that they regulate disability-based discrimination exclusively in their criminal codes. That means that disability based discrimination is prohibited only if it constitutes a criminal offense, which in turn requires the perpetrator to have acted with bad intentions. In reality, however, disability-based discrimination is often carried out by a perpetrator who has the best of intentions. The restaurant owner who doesn't serve wheelchair users because the entrance is inaccessible usually did not intend to deliberately keep out persons with disabilities, and likely has no hostile feelings towards persons with disabilities. Nor does he conceive of himself as a discriminator. While we do not have statistical evidence, it seems probable that criminal disability anti-discrimination law is rarely proven and prosecuted.

---

52 Disability Discrimination Act 1992, §§ 42 & 43.

53 Discrimination Ordinance, 1995, § 47.

54 The Training and Employment of Disabled Persons Act, 1996, § 18.

55 Equal Rights for Persons with Disabilities Law, §§ 15 & 19 (d).

56 Magna Carta for Disabled Persons, 1992, Title IV, § 46.

57 The Persons with Disabilities Act, 1996, § 32.

58 Disabled Persons Act, 1992, § 10 (c).

ii. Using Constitutional Law

A number of countries have constitutional anti-discrimination provisions which explicitly include disability. These are: Austria,[59] Brazil,[60] Canada,[61] Finland,[62] Fiji,[63] Gambia,[64] Ghana,[65] Germany,[66] Malawi,[67] New Zealand,[68] South Africa,[69] Switzerland,[70] and Uganda.[71] These clauses generally prohibit discrimination (via a negative command) against disabled persons without defining exactly what constitutes discrimination. Some equality clauses mention direct and indirect forms of discrimination.[72] The equality clause of Fiji's constitution is exceptionally broad, covering unfair direct and indirect discrimination and in addition stating:

> Every person has the right of access, without discrimination on a prohibited ground [*inter alia* disability], to shops, hotels, lodging-houses, public restaurants, places of public entertainment, public transport services, taxis and public places.[73]

---

59 Federal Constitution, as amended 1997 (art. 7).

60 Constitution of the Federal Republic of Brazil, as amended 1993 (art. 7).

61 Canadian Charter of Human Rights and Freedoms, 1982 (§ 15).

62 Constitution as adopted in 1999 (§ 6).

63 Constitution as of 1997 (§ 38).

64 Draft of a Constitution for the Second Republic of Gambia of 1996 (§ 31). The draft was released for publication in 1997, but we have not ascertained for certain whether the Constitution has been adopted and is presently in force.

65 Constitution as of 1992 (art. 29).

66 Basic Law of the Federal Republic of Germany, as amended in 1994 (art. 3).

67 Republic of Malawi (Constitution) Act 1994 (§ 20).

68 Human Rights Act of 1993 (§ 21).

69 Constitution, as of 1996 (§ 9).

70 Constitution, adopted 1999 (art. 8).

71 Constitution of the Republic of Uganda as of 1995 (art. 21).

72 Fiji: § 38(2), South Africa: § 9 (3), Gambia: § 33, New Zealand: § 65.

73 § 38(4).

The constitutions of Austria, Brazil, Canada, Germany, Ghana, Malawi, South Africa, Switzerland, and Uganda also enable or entrust the legislature to take affirmative action to combat disability discrimination. Affirmative action means preferential treatment, whether in the form of quotas or by other means of positive discrimination. Affirmative action thus targets structural discrimination, which is one of the major obstacles to the equalization of opportunities for disabled persons. In the area of employment, many states have introduced quotas for the advancement of disabled persons, whereby employers have a duty to hire disabled workers as a certain percentage of their total workforce. Employment quotas were initially introduced into disability policy after World War II, and functioned as classic welfare measures. They were founded on the idea that disabled people cannot compete in the real world. With the rise of the civil rights movement in the context of race and gender, quota policies gained a new equality-related meaning. This in turn influenced quota schemes in the disability field. In this respect, it is interesting to note that some of the constitutions provide for quota schemes in the area of employment,[74] whereas others do so in the area of political representation. For example, the constitution of Malawi provides that the Senate, which is a legislative body, shall include representatives of various interest groups, among them disability groups.[75] Similarly, the constitution of Uganda requires the parliament to have a certain number of representatives of persons with disabilities.[76] The Ugandan Parliament has five seats reserved for representatives from the disability community, and the first minister for disability (and women and the elderly), Mrs. Florence Nayiga Sekabiro, is a person with a disability. Based on the affirmative action clause of the constitution, Uganda's legislators passed several acts to increase the representation of disabled people in the public sphere. For instance, the *Local Government Act of 1997* allocates a certain number of seats in elected political bodies at all levels to people with disabilities. As a result there are more than 2,000 disabled elected officials at all levels of government today, from the parish to the

---

[74] Brazil does so with respect to public employment, *see* art. 37 of that country's Constitution.

[75] § 68(2)(i).

[76] Art. 78(1)(c).

district level.[77] Another interesting feature of those constitutions that include disability as a prohibited ground of discrimination, whether as originally drafted or through amendment, is that they also often recognise the right to use sign language. Finland,[78] South Africa[79] and Canada[80] have such provisions in their constitutions.

Constitutional anti-discrimination clauses seem to be more effective in transforming society than criminal anti-discrimination clauses. Since in most countries the constitution is the highest law of the land, constitutional provisions and amendments receive more public attention, and may render lower law unconstitutional and void. Constitutional enactments also bind the judiciary, and thus may lead to reform in disability case law. Yet, there are several reasons why constitutional disability discrimination law can have a limited effect.

First, depending on the legal system, some constitutions fail to give substantive rights to citizens, which means that the anti-discrimination clause may not be invoked by a disabled person in court. Second constitutional rights only apply to public or so called vertical law. That is, constitutional provisions protect disabled persons against discrimination by national or local state entities, but not private employers or private providers of goods and services. Finally constitutional provisions tend to be broad and vague. Neither disability nor discrimination is defined in any of the constitutional provisions except in the constitutional law of New Zealand.[81] This leaves vast discretion to the courts, and their rulings are very much determined by the prevailing legal culture.

---

77 Personal communication with Mrs. Nayiga Sekabiro at an international human rights seminar for young disabled women in New York, June 1–7, 2000.

78 Constitution, adopted in 1999, § 17. Though Portugal's constitution has no anti-discrimination clause that explicitly includes disability, it should be mentioned here that the state's obligation to protect and develop sign language was constitutionally enshrined in 1997 (art. 74.2.h).

79 § 6.

80 § 14 establishes the right to an interpreter for any deaf party or witness in legal proceedings.

81 This is probably because the Human Rights Act of 1993 is an entire statute that deals expressly with discrimination; the Constitution of New Zealand consists of several legislative acts.

For example in Germany, where there is no history of civil rights legislation and litigation, the constitutional anti-discrimination clause has been rendered a toothless tiger by the Federal Constitutional Court. In a 1996 case filed by a girl who uses a wheelchair and was consequently denied access to a regular school, the Court decided that the school authorities did not violate the constitutional anti-discrimination clause.[82] The reasoning of the German Federal Constitutional Court is reminiscent of a case which was decided more than 100 years ago by the U.S. Supreme Court that upheld racial segregation in public railways. As in *Plessy v. Ferguson* in 1896,[83] the German Court reasoned that educational segregation of disabled children is not discriminatory because it is separate but equal. The separate but equal ruling of *Plessy* was struck down in the U.S. in 1954 with the ground-breaking decision of *Brown v. Board of Education of Topeka*,[84] in which the Supreme Court finally acknowledged that separate educational facilities are inherently unequal. The German Federal Constitutional Court, however, has been very reluctant to consider exclusion from education in the context of disability discrimination. While the Court acknowledged that it would be discriminatory to deny admission to a disabled student who did not need any accommodations or special services, it was unwilling to extend its interpretation to include disabled students who need ramps, lifts, sign language interpreters, alternative reading formats, or any kind of special education services. Thus, the medical model of disability was only reinforced by this first decision on Germany's new anti-discrimination clause for persons with disabilities.

While these shortcomings of constitutional anti-discrimination provisions might lead to the conclusion that constitutional amendments are substantively ineffective, the example of Ireland indirectly supports the opposite conclusion. Because the equality clause in the Irish Constitution of 1937 is exceptionally weak, the Irish Supreme Court in 1997 struck down two pieces of civil anti-discrimination legislation that had included disability among other prohibited grounds of discrimination.

---

[82] Bundesverfassungsgericht, decision of October 1996–1 BvR 1308/96 (case No.), *Juristen Zeitung* 1073 (1996).

[83] 163 U.S. 537 (1896).

[84] 347 U.S. 483 (1954).

The court ruled that the statutory requirement to engage in reasonable accommodations violated the property rights of employers,[85] and both laws had to be redrafted and weakened with respect to disability. Therefore, if the lack of a strong constitutional equality provision can act as a bar to the enactment of civil anti-discrimination laws, then the existence of strengthened constitutional anti-discrimination provisions could serve as an important and necessary foundation for statutory anti-discrimination laws.

Finally, a positive example of how to interpret rather vague constitutional equality clauses is found in a 1997 decision of the Supreme Court of Canada. In *Eldridge v. British Columbia*,[86] the plaintiffs brought their case before the British Columbia Supreme Court because the province did not provide medical interpretation services to deaf patients. Robin Eldridge had been unable to communicate with her physician, and John and Linda Warren had undergone the ordeal of giving birth to their twins without being able to fully comprehend what their doctors and nurses were telling them. The plaintiffs framed their action under the equality clause (Sec. 15) of the Canadian *Charter of Rights and Freedoms*, claiming that provincial hospitals legislation discriminated against the deaf by failing to provide for sign language interpretive services when effective communication is an inherent and necessary component of the delivery of medical services. While the lower courts rejected their claim, the Supreme Court of Canada found that the equality clause had been violated. By interpreting the equality clause in a way that recognises that certain groups may need some accommodation in order to enjoy equality, *Eldridge* at least opens the

---

85 *In the matter of Article 26 of the Constitution of Ireland and in the Matter of the Employment Equality Bill*, Judgement of the Supreme Court May 1997; *Re Article 26 and the Equal Status Bill*, Judgement of the Supreme Court, May 1997 [both of these cases were Presidential referrals to the Supreme Court under the Irish Constitution]. *See also* Gerard Quinn, "From Charity to Rights The Evolution of the Rights-Based Approach to Disability: International and Irish Perspectives," *in Access West: A Guide to Services, Supports and A Rights Based Perspective for People with Physical and Sensory Disabilities Living in the Western Health Board Region* (Galway, Enable Ireland Galway & Western Health Board, 2001).

86 Eldridge v. British Columbia (Attorney General) (1997), 151 D.L.R. (4th) 577 (S.C.C.).

possibility that Section 15 of the *Charter* requires governments to take positive and substantive steps to ensure that persons with disabilities and other groups who experience discrimination receive the "equal protection and equal benefit" of the law. However, despite encouraging comments in *obiter dicta*, the Supreme Court of Canada has continued to leave the issue of positive obligations under the equality clause open.[87]

iii. The Enactment of Civil Anti-Discrimination Laws

A third approach is to enact civil anti-discrimination laws for persons with disabilities. A number of countries have adopted such laws and more countries are about to follow this path.[88] Countries with a civil rights oriented disability anti-discrimination law are: Australia,[89] Canada,[90] Chile,[91] Costa Rica,[92] Ethiopia,[93] Ghana,[94] Guatemala,[95] Hong Kong,[96] Hungary,[97] India,[98]

---

[87] *See* Vriend v. Alberta, [1998] 1 S.C.R. 493. For a more comprehensive analysis, *see:* Bruce Porter, "Beyond *Andrews:* Substantive Equality and Positive Obligations After *Eldridge* and *Vriend*," 9(3) *Const. F.* 71 (1998); M. David Lepofsky, "The Charter's Guarantee of Equality to People with Disabilities—How Well Is It Working?", 16 *Windsor Y.B. of Access to Just.* 155 (1998); Martha Jackman, "'Giving Real Effect to Equality': *Eldridge v. British Columbia Attorney General* and *Vriend v. Alberta*," 4 *Rev. of Const. Stud.* 352 (1998).

[88] For example, Austria, Germany, The Netherlands, Portugal, Switzerland.

[89] Disability Discrimination Act of 1992.

[90] Canadian Human Rights Act, R.S.C. 1985, c. H-6.

[91] Act No 19.284 of 1994.

[92] Law 7600 on Equal Opportunities for Persons with Disabilities, 1996.

[93] The Rights of Disabled Persons to Employment, Proclamation No. 101/1994.

[94] The Disabled Persons Act, 1993.

[95] Act for the Protection of Persons with Disabilities, Decree No. 135–96.

[96] Disability Discrimination Ordinance, 1990.

[97] Act No. XXVI of 1998 on Provision of the Rights of Persons Living with Disability and their Equality of Opportunity (hereinafter cited as Act No. XXVI).

[98] The Persons with Disabilities (Equal Opportunities, Protection of Rights and Full Participation) Act, 1995.

Ireland,[99] Israel,[100] Korea,[101] Madagascar,[102] Mauritius,[103] Namibia,[104] Nigeria,[105] the Philippines,[106] South Africa,[107] Spain,[108] Sri Lanka,[109] Sweden,[110] the U.K.,[111] the U.S.,[112] Zambia,[113] and Zimbabwe.[114] With the exception of the law of Chile, all of these statutes cover employment-related discrimination against disabled persons. Some laws are labour laws and thus cover only the area of employment discrimination;[115] the laws differ to a great extent with respect to coverage of all other areas. The most comprehensive disability discrimination laws are from Australia, Canada, Hong Kong, the Philippines, the U.K., and the U.S.

---

99 Employment Equality Act (1998), Equal Status Act (2000), and National Disability Authority Act (1999).

100 Equal Rights for Persons with Disabilities Law, 5758–1998 (hereinafter cited as ERPWDL).

101 Act Relating to Employment Promotion, etc. of the Handicapped, Law No. 4219 (1990) and The Special Education Promotion Law, as amended 1994.

102 Labour Code as of 29 September 1994.

103 The Training and Employment of Disabled Persons Act, 1996 (Act No. 9 of 1996).

104 Labour Act (1992).

105 Nigerians with Disability Decree 1993.

106 Magna Carta for Disabled Persons, 1991.

107 Employment Equity Bill, 1998 and Skills Development Bill, 1998.

108 Workers' Charter of 1980.

109 Protection of the Rights of Persons with Disabilities Act, No.28 of 1996.

110 Law on the Prohibition of Discrimination Against Persons With Disabilities in Employment, SFS No: 1999–132, 1999.

111 Disability Discrimination Act 1995 and Disability Rights Commission Act 1999.

112 Americans with Disabilities Act of 1990, which needs to be read together with that country's earlier disability discrimination laws, *supra* note 47.

113 The Persons with Disabilities Act 1996 (Act No. 33 of 1996).

114 Disabled Persons Act, 1992.

115 Canada (Employment Equity Act, S.C. 1994–95, c. 44), Ethiopia, Ireland

The Australian *Disability Discrimination Act of 1992* prohibits discrimination in the areas of work, housing, education, land possession, the provision of goods and services, and access to premises, clubs, sports and other facilities.[116] The *Canadian Human Rights Act of 1985* covers discrimination in the provision of goods, services, facilities, or accommodations that are available to the general public (including transportation). Furthermore it prohibits discrimination in employment and in the provision of commercial premises or housing.[117] The 1995 *Disability Discrimination Ordinance* of Hong Kong covers the areas of employment, education, premises, goods and services, facilities for the general public, barrister chambers, clubs and sports, and government activities.[118] The 1992 *Magna Carta for Disabled Persons* of the Philippines prohibits disability-based discrimination in the fields of employment, transportation, public accommodation, and goods and services.[119] The British *Disability Discrimination Act of 1995* covers discrimination in employment, in the provision of goods, facilities and services, and to some degree, also covers the areas of education and public transportation.[120] Finally, the *Americans with Disabilities Act* of 1990 prohibits discrimination in the area of employment, state and local government activities (including education, transportation, social services, etc.), public accommodations (goods and services available to the public), and telecommunications.[121]

The civil laws of the other countries are also broad in scope, in that the legislation is often directed at a wide range of every day life activities, but anti-discrimination provisions are not included in every area covered by the law. For instance the 1996 *Act on Equal Opportunities*

(Employment Equality Act), Korea (Act Relating to Employment Promotion, etc), Madagascar, Mauritius, Namibia, South Africa (Employment Equity Bill, 1998), and Sweden.

[116] §§ 3, 15, 22–30.

[117] §§ 5–10.

[118] §§ 11–20, 24, 25–29, 33–37.

[119] Title III, chapters I–III.

[120] §§ 4, 19, 22, 29, 30, 32–39, 40–47.

[121] Titles I–IV.

for Disabled Persons of Costa Rica legislates access to education, employment, public transportation, public services, information and communication, and cultural, sports and leisure activities. However, discrimination is explicitly prohibited only with respect to employment, public health services, and participation in culture, sports and leisure activities.[122]

The Indian *Persons With Disabilities (Equal Opportunities, Protection of Rights And Full Participation) Act, 1995* differs from the other civil rights laws in that it has rather weak non-discrimination provisions, but instead calls for quotas in various areas. Non-discrimination provisions cover transportation, roads, the built environment, and government employment (excluding the hiring process).[123] However, duties to enable access for disabled persons apply only "within the limits of . . . economic capacity and development," and thus are rather easy to evade. A 3 percent quota scheme applies to government employment, government aided educational institutions, and poverty alleviation schemes.[124] The government employment quota system reserves 1 percent of jobs to persons with certain types of impairments, notably visual, hearing and physical impairments.[125] A particularly interesting aspect of the law is that any shortfall under the 3-percent quota requirement in government employment is to be accrued forward to the following year.[126] Theoretically, this could lead to a situation in which any government agency that had been avoiding its quota requirement could only hire or promote disabled employees. Many of the other foreign laws also have quota provisions, particularly in the public employment field. Nonetheless, as our brief overview of comparative European disability laws in Section C.2 shows, employment quota schemes have a long tradition and do not necessarily pertain to the anti-discrimination principle.

Compared to criminal and constitutional anti-discrimination laws, civil disability anti-discrimination legislation tends to be more explicit

---

122 Arts. 24, 31 & 55.

123 Chapter VIII, §§ 44–47.

124 Chapter VI, §§ 33–40.

125 Chapter VI, § 33 (i)–(iii).

126 Chapter VI, § 36.

about the scope of the law and more detailed; most of the laws provide a definition of what constitutes discriminatory practice and/or equality. In addition, all the civil disability discrimination laws make some provision for their enforcement. Both the concepts of discrimination and equality and the different kinds of enforcement mechanisms will be discussed further below.

iv. Social Welfare Laws and Disability

Finally, some countries choose to approach the issue of disability discrimination through the enactment of traditional social welfare laws for disabled persons. Countries that have done so are: Bolivia,[127] China,[128] Costa Rica,[129] Finland,[130] Korea,[131] Nicaragua,[132] Panama,[133] and Spain.[134]

In these laws, anti-discrimination provisions are found next to more traditional provisions on the prevention of disability and rehabilitation. Except for the Finnish 1992 *Act on the Status and Rights of Patients*, which provides that every resident in Finland is entitled to health and medical care without discrimination, these laws are focussed mainly on enacting and enforcing social services and integration principles rather than rights-based anti-discrimination provisions. Non-discrimination provisions found in social welfare legislation tend to be vague and/or restricted in scope, limited to the area of public employment or public

---

[127] Act No. 1678 about the Person with Disability (1985).

[128] Law of the People's Republic of China on the Protection of Disabled Persons (1990).

[129] Decree No. 119101-S-MEP-TSS-PLAN, 1989.

[130] Act on Status and Rights of Patients (785/ 1992).

[131] The Welfare Law for Persons with Disabilities, Law No. 4179 (1989) and The Special Education Promotion Law, as amended 1994.

[132] Act No. 202, Law for the Prevention, Rehabilitation and Equalization of Opportunities for Persons with Disabilities in Nicaragua (1995), *see also* Decree No. 50-97 (regulations).

[133] Family Law Code, Act No. 3 (1994).

[134] Law on the Social Integration of the Disabled (1982).

education for example. The Spanish *Act on the Social Integration of the Disabled* (1982) is typical, in that it deals with the prevention, diagnosis and assessment of disability, the establishment of a system of benefits in cash and kind, medical and vocational rehabilitation, community services, integration at work, etc. The only anti-discrimination provision in the act states that any discriminatory disability-based provision found in labour regulations, collective agreements, individual contracts, or unilateral decisions shall be null and void.[135]

The Chinese *Law of the People's Republic of China on the Protection of Disabled Persons* of 1990 contains a general prohibition on discrimination against disabled persons,[136] but does not specify what that means for how society is organised. A textual analysis of the law gives the impression that the traditional medical model of disability, which relies on institutionalization and segregation, forms the framework of the act. For instance Article 29 stipulates "concentrated employment" for persons with disabilities as a guiding principle. This means that employment opportunities are provided in special welfare enterprises and institutions. Within these special institutions, discrimination against disabled persons regarding recruitment, employment, promotion, the awarding of professional or technical titles, payment, welfare, and other aspects of employment is prohibited.[137] Given that this is the only detailed anti-discrimination provision in the whole act, the law conveys a rather peculiar and limited concept of equality. The medical model underpinnings of the law are also evident in some provisions on the obligations of disabled persons. According to Article 10, Chinese disabled persons "should display an optimistic and enterprising spirit," which implicitly perpetuates the notion that disability fosters negative attitudes and depression.

Some countries, such as the Philippines, have laws that could be characterised as both a social welfare law and a civil rights law. The *Magna Carta* of the Philippines, however, clearly reveals the legislators' intent to move from the medical model to the human rights model of

---

135 Title VII, § 38 (2).

136 Chapter I, art. 3.

137 Art. 34.

disability. Title I, Chapter I, Section 2 (b) states that "[d]isabled persons' rights must never be perceived as welfare services by the Government."

The history of U.S. disability discrimination law shows that states often begin initiating anti-discrimination provisions for disabled persons in social welfare legislation. This is the legal area where disability law tends to be first developed. The United States first prohibited certain forms of discrimination against disabled people in the *Rehabilitation Act of 1973*. The famous Section 504 provides that every entity which receives federal financial assistance, or is conducted by any federal agency, must not discriminate against an "otherwise qualified" disabled person. The 1988 amendment to the *Fair Housing Act*, which prohibits discrimination in housing matters, was the first step towards including disability as a prohibited ground of discrimination in general U.S. civil rights legislation. A final step was taken with the 1990 adoption of the ADA. On a similar path, Costa Rica and Spain have enacted disability anti-discrimination provisions within social welfare legislation as well as civil laws.

In sum, discrimination provisions contained in social welfare legislation tend to be less comprehensive and reform oriented. The paradigm shift from the medical model of disability to the human rights model of disability seems to be less obvious in this type of legislation.

b. Protected Groups: the Disability-Specific Approach or the Trans-Group Approach

Some anti-discrimination laws for persons with disabilities are part of a law that seeks equality for multiple groups, while other laws focus on disability exclusively. The group law approach protects other minorities or groups such as women, homosexuals, children, the elderly, and linguistic or religious minorities that historically have been the targets of discriminatory practices. With the exception of Ghana,[138] all of the constitutional discrimination provisions protect disabled persons as a group among others. The same is true for discrimination provisions in employment laws and criminal laws. Disability discrimination laws that are

---

[138] The general constitutional equality clause (art. 17) does not cover disability, which is dealt with in a special provision (art. 29).

designed as civil or social laws tend to be directed exclusively to persons with disabilities.

In addition to protecting persons who presently have a disability, some laws also protect persons who were disabled in the past (Australia, Canada [*Human Rights Act*], Hong Kong, New Zealand, the Philippines, the U.K., the U.S.), may be disabled in the future (Australia, Hong Kong, Sweden) or who are regarded as being disabled (Australia, Hong Kong, New Zealand, the Philippines, the U.S.). Furthermore, some laws also protect family members or other associates of disabled persons (Australia, Hong Kong, New Zealand, the Philippines, the U.S.[139]), as well as persons who are victimised because they make a complaint about discrimination or exercise their anti-discrimination rights (Australia, Canada [*Human Rights Act*], New Zealand, the U.K.)

Most discrimination laws that are examples of civil or social legislation give a definition of disability. Usually the definition is medically oriented in that disability is defined as a physical or mental impairment that results in some significant functional limitation.[140]

c. The Diversity of Equality and Discrimination Concepts at Play

The underlying equality concepts of the disability discrimination laws here reviewed differ widely. Some laws support a more formal equality model, in that their guarantee of equal treatment is implicitly conditioned on the premise that disabled persons fully adapt to non-disabled culture and society. Some of the constitutional anti-discrimination clauses can be read this way, as shown by the German education case. The formal equality model can also be seen behind those laws that explicitly mention that discrimination may in some circumstances be justified by the factor of disability. For instance, the 1992 *Labour Act* of Namibia provides that a person shall not be regarded as having been unfairly discriminated against if the disabled person, because of his or

---

139 With regards to public accommodations, goods and services (Title III).

140 *See* Aart Hendriks, "Disability as a Prohibitive Ground for Discrimination: Different Definition—Same Problems—One Way Out?" *in* the present collection for an analysis of the issues raised by definitions of disability.

her disability, is unable to perform the job.[141] The 1992 *Disabled Persons Act* of Zimbabwe provides that disability may be a legitimate excuse for employment discrimination,[142] and the denial of any public service or amenity seems to be excused if is "motivated by a genuine concern for the safety of the disabled person concerned."[143] While the Korean *Special Education Promotion Law* as amended in 1994 prohibits discrimination against disabled students in all schools, only special school principals "should take appropriate measures to provide appropriate convenience for entrance examinations and schooling for children with disabilities based on types and degree of disability."[144] Thus, principals at regular schools are implicitly limited in their responsibility for discriminatory omissions when a student with disabilities cannot be schooled or examined "conveniently."

About one fourth of the laws reviewed here, however, are based on a structural equality concept. Therefore this includes the commitment that society has to change in order to guarantee true equal opportunity for persons with disabilities. The key phrase in this respect is reasonable accommodations or reasonable adjustments, which have to be undertaken by the employer, service provider, government, or any other entity under anti-discrimination obligations. The following countries have included such a provision in their anti-discrimination laws, even though it does not always apply to all areas covered by the discrimination prohibition: Australia,[145] Canada,[146] Hong Kong,[147] Hungary,[148] Ireland,[149]

---

141 § 107 (2) (b).

142 § 9(2)(b).

143 § 10(b)(ii).

144 Art. 13(2).

145 As found in various provisions, e.g., § 5 (2) and § 45.

146 § 5 of the Employment Equity Act.

147 As found in various provisions, e.g., § 12, 24–26.

148 §§ 5 to 8.

149 § 16(3)(b) of the Employment Equality Act (1988) and § 4(1) of the Equal Status Act (2000).

Israel,[150] New Zealand,[151] the Philippines,[152] Sweden,[153] the U.K.,[154] the U.S.,[155] and Zimbabwe.[156]

Another indication that the structural equality concept underlies a discrimination law may be found in the presence of affirmative action provisions, as they indicate the understanding that positive actions may have to be taken in order to achieve true equality. Sixteen countries[157] have affirmative action provisions in their laws, most of them relating to quota schemes.

Most anti-discrimination laws focus on the area of employment discrimination. This can be explained by the fact that this is the area in which discrimination law relating to minority groups in general was first developed; anti-discrimination laws relating to race and gender were first adopted in the employment sector. Thus, it makes sense for disabled persons to follow that path. However, we should also recall that employment rights fall into the realm of economic, social and cultural human rights. This is the set of human rights that traditionally has been applied in the context of disability, whereas civil and political rights have usually been neglected in disability policy. It is all the more remarkable, then, that some of the disability discrimination statutes examined here explicitly guarantee non-discrimination with respect to civil and political rights for persons with disabilities.[158] Others do not mention civil

---

150 § 8 (e).

151 As found in several provisions, e.g., §§ 29, 35, 43, 56, 60.

152 Title II, Chapters 1–7 (§§ 5–31).

153 §§ 3 and 6.

154 As found in various provisions, e.g., §§ 6, 21, 32, etc.

155 For instance, § 504 of the Rehabilitation Act, and Title I (§ 102), Title II (§ 202) and Title III (§ 302) of the ADA.

156 §§ 7 and 9.

157 These include Canada (Human Rights Act), Ghana, Ethiopia (very weak), India, Israel, Mauritius, Nigeria, Philippines, South Africa (Employment Equity Act, but specifically excluding quotas), Spain, Uganda, the U.S., Zambia, and Korea.

158 The Nigerians with Disability Decree has provisions on the right to vote and the right to information (§ 12 and 13). The Magna Carta of the Philippines has provisions on the rights to vote, to assemble and to organise (§§ 29–31).

and political rights explicitly, but may still cover them through anti-discrimination provisions directed at ensuring accessibility to public premises, services and accommodations.

The underlying concept of discrimination that underpins a law may be deduced from its statutory definition of disability-based discrimination (if there is one), and the scope of coverage of its discrimination prohibitions. Since the latter has been already discussed in this article, the remainder of this section shall focus on definitions of discrimination, as enacted in approximately half of our reviewed statutes.

A majority of these definitions define discrimination as unfavorable treatment on the basis of disability,[159] whereas a minority of the statutes define discrimination as unjustified differentiation.[160] Some laws distinguish between direct and indirect forms of discrimination,[161] with the latter commonly defined as the general application of requirements or conditions with which disabled persons usually have more difficulty complying. The aforementioned key phrase in the structural equality concept is explicitly incorporated in the discrimination concept of 12 statutes, which make the "denial of reasonable accommodations" discriminatory.[162] Interestingly, some discrimination acts have provisions requiring access to public places, buildings, transportation, etc., but the fact of inaccessibility is not defined as a discriminatory practice.[163] In the result, accessibility seems to be granted as a welfare service where access is not formulated as an individual right.

---

[159] Australia (§ 5), Canada (HRA, §§ 5–11), Fiji (art. 38), Germany (art. 3), Guatemala (arts. 35 & 44), Hong Kong (§ 6), Ireland (EEA, § 6 and ESA, § 3), Namibia (§ 107), Mauritius (§ 16), New Zealand (as found in various sections, e.g., §§ 22, 37, 42, 53, etc.), Philippines (§ 32), South Africa (Constitution, § 9), Sweden (§ 3), the U.K. (§ 5), and Zambia(§ 19).

[160] France (art. 225–1), Luxembourg (art. 454), Ethiopia (§ 3), Uganda (art. 21(3)).

[161] Australia (§ 6), Fiji (art. 38), Namibia (§ 107), New Zealand (§ 65), the Philippines (§ 32), South Africa (§ 9), Sweden (§ 3 and 4), and Zambia (§ 19).

[162] *Supra* notes 145–156.

[163] Brazil, China, Costa Rica, Ghana, Guatemala, Israel, and Nicaragua.

Some of the discrimination laws characterise acts of harassment and victimization as prohibited forms of discrimination.[164] The Canadian *Human Rights Act*, additionally bans discriminatory public communications, publications and hate messages.[165] Another interesting finding is that a significant number of discrimination laws also address the issue of exploitation or abuse of persons with disabilities.[166]

While few anti-discrimination laws actually support the principle of segregated education for students with disabilities,[167] only a minority of the acts contain a clear statement that separate education is inherently unequal and a classic form of disability discrimination.[168] The most comprehensive definitions of disability discrimination can be found in the laws of Australia, Canada, Hong Kong, New Zealand, the Philippines, the U.K., and the U.S. These laws define discrimination with respect to every area covered by the law, including employment, public accommodation, and goods and services. Within each area, the definitions give long lists of the kinds of actions that would be considered discriminatory, and specify such aspects of discrimination as the denial of participation, granting participation under unequal conditions, or the award of separate benefits.[169] In addition to the factor of disability itself, some of the laws explicitly include the use or accompaniment of such auxiliary aids as guide dogs or interpreters as illegitimate reasons for discriminatory treatment (e.g., Australia, Hong Kong).

---

[164] Australia (§§ 35–40), Canada (HRA, § 14) Hong Kong (§ 7), Israel (§ 10), Sweden (§ 9), and the U.K. (§ 55).

[165] §§ 12 & 13.

[166] Costa Rica (Law 7600 on Equal Opportunities: art. 4), Ghana (Constitution: art. 29(1)(4)) and Panama (art. 520).

[167] For example, Brazil and Nigeria.

[168] In the authors' opinion, the laws of the following countries can be read this way: Australia, Canada, Hong Kong, Hungary, the Philippines, the U.S., and Zambia.

[169] *See* for example, § 302, Title III of the ADA, which details various aspects of what would constitute discrimination in the area of public accommodations.

d. A Variety of Enforcement Mechanisms

The enforcement of legislation is commonly the task of public administrative agencies and the courts. Legislation that seeks to transform society to some extent, such as human rights and anti-discrimination laws, usually establish some kind of special enforcement body. This could be a human rights or an equal opportunity commission, an ombudsperson, a national council, or a public agency. Among the disability legislation under review, only the civil or social law statutes include specific provisions on the enforcement or monitoring of the law.

Thus, the Australian *Disability Discrimination Act* establishes the Human Rights and Equal Opportunity Commission and a Disability Discrimination Commission.[170] The Canadian *Human Rights Act* is enforced by a Human Rights Commission and a Human Rights Tribunal.[171] The *Equal Rights for Persons with Disabilities Law* of Israel entrusts various ministries with the enforcement of the law, and additionally establishes a Commission for Equal Rights.[172] In the U.K., a Disability Rights Commission is the watchdog of the *Disability Discrimination Act*.[173]

A significant number of acts entrust representatives of disability organizations with the monitoring of the law. For instance, the *Law of the People's Republic of China on the Protection of Disabled Persons* establishes the China Disabled Persons' Federation, which has the responsibility to represent and protect the rights and interests of disabled persons in China.[174] The Hungarian discrimination act establishes a

---

[170] §§ 67 &113.

[171] §§ 26 & 48.

[172] §§ 20–25.

[173] Established by the Disability Rights Commission Act of 1999. This new body replaces the former National Disability Council that was established by the DDA, but was much weaker. *See* Simon Minty, "Governance and Legislation: Introducing the UK Disability Rights Commission," 3 *Disability World* (2000) *at* http://www.disabilityworld.org/June-July2000/Governance/UKDisabilityRights.htm (visited July 10, 2000).

[174] Art. 8.

National Disability Affairs Council in which disability organisations must be represented.[175] The Indian law establishes a rather elaborate multi-sectoral planning and monitoring mechanism: a Central Coordination Committee is headed by the Chief Commissioner for Persons with Disabilities, and several State Coordination Committees manage disability matters at the state level. The law also requires a certain number of seats in each committee to be filled by disabled persons.[176] The Nigerian discrimination law establishes a National Commission for Persons with Disabilities, whose chairman must be a disabled person, and within which all major disability groups need to be represented.[177] Similarly, the *Disabled Persons Act* of Ghana establishes a National Council on Disabled Persons in which six seats are reserved for representatives of disability organisations. The law of Zimbabwe establishes a Disability Board in which at least half of the seats must be filled by representatives of disability organisations.[178] Similar requirements hold for the Zambian Agency for Persons with Disability, which is the enforcement body of the Zambian discrimination law.[179]

The functions of these monitoring bodies are manifold, and vary from advising and information gathering for the government to awareness raising in the general public to investigation and complaint filing. The Disability Board in Zimbabwe and the Zambian Agency for Persons with Disabilities also have the mandate to issue "adjustment orders," requiring specific action from owners whose premises and/or services are inaccessible to persons with disabilities.

---

[175] § 24.

[176] §§ 3, 9, 13. The disability movement in India is rather disappointed with the slow implementation of these provisions. *See* Anuradha Mohit, "Governance and Legislation: Initiatives of the Government of India to Advance Asia & Pacific Decade of Disabled Persons," 2 *Disability World* (2000) *at* http://www.disability-world.org/April-May2000/Governance/India.htm (visited May 15, 2000).

[177] § 14.

[178] §§ 4–6.

[179] §§ 3–7.

e. Conclusions on the Trends Within Comparative Law

Disability anti-discrimination laws around the world take various approaches. Disabled persons may be protected against discrimination in constitutional, criminal, civil, or social law. From our review, the most comprehensive legal approach to preventing and protecting against disability-based discrimination seems to be the enactment of civil rights legislation. However, it must be kept in mind that our main method for the evaluation of these laws was textual analyses of the legislation itself. The few cases analyzed and cited above reveal that the impact an anti-discrimination law may have on society depends on judicial interpretation to a large extent, along with a political and social commitment to enforcement, and not only the text itself.

Today there is no universal definition of disability-based discrimination, and no universal concept of what equalization of opportunities for disabled persons actually entails. Definitions of discrimination range along the gamut from unjustified differentiation to direct or indirect unfavorable treatment to detailed lists of discriminatory practices. However, we can conclude that modern disability discrimination laws generally adhere to the principles of desegregation, de-institutionalization, and reasonable accommodation, which together work to actively abolish structural as well as overt discrimination. In addition to a strong definition of discrimination, laws need to provide clear and effective enforcement mechanisms in which disabled persons individually or as a group play a major role.

Not all disability laws that act to improve the living conditions and social integration of disabled persons have been analyzed in this article. Many countries have laws that have the effect of advancing the integration of persons with disabilities into the community and public life. For example, many building laws require (new) buildings designed for the general public to be accessible to disabled people. Education laws often provide for integrated education as a fundamental principle of education policy. In Scandinavia, social welfare laws secure a minimum income for persons with disabilities, thus facilitating their economic independence. Other countries have strong legal provisions explicitly establishing independent living services for disabled persons. The Finish *Services and Assistance for the Disabled Act* of 1987 is especially notable for giving severely disabled persons in that country the right to independent living services such as transportation, housing, interpretation services, and to some extent, personal assistance services. Because the act's main purpose is to enable disabled persons to live as independent members of society on an equal footing with others, the act is also called the *Disabled Person's Equality Act*.[180] However, these disability laws have not been reviewed here because they do not fall within the concept of anti-discrimination laws. Even though these laws aim to establish equal opportunities for disabled persons, they do not identify and prohibit inaccessibility, segregation, or the denial of independent living as forms of discrimination. It should be remembered that anti-discrimination law is not the only route to equality for persons with disabilities, but the rights-based approach is one of the most prominent legal methods being used by many states around the world today, and is the subject of the present review.

This global overview of discrimination laws for persons with disabilities give rise to both hope and concern. The concern is that not every instance of anti-discrimination language in legislation may actually achieve or even aim at equal rights for disabled persons. National and international disability organizations need to act as watch dogs to ensure that their legislators do not use anti-discrimination language as a pretext while fundamentally adhering to a medical model of disability policy. But there is also clear evidence that anti-discrimination legislation for disabled persons is on the rise all over the world. With that fact, persons with disabilities can have real hope that disability policy will finally achieve the ideals of human rights and structural equality.

---

180 Jari Korpi, "Finland" *in European Day of Disabled Persons 1995, Disabled Persons' Status in the European Treaties: Invisible Citizens* 67–70 (Brussels, Secretariat of European Day of Disabled Persons,1995).

Part 2
Case Study: Using Regional Law as a Catalyst for Change—Towards a "Europeans with Disabilities Act"

A. INTRODUCTION

This part focuses in from the global to survey major human rights and anti-discrimination developments in the European region, with a view to establishing whether there are realistic prospects for the adoption of a Europeans with Disabilities Act similar in depth and scope to the Americans with Disabilities Act (ADA).

In the aftermath of the Second World War, two very different and yet complementary regional organizations were established in Europe: the Council of Europe (1949) and the European Economic Community or EEC (1957), now known as the European Union (EU). The formal competencies of both these organizations extend to the issue of disability.

In fact both organizations have taken an active interest in disability law and policy over the last several decades, and especially from the early 1990s onwards. The paradigm shift from welfare to rights that is so characteristic of the ADA of 1990, and which was ratified at an international level in the UN Standard Rules in 1993, is also strikingly evident in changes that first took place in national and regional European policy over the last decade.

The fact that new and reforming ideas in this area should come from the Council of Europe is no surprise since the very *raison d'etre* of this body is to advance and protect human rights. That the European Union should concern itself with the issue is of some initial surprise since this body is better known for its success (and near preoccupation) with the establishment of an internal market common to the national markets of its member states. Nonetheless, its newly found interest in the subject is of profound significance. The EU's openness to new thinking on disability could perhaps be explained by its tendency to view appropriately tailored equality strategies as a "productive factor" in an advanced market economy. We recall that this market-perfecting rationale was also one of the most powerful impulses behind the enactment of the ADA.

In purely legal terms, the involvement of the EU is significant in that it has at its disposal much more powerful legal weapons compared to those wielded by the Council of Europe. Indeed, the EU could potentially enact a *Europeans with Disabilities Act* to rival the ADA in scope and depth. As will be seen, the first steps toward such a comprehensive measure have already been taken in Brussels.

The relevant laws and policies of the Council of Europe and the European Union both reflect the pattern of change taking place within their respective member states, and also help to further augment and drive the overall process of reform across the continent. The chief animating ethic of this reform process stems directly from broad notions of equality and non-discrimination, though the specific manifestation of this agenda in the legal and policy initiatives of both organizations is quite bewildering, even to those who are seasoned watchers of these bodies. Nonetheless, these initiatives can be usefully clustered under the following themes.

First, since this reform process aims to honor human dignity, it aims to restore the visibility of the person, especially in those contexts where they are most vulnerable. A good example of an initiative that follows this theme is the mental health law reform process underway throughout Europe. It seeks to restore human visibility by extending the full benefits of the rule of law and legal protections to those who have been involuntarily detained. Equal attention is now being paid to the conditions of confinement, to ensuring adequate rights to treatment, and to the prohibition of certain forms of treatment that degrade the dignity of the person. Underlying this trend is the ethic of equal human self-worth, leading quite naturally to a deliberate policy dedicated to restoring equal visibility to all people. The Council of Europe plays a leading role in this regard.

Secondly, the reform process is leading to a new awareness of the rights of persons who are incapable of vindicating their own rights and interests, and who have a need for flexible legal responses. A good example is the radical reform of incompetency law currently underway throughout Europe. The European Parliament (a body of the European

Union) has taken an active interest in this area in the past, but the Council of Europe has also taken a lead role in helping to spur the process of internal law reform. None of this could take place without an overall strategy of equality.

Thirdly, the reform process is founded on a gradual acceptance that one of the most important entailments of equal citizenship is that the lifeworld should be open to all on genuinely equal terms. A good example is the broad movement toward equal opportunities and non-discrimination laws and programs that are intended to help people take power in their own lives, and to participate on terms they set for themselves. This is leading to the proliferation of specific non-discrimination laws in diverse fields such as education, employment, transport, telecommunications, etc. Both the Council of Europe and the European Union have taken a very active interest in this dimension of the reform process. The European Union is actually poised to adopt hard legal measures to guarantee the right of non-discrimination (including the associated concept of reasonable accommodation) in the important employment context.

Fourthly, the reform process is leading to the awareness that economic and social programs that traditionally have been part of the problem could become part of the solution if they were re-oriented to facilitate participation and choice. This awareness is reflected in the reform of the European social model currently under way, and is especially prevalent within the European Union. Just as American policy makers are coming to the realization that formal freedoms need to be augmented with social supports to make freedom real, so too are European policy makers coming to the realization that social protection is devoid of purpose unless it is tied to a strategy that liberates people and ensures their civil rights.

What follows is an account of how the equal opportunities and non-discrimination model is taking hold in European disability policy as reflected in the Council of Europe and the European Union. After looking at the relevant laws and policies of the two organizations, we will conclude by drawing some analytical strands together and assessing the possibility for the enactment of a Europeans with Disabilities Act.

B. THE COUNCIL OF EUROPE AND DISABILITY

1. Background: The Legal Tools and Policy Instruments of the Council

The Council of Europe was established in 1949 and is the older of the two organizations. Its membership is much broader than that of the EU, and currently stands at 41. Significantly for the reach of disability-related activities, its membership includes most East European countries; Georgia is the latest member state. The United States, Canada and Mexico have consultative status.

The main object of the Council is as stated in Article 1 of its founding statute:

> 1. (a) . . . to achieve a greater unity between its Members for the purpose of safeguarding and realising the ideals and principles which are their common heritage and facilitating their economic and social progress.
>
> These aims are pursued through the organs of the Council by:
>
> 1. (b) . . . discussion of questions of common concern and by agreements and common action in economic, social, cultural, scientific, legal and administrative matters and in the maintenance and further realisation of human rights and fundamental freedoms.[181]

The fundamental philosophy of the Council of Europe seeks to augment the nation-state in order to avoid any repetition of a slide into totalitarianism and consequential conflict between European states. Hence the Council traditionally has laid heavy emphasis on maintaining high (if not exactly uniform) human rights standards throughout Europe.

In terms of its jural character, the Council is a classic inter-governmental organization. That is, it has no power over states except the authority that states are willing to cede to it voluntarily. This emphasis

---

[181] *Statute of the Council of Europe*, 5 May 1949, E.T.S. No. 1.

on inter-governmentalism is reflected in the organs of the Council. The main political organ is the Committee of Ministers, which has a Presidency that rotates every six months. The Council possesses its own expert Secretariat (permanent international civil servants), presided over by a Secretary General (currently Walter Schwimmer of Austria).

The Council also has a Parliamentary Assembly (previously called a Consultative Assembly), whose members are drawn on a pro rata basis from the national parliaments of member states. The Assembly sometimes debates important disability-related matters.

The competence of the Council is broad, though matters of national defense are explicitly excluded under Article 1(d) of the founding statute. In keeping with the character of the Council, the instruments used by it are classically inter-governmental in nature. The most important tool at its disposal is the adoption of conventions or legally binding treaties that are open for signature to all member states. Some conventions are in fact open for signature to non-member states. At least 177 treaties have been concluded in this way on topics ranging from transfrontier television[182] to insider trading[183] to a broad range of human rights. By far the most important of these conventions is the world-famous European Convention for the Protection of Human Rights and Fundamental Freedoms (ECHR), though virtually all of the human rights conventions have either direct or indirect relevance in the context of disability, including disability-based discrimination.

The Committee of Ministers can also adopt Recommendations directed to member state governments, dealing with the formulation of their policies. Though such Recommendations are non-binding in law, they can be extremely influential. Sometimes the inspiration for the adoption of a Recommendation comes from leading cases decided in the European Court of Human Rights. Often, these cases reveal wide gaps in European law that could be addressed effectively through uniform law reform. As will be seen, some leading cases in the field of mental health have prompted important Recommendations. Often the impetus for a Recommendation comes in response to a spontaneously

---

182 *Convention on Transfrontier Television*, 5 May 1989, E.T.S. No. 132.

183 *Convention on Insider Trading*, 20 Apr. 1989, E.T.S. No. 130.

initiated reform process that shows signs of diverging or veering off course and requires a firm conceptual steer from Strasbourg.

Finally, the Council of Europe hosts a bewildering web of inter-governmental activities that provides *fora* for the discussion of a broad range of issues. Where an issue does not seems to fall squarely within the remit of the Council, or where only a few member states wish to pursue a certain policy matter, the Council may nevertheless facilitate discussion of the issue by concluding what is called a Partial Agreement. Under such Partial Agreements the machinery of the Council is made available to those member states that wish to use it for the purposes of the agreement. Under one such Partial Agreement, the Partial Agreement in the Social and Public Health Field, many relevant disability matters (including discrimination based on disability) have been discussed and studied.[184] Steerage is provided for these activities by the Committee on the Rehabilitation and Integration of People with Disabilities (CD-P-RR).

One interesting result from the end of the Cold War was that the Council of Europe, as a matter of necessity, began to revise its own self-understanding. It no longer saw itself as a "democratic club," but also was forced to act as a "democratic school," especially with respect to newer member states from the former soviet bloc. The fall of the Berlin Wall led to the emergence of new democracies out of the former communist bloc. With the urgent need—born of political imperative—to admit these new states, the Council realised that its role also had to change.[185] It was increasingly called upon not merely to police standards but also to promote standards, and to actively facilitate democratisation of the new regimes. To achieve these aims, the Council acquired new tools and bodies such as the ADACS Program.

---

[184] This Partial Agreement dates back to Resolution (59) 23 of 16 Nov. 1959 concerning *Extension of the Activities of the Council of Europe in the Social and Cultural Fields*. The membership of the Partial Agreement was increased in 1996: Resolution (96) 34, *Authorising the States Concerned to Revise the Partial Agreement in the Social and Public Health Field*, 2 Oct. 1996.

[185] The political events of the late 1980s and early 1990s and the response of the Council of Europe are treated extensively in Denis Huber, *A Decade Which Made History: The Council of Europe 1989–1999*, (Strasbourg, Council of Europe Pub., 1999).

ADACS stands for Activities for the Development and Consolidation of Democratic Stability. Its current programs include *Demosthenes* (institution-building through the training of policy makers), *Themis* (training of the judiciary), and *Lode* (development of local democracy). The 2000 ADACS Program; dealing with social cohesion, supports a number of disability-related projects. Interestingly, one such project has to do with the training of officials in Bosnia in the drafting of disability-rights legislation.[186] Other projects include a program for the de-institutionalization of children with disabilities in Russia. Curiously, a recent Council of Europe Strategy on Social Cohesion does not appear to mention disability.[187]

Other relevant Council of Europe post-Cold War developments include the Venice Commission on Democracy through Law,[188] the Office of the Commissioner for Human Rights,[189] and the creation of a process within the Secretariat for the monitoring of the human rights situation in member states, etc. All of these bodies have an interest in the disability field.

Parenthetically, in keeping with their inter-governmental nature, these *fora* traditionally did not actively involve non-governmental organizations (NGOs) or INGOs (i.e., NGOs that span several European countries) in their deliberations. Currently, however, and due in no small part to the equal opportunities philosophy, the Council consults actively with disability NGOs.

---

186 *See* P-SG (2000) 8: ADACs (2000) 1.

187 European Committee for Social Cohesion, *Strategy for Social Cohesion*, CM (2000) 92, 20 July 2000.

188 *See Partial Agreement Establishing the European Commission for Democracy Through Law (Venice Commission)*, adopted by the Committee of Ministers in Resolution 90(6) on May 10, 1990.

189 The decision to establish such a post was taken at the Council of Europe's Second Summit in Oct. 1997. Mr. Gil Robles (former President of the European Parliament) was elected by the Parliamentary Assembly in Aug., 2000 as the first and incoming Commissioner.

2. Council of Europe Conventions in the Context of Disability

The Council of Europe has passed a web of conventions that protect a very broad range of rights, including the right to be free from discrimination. Most of these conventions have either direct or indirect relevance in the context of disability.

a. Disability and the Council of Europe Convention for the Protection of Human Rights and Fundamental Freedoms (1950)[190] (ECHR)

This convention is the European regional equivalent to the UN's International Covenant on Civil and Political Rights. It sets out a full and detailed list of civil and political rights, and—equally important—establishes an elaborate process of judicial enforcement through the European Court of Human Rights. Until 1994, the European Commission of Human Rights assisted the Court. Protocol No. 11 of 1994 dissolved the Commission, but its jurisprudence remains persuasive before the Court.[191] In essence, the Court provides a "system of outer" judicial supervision that is intended to complement rather than supplant national judicial systems, which are still considered primary.

Proceedings before the European Court of Human Rights must be initiated within six months of a final domestic judicial decision. A decision is first made on admissibility, and then on the merits. Adverse judgments are "enforced" politically by the Committee of Ministers, which "supervises their execution."[192]

Several rights from the ECHR have figured quite prominently in the case law of the Court with regards to disability. In particular, the rights to liberty (Article 5), fair trail (Article 6), and to freedom from torture,

---

[190] 4 Nov. 1950, E.T.S. No. 005.

[191] See Andrew Drzemczewski, "A Major Overhaul of the European Human Rights Convention Control Mechanisms: Protocol No 11," *in* 6(2) *Collected Courses of the Academy of European Law* 126 (1997).

[192] *Supra* note 190, at art. 46.2.

inhuman or degrading treatment (Article 3) have given rise to a very rich jurisprudence in the context of mental disability, and civil commitment in particular.[193]

Article 5.1(e) of the ECHR specifically allows for the "lawful detention of persons of unsound mind" (i.e., civil commitment as an exception to the general right to liberty), but a series of important judgments have refined this exceptional power. This is important since the traditional civil commitment process was highly disadvantageous, even in comparison to the corresponding criminal process. Unlike the criminal process, the ground of incarceration in a civil commitment could simply point to a condition *as such*, and not to a condition as manifested in certain behaviour. The decision-making process was generally reflexive and not reflective. Very few substantive or procedural rights were allowed to the person being incarcerated. The length and degree of the loss of liberty was indeterminate, and the consequential effect on remaining rights was severe. Typically, civil commitment in the past led to a near complete forfeiture of civil capacity.

One example of how the Court of Human Rights has narrowed the potential misuse of the civil commitment exception in the ECHR is found in *Winterwerp v Netherlands*.[194] In its decision, the Court refused to adhere to any single definition of mental illness, and instead tied the definition to advances in medical science. It insisted that the term "unsound mind" should never be used as a subterfuge with which to incarcerate those who simply deviate from social convention or who hold unpopular political views. The Court has also devised an elaborate jurisprudence on the criteria of "lawfulness" as required for the detention of a person under Article 5.1(e). The evidence must be credible and objective. The party bringing the motion must not be the same as the receiving party (or institution). Domestic law must be fully complied with, and any failure to comply will amount to a separate breach of the Convention. Furthermore, Article 5(4) requires a periodic review of commitment, and Article 6 guarantees a right of reasonable access to the ordinary courts for the hearing of any general civil claim or argu-

---

193 *See* Gerard Quinn, "Civil Commitment and the Right to Treatment under the European Convention on Human Rights," 5 *Harv. Hum. Rts. J.* 1 (1992).

194 (24 Oct. 1979), A-33.

ment against the lawfulness of detention. The mere fact of civil commitment is not in itself enough to warrant denying a person's legal capacity. Placing a sane person in a mental institution raises issues under both Article 5(1)(e) and Article 3. Likewise, placing a person "of unsound mind" in a prison without treatment raises similar issues.

In general, Article 5 (alone, as well as in combination with Articles 6 and 3) has given rise to what has been termed the "creeping criminalization" of civil commitment law in Europe. The phrase refers to the manner in which many of the substantive and procedural safeguards that normally attend criminal incarceration proceedings are gradually being grafted on to the civil commitment process.

By far the most serious weakness of the ECHR in the context of disability concerns the inadequacy of its non-discrimination provision. The main equality/non-discrimination norm of the Convention is contained in Article 14, which states:

> 14. The enjoyment of the rights and freedoms set forth in this Convention shall be secured without discrimination on any ground such as sex, race, colour, language, religion, political or other opinion, national or social origin, association with a national minority, property, birth or other status.

The first overall limitation stems from the fact that the critical bite of Article 14 is reserved exclusively for the enjoyment of rights contained in the Convention itself. That is, it does not provide for a general anti-discrimination clause that could apply, for example, in the field of public transport. Secondly, the grounds on which discrimination is prohibited do not explicitly include disability. It is, of course, entirely possible to interpret the phrase "other status" as one which sweeps in persons with disabilities. But it would have been easier to make a case for coverage under the ECHR if disability were explicitly mentioned.

The weaknesses of Article 14 are universally and frankly acknowledged. It could be broadened if it referred to more grounds than those listed. It could be deepened if it stretched beyond the convention rights themselves so as to prohibit discrimination in a broad range of fields. In fact, an opportunity to broaden and deepen the protection of Article 14 arose recently. The main impulse for this process of reform came from persons and organizations primarily concerned with issues of gender and race. From the gender perspective, the need for reform arose from the concern that Article 14 could not sustain even mild measures of affirmative action. From the race perspective, the need for reform arose because the narrow scope of Article 14 (confined to the equal enjoyment of convention rights) failed to secure real equality in those contexts where it mattered most, including the areas of employment and the enjoyment of social services.

The end product of this reform process was Protocol 12 to the Convention,[195] Article 1 of which reads:

> 1. The enjoyment *of any right set forth by law* shall be secured without discrimination on any ground such as sex, race, colour, language, religion, political or other opinion, national or social origin, association with a national minority, property, birth or other status. [emphasis added]

It is important to note that Protocol No. 12 is additional to the ECHR. That is, it does not replace Article 14 of the Convention as such, but stands as a separate option. For those member states that choose to ratify it, the Protocol merely adds to Article 14. For those states that do not ratify it, only the original Article 14 (and nothing else) applies.

The text italicised in Article 1 of Protocol No. 12, above, is the only change from the original Article 14. As such, the Protocol is clearly intended to carry the protective coverage of the Article 14 non-discrimination norm beyond the rights secured by the convention itself, but does not add to or extend the grounds of prohibited discrimination as originally drafted. Therefore disability is still not explicitly covered under the Council of Europe's main legal weapon against discrimination. This situation stands in vivid contrast to that in the European Union, see below, and if only because of the unfavorable comparison

---

[195] For the reasoning behind its enactment, *see* Steering Committee for Human Rights, *Draft Protocol No. 12 to the European Convention on Human Rights and Draft Explanatory Report*, 766 *bis* meeting 27–28 July 1999, Appendix 8, H (98) 8.

with the EU, the ECHR's current shortcomings must surely rank as a standing embarrassment to the Council of Europe.

Certain other rights that are additional to those set out in the original convention have been added by Additional Protocols. Of special interest in the context of disability is the right to education that is contained in the First Protocol (1952).[196] The right reads as follows:

> 2. No person shall be denied the right to education. In the exercise of any functions which it assumes in relation to education and to teaching, the State shall respect the right of parents to ensure such education and teaching in conformity with their own religious and philosophical convictions.

The combination of Article 2 of the First Protocol (education) and Article 14 of the ECHR (non-discrimination) should have been a fruitful source of jurisprudence in the context of education discrimination against students with disabilities. This has not been the case so far for two main reasons.

First of all, in an area of law or in circumstances where there is ambiguity, the interpretation of the ECHR will depend in part on the state of domestic law throughout Europe. That is, the evolving norms are pegged at the current state of European law generally. The European Court does not typically or lightly use the norms of the Convention to strike out boldly and require wholesale reform from member states. The harsh reality is that education across Europe has tended to be largely exclusionary and discriminatory in the past. It was perhaps inevitable that the organs of the ECHR would come to reflect this by timidly interpreting the right to an equal education. Secondly, any meaningful enforcement of the right would demand a critical examination of current European educational systems, and inevitably result in adverse judgments that would have a bearing on how state resources are allocated and used. In other words, full compliance with an adverse judgment would require better planning, new legislation, and the allocation

---

[196] *Protocol to the Convention for the Protection of Human Rights and Fundamental Freedoms*, 20 Mar. 1952, E.T.S. No. 009.

of fresh resources. Put bluntly, such requirements would threaten or at least appear to constrain the executive prerogatives of the state.

In at least two applications the European Commission on Human Rights could have taken a bold line with respect to educational discrimination against students with disabilities, but chose not to consider the substantive issues by refusing admissibility.[197] While strict separation of powers concerns have not acted as a bar to admissibility for the Commission or Court in the past where they were inclined to be activist toward a member state, they evidently have chosen not to be activist on this issue.

However, the right kind of test case strategy could still create some positive jurisprudence on educational issues in the future, for the simple reason that domestic law and policy in this area is changing in the member states and the Court is bound to take some cognizance of this trend.

b. Disability and the European Social Charter (1961),[198] the Additional Protocol to the European Social Charter Providing for a System of Collective Complaints (1995),[199] and the Revised European Social Charter (1996)[200]

Civil and political rights do not fully exhaust the field of human rights. Indeed the non-discrimination ideal places just as much emphasis on economic and social supports as it does on the enjoyment of classic civil and political rights. Economic, social and cultural rights are also implicated by the broad notion of human rights and have particular resonance in the context of disability. Indeed, disability is one of the best fields in which to establish (and not just assert) the much-vaunted interdependence and indivisibility of both sets of rights.

---

[197] *See* S.P. v. United Kingdom, Application No. 28915/95, decision of the Commission, 17 Jan. 1997 and Cohen v. United Kingdom, Application No. 25959/94, decision of the Commission, 28 Feb. 1996.

[198] 18 Oct. 1961, E.T.S. No. 035.

[199] 9 Nov. 1995, E.T.S. No. 158.

[200] 3 May 1996, E.T.S. No. 163.

The European Social Charter of 1961 is the European regional equivalent to the UN's International Covenant on Economic, Social and Cultural Rights (1966). The title of the Charter is misleading since it is in fact a legally binding treaty, though it was quite weak as originally drafted.

Part I outlines 19 general principles which contracting parties undertake, to respect the formulation of relevant domestic economic and social policies. Part II states, in greater detail, the rights (Articles 1–19) that correspond to these principles. Part III (Article 20) deals with the kinds of "undertakings" that contracting parties assume upon their ratification of the text. Part IV (Articles 21–29) details the reporting requirement that accompanies the undertakings entered into by particular contracting parties. According to Part 1:

> The Contracting Parties accept as the aim of their policy, to be pursued by all appropriate means, both national and international in character, the attainment of conditions in which the following rights and principles may be effectively realised: [19 principles follow]

Most of the principles have general relevance for all rights and considerable indirect relevance in the context of disability. They include principles such as the opportunity to earn a living in an occupation freely entered into (Principle 1), the right to just conditions of work (Principle 2), the right to appropriate facilities for vocational training (Principle 10), the right to benefit from measures enabling the person to enjoy the highest possible standard of health attainable (Principle 11), and the right to benefit from social services (Principle 14). Persons with disabilities are mentioned explicitly in both Articles 9 and 10, and Principle 15 and Article 15 apply specifically to the case of persons with disabilities.

The Charter was subject to three structural weaknesses that deserve mention. The first weakness had to do with the critical bite of the norms. The relevant norms of the original Charter were fairly hollow, and seemed designed to act as lip service to the contemporary reality of social policy across Europe at a particular point in time, rather than as the engine driving any process of real social change.

A second weakness had to with the *a la carte* nature of the obligations entered into. Apart from being required to abide by certain core rights (which did *not* include Article 15), any contracting party had discretion over which of the remaining articles it would agree to be bound by.[201] In the result, a Contracting Party could even opt out of the original Article 15.

Yet a third weakness had to do with the "enforcement mechanism" of the Social Charter, which merely entailed periodic reporting to the Council of Europe and to a committee of independent experts (formerly styled the Committee of Independent Experts on the European Social Charter and now the European Committee of Social Rights). However, even though the Committee lacks the authority to issue "binding" judgments, it has built up a considerable body of "case law" that consists of interpretations of the Charter. The Committee of Ministers adopts a resolution at the end of each supervision cycle that covers named articles and named countries. It also has the power to issue more specific recommendations directed at particular contracting parties that fail to comply with their obligations under the Charter.

With specific reference to disability Principle 15 stated:

> 15. Disabled persons have the right to vocational training, rehabilitation and resettlement, whatever the origin and nature of their disability.

The emphasis on vocational training was in keeping with the thinking of the times. The corresponding Article 15 read:

> 15. With a view to ensuring the effective exercise of the right of the physically or mentally disabled to vocational training, rehabilitation and resettlement, the Contracting Parties undertake:
> (1) to take adequate measures for the provision of training facilities, including, where necessary, specialized institutions, public or private;
> (2) to take adequate measures for the placing of disabled persons in employment, such as specialized placing services,

201 *Supra* note 198, at art. 20.

> facilities for sheltered employment and measures to encourage employers to admit disabled persons to employment.

Obviously both Principle 15 and Article 15 as originally conceived flow from a welfare mentality, and not from a human rights or equal opportunities mentality. This was the case despite the fact that Article 15 occurred in an instrument ostensibly dedicated to human rights. There was nothing unusual in this since the Charter dates back to a time when the paradigm shift to full and equal rights in the disability context was not even on the distant horizon. Granting access to welfare and rehabilitation was seen as exhausting the human rights entitlements of persons with disabilities.

Nevertheless, to its credit, the European Committee of Social Rights has interpreted Article 15 generously. In its very first cycle of conclusions (reports on the Charter's implementation that are periodically issued by the Committee), the Committee gave its understanding of Article 15 as follows:

> For a long time aid to the handicapped was classed together with aid to the aged; since the second world war, aid to handicapped persons has developed on separate lines, under the influence of Anglo-Saxon legislation. Traditional assistance policies are now out of date and in legislation the emphasis regarding this category of persons has shifted to vocational training and rehabilitation, [and] . . . reintegration within society.[202]

According to the above interpretation, the overriding purpose behind Article 15 was to enable the persons addressed in it to work and be independent. Overall the Charter reflects this trend, and after referring to handicapped persons in Articles 9 and 10, raised the rights of physically or mentally disabled persons to training, vocational rehabilitation and social resettlement to the level of being separate social rights. Such rights are inconceivable in the absence of the means of bringing

---

202 Conclusions Cycle I, at 72 (1970). *See generally* Lenia Samuel, *Fundamental Social Rights: Case Law of the European Social Charter* 338–47 (Strasbourg, Council of Europe Pub., 1997).

them into effect, and the Charter therefore incorporated some of the provisions already contained in relevant International Labour Organization (ILO) recommendations. Under Article 15 of the Charter, the contracting parties undertook to guarantee to disabled persons:

- training facilities, including, where necessary, specialised institutions (paragraph 1);
- that their placing shall be promoted by means of specialised services, sheltered employment and measures to encourage employers to admit physically or mentally disabled persons to employment (Paragraph 2).[203]

Even though the intention may have been to broaden the traditional approach, the fact remains that the text harboured a contradiction between reliance on specialised, separate and/or targeted measures, and integrationist measures. Furthermore, the actual operation of Article 15 failed to keep pace with the range of disability discrimination issues that could arise. For example, in the analysis of state party reports by the European Committee on Social Rights, a prominent issue has been the treatment of non-nationals with disabilities. Italy was found in violation of Article 15 on account of the excessive and unexplained large amount of persons with disabilities who were unemployed, but who were actively seeking entry to the labour market.[204]

It was clear by the mid-1990s that the Charter was woefully out of date. For one thing, many European constitutions had by then made at least some of the economic and social rights guaranteed within them justiciable. Perhaps the best example is the recent Finnish Constitution of 1995. The flood of emerging democracies into the Council meant that more emphasis had to be placed on the real enjoyment of these rights and not just on rhetorical enjoyment.

Two concrete results ensued from the process of reflection initiated in the early 1990s. The first result has to do with "enforcement." An Additional Protocol was concluded in 1995 that, once ratified by a par-

---

[203] *Id.*

[204] Conclusions Cycle XIII-3, at 190 (1996).

ticular member state, would enable any INGO that held consultative status with the Council of Europe to lodge a "collective complaint" against that state with the European Committee of Social Rights (Article 1).[205] At least three European level disability INGOs have that entitlement at present.[206] More European INGOs can and should apply. Under Article 2 of the Additional Protocol, contracting parties may also opt to vest purely national NGOs with such an entitlement (for example, the Forum of People with Disabilities, which is a purely national disability organization in Ireland).

Sufficient ratifications have now been garnered to enable this Additional Protocol to become operative with respect to those member states that have signed it. Indeed, eight collective complaints have already been lodged. The first concerned child labour law, and was made by the International Commission of Jurists (based in Geneva) against Portugal.[207] None of the complaints relate to disability so far, but it is probably only a matter of time before they do. This convention could therefore serve as a useful forum for INGOs and NGOs to discuss discrimination with respect to economic, social and cultural rights and programs.

The second concrete result has to do with substance. The norms were completely reworked, and the result was the Revised European Social Charter of 1996.[208] Most significant for our purposes, Principle 15 has been completely modernised and reworded to embrace the equal opportunities philosophy (albeit imperfectly). It now reads:

---

205 *Additional Protocol to the European Charter Providing for a System of Collective Complaints*, *supra* note 199.

206 European Action of the Disabled—EAH (as of Jan. 1, 2000); International Association Autism—Europe (as of July 1, 1998); International Federation for Hydrocephalus and Spina Bifida (as of July 1, 1998).

207 Decision on Admissibility, Complaint No. 1/1998 from the International Commission of Jurists against Portugal, European Committee on Social Rights. The complaint was declared admissible.

208 *European Social Charter (Revised)*, *supra* note 200.

Principle 15.

Disabled persons have the right to independence, social integration and participation in the life of the community.

The corresponding Article 15 now reads:

15. With a view to ensuring to persons with disabilities, irrespective of age and the nature and origin of their disabilities, the effective exercise of the right to independence, social integration and participation in the life of the community, the Parties undertake, in particular:
    1. to take the necessary measures to provide persons with disabilities with guidance, education and vocational training in the framework of general schemes whenever possible or, where this is not possible, through specialised bodies, public or private;
    2. to promote their access to employment through all measures tending to encourage employers to hire and keep in employment persons with disabilities in the ordinary working environment and to adjust the working conditions to the needs of the disabled or, where this is not possible by reason of the disability, by arranging for or creating sheltered employment according to the level of disability. In certain cases, such measures may require recourse to specialised placement and support services;
    3. to promote their full social integration and participation in the life of the community in particular through measures, including technical aids, aiming to overcome barriers to communication and mobility and enabling access to transport, housing, cultural activities and leisure.

It is fairly plain that the drafters of the revised Article 15 took cognizance of the paradigm shift from welfare to rights taking place around the world.

Apart from a reference in its preamble, the original Charter of 1961 did not contain any legal provision relating to discrimination.[209] Interestingly, a new and specific provision was added to the Revised Social

---

209 The preamble to the 1961 Charter reads in the relevant part:

Charter (1996) to guarantee non-discrimination with respect to the rights set out in the Charter (Part V, Article E). The text copies that of Article 14 of the ECHR almost word by word. It does not, therefore, explicitly list disability as one of the prohibited grounds of discrimination. However, the European Committee of Social Rights has emphasised in its case law that the enumerated grounds set out in the Charter's non-discrimination clause are not exhaustive.[210] It is therefore likely that if a proper case were presented, the European Committee of Social Rights would interpret the phrase "other status" as including persons with disabilities.

Equally important, the Additional Protocol will apply to the Revised Social Charter for those states that ratify both instruments (Part IV, Article D of the Revised Charter). The Revised Charter in combination with the Additional Protocol could be of great value. With the right kind of ratification, it is entirely possible that disability INGOs and NGOs, who are already on the frontlines monitoring for rights abuses, will be able to use the collective complaints mechanism to argue non-discrimination issues before the European Committee on Social Rights. This means that discrimination issues covering a broad range of social policy fields could be ventilated in Strasbourg, once we work out details about how the mechanism will work and precisely which ratifications will be needed.

c. Council of Europe Convention for the Protection of Human Rights and Dignity of the Human Being with Regard to the Application of Biology and Medicine: Convention on Human Rights and Biomedicine (1997)[211]

This convention is highly relevant in the context of disability for a number of reasons. First of all, science can generate information that can be

---

> Considering that the enjoyment of social rights should be secured without discrimination on grounds of race, colour, sex, religion, political opinion, national extraction or social origin. . . .

210 *See* Council of Europe, *The Revised European Social Charter and Explanatory Report* (Strasbourg, Council of Europe Pub., 1996), and *The Additional Protocol to the European Social Charter Providing for A System of Collective Complaints and Explanatory Report* (Strasbourg, Council of Europe Pub., 1997).

211 4 Apr. 1997, E.T.S. No. 164.

used to the detriment of individuals. The interesting thing about "objective" scientific facts is that they tend to fit with social determinism. Therefore, some mechanism is needed to deal with the uses and abuses of such information.

Secondly, human vulnerability brings many risks. It can exacerbate the "normal" risks that attend the inherently unequal relationship between patient and doctor. It tends to render individuals invisible in decision-making processes that affect them, and this in turn unfortunately tends to have drastic consequences for the attitudes of those who are in positions of power and responsibility. In a worst case scenario drawn from history, the vulnerability of persons with disabilities has been exploited to excuse the conduct of vicious experiments and to subject disabled persons to pointless or evil clinical trials. Careful controls are therefore called for to protect the rights and interests of vulnerable persons, even where the procedures in question can potentially lead to advances in medical understanding and treatments. The role of law is to draw a line—to insist on the dignity and equal inherent worth of all human beings.

The Council of Europe's Biomedicine Convention unfortunately fails to reach this goal. It pays lip service to important human rights principles, for example, by stating in Article 1 that the parties shall:

> protect the dignity and identity of all human beings and guarantee everyone, *without discrimination*, respect for their integrity and other rights and fundamental freedoms with regard to the application of biology and medicine. [emphasis added]

However, the Convention fails to protect the human rights of disabled persons in the context of genetic research and medical experimentation. In particular, the Biomedicine Convention allows non-therapeutic medical experimentation to be carried out on persons who cannot give informed consent.[212] Human rights groups, such as the International Commission of Jurists, and other non-governmental organizations, such as Disabled Peoples' International, criticised the treaty while it was drafted by the Parliamentary Assembly because of these and other short-

---

212 *Id.* art. 17.2.

comings. Some national disability groups, notably organizations in Germany, convinced their governments not to sign the treaty after it was adopted in 1997. At an international UN expert meeting on International Norms and Standards Relating to Disability, which took place December 13–17, 1999 in Hong Kong (Special Administrative Region), People's Republic of China, the European Biomedicine Convention was reviewed from a disability rights perspective. In particular, the provision relating to non-therapeutic experimentation was singled out for being incompatible with article 7 of the ICCPR[213] and the Nuremberg Code of 1947.[214] Both of these latter human rights documents state that medical research shall never be performed without informed consent.

d. Disability and the Council of Europe Convention for the Prevention of Torture and Inhuman or Degrading Treatment or Punishment (1987) (CPT)[215]

The formal prohibition of torture, inhuman and degrading treatment is contained in Article 3 of the ECHR. The adoption of an entire convention in the area was intended to augment Article 3 by providing a proactive (non-judicial) mechanism that would enable the international community to prevent the occurrence of torture in the first place.

This convention has obvious and important applications in the context of persons with disabilities who are deprived of their liberty by a public authority. It covers persons with disabilities who are held for police interrogation, imprisoned in the penal system, or incarcerated in a mental institution or some other place of residential care.

The Convention establishes a European Committee for the Prevention of Torture, Inhuman and Degrading Treatment (CPT). Article 1 asserts that the Committee shall:

---

213 *International Covenant on Civil and Political Rights, supra* note 13.

214 For the text of the Code, *see The Nazi Doctors and the Nuremberg Code: Human Rights in Human Experimentation* 2 (George J. Annas & Michael A. Grodin eds., New York, Oxford University Press,1992).

215 26 Nov. 1987, E.T.S. No. 126.

> by means of visits, examine the treatment of persons deprived of their liberty with a view to strengthening, if necessary, the protection of such persons from torture and from inhuman or degrading treatment or punishment.

The CPT's members are independent and impartial experts from a variety of backgrounds, including law, medicine and public policy. They conduct periodic visits to places of detention located in the contracting parties and can conduct ad hoc visits; 72 periodic visits and 32 ad hoc visits had taken place as of August 2000. Prior notification of a visit must be given to the contracting party, but once given, the visit can occur immediately thereafter (Article 8). The contracting party in question must make all facilities available to the Committee, including full access to the place of detention. The Committee has the right to interview any person detained in private, and indeed has the right to receive information from any other person whom it believes can supply relevant information (for example, members of relevant NGOs). A contracting party may resist a visit, but only on such exceptional grounds as national security, public safety or the fear of public disorder, the medical condition of the person involved, and the need to carry out urgent interrogation (Article 9.1). None of these (except possibly the medical ground) would appear to apply in the case of persons with disabilities. The right to resist visits is not absolute, and the Committee is empowered to enter negotiations to try to reach an agreement about access.

The Committee works on the basis of confidentiality. After each visit it draws up a report outlining its factual findings as well as any recommendations for reform. These reports are shared with the contracting party and are not published unless the party so requests. Most reports—together with the responses of the contracting party in question—are, in fact, published at the request of the contracting parties. If a contracting party does not cooperate or fails to introduce adequate reforms, the Committee may make a public statement to this effect.

Subject to the strictures of confidentiality, the Committee makes a general report available to the Committee of Ministers of the Council of Europe each year. This report is conveyed to the Parliamentary Assembly and is made public (Article 12). It contains a detailed account of the activities of the CPT in the preceding year, and it also draws together the distilled essence of its observations and recommendations in a substantive section that follows a selected theme.

The CPT nearly always visits psychiatric institutions during each periodic visit. On at least two occasions thematic sections have included disability issues. The 3rd Annual Report, covering 1992, contains a detailed section on health care services in prisons, including a significant part that deals with adequate standards of psychiatric care and provision for prisoners.[216] The 8th Annual Report, which covers 1997, contains a specific and detailed section on visits by the Committee to places of psychiatric detention.[217] It spans issues such as the prevention of ill-treatment, patient living conditions and treatment, staff, means of restraint, and safeguards in the context of civil commitment.

With respect to ill-treatment, the Report states in part:

> the CPT's own on-site observations and reports received from other sources indicate that the deliberate ill-treatment of patients in psychiatric establishments does occur from time to time.[218]

The report drawn up by the CPT on its second periodic visit to Ireland in 1998 contains an interesting case study. Amongst other establishments, the CPT visited the Central Mental Hospital, which is Ireland's main center for the detention of those who are found "criminally insane" by the courts. The CPT made several recommendations concerning quality and adequacy of service in relation to such areas as staffing, the treatment of patients, patient's living accommodation, seclusion, and safeguards for involuntary patients. The report was published with the consent of the Irish government in December 1999.[219] The government

---

216 *3rd General Report on the CPT's Activities Covering the Period 1 January to 1 December 1992*, CPT/Inf (93) 12, at ¶¶ 41–44.

217 *8th General Report on the CPT's Activities Covering the Period 1 January to 31 December 1997*, CPT/Inf (98) 12.

218 *Id.* at ¶ 27.

219 *Report to the Irish Government on the Visit to Ireland Carried Out by the European Committee for the Prevention of Torture and Inhuman or Degrading Treatment or Punishment (CPT) from 31 August to 9 September 1998*, CPT/Inf (99) 15, at ¶¶ 140–45.

in turn published its own responses (including an outline of the actions it proposed to take with regard to the Central Mental Hospital) on the same day.[220]

At the very least, the publication of the two reports has spurred further and better domestic law reform as well as provisions for safeguarding the human rights of persons with disabilities who have been involuntarily detained. It also afforded NGOs with a focused opportunity to raise relevant issues in the public domain. In short, the Convention and the watchdog mechanism of the CPT establishes a developed system to assess the conditions of confinement of those European citizens with disabilities who are confined in residential care or otherwise incarcerated.

e. Framework Convention on the Protection of National Minorities (1995) in the Context of Disability

The Council of Europe has had a long history of concern for national or ethnic minorities.[221] However, the Council did not adopt a convention as such until the mid-1990s. This timing coincides with the collapse of the Soviet Empire, and the influx of new member states into the Council of Europe. The Council feared that the national minority problem, which has been driven underground for so long in Eastern Europe, would explode and cause violence and political instability. Therefore, a convention finally was adopted, and remains the only "hard law" legal instrument in the world on the topic.

The philosophy behind the Council of Europe Convention on the Protection of National Minorities is quite clear, and resonates well with the core theme of the disability rights movement (equal opportunities

---

[220] *Response of the Irish Government to Report of the European Committee for the Prevention of Torture and Inhuman or Degrading Treatment or Punishment (CPT) on its visit to Ireland from 31 August to 9 September 1998*, CPT/Inf (99) 16, Part C.

[221] *See* Patrick Thornberry & Maria Amor Martin Estebanez, *The Council of Europe and Minorities* (Strasbourg, Council of Europe Pub., 1994); and John Murray & Jan Niessan, *The Council of Europe and the Protection of the Rights of Migrants, Refugees and Minorities* (CCME Briefing Paper No. 13) (Brussels, Churches' Commission for Migrants in Europe, 1993).

for all). Underlying the convention is the notion that the just polity is one that is defined inclusively, on the basis of both non-discrimination and the understanding that positive space is sometimes required for the expression of difference. In a sense, the philosophy of the convention flows from the same broad concept of equality that animates the disability reform process.

Part I of the Convention sets out certain principles (Articles 1–3). Part II sets out the various rights that members of national minorities may enjoy. It tacks back and forth along the non-discrimination/positive action continuum. Neither collective rights nor individual complaints, *per se*, are created. Enforcement is accomplished through the requirement of periodic reports to the Committee of Ministers, which is assisted by an expert advisory committee.

The remarkable thing about the Convention is that the definition of what constitutes a national minority is left open. Thus, the drafters intended to make it plain that the meaning of the term is capable of evolving through time. As a result, one could conceivably argue that if a group suffers the same kind of marginalization undergone by a classic national minority (e.g., the Roma people) in the past, then that group should be considered a "national minority" for the purposes of the convention.

Since the definition of a national minority is open, contracting parties are left with the choice of which groups to include in their periodic reports. While there is nothing to compel them to include situations pertaining to persons with disabilities in their reports, there equally is nothing to prevent them from doing so either.

This flexibility is particularly relevant in the context of those who are hearing impaired, and who have long argued that they constitute a linguistic minority. Many state reports have included detailed commentary on the treatment of linguistic minorities within their jurisdiction, and the Convention is very explicit on the kinds of rights linguistic minorities can claim (Article 10). In actual fact, Finland in its first report made oblique reference to the deaf or hard of hearing as a "national minority." Although the reference was hardly unambigous, and certainly did not set a precedent, it nevertheless shows what would be possible if the analogous situation of the hearing impaired as a distinct group was taken seriously.

Under the terms of the Convention, if the relevant European NGOs could persuade a contracting party to include the hearing impaired in the category of "national minority," there would be little to stop the contracting party from so reporting. Indeed, if the relevant NGOs could persuade their own contracting parties that people with disabilities suffer the same kind of discrimination that previously has been meted out to traditional national minorities, then likewise, there would be nothing to stop the parties from reporting on the entirety of persons with disabilities as a minority group under the Convention. Nonetheless, the former scenario is more likely than the latter since the gap between traditional "national minorities" and all people with disabilities seems too large to traverse, at least at present.

3. Council of Europe Policy Recommendations in the Context of Disability

Recommendations serve a useful function in any reform process by getting member states both to address the central issues and to orient their policies toward more or less uniform European solutions. The following exemplify the wide variety of Recommendations that exist in the field of disability.

a. Recommendation R (92) 6 on a Coherent Policy for Persons with Disabilities

This Recommendation is by far the most important issued by the Council of Europe in the context of disability. It was adopted on April 9, 1992 by the Committee of Ministers within the framework of the Partial Agreement in the Social and Public Health Field, and is roughly contemporaneous with the drafting of the UN Standard Rules. In a sense, it attempts to apply the equal opportunities and non-discrimination model in a European environment. It replaced its 1984 forerunner, Resolution AP (84)3 "On a Coherent Policy for the Rehabilitation of Disabled People,"[222] which was much more welfare oriented.

---

222 Adopted by the Committee of Ministers on Sept. 17, 1984.

The principles that animate Recommendation R(92)6 are set out in Part I which deals with General Policy as follows:

> A coherent and global policy in favour of people with disabilities or who are in danger of acquiring them should aim at:
>
> - preventing or eliminating disablement, preventing its deterioration and alleviating its consequences;
> - guaranteeing full and active participation in community life;
> - helping them to lead independent lives, according to their own wishes.
>
> It is an ongoing and dynamic process of mutual adaptation, involving on the one hand people with disabilities living according to their own wishes, choices and abilities, which must be developed as far as possible, and on the other hand, society which must demonstrate its support by taking specific and appropriate steps to ensure equality of opportunity.

The "aims" of both people with disabilities and policymakers are set out in this General Policy section, and include the following:

> - [to] retain as much personal responsibility as possible in the planning and implementation of rehabilitation and integration processes;
> - [to] exercise their rights to full citizenship and have access to all institutions and services of the community including education;
> - [to]have as much personal self-determination and independence as possible, including independence from their own families, if they so desire.
> - the special situation faced by women and elderly people with disabilities should receive particular attention.

The body of Recommendation R (92) 6 comes in 12 parts: (1) general policy, (2) prevention and health education, (3) identification and diagnosis, (4) treatment and therapeutic aids, (5) education, (6) vocational guidance and training, (7) employment, (8) social integration and environment, (9) social, economic and legal protection, (10) training of rehabilitation personnel, (11) information, and (12) statistics and research.

Various "fields of intervention" are identified in the general policy part, and the succeeding 11 substantive parts set out more specific recommendations sector by sector. The non-discrimination idea pervades all the identified "fields of intervention," and the provisions in Part 5 dealing with education are especially impressive in this respect. Part 9 is also particularly important since it examines the legal framework that needs to underpin a coherent disability policy model. Paragraph 3 of Part 9 states:

> The exercise of basic legal rights of people with disabilities should be protected, including being free from discrimination. . . .

b. Recommendation R (83) 2 Concerning the Legal Protection of Persons Suffering from Mental Disorder Placed as Involuntary Patients[223] and Subsequent Developments

The Parliamentary Assembly of the Council of Europe published a landmark report in 1977 on the situation of the mentally ill in Europe.[224] It led to a Recommendation from the Parliamentary Assembly (Recommendation 818 (1977)) that calls for Member States:

> to review their legislation and administrative rules on the confinement of the mentally ill [*inter alia*] . . . by reducing to the minimum the practice of compulsory detention for an "indeterminate period," . . .[225]

Recommendation 818 also calls on the Committee of Ministers to set up a working group of experts to prepare a draft Recommendation to member states. The need for this policy Recommendation was evident after a number of leading cases in the European Court of Human

---

[223] Adopted by the Committee of Ministers on Feb. 22, 1983.

[224] Council of Europe, Parliamentary Assembly, 3 *Documents*, 29th Sess. (2nd Part), *Report on the Situation of the Mentally Ill: Draft Recommendation Presented to the Committee on Social and Health Questions*, prepared by Rapporteurs MM. Tabone & Voogd, Doc. No. 4014 (12 Sept. 1977).

[225] Recommendation 818(1977), adopted 8 Oct. 1977, at ¶ 13.I.i.

Rights brought substantive and procedural deficiencies in European civil commitment law to light.

The group of experts was duly convened and produced a text which was adopted by the Committee of Ministers in 1983 (Recommendation R (83) 2). The norms of the Recommendation are quite advanced for their day and refer to the grounds for involuntary loss of liberty, the procedure to be followed in such an event, and the substantive rights of those subjected to this exceptional power. This Recommendation was very influential throughout Europe.

The Parliamentary Assembly adopted another Recommendation on April 12, 1994 (Recommendation 1235(1994) on psychiatry and human rights), which invited the Committee of Ministers to update Recommendation R (83) 2 in light of medical and legal advances. The Recommendation of the Parliamentary Assembly included a list of principles, which was put forward as a guide to the revision of the 1983 instrument.

The Committee of Ministers duly convened a group of experts (Working Party on Psychiatry and Human Rights [CDBI-PH], created as a subordinate body under the authority of the Steering Committee on Bioethics) to update Recommendation R (83) 2. In March 2000, the Committee of Ministers published a discussion paper on reform options that had been produced by the Working Party[226] for consultation purposes. Misleadingly, the paper is styled a "white paper," and the deadline for submissions was October 2000. Although technically beyond the scope of this article, the "white paper" is a fascinating document and deserves extensive analysis by the European NGO community. A wholly revised Recommendation on this topic was expected from the Committee of Ministers later in 2000 or early in 2001.

c. European Charter on Sport for All: Disabled Persons (1986)

The Council of Europe has long viewed sport as a key element in helping to bring about greater social cohesion. A conference of European Ministers for Sport adopted the European Sport for All Charter in 1975,

---

[226] *White Paper on the Protection of the Human Rights and Dignity of People Suffering from Mental Disorder, Especially Those Placed as Involuntary Patients in a Psychiatric Establishment*, CM(2000) 23 Addendum, 10 Feb. 2000.

and this remains the baseline document in this field. Article 1 of that Charter asserts that "[E]very individual shall have the right to participate in sport." No distinction is made on the grounds of disability or capacity.

The third Sports Ministerial conference adopted a more specific resolution dealing with persons with disabilities in 1981: Resolution on Sport for Handicapped Persons (81/5). It reads in part:

> [The Conference of Ministers] . . .
>
> Consider that sport is of paramount importance in preparing for life, restoring and maintaining health, rehabilitating motor functions . . .
>
> Recognise sport as a valuable means of education, rehabilitation, enhancement of leisure activities and social integration . . .

In the Resolution, the Conference of Ministers for Sport undertook to do their utmost to introduce physical activities and sport to the education, rehabilitation and preventative treatment of the handicapped, and to take measures to make (existing) sports facilities easily accessible. The Conference called on the Committee of Ministers of the Council of Europe to, *inter alia*, draw up guidelines and establish priorities on this topic.

Gradually the emphasis shifted from rehabilitation to equal opportunities, non-discrimination and integrated sport. The 4th Conference of European Sports Ministers invited the Committee of Ministers to recommend to the Member States, *inter alia*,

> 1. when building or converting sports facilities, to ensure that there is suitable access for these groups, thus increasing their participation opportunities in physical education and sport . . .
> 4. [to] promote the adequate representation of [disability NGOs] in the decision making bodies concerning physical education and sport . . .

Eventually the Committee of Ministers adopted the *European Charter on Sport for All: Disabled Persons* in a Recommendation of

1986.[227] The body of the Charter is in two parts. Part A outlines certain actions appropriate for the member states. Part B contains actions that are appropriate for sporting bodies to take themselves.

The following sections of Part A are worth noting as they fit in neatly with the principles of the equal opportunities/non-discrimination model. Among other things, the governments of the members states are exhorted to:

1. take the necessary steps to ensure that all relevant public authorities and private organisations are aware of the sporting and recreational wants and needs . . . of all disabled people;
2. orient their policies for such persons so that they may have adequate opportunities to take part in recreational physical activities which will:
   a) encourage their feeling of well being . . .
   b) encourage social communication both between themselves and between them and able-bodied persons;
3. encourage the appropriate authorities to seek to ensure that public sports facilities are accessible to and useable by disabled persons and to incite those authorities to:
   a) [consider setting aside public monies to help facilities meet accessibility guidelines provided in an explanatory memo to the Charter]
   b) ensure as far as possible that future sports facilities will meet [the accessibility guidelines] or equivalent national standards.

Part B of the Charter essentially states that member states should, *inter alia*, work closely with sporting organizations to find ways to integrate sporting opportunities for persons with disabilities into mainstream sport (B:2), and to recognize that such persons can legitimately aspire to elite sport involvement (B:5).

In 1999 the Committee of Ministers adopted a Recommendation "On the Role of Sport in Furthering Social Cohesion."[228] It exhorts

---

227 Recommendation R (86) 18, adopted 4 Dec.1986.

228 Recommendation R (99) 9, adopted 22 Apr. 1999.

member states to adopt global and integrated sports policy for all, and then proceeds to target certain disadvantaged or excluded groups, including persons with disabilities, for specific recommendations. Section 1(a) deals with disability and states:

> with regard to the disabled:
> - adapt sporting facilities and facilitate access and transport to these facilities and recreation areas as set out in Recommendation No. R (86) 18 . . . ;
> - set up projects designed for the disabled to stimulate self-confidence in their own physical abilities, together with programmes which make them aware of the potential physical, psychological and social benefits of sport;
> - encourage mainstream sporting bodies to make provision for, and contact with, disabled sporting bodies and to take measures toward eliminating the distinction between disabled and mainstream sport in order to provide acceptance and integration for the disabled in the world of sport;

d. Recommendation AP (95) 3 on a Charter on the Vocational Assessment of People with Disabilities

This very interesting instrument clearly demonstrates the effects of the shift from welfare to rights. It recalls (in the opening recitals) that the principle underlying rehabilitation is to ensure that persons with disabilities achieve "the greatest possible measure of social and economic participation as well as independence."

The equal rights philosophy is also reflected in the way the Recommendation seeks to re-orient vocational assessment to the *abilities* of persons with disabilities (Principle 2.2.4), and recognizes the need to rationally match those abilities with job openings in the labour market (Principle 2.2.5). Interestingly in the context of the debate over definitions of disability, it states:

> 2.2.3. Some classifications in medicine and other scientific fields focus on deviation from norms and on deficiencies. Such classifications do not appear to do justice to the abilities of peo-

> ple with disabilities. In only focusing on their weak points, they can hinder their social integration, put them at a disadvantage and lead to their exclusion.

For years NGOs have made this assertion, which flows visibly from an equal opportunities philosophy. The rest of the Charter goes on to specify how to facilitate a better fit between supply (i.e., a more accurate assessment of abilities) and demand (i.e., available jobs).

e. Recommendation R (98) 3 on Access to Higher Education[229]

A three-year project on access to higher education was conducted under the auspices of the Council of Europe between 1993 and 1996. The Project Group carried out an in-depth study that compared the access policies of all member states along several access axes, and presented its findings at a closing conference in Parma in 1996. Recommendation R (98) 3 was the main policy output of this process. It has particular resonance in the context of disability discrimination and access to higher education.

For the Purposes of the Recommendation, "access policy" is defined broadly in Article 1 as follows:

> 1.1 A policy that aims both at the widening of participation in higher education to all sections of society, and at ensuring that this participation is effective (that is, in conditions which ensure that personal effort will lead to successful completion).

The relevant section in the accompanying explanatory amplifies the above as follows:

> The term "access policy" includes not just admission to and participation in higher education, but the dimensions of equitable distribution and a reasonable chance of success by individuals. Large-scale under-representation of certain social groups, and large-scale under-performance or dropout by

---

[229] Adopted by the Committee of Ministers on Mar. 17, 1998.

> committed students, are thus both symptoms of a failure in access policy . . .[230]

The term "equal opportunities" is defined in the Recommendation as:

> 1.3. . . . one that is designed to meet all requirements of the principle of equality, not only formal or *de jure* equality and the absence of discrimination, but also full and effective equality in the sense of enabling all individuals to develop and fulfill their potential. The promotion of effective equality may require the adoption of special measures where this is necessary and consistent with the principle of non-discrimination to take account of the specific conditions of individuals or groups in society.

Among the accessibility objectives in Article 2 that are recommended both to governments and institutions of higher education are the following:

> 2.1 [that] All who are able and willing to participate in higher education should have fair and equal opportunities to do so;
>
> 2.2 [that the] higher education population as a whole should increasingly reflect the diversity of a changing society in each member state . . .

The Recommendation deals with the age-old tension between the need to maintain high academic standards and the achievement of equal opportunity for all in an interesting way. It asserts in Article 2 that:

> 2.4. Efforts to maintain and raise the quality of higher education . . . should include the criterion of effective access offered to all groups in society, as well as that of excellence in teaching and research.

---

[230] Council of Europe's Higher Education and Research Committee, "Explanatory Memorandum to Recommendation R (98) 3" at ¶ 21, in CM (98)28, Appendix IV, *Draft Recommendation of the Committee of Ministers to Member States on Higher Education.*

In other words, it treats the achievement of equitable access as a factor in the overall assessment of educational quality.

Article 3 of the Recommendation deals specifically with discrimination and explicitly includes the situation of students with disabilities. It states in the relevant parts:

> 3.1. Member States are recommended to consider the need for legislation to outlaw discrimination in higher education on grounds of [*inter alia*] . . . disability. Account should be taken of [*inter alia*] . . .
>
> - the relevant Council of Europe instruments which Member States have adopted concerning [*inter alia*] policies for persons with disabilities . . .
> - the need for a balanced mix of measures between that empower individuals to gain redress against proven discrimination with those which tackle structural causes and promote institutional change;

In terms of areas of substantive concern the Recommendation goes on to deal with admissions policies and access (Article 4), student progress after entry (Article 5), access and lifelong learning (Article 6), staffing and staff development (Article 7), funding (Article 8), and monitoring of progress toward equal opportunity (Article 9). All of these standards have applications in the context of disability, with Article 5.3 having particular importance (student progress) when it states in the relevant part:

> 5.3. To enable all sectors of a diverse student intake to achieve academic success, steps should be taken:
>
> - to reorganise curriculum content where appropriate and modify its delivery as necessary to reflect the diversity of a multicultural society, taking account of the views of those from minority cultures
>
> . . .
>
> - to promote a climate of tolerance, solidarity and democracy.

The modification of curriculum content and design is a contentious subject throughout Europe, but at least this Recommendation comes down firmly on the side that views curriculum adjustment as necessary for ensuring genuinely equal opportunities to education. There is a specific reference in the provision dealing with staffing (Article 7.1) that adverts to the need to increase the number of staff with disabilities.

A further perspective on integrated education is found in an interesting Declaration adopted by the Committee of Ministers in 1999, titled a *Declaration and Programme on Education based on Democratic Citizenship, based on the Rights and Responsibilities of Citizens.*[231] Among other things the Declaration asserts that one of the roles of education is to "prepare(s) people to live in a multicultural society and to deal with difference knowledgeably, sensibly, tolerantly and morally."[232] In a sense this supports the point that the integration of children with disabilities (indeed all children who are "different") into mainstream education benefits everyone in society.

f. Recommendation R (99) 4 on Principles Concerning the Legal Protection of Incapable Adults

Part of the disability reform agenda in Europe is devoted to reviewing how the rights and interests of incapable adults are handled. If citizens with disabilities are generally invisible, then those within this group who cannot vindicate their own rights or interests are the most invisible. Generally, the law has either neglected their concerns or abandoned them to the fate of unscrupulous family members or others. Incapacity in one area of life has generally translated into an assumption of incapacity in all areas.

In keeping with the newer philosophy of equality (i.e., a belief in the equal inherent worth of all citizens regardless of capacity), the Council of Europe has been taking a close look in recent years at the reform of European incompetency law. The Directorate of Legal Affairs held a major conference on the subject in Cadiz in 1994.[233] A survey was carried out among the member states regarding the state of their

---

231 Dec-7.5.99, adopted by the Committee of Ministers on May 7, 1999.

232 *Id.*, art. 11.iv.

233 *3rd European Conference on Family Law: Family Law in the Future: Proceedings [Cadiz, 20–22 April 1995]* (Strasbourg, Council of Europe Pub., 1995).

laws and any proposals for law reform. Finally, a very eminent consultant, Professor Eric Clive of Edinburgh University, prepared a model Recommendation with an accompanying report.[234] Recommendation R (99) 4 is the result of the foregoing activity.

In essence, the reform process in this area is concerned with restoring the indicia of legal personhood (and *equal* personhood) to the individual concerned. This entails abandoning absolute distinctions, and adopting a graded response that recognizes that competence and incompetence can subsist within the one person. Such an approach favors taking a proactive approach to maintaining the person's existing levels of competence, while simultaneously providing adequate protections to the extent that the person is genuinely incompetent (assuming such a phrase remains appropriate). It is a reform process that is long overdue and is being inspired by the equal rights philosophy of the disability movement.

Recommendation R (99) 4 is a remarkable and forward-looking document. Part II sets out certain governing principles (i.e., principles that ought to govern the law reform process). The Recommendation asserts that the very first "governing principle" in the reform process is respect for human rights as follows:

> *Principle 1—Respect for Human Rights.*
>
> In relation to the protection of incapable adults
>
> The fundamental principle, underlying all the other principles, is respect for the dignity of each person as a human being. The laws procedures and practices relating to the protection of incapable adults shall be based on respect for their human rights and fundamental freedoms . . .

The second governing principle has to do with the need for flexibility (i.e., the abandonment of the old black and white distinction between legal competence and incompetence). Among other things, it states that "the range of measures should include . . . those which do not

---

[234] *Group of Specialists on Incapable and other Vulnerable Adults, Report Prepared by Dr Eric Clive* (CJ-S-MI, 21 Jan. 1997).

restrict the legal capacity of the person concerned." The third principle has to do with maximum preservation of existing levels of competence. The fourth concerns the need for publicity to attend any public measures. The fifth discusses the standards of necessity and subsidiarity with respect to protective measures. The sixth adds the extra safeguard of proportionality. The seventh enshrines the requirement for procedural fairness and efficacy. The eighth establishes the interests and welfare of the person concerned as paramount in determining protective measures. The ninth deals with the need to respect the wishes and feelings of the person, and the last sets out the need to consult with all interested parties before measures are adopted.

Part III covers procedural principles in detail. Part IV focuses on the role of representatives (i.e., what should be the legitimate scope of their decision-making authority over the person concerned). Part V deals with principles governing interventions in the health field.

A fuller treatment of this Recommendation is out of place here, but it should properly be viewed as part of the larger project of rendering people with disabilities visible in the legal order—a project that is largely a result of the shift from welfare to rights and equal opportunities.

4. Council of Europe Working Groups, Studies, etc., in the Context of Disability

The Council of Europe has engaged in extensive research on disability issues over a number of years. Many of them take their cue—if not their exact terms of reference—directly from Recommendation R (92) 6. The following are particularly noteworthy.

a. Periodic Review of European Disability Legislation

The Council of Europe publishes a periodic review of disability legislation throughout Europe. It is currently in its sixth edition.[235]

[235] Committee on the Rehabilitation and Integration of People with Disabilities, *Legislation on the Rehabilitation of People with Disabilities in Sixteen Member States of the Council of Europe* (5th Ed., Strasbourg, Council of Europe Pub., 1993).

b. Group of Experts on the ICIDH

Under the auspices of the Partial Agreement, the Council of Europe established in 1987 a committee of experts on the World Health Organization's (WHO) International Classification of Impairments, Disabilities and Handicaps (ICIDH). Over the years, this group has taken a lead role in Europe in assessing and proposing reforms to the WHO's ICIDH. They also have produced valuable reports on a wide variety of topics connected with the ICIDH.[236]

The key issue here from an equal rights perspective concerns the need for continuing socialization of the ICIDH's three-pronged definition of disability so as to reflect the equal opportunities agenda and the centrality of the dignity and autonomy of the person. In a major initiative, the Council of Europe hosted a joint seminar between the WHO and the various European disability NGOs on this topic in 1996.[237] The seminar and the process of dialogue that it initiated between the WHO and European NGOs was, at the very least, one factor that led ultimately to the reform of the ICIDH.

c. Disability Employment Studies

The employment of persons with disabilities has also been a long-standing concern of the Council of Europe. From 1993–1996, the Council's activities in this area concentrated on the transition from sheltered to

---

236 *See* for example, S.C. van Stokkom, *The Use and Usefulness of the ICIDH in the Maintenance of People with Disabilities at Home and in Their Communities* (1998) (Strasbourg, Council of Europe Pub., 1998); H. Gardent, *Use of the ICIDH in Relation to Elderly People (1997)* (Strasbourg, Council of Europe Pub., 1997); O. Sjogren, *The Use and Usefulness of the ICIDH for the Education of Children with Impairments or Disabilities (1997)* (Strasbourg, Council of Europe Pub., 1997); D.W. Kraijer, *The ICIDH in the Field of Mental Retardation (1993)* (Strasbourg, Council of Europe Pub., 1993); F. Chapireau, *The Conceptual Framework of the ICIDH (1992)* (Strasbourg, Council of Europe Pub., 1992); etc.

237 *See The Use and Usefulness of the International Classification of Impairments, Disabilities and Handicaps (ICIDH): Proceedings, International Workshop, Strasbourg, France, 25–27 March 1996* (Strasbourg, Council of Europe Pub., 1999). Note the presentation made on behalf of the European Commission at that seminar was strongly in favour of reform of the ICIDH.

open employment. From 1996 onwards, they concentrated on the penetration of people with disabilities into the mainstream jobs market.

Useful studies have been published by the Council of Europe on a broad range of employment-related topics, including the transition from sheltered employment to ordinary employment (1996), the state of sheltered employment in certain member states (1997), and comparative analysis of vocational training and assessment (1997). A document on employment strategies to promote equal opportunities for persons with disabilities in the open labour market is presently being prepared for publication.

d. Group of Experts on Violence Against Persons with ` Disabilities

A Group of Experts on violence against persons with disabilities was established in 1999. It was established to study the problem of violence against people with disabilities, and to make concrete recommendations on how to combat and prevent the problem. It held its fourth meeting in November 2000. Violence is broadly defined to include physical violence, sexual abuse, psychological harm, financial abuse, and neglect. The group consults with INGOs, and their work is due to be completed in 2001. A Recommendation from the Committee of Ministers on this topic might well ensue.

e. Working Group on Universal Design

The Council of Europe is preparing new accessibility guidelines, as well as working on a recommendation to incorporate the principle of universal design into the curriculum of all professions involved in the built environment.

A separate Working Group of Experts is also engaged in developing concrete recommendations for gaining maximum utilisation of new technologies for the benefit of people with disabilities. Yet another Working Group of Experts is developing uniform assessment methods for allowances (e.g., social insurance benefits), in order to avoid the need for fresh assessment once individuals migrate across borders. Their report was due in 2000.

f. Working Group on Discrimination Against Persons with Disabilities

Obviously, the philosophy of equal opportunities and non-discrimination is the guiding principle in all the above activities. More specifically, the Council of Europe established a Working Group on Discrimination against Persons with Disabilities in November 1996. It has conducted a comparative analysis of disability discrimination law throughout the 41 member states of the Council of Europe (unpublished as of September 2000), and also has surveyed the positions of NGOs, as well as employer federations and trade unions.

The Working Group is focusing particularly on anti-discrimination legislation, positive action (i.e., measures that tackle structural causes of discrimination), and the participation of people with disabilities in decision-making processes. The Group's final report was adopted by the Council of Europe Committee on the Rehabilitation and Integration of People with Disabilities in spring 2000. The report is due to be published in October 2000, and many hope that its publication will lead to a Committee of Ministers Recommendation on disability discrimination.

G. THE EUROPEAN UNION AND DISABILITY

1. Background: The Legal Tools and Policy Instruments of the European Union[238]

a. The Economic Focus of the EU

From an historical perspective the European Union is an odd source of law and policy in the context of disability. The Union has its origin in three separate treaties which originally created three separate "communities": the European Coal and Steel Community (Paris, April 18, 1951, Treaty establishing the European Coal and Steel Community—ECSC), the European Economic Community (Rome, March 25, 1957, Treaty establishing the European Economic Community—EEC [renamed the European Community Treaty in 1992 by Article G(1) of the Treaty on European Union—TEU]), and the European Atomic Energy Agency

---

[238] *See generally The Evolution of EU Law* (Paul Craig & Gráinne de Búrca eds., Oxford, Oxford University Press, 1999).

(Rome, March 25, 1957, Treaty establishing the European Atomic Energy Community—EURATOM). The EEC was officially transformed into the European Community or EC in 1965 after the merger of core provisions and institutions from the three original treaties (Treaty on the European Community—TEC).

The main idea behind the original EEC was to seek European unity through the unification of its disparate national markets into one common market (the theory of "functional integration"). The theory rests on the depressing (but very successful) insight that men cooperate best where they calculate such cooperation to be in their own self-interest. The forging of national markets into one common market thus serves to integrate not only economies but also people.

b. EC/EU Treaty Law as the Basis of the EU "Constitutional Order"

EEC law focused in the main on the economic tools needed to create a great commercial republic in Europe. Among other things, this entailed protecting those core economic "freedoms" that help establish and augment a common market, such as the freedom of movement of workers (Articles 48–51, TEC), free movement of capital (Articles 76–73, TEC), free movement of goods (Articles 9–37, TEC), and the right of establishment (i.e., the right to set up as a professional in another member state—Articles 52–58, TEC). It is, of course, theoretically possible to subsume at least some of these economic freedoms under the more general rubric of human rights—but they were not conceived or intended as such at the outset.

At the time of the drafting of the Treaty of Rome (the original EEC) in the late 1950s, there was some debate about whether the achievement of human rights as such should be added to the treaties as an objective of the Community.[239] Among other things, this would have created an unambiguous legal basis for enacting legislation on disability discrimination. However, for a variety of political reasons, the member states decided to focus solely on the use of economic means toward functional

---

239 *See generally* Alina Kaczorowska, *EU Law Today* (London, Old Bailey Press, 1998).

integration. So, although the underlying goal of the EC was the integration of peoples, its foundational treaties concentrated only on achieving economic means to this end. From the narrow perspective of treaty law, the means toward the end were more important than the unstated end itself.

In purely institutional terms, the EC contrasts vividly with the Council of Europe. In order to obviate the natural temptation of member states to preserve national competitive advantage, the EC conceived of a new institution that could assert the overall "European public interest"—the European Commission (Articles 155–163, TEC).[240] The members of the Commission are nominated by the member states, but serve in an independent capacity (Article 157.1, TEC). In addition to guarantees of autonomy from member states, the Commission has the sole (and jealously guarded) prerogative to make legislative proposals. Depending on which treaty provisions have been relied on for a legal basis, these proposals can then go to the European Parliament (directly elected by the people of Europe since 1979), and ultimately come up for adoption before the Council of Ministers (comprised of relevant Ministers from the member states). A separate European Court of Justice (ECJ), based in Luxembourg, is charged with the task of interpreting and applying treaty law (Articles 164–188, TEC). This court is often confused with the European Court of Human Rights, based in Strasbourg, which interprets one treaty of the Council of Europe (the European Convention on Human Rights). As well, formal and informal issue-specific groups within the Community produce frequently influential findings and reports; such an informal grouping exists in the European Parliament that deals with a range of disability rights issues.[241]

---

[240] *See generally* Michelle Cini, *The European Commission: Leadership, Organisation and Culture in the EU Administration* (Manchester, New York, Manchester University Press, distributed exclusively in the United States by St. Martin's Press, 1996).

[241] The informal grouping has produced some influential reports on the status of persons with disabilities in Europe: *see* for example, Committee on Petitions (Rapporteur Mary Elizabeth Bannotti, MEP), *Resolution on the Rights of Disabled People*, PE 218.897/DEF 1996 (adopted 13 Dec. 1996).

All of this gives rise to a rich (if not confusing) and multi-layered patchwork of governance in Europe whereby legal competencies can either be reserved to the member states, shared with the Community, or transferred to the Community. Until the Treaty of Amsterdam in 1997, disability matters lay within the sole prerogative of the member states. This is no longer the case—as will be seen.

A chief difference between the EC and the Council of Europe is that in the EC, once a requisite majority in the Council of Ministers (in consultation with the directly elected European Parliament) adopts a legislative proposal by the Commission, this legislation takes precedence over any law to the contrary in the member states, including domestic constitutional provisions (the doctrine of the "supremacy of Community law").[242] There are two types of EC law: Regulations that are directly and automatically effective, and Directives that typically grant member states both discretion as to the method of transposition or implementation and some time before full implementation (usually between three to five years).

The underlying treaties that constitute the EC have been re-visited on many occasions. The member states periodically consider revisions to the treaties in a forum, called Inter-Governmental Conferences (IGCs), that lies outside of the Institutions established by the Union. This cumulative succession of amending treaties is said to form the basis of the EU's "constitutional order."[243]

One such IGC produced the Treaty of Maastricht in 1992.[244] The treaty basically created a new legal entity on the world stage called the European Union (EU or Union). Simply put, the EU comprises three pillars of operations: (1) the existing European Community (Treaty on the European Community or TEC), which specialises in economic affairs, (2) justice and home affairs, and (3) common foreign and security policy. Only the first pillar entails supranational competencies of the type

---

[242] *See* Penelope Kent, "The Supremacy of Community Law," *in Law of the European Union* Ch. 5 (London, Pitman Pub., 1996).

[243] *See* Craig & de Búrca, *supra* note 238.

[244] For a general guide *see* Alexander Noble, *From Rome to Maastricht: The Essential Guide to the European Union* (London, Warner Books, 1996).

described above. The latter two pillars operate on a purely inter-governmental basis in a similar fashion to the Council of Europe. Only the first pillar is relevant in the context of disability.

Like all treaties, the Treaty of Maastricht had to be ratified in accordance with national law. The Danish people voted against it (thus delaying its operation), and the French nearly did so as well. There were two basic reasons for this. First, the EC or Union was seen as obsessed with markets and not with people. In other words, the human face of the EC or Union was completely undeveloped, giving rise to an imbalance between social Europe and economic Europe. Secondly, many ordinary citizens were particularly incensed by the fact that although unemployment remained high throughout the EU, there were no specific competencies at the level of the Union that would enable it to become involved. This clouded the legitimacy of the enterprise. The answer from the political establishment was the 1997 Treaty of Amsterdam (see below).

c. Weak Human Rights Provision in the Original Treaties—The Significance of "General Principles of Community Law" in the Context of Disability

Although extensive powers were ceded to the Brussels Institutions to forge a common market out of disparate national markets, no such competency was ceded in the general field of human rights.[245] While Article 100a of the TEC gave the Union an equivalent to the U.S. federal government's Inter-State Commerce Clause in Article 1(8)(3) of the American Constitution, it never had a full equivalent to the U.S. 14th Amendment guarantee of equal protection. This proved to be a large gap. Both the Inter-State Commerce Clause and the 14th Amendment were cited in the ADA as grounds for that law's underlying constitutional authority. The partnering of a power that enabled the U.S. federal government to reach deep into the private sector (Inter-State Commerce Clause) with the imperative of equality (14th Amendment) was simply unavailable in the EU until very recently.

---

245 *See generally* Lamy Betten & Nicholas Grief, *EU Law and Human Rights* (European Law Series) (London, New York, Longman, 1998).

No less than three EU *"comité des sages"* reports have been issued in recent years on the role of the EU in the human rights field[246]—all advocate the development of a more human face to the Union. The gradual rise of interest in disability policy in the EU can only be understood against the backdrop of this public clamor for a more human face to the Union and for an increased commitment to general human rights. The idea that the Community is bound by general principles that include respect for human rights was initiated during the 1960s in a "turf war" between the European Court of Justice and national constitutional courts. Basically, the ECJ began to insist on a doctrine favoring the supremacy of Community Law even over national constitutions. This was deemed necessary for the integrity of the Community legal order, and to prevent the inevitable tendency toward fragmentation that would result if national courts could have an equal say over the interpretation of Community Law. In a sense, the ECJ was engaged in trying to achieve the result of *Marbury v Madison*[247] for the EEC.

A major problem with such a result was the fear that acknowledging the supremacy of EEC law could well lead to the setting aside of those human rights norms that were protected in national constitutions. Constitutional courts threatened to revolt. To assuage them, the ECJ bounded EEC Community Law with the "general principles of Community Law"—principles which include respect for human rights. The Court was clearly not obligated to do so under the Community's founding treaties, but felt impelled to do so in order to maintain the market integration project. The formula used by the ECJ to divine those "general principles of Community Law" by which it will be bound embraces laws that form part of the constitutional traditions common amongst the member states and are subscribed to internationally.

---

[246] The two most recent reports were *Leading by Example: A Human Rights Agenda for the European Union for the Year 2000—Agenda of the Comité Des Sages and Final Project Report* (Vienna, European University Institute, 1998), also available *at* http://www.iue.it/AEL/events.htm; and *Affirming Fundamental Rights in the European Union: Time to Act—Report of the Expert Group on Fundamental Rights* (Brussels, European Commission, 1999).

[247] 5 U.S. 137 (1803). In this case, the United States Supreme Court stated that the U.S. Constitution is the supreme law of the land, and the Supreme Court was the body with the final word on its interpretation.

Unfortunately, the utility of such general principles in the disability field was quite limited. Since most European Constitutions do not ban discrimination based on disability, this otherwise fascinating legal development was of little use to persons with disabilities. Indeed, since the main instrument used by the ECJ for inspiration was the ECHR, even less could be expected due to the weaknesses of Article 14 of that Convention, discussed above.

Any real change for people with disabilities would have to come through a revision of the underlying treaties. Pending such treaty changes, any innovations would have to come from an anomalous field—namely EU social policy. This was an anomalous source only in the sense that many disability NGOs felt that social policy continued to be a part of the problem, and not part of the solution.

2. EU Disability Policy in the 1980s

a. The Social Policy Field as the Initial Basis for EU Disability Policy

The original TEC provides barren ground from which to begin addressing disability issues. The only colourable area where disability might arise concerns "social policy" (Articles 117–125). Indeed, disability first registered as an EU issue in the context of EU social policy, but EU social policy is rather peculiar.[248]

Essentially it deals with the social dimension to the creation of the single or common market. Therefore, the 1965 TEC tends to concentrate on the social protections necessary for enabling a free market of workers to come into existence. It focuses in the main on the free movement of workers. There are two non-discrimination provisions, but they have proven to be of little avail for redressing most grounds on which persons suffer discrimination.

Article 6 of the TEC secures the right to non-discrimination with respect to the treatment of other member states' nationals. This is only of use in the disability context if Country A treats its own disabled

---

[248] *See* Tamara K. Hervey, *European Social Law and Policy* (London, New York, Longman, 1998).

citizens in a favorable way, and refuses to extend that treatment to a disabled national from another EU country who is lawfully resident in Country A. Quite apart from the fact that Article 6 is of little use if the disability laws and policies of Country A are underdeveloped, it only inures to the benefit of that tiny proportion of European citizens with disabilities who migrate to seek work in another member state.

Article 117 of the TEC secures the right to equal pay for equal work as between men and women. Its presence in the treaty is due entirely to the desire of the French government to maintain high French labour standards for women as opposed to the corresponding German standards in this area. Article 117 is only of use when an employer treats female workers with disabilities differently than it treats male workers with disabilities. Since many employers (public and private) treat both sexes with disabilities equally unfairly, there is nothing for Article 117 to object to in the disability context.

In any event, these two prohibitions on discrimination were not subsumed under any broader or deeper equality provision, and as a result, no general prohibition existed under EC law against discrimination (whether direct or indirect) based on characteristics such as age, sexual orientation or disability. Of course, it was always theoretically possible to construct such a prohibition from general principles of Community Law, but this would be a pale substitute for an explicit provision in the text of the EC Treaty.

The European Social Fund has, of course, contributed greatly to the development of human resources in the disability field. But such provisions are completely distinct from the creation of any norms of non-discrimination.[249]

In short, the absence of hard legal rules in the TEC against discrimination on the grounds of disability meant that many Directives, dealing with the design of lifts for example, could safely ignore the needs of people with disabilities without incurring any censure.

---

[249] *See generally* Andrew Evans, *The EU European Structural Funds* (Oxford, New York, Oxford University Press, 1999).

b. The Successive HELIOS Programmes (1983–1996)

Article 235 of the TEC allows Council to adopt measures that fall within the broad objectives of the EC, but for which no specific competence has been provided elsewhere in the text of the treaties. However, unanimity in Council is required before Article 235 can be invoked, since otherwise the treaties themselves could be extended simply through majority voting.

This article was used to initiate an action programme dealing with disability in the social affairs field. The programme was first created as the Community's response to the United Nations International Year of the Disabled (1981), but has since gained an independent impetus. Indeed, ever since the early 1980s the European Commission has had a dedicated unit within DGV (now called DG Employment and Social Affairs) that specifically deals with disability integration issues.

Three such programmes in the field of disability have existed.[250] The main result (even if this was not a prior aim) was to energize the European NGO community. Prior to these programmes, many NGOs had not developed links across national borders, and many of the impairment-specific NGOs had not engaged in dialogue with other impairment sectors to seek common ground. The HELIOS programmes at least contributed to the opening of minds, and therefore paved the way for reception of the equal opportunities and non-discrimination model into the European context. The main European NGOs are now affiliated with the Europeans with Disabilities Forum (EDF), which is headquartered in Brussels. Since 1993 the EDF (or a consortium of NGOs affiliated

---

[250] *Council Resolution of the Representatives of the Governments of the Member States of the European Communities Meeting with the Council of 21 December 1981 on the Social Integration of Handicapped People* [1983–88], O.J. C347/1 (1981); *88/231/EEC: Council Decision of 18 April 1988 Establishing a Second Community Action Programme for Disabled People (Helios)* [1988–1992], O.J. L104/38 (1988); *93/136/EEC: Council Decision of 25 February 1993 Establishing the Third Programme to Assist Disabled People (Helios II 1993 to 1996)*, O.J. L56/30 (1993). For a comprehensive collection of these and other EU texts on disability, *see European Disability Law* (Colección Solidaridad 8) (Santiago Munoz Machado & Rafael de Lorenzo eds., Madrid, Fundación ONCE, Escuela Libre Editorial, 1997).

with the EDF) helps to prepare an annual European Day of Disabled People, which adopts a different theme each year.[251]

The HELIOS II programmes ceased at the end of 1996 when it was clear that there was no prospect of securing sufficient unanimity in the Council for a continuation. In a sense, they had already done their work by preparing the ground. The programmes generated a wealth of material and literature, including guides of good practice in a variety of sectors,[252] and much of this literature has influenced the evolution of disability thinking and policy at an EU level.

c. Council Recommendation on the Employment of Persons with Disabilities (1986)[253]

Although the Council of Ministers had no formal competency until the Treaty of Amsterdam in 1997 to adopt legal measures in the disability field, this did not stop it from adopting non-binding recommendations and resolutions on disability issues. One such recommendation was issued in 1986 dealing with the "employment of disabled people in the Community."[254] It was an interesting instrument that, *inter alia*, urged the member states:

> To take all appropriate measures to promote fair opportunities for disabled people in the field of employment and vocational training, . . .[255]

A guideline framework for positive action was appended.

---

[251] *See*, for example, European Commission, Employment and Social Affairs, European Day of Disabled People 1999, *Conference Report on Violence and Disabled People: Root Causes and Prevention* (Brussels, 3 December 1999).

[252] An independent evaluation of the HELIOS II program has been carried out: *see The Evaluation of Helios II—Final Report* (London, Tavistock Institute, 1997). *See also Report from the Commission to the Council, the European Parliament, the Economic and Social Committee, and the Committee of the Regions on the Evaluation of the Third Community Action Programme to Assist Disabled People (HELIOS II 1993–1996)* COM (98) 0015 FINAL (Brussels, 20 January 1998).

[253] *86/379/EEC: Council Recommendation of 24 July 1986 on the Employment of Disabled People in the Community*, O.J. L225/43 (1986).

[254] *See generally*, Waddington, *supra* note 7.

[255] *Supra* note 253, at ¶ 1.

d. Council Resolution on the Integration of Children and Young People Within Ordinary Systems of Education (1990)[256]

Another resolution was adopted on May 31, 1990 that addressed mainstreaming in education. In it the member states agreed that:

> Full integration into the system of mainstream education should be considered as a first option in all appropriate cases, and all education establishments should be in a position to respond to the needs of pupils and students with disabilities.[257]

Very little progress, however, had been reported on integration by 1992.[258] The basic problem is that education was (and largely continues to be) an issue within the exclusive competency of member states, so the Union is limited in what it can require.

3. The Shift to the Equal Opportunities/Non-Discrimination Model in the 1990s

a. The Lead Up to the Shift

i. The Reshaping of EU Social Policy— from Welfare to Active Citizenship (1993–1994)

EU social policy was substantially restated by the European Commission in the early 1990s in anticipation of treaty changes. This restatement fit neatly with the disability agenda, although there was little consciousness of this at the time.

The problem that first initiated social policy changes concerned the financial viability of the so-called "European Social Model." Financial problems forced reconsideration of the nature of social policy and its

---

[256] *Resolution of the Council and the Ministers for Education Meeting within the Council of 31 May 1990 Concerning Integration of Children and Young People with Disabilities into Ordinary Systems of Education*, O.J. C162/2 (3 July 1990).

[257] *Id.* at ¶ 2.

[258] *Report of the Commission on Progress with Regard to the Implementation of the Policy of School Integration in the Member States (1988–1991)*, SEC/92/1891 FINAL (Brussels, 5 Nov. 1992) [Com(92) 1981].

goals. Basically, the Commission recast social policy in terms of empowering people for active citizenship. Active social policy was defended as a "productive factor" in a market economy, and also as a "civilizing factor" in a just society.

Relevant policy documents that were drafted at the time had specific references to disability. In a remarkable paragraph dealing with disability in the Green Paper on the Future of Social Policy (1993), the Commission stated:

> Social segregation *even with adequate income maintenance and special provision*, is contrary to human dignity and corrosive of social solidarity and community morale. Special facilities, institutions and legal rights are obviously necessary, but they should not be an obstacle or an alternative to the principle of "mainstreaming." . . .[259] [emphasis added]

This was a daring statement even in 1993. The White Paper of 1994 was even more forthcoming. It stated:

> [A]s a group, people with disabilities undoubtedly face a wide range of obstacles which prevent them from achieving full economic and social integration. There is therefore a need to build the fundamental right to equal opportunities into Union policies.[260]

It was clear from this policy reconsideration that the Commission was already moving decisively towards recasting social policy in light of imperatives that are normally the preserve of civil rights. This shift was to pay handsome dividends in the context of disability.

---

259 *Green Paper on European Social Policy—Options for the Union*, COM (93) 551 (1993), at 48.

260 *White Paper: European Social Policy—A Way Forward for the Union*, COM(94) 333 (1994), at 51.

ii. The Political Adoption of the Equal Opportunities Model in the Disability Field by the European Commission and Council of Ministers (1996)

Among other things, the 1994 White Paper promised that the Commission would "prepare an appropriate instrument endorsing the UN Standard Rules on the Equalization of Opportunities for Persons with Disabilities."[261] In response the Commission adopted a landmark policy statement or Communication in 1996,[262] in which it firmly committed itself to the rights-based perspective on disability manifested in the UN Standard Rules. The Council of Ministers responded in late 1996 with an equally fulsome Resolution in which they collectively rededicated themselves at a European level to the pursuit of the equal opportunity approach that member states had previously acceded to individually within the United Nations system.[263]

A number of positive steps were taken as a result of the Communication. First of all, the Commission established (or reinvigorated) an inter-service working group with the aim of "mainstreaming" disability issues into the Commission's policy and legislative process. Another positive step was the creation of a High Level Group of representatives of the member states to deal with disability issues. Incredible as it may seem, such a forum had never existed before. The basic idea was to allow for the ongoing exchange of views on how to achieve equal opportunities for persons with disabilities.[264] Yet a third positive step involved

---

261 *Id.*

262 *Communication of the Commission on Equality of Opportunity for People with Disabilities—A New European Community Disability Strategy*, COM (96) 406 FINAL (20 Dec. 1996).

263 *Resolution of the Council and of the Representatives of the Governments of the Member States Meeting within the Council of 20 December 1996 on Equality of Opportunity for People with Disabilities*, O.J. C012/1 Vol. 40 (13 Jan. 1997).

264 As an example of their output *see Employment and People with Disabilities—Report of the Special Meeting of the High Level Group on Disability* (Brussels, 15 October 1997); *High Level Group on Disability Compendium on Member States' Policies on Equality of Opportunity for People with Disabilities* (Oct. 1998).

the increasing attention paid by "social partners" (EU level trade unions and employers) to the issues.[265]

Perhaps the most positive outcome was the foreclosing of any more arguments about whether the equal opportunities/non-discrimination model was the correct one. The Commission has since adopted a detailed blueprint on mainstreaming, and continues to stimulate the member states with thought-provoking policy documents on employment.[266]

iii. The NGO Arguments for Treaty Changes Generally and Specifically in the Field of Disability Discrimination

The late 1990s seemed to provide the ideal conditions for addressing the troubling absence of general human rights provision in the treaties, as well as the absence of any powers to tackle discrimination based, *inter alia*, on disability. The economic agenda of the EU had reached its natural end-point with the completion of the Internal Market in 1992 and the advent of Economic and Monetary Union in 1999. It was therefore entirely logical to expect the Union to either return to its political roots or to move forward to more humanitarian concerns (depending on how one interprets the evolution of the Union).

The stage was therefore set for sweeping changes. European NGOs (both general and disability specific NGOs) took advantage of this opportune time to submit four sets of inter-acting claims. The first set concerns the need for general human rights clauses in the treaties, and specifically with the need to create a power to suspend member states that fail to consistently respect human rights.

---

[265] The combined social partners adopted a *Declaration of the Social Partners on the Employment of People with Disabilities* (19 May 1999), and actually compiled a compendium of good business practice throughout Europe.

[266] *See* European Commission A DG V Services Working Paper, *Mainstreaming Disability within EU Employment and Social Policy* (1998); European Commission Staff Working Paper, *Raising Employment Levels of People with Disabilities: The Common Challenge*, SEC (98) 1550 (Brussels, 22 Sept. 1998); *Communication from the Commission to the Council, the European Parliament, the Economic and Social Committee and the Committee of the Regions: Towards a Barrier Free Europe for People with Disabilities* COM(2000) 248 FINAL (Brussels, 12 May 2000).

The second set has to do with the need to broaden and deepen existing anti-discrimination clauses to (1) make them applicable to areas additional to the labor market (e.g., education, transport), and (2) include more groups within the provisions (including persons with disabilities). These disability-specific arguments were spelled out in detail by the EDF in the period leading up to the negotiation of the Treaty of Amsterdam;[267] the EDF campaign literature from the time makes compelling reading. Basically, the EDF wanted a new judicially enforceable Article 7 in the TEC to deal with broad issues of discrimination. Closely allied to this requirement was the argument that Article 100a (the legal basis for legislation harmonizing the internal market—for example, setting a standard design for lifts) should be amended so that the needs of persons with disabilities should be factored into all harmonizing proposals.

The third set claims a clearer legal base from which to authorise the administration of EU financial aid to NGOs and civil society. The fourth set concerns the need to add a new employment chapter to the TEC to deal with the legitimacy issue.

b. The Shift in Treaty Law: The Treaty of Amsterdam (1997)

i. The Report of the Westendorp Reflection Group (1996) and Disability

Before formal negotiations opened at the IGC, the member states created a high level Reflection Group to prepare the ground for negotiations to take place. The IGC Reflection Group (called the Westendorp Group after its chair) supported the claims being made by disability

---

[267] Two key documents are vital background reading in this regard: *European Day of Disabled People 1995, Disabled Persons Status in the European Treaties: Invisible Citizens*; and *European Day of Disabled People 1996, How Can Disabled Persons in the European Union Achieve Equal Rights as Citizens: The Legal and Economic Implications of a Non-Discrimination Clause in the Treaty on European Union*. *See also* the following European Day Reports: *Towards Equalisation of Opportunities for Disabled People: Into the Mainstream* (1996); *Disabled People: Consumers* (1998); the theme of the 1999 European Day was violence against people with disabilities (*see supra* note 251).

NGOs.[268] Only one dissenting voice was heard (widely presumed to be the U.K. Conservative Government of the time).

ii. Positive Developments in the Treaty of Amsterdam—Article 13 on Non-Discrimination in the Disability Field

The Treaty of Amsterdam added new and very general human rights provisions to the TEU. Full treatment of these developments is out of place here. Suffice it to say that respect for human rights is now stated to be a founding principle of the Union, and a new mechanism is in place to suspend the rights of member states that persistently violate those rights. Nevertheless, any alleged violation would probably have to meet a high factual and evidentiary threshold before these provisions would be triggered in the context of disability.[269]

The basic claim made by European disability NGOs (i.e., through EDF) was the need for a general non-discrimination provision—one that was legally enforceable through the courts and explicitly included disability as one of the prohibited grounds of discrimination. Negotiating member states accepted the political argument for the necessity behind such a provision. However, the new provision that finally emerged (Article 13) only creates the possibility that a unanimous Council might take action to combat discrimination based on one of several listed grounds, including disability.[270]

Article 13 of the TEU reads:

> Without prejudice to the other provisions of this treaty and within the limits of the powers conferred by it upon the Community, the Council, acting unanimously on a proposal from the Commission and after consulting the European Parliament, may take appropriate action to combat discrimination based on [*inter alia*] disability . . .

---

[268] *Reflection Group's Report* (Brussels, 5 Dec. 1995).

[269] *See generally The EU and Human Rights*, *supra* note 7.

[270] *See Amsterdam: What the Treaty Means* (Ben Tonra ed., Dublin, Institute of European Affairs, 1997).

Clearly Article 13 will need to be refined at the next Inter-Governmental Council, which will take place some time after the admission of new Eastern European Members (probably in about four to five years time). Nevertheless, the inclusion of Article 13 is a significant breakthrough since it represents the first time that European governments have acknowledged the reality of the discrimination experienced by people with disabilities. The related disability-specific claim concerning harmonization under Article 100a was also accepted politically. However, the text that eventuated was weak. A Declaration was added to the Treaty of Amsterdam, amending what is now Article 95 of the TEU (ex-Article 100a) as follows:

> The Conference agrees that, in drawing up measures under Article 95 of the Treaty establishing the European Community, the institutions of the Community shall take account of the needs of persons with a disability.[271]

On the downside, the Treaty of Amsterdam did not acknowledge the role played by NGOs in civil society, and failed to provide a solid legal basis for the adoption of social action programs to support the same. This was a grave disappointment to many. Interestingly, disability was specifically mentioned in a draft clause dealing with social exclusion, but was removed at virtually the very last moment in negotiations in Amsterdam; the apparent reason for this concerned perceptions about cost.

The Treaty of Amsterdam also added a completely new employment chapter to the TEU. Article 125 of the TEU (ex-Article 109n) states in part that the member states and the Community will:

> work towards developing a coordinated strategy for employment and particularly for promoting a skilled, trained and adaptable workforce.

---

[271] *Declaration (No. 22) Regarding Persons with a Disability*, Declarations Annexed to the Final Act of Amsterdam.

The member states are required by Article 126(2) (ex-Article 109o) to:

> regard promoting employment as a matter of common concern and shall coordinate their action in this respect within the Council. . . .

For its part, the Community is required by Article 127(1) (ex-Article 109p) to:

> contribute to a high level of employment by encouraging cooperation between Member States and by supporting and, if necessary, complementing their action. . . .

In sum, the real breakthrough at Amsterdam was the recognition that discrimination against people with disabilities does happen. For the first time, people with disabilities are specifically mentioned in the text of the Treaties. No doubt this will prove to be a valuable stepping stone on the way to a general equality and non-discrimination clause. The Treaty of Amsterdam, like the Treaty of Maastricht, must itself be reviewed when additional member states are admitted to the Union, giving disability NGOs a full agenda to ponder over the next few years.

c. Making the Shift a Reality for European Citizens with Disabilities

i. Tackling Disability Discrimination Proper: Commission Proposal for a Directive on Article 13 Banning Disability Discrimination in the Context of Employment (1999).

On November 26, 1999, primarily on the basis of Article 13 of the Treaty of Amsterdam, the European Commission proposed two draft Directives on non-discrimination for adoption by the Council.[272] These Directives were adopted by the Council in June and November of 2000, and consequently will be binding on all member states, regardless of

---

[272] For an overview of the Commission package, *see generally*, *Communication from the Commission to the Council, the European Parliament, the Economic and Social Committee and the Committee of the Regions on Certain Community Measures to Combat Discrimination*, O.J. C369/3 (Brussels, 26 Oct. 1999).

whether they have any domestic constitutional norms to the contrary. The fact that the Directives achieved adoption is particularly significant since unanimity was needed in Council for all proposals coming under Article 13. Each Directive will allow for a period of time before national governments will be required to transpose them into national law.

The first Directive covers the ground of race only, and extends to all spheres including employment, education, cultural activities and the provision of goods and services (Article 3).[273] The second Directive covers all other grounds of discrimination mentioned in Article 13 except gender (which already has accreted a web of directives under Article 117 TEC) and race (which has a whole directive dedicated to it), but applies only in the area of employment.[274]

This second Directive will therefore include disability. It not only forbids direct discrimination but also prohibits indirect discrimination against people with disabilities (as well as others). Article 2.2(b) states that indirect discrimination is taken to occur:

> where an apparently neutral provision, criterion or practice would put persons having a particular religion or belief, a particular disability, a particular age, or a particular sexual orientation at a particular disadvantage compared with other persons unless:
>
> (i) that provision, criterion or practice is objectively justified by a legitimate aim and the means of achieving that aim are appropriate and necessary, or
>
> (ii) as regards persons with a particular disability, the employer or any person or organisation to whom this Directive applies, is obliged, under national legislation, to take appropriate measures in line with the principles contained in Article 5 in order to eliminate disadvantages entailed by such provision, criterion or practice.

---

273 Council Directive 2000/43/EC of 29 June 2000, O.J. L180/22 (19 July 2000).

274 Council Directive 2000/78/EC of 27 November 2000, O.J. L303/16 (2 Dec. 2000).

Article 5 then provides for the principle of "reasonable accommodation" as follows:

> In order to guarantee compliance with the principle of equal treatment in relation to persons with disabilities, reasonable accommodation shall be provided. This means that employers shall take appropriate measures where needed in a particular case to enable a person with a disability to have access to, participate in, advance in employment, or to undergo training, unless such measures would impose a disproportionate burden on the employer. This burden shall not be disproportionate when it is sufficiently remedied by measures existing within the framework of the disability policy of the Member State concerned.

The explanatory memorandum accompanying the draft Directive amplifies this as follows:

> Essentially the concept ("reasonable accommodation") stems from the realisation that the achievement of equal treatment can only become a reality where some reasonable allowance is made for disability in order to enable the abilities of the individual to be put to work. It does not create any obligations with respect to individuals who, even with reasonable accommodation, cannot perform the essential functions of any given job. The obligation is limited in two respects. First, it only pertains to what is reasonable. Secondly, it is limited if it would give rise to undue hardship.

The Directive is stated to be without prejudice to the right of any member state to maintain or adopt measures intended to prevent or compensate for disadvantage (i.e., take positive action).

The Commission has also proposed a well-funded Community Action Programme to complement the two Directives. The objects of the draft programme are: (i) to improve understanding of discrimination issues, (ii) to develop the capacity of target actors, and (iii) to promote and disseminate the values and practices that underlie the fight against discrimination (Article 3). The program proposes achieving its objects through transnational cooperation involving NGOs, as well as others primarily involved in fighting discrimination on specific grounds (excluding those of race and gender). Two pan-European networks of legal experts have now been formed under the Commission's action program. One deals with racial discrimination and the other deals with disability discrimination. Other networks are expected to be established in 2002. The disability discrimination network is directed by the Disability Law and Policy Research Unit of the School of Law at the National University of Ireland (Galway) under Professor Gerard Quinn, and includes as network members several participants at the DREDF (Disability Rights and Education Defense Fund, Inc.) hosted *Principles to Practice* symposium for which this article was commissioned. The network aims to produce a baseline study of disability discrimination legislation and practice covering the EU member states by early 2003. A five-year work program is being developed for the network.

ii. Increasing Equal Opportunities in Employment: Systematic Evaluation of the Employment Situation for People with Disabilities

The new TEU employment chapter added by the Treaty of Amsterdam does not confer hard legal powers as such, but it is nevertheless being put into operation in an interesting way. Essentially, the Commission and Council prepare guidelines according to which member states must report on their employment policies. The original set of guidelines was formally adopted by the Heads of State on December 15, 1997, organised under the following four general headings:

- improving employability;
- developing entrepreneurship;
- encouraging adaptability in business and among their employees; and
- strengthening policies for equal opportunities.

Disability is explicitly addressed under the fourth heading (equal opportunities). The relevant part of heading (IV) reads:

The Member States will:

- give special attention to the problems people with disabilities may encounter in participating in working life.

National action plans (NAPs) based on the Guidelines were drawn up and submitted first in early April 1998 and annually thereafter. They are a very rich source of information on the employment strategies that have been developed by member states with respect to the employment of persons with disabilities. In a background report analysing the detail of the various NAPs the Commission stated:

> All Member States implement a wide range of measures *to promote the participation of disabled people in the mainstream labour market*. Although it is not uncommon for people with disabilities to be given early access to employability measures for the unemployed, priorities vary considerably from one Member State to another. Measures for people with disabilities include anti-discrimination legislation against disabled people, quota systems, rehabilitation and vocational programmes, wage subsidies, subsidies for the acquisition of technical aids or tools, information and awareness campaigns against prejudices affecting people with disabilities.[275]

The latest version of the Guidelines (adopted by the Heads of State in 1999) now deals with disability under the general heading of employability. A specific section under that heading is entitled "Promoting a Labour Market Open to All," and the relevant 1999 Guideline reads:

> Many groups and individuals experience particular difficulties in acquiring relevant skills and in gaining access to, and remaining in, the labour market. A coherent set of policies promoting the integration of such groups and individuals into the world of work and combating discrimination is called for. Each Member State will:

---

[275] European Commission, *Background Report—From Guidelines to Action: The National Action Plans for Employment* (1998).

9. Give special attention to the needs of the disabled, ethnic minorities and other groups and individuals who may be disadvantaged, and develop appropriate forms of prevention and active policies to promote their integration into the labour market.

A new draft Guideline incorporating several different "socially excluded Groups" has been proposed recently by the European Commission. It reads:

Combating Discrimination and Promoting Social Inclusion by Access to Employment.

> Many groups and individuals experience particular difficulties in acquiring relevant skills and in gaining access to, and remaining, in the labour market. This may increase the risk of exclusion. A coherent set of policies which promote social inclusion by supporting the integration of disadvantaged groups and individuals into the world of work, and combat discrimination in access to, and on, the labour market is called for.

. . .

8. Each [Member State] will

- develop pathways consisting of effective preventive and active policy measures to promote integration . . .
- identify and combat discrimination on grounds of . . . disability . . . in access to the labour market and education and training
- implement appropriate measures to meet the needs of the disabled . . . as regards their integration into the labour market and set national targets for this purpose . . .

Under the Guideline, the Council of Ministers can direct very specific recommendations to particular member states whose policies are deemed inadequate. A sort of "case law" on disability therefore has the potential to emerge. In short, the new employment provisions are useful because they help maintain momentum in the field of disability policy. The NAPs are also a very useful source of information on the current status of the employment situation for persons with disabilities throughout Europe.

iii. Creating Equal Access to the Tools of the Information Society: Equal Opportunity Policy Proposals in the Area of Access to the Information Society for Persons with Disabilities (2000)

Europe was much slower than the United States to realise the liberating potential of new Information and Communications Technologies (ICTs)—the tools of the Information Society—for people with disabilities. The European Commission set up a High Level Group of Experts to ponder the future of EU social policy in the context of the coming revolution. In their interim report of 1996, the Group identified the disabled as a disadvantaged group and stated:

> ICTs can indeed substantially contribute to the quality of life and autonomy of many people who have had problems gaining access to services or caring for themselves . . . This would be particularly valuable for people with disabilities or chronic health problems . . . [276]

Clearly the Group was thinking more in terms of access to services than in terms of personal liberation. Their final report referred to the risk of increasing isolation posed by ICTs, and recommended a number of proactive measures to ensure that the "socially excluded" are not forgotten.[277]

---

[276] *Building the European Information Society for Us All: First Reflections of the High Level Group of Experts: Interim Report 33* (Brussels, European Commission, Directorate V, Employment, Industrial Relations & Social Affairs; Secretariat of the High Level Group of Experts, 1996).

[277] European Commission, Directorate-General for Employment, Industrial Relations & Social Affairs; European Social Fund—Policy Development; Adaptation to Industrial Change, *Building the European Information Society for Us All: Final Policy Report of the High Level Expert Group*, 51 (Luxembourg, Office for Official Publications of the European Communities, 1997).

The European Commission issued its own Green Paper on the Information Society in 1996.[278] Among other things, it adverted to the potential of ICTs:

> to improve the quality of life of older people and people with disabilities by facilitating independent living in the community and helping to open up new possibilities for access, participation and socio-economic integration.[279]

The Commission then issued a White Paper in 1998. It was much more forthcoming on the topic of ensuring equal access to ICTs by people with disabilities, and included a separate section on disability. The Commission's objective in this regard was to "promote access and full integration of people with disabilities in the Information Society." The White Paper recommended a series of "actions" for member states, including collaboration with industry and NGOs. In fact a major transatlantic conference on this theme was organised by the European Commission, in conjunction with the U.S. Department of Labor and the President's Committee on the Employment of People with Disabilities, in October 1998 (held in Madrid).[280]

Little happened subsequent to this until January 2000, when the incoming President of the European Commission (Romano Prodi) suddenly issued a Communication on *e*Europe: An Information Society for All.[281] Interestingly and remarkably, a specific section was set out on "*e*Participation for the Disabled." This time, instead of talking about access to services, the policy statement went:

---

[278] *Green Paper on Living and Working in the Information Society: People First*, COM(96) 389 FINAL (Brussels, 22 July 1996).

[279] *Id.* at ¶ 111.

[280] *See Harnessing the Information Society to Raise Employment Levels for People with Disabilities—A New Transatlantic Agenda Sponsored EU/US Conference* (Madrid, 26–27 October, 1998); the conference participants, program and conclusions are available *at* http://www.conf-us-ue-disability.org/frames.htm.

[281] Com (2000) 22.

> Developments in digital technologies offer extensive opportunities to overcome barriers (socio-economic, geographical, cultural, time, etc.) for people with disabilities. Accessible technologies which address their specific needs enable their participation in social and working life on an equal basis.[282]

A number of important targets were proposed in the Communication, including the review of legislation and standards to ensure the inclusion of persons with disabilities, the development of a policy recommendation to member states on their procurement policies, the making of all public web sites accessible, etc.

At a meeting of the Council in March 2000, the Council and the Commission concluded that they jointly should prepare an "Action Plan" on this topic for further consideration.[283] The official conclusions of the Presidency included a specific reference to disability.[284]

To help them draw up the draft Action Plan, the Presidency and the Commission organised a major Ministerial Conference on Knowledge and the Information Society that took place in Lisbon on April 10–11, 2000. For the first time at a Ministerial Conference of this sort, a full panel on "citizens with special needs" was convened that included quite a lot of participation from the United States.

A draft Action Plan on overall vision was duly prepared by the European Commission in May 2000 for consideration by the Council of Ministers at their July meeting in Portugal.[285] Included among the specific "actions" proposed were:

---

282 *Id.* at 13.

283 Lisbon European Council, *Presidency Conclusions—Preparing the Transition to a Competitive, Dynamic and Knowledge-Based Economy*, 23–24 Mar. 2000, at 3.

284 *Id.* at 3: "Special attention [in the drafting of the Action Plan] must be given to disabled people."

285 Com (2000) 330, also *at* http://europa.eu.int/ISPO/docs/policy/docs/e_europe/actionplan_en.pdf.

- The publication of "design for all" standards for ICT accessibility, particularly aimed at improving the employablity of people with disabilities (by the end of 2002);
- A review of legislation and standards to ensure conformity with accessibility principles;
- Adoption of the W3C WAI (Web Accessibility Initiative) guidelines for public web sites;
- Setting up public access points in all Member States;
- Establishing a network of national centres of excellence in design-for-all, and creating a European curriculum on the subject.[286]

On the other hand, the reference to developing a recommendation on public procurement policies (which was in the original *e*Europe Communication) was abandoned

The issue of accessible access to the Information Society is likely to prove crucial in the years ahead. It is noteworthy that the disability perspective has registered from the very outset (albeit not perfectly). This is testament to the power and reach of the equal opportunities model across a broad range of policy sectors. Further policy exchanges between the United States and Europe on this topic would prove most beneficial.

iv. The Fit with New EU Human Rights Initiatives: The Draft EU Charter on Human Rights and Disability

Although the Treaty of Amsterdam elevates the status of human rights in the Union, it does not set out a catalog of such rights. Interestingly, the German Presidency in 1999 proposed the drafting of an EU Charter on Fundamental Rights. A specialised body composed of government representatives—representatives of the European Parliament and National Parliaments as well as the Institutions of the Union—have begun drafting such a Charter and plan to present it for adoption to Council in December 2000. It is still unclear whether the Charter will have some kind of legal status. Even if it does not, a Charter can still be used as a source of inspiration by the European Court of Justice, and could eventually form the basis of a Bill of Rights to be added to the treaties.

---

[286] *Id.* at 17–18.

The Charter is in its second draft. Draft article 24 deals with disability and states:

> 24. Persons with disabilities have the right to benefit from measures designed to ensure their independence, social and occupational integration and participation in the life of the community.

This is clearly deficient. It shows the continuing power of the social services model. Nevertheless, the fact that disability is mentioned at all in such a high profile document means that the issue finally has reached the top policy echelon and cannot be ignored. For the moment, this is the real significance of the Charter in the disability field. There is much current speculation on whether the treaties will be integrated in the next few years into a written Constitution for the Union. If so, that will the occasion at which the real battle lines will be drawn.

D. CONCLUSIONS—THE PROSPECTS FOR A EUROPEANS WITH DISABILITIES ACT (EDA)

As is obvious, the European system of governance is complex. Legal competency is shared between two very different regional organisations and their respective member states, with all parties engaged in a constant dialectic process. The new and encouraging factor is that disability issues have begun to surface at levels above the nation state.

The Council of Europe has adopted and tried to propagate the human rights or equal opportunities approach. This is to be expected given that organization's overall commitment to basic human values and human rights. Unfortunately, its main weapon—the European Convention on Human Rights—still lacks an equality clause with real bite, both generally as well as in the specific context of disability. If there is a mismatch within the Council of Europe, it is between the thrust of the excellent work being done under the Framework of the Partial Agreement in the Health and Social Policy field, and the ongoing activities of the other human rights instruments and bodies. In other words, the Council of Europe still has some distance to go in mainstreaming disability issues into the broad spread of its ongoing work.

The American experience shows that holding a principle is not enough. Principles need to be married to power to bring about real change. Whereas the Council of Europe has had plenty of principle but little power, the reverse tended to be true for the European Union. But this is true no longer. The Union is now said to rest on a foundation of basic principles that include respect for human rights. New supranational legal competencies—albeit inchoate—are conferred on the Union to combat a range of discrimination, including disability discrimination, and the Commission seems eager to press ahead with legislative proposals in the employment field. As a matter of law, more can and should follow, though Treaty amendments are needed to clarify and purify this competency.

If the Union can contribute to the overall development of the equal opportunities model, it will be in the way it reconciles its traditional "European social model" (with its emphasis on social support, including health care) with the newer civil rights model. Formal freedoms need to be made real, with sufficient practical supports to enable people to take their rightful place as citizens. This is the challenge that lies ahead for both the United States and the European Union.

Part 3
Current Trends and Future Prospects

What conclusions, if any, can one garner from the analyses in the two preceding parts? Five particular conclusions strike the authors as significant.

First of all, the war of ideas is over. The paradigm shift to the human rights perspective is now nearly universal. Most countries are beginning to view disability as a human right issue. Admittedly, there is uneven commitment to, or even understanding of, the model worldwide. But its gradual ascendancy has been inexorable. The moral authority of the UN Standard Rules has helped to legitimate the shift, and the enactment of the ADA powerfully demonstrates that change is possible and beneficial both for individuals and for their communities. If there is a broader message in the disability rights movement, it is that citizenship means equal effective access to all dimensions of the lifeworld.

Secondly, recognizing a paradigm shift at the level of ideas is one thing, making it a reality is quite another. Our comparative survey found a wide diversity of legal approaches. To a degree, this is quite understandable given the diversity of the world's cultures and legal systems. The world is as diverse as is the population of people with disabilities. Yet, amid this diversity, one key factor emerges. The best legislation (of whatever variety) tends to be that which creates social, economic and public space for the difference of disability. That is, the law must recognise that strictly identical treatment, in and of itself, places a yoke of inequality upon people with disability. Furthermore, this inequality cannot be removed without requiring some accommodation for the difference of disability. Hence the overarching significance of the concept of "reasonable accommodation." This, the crowning achievement of the ADA, is the critical element that permeates all effective legislation. Clearly, significant work needs to be done in educating people across different legal cultures about the nature and operation of this concept, without which legislation will either fail or not achieve as much as it could.

Thirdly, regional organizations—like the Council of Europe and the European Union—can act as powerful carriers of the fighting faith. They can facilitate the reception of equal opportunities and human rights ideas into national policy-making apparatuses. And they can, within their own sphere of competencies, adopt measures that can make a difference. Any strategy aimed at change must factor in the role (catalytic or otherwise) of such regional bodies, and seek to harness their moral, as well as legal and political, authority.

Our fourth conclusion is that the discrimination agenda—important though it is—does not exhaust the complete spectrum of issues that affect the full enjoyment of human right by persons with disabilities. Anti-discrimination law is an indispensable tool, but it has to be frankly admitted that although effective legislation can open doors, it cannot facilitate people entering through those doors if other needs are not met. In other words, a concern for formal freedom must be matched with a concern for the means by which that freedom is exercised. The importance of achieving actual economic, social and cultural rights for people with disabilities should not be forgotten. By this, we do not mean a social policy agenda that effectively traps people in a gilded cage of passive maintenance, as has been the case in the past. Rather, we mean a social policy that aims to put positive supports in place that will truly enable people to maximise their formal freedoms.

Lastly, most progressive disability legislation has been marketed politically on the basis that it is a "productive factor" in market economies. In other words, such legislation contributes to more rational labour market decisions and greater overall economic activity. We strongly agree. But we also feel that such legislation acts as a "civilizing factor" in any society that respects difference and aims to create societies that are truly open to all.

Annex I
List of Laws*

1. Australia:	Disability Discrimination Act of 1992
2. Austria:	Federal Constitution, as amended 1997
3. Bolivia:	Act No. 1678 about the Person with Disability (1985)
4. Brazil:	Constitution of the Federal Republic of Brazil, as amended 1993
5. Canada:	(a) Canadian Charter of Human Rights and Freedoms, Schedule B, Constitution Act 1982 (b) Canadian Human Rights Act, R.S.C. 1985, c. H-6 (c) Employment Equity Act, S.C. 1994–95, c. 44
6. Chile:	Act No. 19.284
8. China	Law of the People's Republic of China on the Protection of Disabled Persons (1990)
9. Costa Rica	(a) Law 7600 on Equal Opportunities for Persons with Disabilities, 1996 (b) Decree No.19101-S-MEP-TSS-PLAN, 1989
10. Ethiopia:	The Rights of Disabled Persons to Employment, Proclamation No. 101/1994
11. Fiji:	Constitution, as amended 1997
12. Finland:	(a) Constitution as adopted in 1999 (2000) (b) Penal Code as amended 1995 (c) Act on Status and Rights of Patients (785/1992)
13. France:	(a) Law No. 90-602 of 12 July 1990
14. Gambia:	Draft of a Constitution for the Second Republic of Gambia (1996)
15. Germany:	Basic Law of the Federal Republic of Germany, as amended 1994

---

* Note that some of the names of the laws may not be the official name. Translation in some cases by the author (TD).

16. Ghana:	(a) Constitution as of 1992 (b) The Disabled Persons Act, 1993
17. Guatemala:	Act for the Protection of Persons with Disabilities, Decree No.135-96
18.Hong Kong:	SAR Disability Discrimination Ordinance, 1990
19. Hungary:	Act No. XXVI of 1998 on Provision of the Rights of Persons Living with Disability and their Equality of Opportunity
20. India:	The Persons with Disabilities Act (Equal Opportunities, Protection of Rights and Full Participation) Act, 1995
21. Ireland:	(a) Employment Equality Act (#21 of 1998) (b) Equal Status Act (#8 of 2000) (c) National Disability Authority Act (#14 of 1999) (d) Comhairle Act (#1 of 2000)
22. Israel:	Equal Rights for Persons with Disabilities Law, 5758–1998
23. Korea:	(a) The Welfare Law For Persons with Disabilities, Law No.4179 (1989) (b) Act Relating to Employment Promotion, etc. of the Handicapped, Law No. 4219 (1990) (c) The Special Education Promotion Law, as amended 1994
24. Luxembourg:	Penal Code, as amended 1997
25. Madagascar:	New Labour Code as of 29 September 1994
26. Malawi:	Republic of Malawi (Constitution) Act, 1994
27. Mauritius:	The Training and Employment of Disabled Persons Act, 1996 (Act No. 9 of 1996)
28. Namibia:	Labour Act (1992)
29. New Zealand:	Human Rights Act 1993
30. Nicaragua:	(a) Act No. 202, Law for the Prevention, Rehabilitation and Equalization of Opportunities for Persons with Disabilities in Nicaragua (1995) (b) Decree No. 50-97, Regulations and Policies for Act No. 202
31. Nigeria:	Nigerians with Disability Decree 1993
32. Panama:	Family Law Code, Act No. 3 (1994)

33. Philippines:	Magna Carta for Disabled Persons, 1991
34. South Africa:	(a) Constitution, as of 1996 (b) Employment Equity Bill, 1998 (c) Skills Development Bill, 1998
35.Spain:	(a) Workers' Charter as of 1980 (b) Law on the Social Integration of the Disabled (1982) (c) Law on Infringements and Penalties of a Social Nature, 1988
36. Sri Lanka:	Protection of the Rights of Persons with Disabilities Act, No.28 of 1996
37. Sweden:	Law on the Prohibition of Discrimination Against Persons with Disabilities in Employment, SFS No: 1999-132, (1999)
38. Switzerland:	Constitution, adopted 1999
39. Uganda:	(a) Constitution of 1995 (b) Local Government Act of 1997
40. United Kingdom:	(a) Disability Discrimination Act 1995 (b) Disability Rights Commission Act 1999
41. United States of America:	(a) Americans with Disabilities Act of 1990 (b) Rehabilitation Act of 1973
42. Zambia:	The Persons with Disabilities Act, 1996 (Act No. 33 of 1996)
43. Zimbabwe:	Disabled Persons Act, 1992

Annex II
List of Useful European Disability Web Sites

THE COUNCIL OF EUROPE DISABILITY WEB SITE.

The main Council of Europe site is at [www.coe.int]. The disability site is captured under the heading "Social" on the right hand margin. Click on "Social-Public Health," which opens a page entitled "Partial Agreement in the Social and Public Health Field." One of the sites in the left hand margin of the page is entitled "Integration of People with Disabilities" and leads to a number of useful links.

THE EUROPEAN COMMISSION (EU) DISABILITY WEB SITE.

Directorate General Employment and Social Affairs can be found directly at [www.europa.eu.int/comm/dgs/employment_social/index_en.htm]. From the opening page, click on "Employment and Social Affairs Website," and then click on "social security and social integration." One among many items will be "people with disabilities."

THE EUROPEAN DISABILITY FEDERATION (EDF) WEB SITE.

This is at (www.edf-feph.org).

Part II: Foundational Issues in the Use of Anti-Discrimination Law

Where Prejudice, Disability and "Disablism" Meet

*Silvia Yee**

A. INTRODUCTION

In many ways, this collection of articles on the burgeoning field of national, regional and international instruments directed towards the redress of disability discrimination is really about the existence of disability prejudice. Most of the articles focus on practical or theoretical issues raised by the laws themselves, or the jurisprudential, social and political choices that shape the drafting and enactment of laws. Nonetheless, every article is built on the conviction that disability prejudice is a fundamental force behind the exclusion of people with disabilities from a myriad of social and economic opportunities, and one author in particular writes in detail about the personal and systemic consequences of persistent disability prejudice and stereotypes.[1] This article certainly does not dispute the existence of disability prejudice, but it does seek to take a direct look at disability prejudice to argue that the phenomenon of disability prejudice is not widely understood or truly accepted among the political, legal and social institutions that are counted upon to put anti-discrimination laws into practice.

It is my claim that disability prejudice has been viewed through the lens of prejudices such as anti-Semitism, racism, feminism and homophobia—intolerances that may not be pre-existing, but have been generally recognised and theorised earlier in time. While many prejudices may share certain elements of behaviour or even a common trajectory

* LL.B. 1989; B.MUS. 1995; M.A. 1997, University of Alberta. Silvia Yee is the International Law and Policy Fellow with DREDF.

1 David Ruebain, "What is Prejudice as it Relates to Disability Anti-Discrimination Law?", *infra* in this volume at Part IV.

of development, they are not equivalent in their historical, social or psychological dynamics. To assume that they are equivalent poses a theoretical straitjacket on prejudices, allowing us to fall into the habit of believing that perpetrators of prejudice all act and think a certain way, and victims of prejudice share inherent characteristics. We confidently set legal and social prohibitions on the former in order to protect the latter, and we are then surprised to learn that there is a disjunction between the goals we set for disability discrimination laws and the experiences of prejudice that people with disabilities continue to undergo.

The claim that modern society is unfamiliar with disability prejudice may seem incredible in the face of governmental findings, the reports of non-governmental organizations (NGOs) and United Nations (UN) bodies, and the enactment of national and international disability anti-discrimination laws. In the United States, the Americans with Disabilities Act of 1990[2] (ADA) declares that the "continuing existence of unfair and unnecessary discrimination and prejudice denies people with disabilities the opportunity to compete on an equal basis . . . and costs the United States billions of dollars in unnecessary expenses resulting from dependency and non-productivity."[3] Even prior to the enactment of the ADA, the United States Supreme Court stated that:

> By amending the definition of "handicapped individual" [in the Rehabilitation Act] to include not only those who are actually physically impaired, but also those who are regarded as impaired and who, as a result, are substantially limited in a major life activity, Congress acknowledged that society's accumulated myths and fears about disability and disease are as handicapping as are the physical limitations that flow from actual impairment.[4]

---

2 42 U.S.C.A. §§ 12101 *et seq*.

3 42 U.S.C. § 12101(a)(9).

4 School Bd. of Nassau City v. Arline, 480 U.S. 273 (1987); discussing the "regarded as" prong of the Rehabilitation Act's definition of disability (which was also incorporated as the ADA's definition of disability). At this point in the article, I am putting aside the matter of how this same court has been strictly and narrowly interpreting other aspects of the ADA, such as the actual scope of the definitions

This seemingly unambiguous understanding that people with disabilities are bereft of social, educational and economic opportunities not because of individual medical conditions, but because of external social conditions is reiterated throughout numerous international instruments as well.[5] In 1993, a major UN conference on human rights found that:

> The place of disabled persons is everywhere. Persons with disabilities should be guaranteed equal opportunity through the elimination of all socially determined barriers, be they physical, financial, social or psychological, which exclude or restrict full participation in society.[6]

The work of such NGOs as Mental Disability Rights International (MDRI), which has documented the wide-spread and commonly overlooked denial of the most basic human rights of people with mental disabilities in numerous countries,[7] has provided further evidence of discrimination and prejudice against people with disabilities.[8] With the new millennium, the denunciation of disability prejudice and discrimi-

---

contained in the law, or the reach of disability civil rights in the face of constitutional principles such as state sovereign immunity. *See* Toyota Motor Mfg. v. Williams, 534 U.S. 184 (2002); Board of Trustees of the University of Alabama v. Garrett, 531 U.S. 356 (2001).

5 The gradual but steady recognition in European and international law that disability issues extend beyond medical rehabilitation and welfare concerns to encompass human rights discrimination issue is documented by Theresia Degener & Gerard Quinn, "A Survey of International Comparative and, Regional Disability Law Reform," *supra* in this volume at Part I.

6 U.N. World Conference on Human Rights, *Vienna Declaration and Programme of Action*, U.N. Doc. A/CONF.157/23 (1993) ¶ 64.

7 Eric Rosenthal & Arlene Kanter, "The Right to Community Integration for People with Disabilties Under United States and International Law," *infra* in this volume at Part III, at notes 167–73 and accompanying text.

8 For example, MDRI's *Human Rights and Mental Disability: Mexico* (2000) is specifically cited in the Inter-American Commission on Human Rights, Annual Report of the Inter-American Commission on Human Rights 1999, III, para. 20, Doc. 6 Rev, OEA/Ser.L.V/II.106 (Apr. 13, 1999). The report is available *at* www.cidh.oas.org/annualrep/99eng/Chapter5b.htm.

nation in all aspects of life has advanced beyond an exercise in political rhetoric and moved towards the enactment of national laws and international instruments. The first binding regional convention concerning discrimination against people with disabilities finally entered into force last year,[9] and the UN General Assembly has just convened an Ad Hoc Committee to actively investigate and set proposals for a binding international instrument concerning discrimination against people with disabilities.[10]

Even international human rights tribunals have shown a corresponding willingness in recent years to interpret general human rights instruments in a way that recognises the failure to extend human rights to people with disabilities as a clear violation of international law, and not simply an unfortunate consequence of an individual's impairment. Both the Organization of American States' (OAS) Human Rights Commission[11] and the European Court of Human Rights[12] have denounced

---

9 Inter-American Convention on the Elimination of Discrimination Against Persons with Disabilities, AG/RES. 1608 (XXIX-0/99), 29th Sess. of the General Assembly; *opened for signature* June 7, 1999, *entered into force* Sept. 14, 2001 [not published]. For the full text, visit the official Inter-American Commission on Human Rights web site <http://www.cidh.org>.

10 G.A. Res., 56th Sess. [on the report of the 3rd Committee on the draft resolution concerning a comprehensive and integral international convention to promote and protect the rights and dignity of persons with disabilities (A/56/583/Add.2)], U.N. Doc. A/RES/56/168 (2001).

11 *The Case of Victor Rosario Congo, Annual Report of the Inter-American Commission on Human Rights*, Report 63/99, Case 11.427, Ecuador, OEA/Ser.L/V/II.102 Doc. 6 rev. Apr. 13, 1999, in which the Commission stated that "the right to physical integrity is even more serious in the case of a person held in preventative detention, suffering a mental disease, and therefore in the custody of the State in a particularly vulnerable position." At ¶ 67. The Commission concluded that the detention in question constituted a violation of the American Convention on Human Rights, s. 2" which states that "No one shall be subjected to torture or to cruel, inhuman, or degrading punishment or treatment."

12 *Case of Price v. United Kingdom*, Judgement of 10 July 2001, Application No. 00033394/96, HUDOC REF00002640, available *at* http://hudoc.echr.coe.int/Eng/Judgements.htm. The European Court of Human Rights was considering the alleged violation of Article 3 of the Convention for the Protection of Human

the prejudicial mistreatment and particularly high potential for the denial of human rights faced by people with disabilities in situations of involuntary confinement. In the European case, the Court specifically noted that there was "no evidence in this case of any positive intention to humiliate or debase the applicant," but nonetheless found a violation of the Convention: "to detain a severely disabled person in conditions where she is dangerously cold, risks developing sores because her bed is too hard or unreachable, and is unable to go to the toilet and keep clean without the greatest of difficulty, constitutes degrading treatment contrary to Article 3."[13] In the face of such escalating activity and official acknowledgment, how can it be asserted that disability prejudice is unheard of?

In fact, I do not believe that disability prejudice is *unheard* of, at least in modern Western society, and all over the world, nations are paying attention to the reality of discrimination claimed by people with disabilities. I do, however, believe that the precise inability or unwillingness of many people, including people who have suffered from other kinds of prejudices themselves, to truly grapple with the what and why of disability prejudice lies at the heart of much of the resistance and backlash that disability discrimination legislation and policies have recently faced in the United States.[14] While this paper certainly does not purport to

---

Rights and Fundamental Freedoms: "No one shall be subjected to torture or to inhuman or degrading treatment or punishment."

[13] *Id* at ¶ 30. The separate concurring opinion of Judge Greve in the case is interesting for his explicit acknowledgment of a key tenet of the disability rights movement: "The applicant's disabilities are not hidden or easily overlooked. It requires no special qualification, *only a minimum of ordinary human empathy*, to appreciate her situation and to understand that to avoid unnecessary hardship—that is, hardship not implicit in the imprisonment of an able-bodied person—she has to be treated differently from other people because her situation is significantly different." In other words, discrimination can lie in the refusal to treat differently situated persons differently. To take this one step further, I submit that prejudice can lie behind the refusal to either recognise or assess individual difference, unbiased by myth and stereotype.

[14] Negative ADA news coverage and unfavorable editorials abound in the media. *See* for example, "Disabilities Act Unreasonable Law" [editorial], *Daily News [Bowling Green, Kentucky]*, Apr. 30, 1993; Joseph Perkins, "ADA Well-intentioned, but Its Implementation Is Increasingly Unreasonable," *West County Times*

supply final answers to such critical questions as what disability prejudice is, how it operates and is communicated, and how to combat it, I hope to initiate a closer examination of the many assumptions inherent in the way we currently answer these questions.

The first part of my article will look briefly at the development of disability studies with regard to the idea of prejudice. Second, I will examine how studies of prejudice as a social, psychological and cultural phenomenon have evolved since the area's first large influx of work in the post-World War II period. These fields of study can inform one another, but they have so far generally failed to do so. This part will also focus on some of the complicating social and historical factors that make disability prejudice such a complex topic of study *as* an area of prejudice. The failure to study or even to see this theoretical gap threatens the future of disability anti-discrimination, because laws and policies are only effective in so far as they are maintained, enforced and accepted by a society that understands the underlying need for such laws. Finally, I will review how the historical emergence of disability rights awareness and its specificity as an area of prejudice has influenced the social and legal acceptance of disability prejudices. A short conclusion will consider areas for future development.

B. PREJUDICE IN DISABILITY STUDIES

The idea that society fails to perceive disability prejudice is hardly news to anyone who has or has had experience living with a disability. The increasing unification, political identity and self-advocacy of people

---

[Contra Costa], May 15, 1997; "Review and Outlook: The Actively Sick" [editorial], *The Wall St. J. Interactive Edition*, Aug. 26, 1997; "A Judge Blows a Chip Shot" *at* http://www.chicago.tribune.com/print/editoria/9801/18/editoria/9801180006.html Jan. 18, 1998; Meredith May, "Disability Act Being Redefined," *West County Times [Contra Costa]*, Apr. 5, 1999; Marianne M. Jennings, "Disabled Should Play Hand Dealt, Not Demand New Rules, <Desertnews.com> Feb. 19, 2001. For responses to negative media coverage *see* Nina Schuyler, "Disability Rights Advocates Redouble Efforts in an Atmosphere of Hostility," *San Francisco Daily J.*, Dec. 1, 1994 at 1 & 8; Ruth Colker, "The Americans with Disabilities Act: A Windfall for Defendants," 34 *Har. C.R.-C. Lib. L. Rev.* 99 (1999); "Backlash Against the ADA—Interdisciplinary Perspectives and Implications for Social Justice Strategies," 21 *Berkeley J. Emp. & Lab. L.* (2000) [entire volume].

with disabilities has occurred with remarkable momentum over the last four decades, and a key component in this swift progression has been the re-conceptualization of disability as a product of relations between people and not as an individual characteristic. One critical turning point in this process of re-conceptualization occurred in 1976 with the work of the Union of the Physically Impaired Against Segregation (UPIAS) in Britain. UPIAS clearly distinguished between *impairment*, which it defined at the time as "lacking part of or all of a limb, or having a defective limb, organism or mechanism of the body," and *disability:* "the disadvantage or restriction of activity caused by a contemporary social organisation which takes no or little account of people who have physical impairments and thus excludes them from participation in the mainstream of social activities."[15] The resulting view of disability as a socially created mandate was later coined the "social model of disability" by Michael Oliver, a leading British disability academic.[16]

If the gravamen of disability is located in contemporary social organization, then it logically follows that society holds perceptions about people with impairments[17]—whether subconscious or cognitive, socially or psychologically caused, individually communicated or culturally preserved—that appear to justify the exclusion of people with disabilities.

---

[15] Union of the Physically Impaired Against Segregation, *Fundamental Principles of Disability* 14 (London, UPIAS, 1976).

[16] *See* Michael Oliver, *Social Work with Disabled People* (London, MacMillan, 1983). With only a few exceptions, this article looks at disability studies as developed by the work of British and U.S. schools. This is a reflection of my own limitations of time and knowledge, and not a comment on the thinking of disability academics from such other countries as Canada, Australia or the Netherlands.

[17] The marked distinction between (medical) impairment and disability is usually found in British disability scholarship, as is the term "disabled people" to connote people with impairments who are burdened by an oppressive and discriminatory social environment. In the United States, the term "people with disabilities" is preferred, for its person-centered emphasis on individuals who share the characteristic of experiencing life with a physical, mental, sensory or cognitive disability. In general, I adhere to U.S. terminology in this article, and will not therefore be preserving the sharp distinction between the terminology of impairment and disability, although I endorse distinguishing between an individual's functional capacity and the discriminatory consequences that social, cultural and built norms impose upon that individual.

If these perceptions, often deeply imbedded and naturalized over time, are based on over-generalization or myth or stereotype, or fail to accord with reality or the actual experiences of people with disabilities, then the result is aptly called prejudice.

Interestingly, disability studies have tended to focus on discrimination and stereotype far more than what could be considered the more primary study of disability prejudice. That is, the focus has been on re-interpreting overt acts that exercise control over the options available to people with disabilities, rather than on theorisation of the attitudes presumed to be behind the actions.[18] I posit at least two reasons for this. First, people with disabilities were living lives that were always imminently and profoundly circumscribed by social rules established by people without disabilities; regardless of *attitudes*, people with disabilities needed the rules to be changed before they could hold any hope for a future free from prejudice. Second, people with disabilities are historically one of the last groups to come to a sense of self-conscious political and social awareness.[19] An abundant academic and theoretical

---

18 I will be examining prejudice studies in greater detail in Part C, *infra*, but for the purposes of the discussion at this point I will simply advert to the basic distinction used in social psychology that prejudice is something that relates to attitudes while discrimination relates to overt behaviour; *see* for example Edward E. Sampson, *Dealing with Differences: An Introduction to the Social Psychology of Prejudice* 5–7 (Fort Worth, Harcourt Brace, 1999). Numerous studies have found that the actual relationship between prejudice, stereotypes and discrimination is surprisingly weak, prompting the conclusion that "cognitive, affective, and behavioral orientations to individuals and social groups represent different, independent response systems whose interrelationships are more complex than previously thought.": *see* M.B. Brewer, "The Social Psychology of Prejudice: Getting It All Together," *in The Psychology of Prejudice*, Ontario Symposium on Personality and Social Psychology, v. 7, 315 at 321 (M.P. Zanna & J.M. Olson eds., Hillsdale, NJ, Lawrence Erlbaum, 1994).

19 The phrase "last civil rights movement" was tapped by Diane Dreidger in *The Last Civil Rights Movement: Disabled People's International* (London, Hurst, 1989). However, even prior to political self-awareness and the move of people with disabilities to assert control over the term, recognition of "the disabled" as a human category does not have deep historical roots. "The idea that individuals with physical, sensory, and cognitive impairments together form a class of 'the disabled' is an invention of the current century. . . . Persons were described as crippled or deaf or blind or mad or feebleminded, but only in the first part of this century was the

discourse concerning the nature and effects of prejudice and its root role in the social oppression of ethnic and racial minorities, as well as women and gay people, already existed and continues to grow. Rather than contribute to this often psychologically focussed exploration of the types of individuals who hold prejudice, people with disabilities concentrated on recognizing commonalities between their own experiences of oppression and those of other minority groups, and on revealing the social treatment of people with disabilities *as* discrimination, and not simply as something objectively and inescapably dictated by the physical, mental or cognitive conditions of people with disabilities.

This is the approach taken by Paul Hunt, a first-generation disability activist, who in the 1960s chose to write:

> . . . largely in terms of our relation with others, our place in society. This is essentially related to the personal aspect of coping with disablement, which I hope it will at the same time illuminate, since the problem of disability lies not only in the impairment of function and its effects on us individually, but also, more importantly, in the area of our relationship with "normal" people. If everyone were disabled as we are, there would be no special situation to consider.[20]

Hunt was discussing his own specific situation of being a person with a physical impairment that is commonly considered severe, and identified five distinct facets of this situation: society considered people with such impairments as "unfortunate, useless, different, oppressed and sick." In his experience, people without disabilities believed that people with disabilities were "unfortunate" because the latter led

---

term *disabled* introduced to characterize and collectivize them." Anita Silvers, "Formal Justice," *in* Anita Silvers, David Wasserman & Mary B. Muhowald, *Disability, Difference, Discrimination: Perspectives on Justice in Bioethics and Public Policy* 54 (Lanham, MD, Rowman & Littlefield, 1998); *see also* Deborah Stone, *The Disabled State* 25–28 (Philadelphia, Temple U. Press, 1984).

20 Paul Hunt, "A Critical Condition" *in Stigma: The Experience of Disability* (London, Geoffrey Chapman, 1966) reprinted *at* http://www.leeds.ac.uk/disability-studies/archiveuk/Hunt/critical%20condition.pdf, 1–2.

"cramped lives" in which they were deprived of such things as freedom of movement, independence and the enjoyment of material goods. People with disabilities were also considered "useless" because they were "unable to contribute to the economic good of the economy." Both of these aspects contributed to the assessment that people with disabilities were "different"—"abnormal, marked out as members of a minority group." Hunt drew an analogy to the situations of other minorities, among which he included Jews, Blacks, homosexuals and the mentally disabled, who also feel the "constant experience of the pressure towards unthinking conformity." He also explicitly evokes a correlation to the better-recognised racial and ethnic minorities when he concludes that the fact of being "different" subjects people with disabilities to "prejudice which expresses itself in discrimination and oppression." The final aspect of being considered "sick" arose from disability's uncomfortably close association with such things as depression, pain, loneliness, poverty, and other aspects of tragedy and the unknown in the minds of non-disabled people.[21]

By linking disability prejudice with both general cultural expectations for such things as material goods and employment, and social perceptions concerning the inability of people with disabilities to achieve such expectations, Hunt was one of the first activists to cast an alternative light on the social segregation and lack of life alternatives hitherto assumed endemic in the mere fact of having an impairment. In Britain, where Hunt continued his work with UPIAS colleagues in the 1970s, disability studies developed as an independent academic area that conceived of disability as "a complex and sophisticated form of social oppression or institutional discrimination on a par with sexism, heterosexism and racism,"[22] and criticized disciplines such as medical sociol-

---

21 *Id.* at 2–6. Hunt's use of the word "sick," and the taxonomy used in British disability studies, can be compared with the terminological distinctions made by medical sociologists between "sickness" (a social role imposed from without), "illness" (involving self-perception of the individual) and "disease" (cause by biological agent).

22 Colin Barnes, "Theories of Disability and the Origins of the Oppression of Disabled People in Western Society" *in Disability and Society: Emerging Issues and Insights* 43, (Len Barton ed., Harlow, Essex, Addison Wesley Longman, 1996). *See also* Michael Oliver, "Social Policy and Disability: Some Theoretical Issues,"

ogy that "have been unable to distinguish between illness and disability and have proceeded as if they are the same thing."[23]

Building on the powerful and liberating idea that disability discrimination is based on larger social relations rather than individual impairment, British academics—many of whom had disabilities and a number of whom were sociologists—drew heavily on Marxist materialist theories to trace disability oppression to the historical emergence of modern capitalist society and the cultural ideology of industrialism. According to Michael Oliver, capitalist ideology's emphasis on individual entrepreneurship and achievement, aided by "peripheral ideologies associated with medicalisation and underpinned by personal tragedy theory, have presented a particular view of the disabled individual." The social construction of disability as "dependence" is not derived from "functional limitations on [people with disabilities'] capacities for self-care," but because dependence is shaped by "politicians, planners and professionals who have to manage (control) this dependency in accord with current social values and economic circumstance."[24] Later British academics such as Tom Shakespeare have taken a somewhat different approach to studying the role of culture in the social construction of disability, focusing on discursive practices related to disability and cultural representation of disability "in the broader linguistic and artistic environment."[25] Regardless of the precise emphasis, British academics and scholars are united in their conviction that impairment is disabling because a social and physical environment historically created by non-impaired people makes it so.

U.S. accounts of disability equally refute the individual, impairment-based medical model of disability in favor of a social model, but the

---

1:1 *Disability, Handicap & Society* 5 (1986); Colin Barnes, *Disabled People in Britain and Discrimination: A Case for Anti-Discrimination Legislation* (London, Hurst & Co., 1991).

23 Michael Oliver, *The Politics of Disablement: A Sociological Approach* xi (New York, St. Martin's Press, 1990).

24 *Id.* at 78, 94.

25 Tom Shakespeare, "What is a Disabled Person?" *in Disability, Divers-Ability and Legal Change* 24, 33 (Melinda Jones & Lee Ann Basser Marks eds., The Hague, Boston, London, Martinus Nijhoff, 1999).

most powerful and well-known of these accounts tend to accomplish this refutation through the immediacy of experiential narrative rather than the direct exposition of social theory.[26] One of the first disability studies scholars, the political scientist Harlan Hahn, writes of people with disabilities as subject to "the pervasive sense of physical and social isolation produced not only by the restrictions of the built environment but also by the aversive reactions of the nondisabled that often consign them to the role of distant friends or even mascots rather than to a more intimate status as peers, competitors, or mates."[27] Jenny Morris, a successful political activist and feminist when she became disabled as an adult, argues that the lack of an inclusive forum in which people with disabilities can express their views of themselves and their social relationships enables the medical model's view of impairment to be self-perpetuating. "Disabled people—men and women—have little opportunity to portray our own experiences within the general culture . . . [and t]his lack of a voice, of the representation of our subjective reality, means that it is difficult for non-disabled [people] to incorporate our reality into their research and their theories, unless it is in terms of the way the non-disabled world sees us."[28]

How do we determine what is interesting, what is "newsworthy" or significant? In the late 1980s, journalists increasingly began to give press coverage from the viewpoint of people with disabilities. The journalist Joseph Shapiro recounts that in 1988, a public relations woman from the National Multiple Sclerosis Society called him with a story about how New York's lack of accessability had forced the Society to take extraordinary measures just to get their "Man of the Year" from his hotel room across the street to the club where he was to be honored. Shapiro declined, asserting that he was seeking a story "with broad national significance, something important that was happening in the lives of all

---

[26] The work of anthropologist Robert Murphy, who performs an ethnography on his own body after becoming paraplegic as an adult, explicitly combines personal expression and theory: *The Body Silent* (New York, Holt, 1987).

[27] "Civil Rights for Disabled Americans" *in Images of the Disabled, Disabling Images* 198 (A. Gartner & T. Joe eds., New York, Praeger, 1987).

[28] *Pride Against Prejudice: Transforming Attitudes to Disability* 8 (Philadelphia, New Society, 1991).

disabled people throughout the country." The woman then told him about the efforts of something called the disability rights movement, and about an upcoming meeting in Washington, D.C. to consider a bill called the Americans with Disabilities Act. Shapiro went to Washington to watch as "an utterly anonymous presidentially appointed council" put together "dreamy, pie-in-the-sky legislation." He found the council's impassioned discussion about rights, and the irony of a sweeping civil rights bill being proposed by a council that had been appointed under then-President Reagan, not known for his support of civil rights causes, "interesting" but was still "not sure that [he] saw a story." Later, standing in line for a taxi after checking out of his Washington hotel, Shapiro witnessed a taxi driver make an abrupt U-turn to avoid picking up the next person in the queue, a well-dressed young man in a wheelchair. Shapiro writes:

> His face showed no anger, no emotion at all, as if getting passed by cabdrivers was an everyday occurrence. I was reminded of the MS Society's Man of the Year, unable to cross the street in one of the world's most modern cities, stranded without transportation. . . . If not for cabs, how would this man get back to his office or to his home? Few buses in Washington had wheelchair lifts. The subway system was accessible, assuming the elevator at his stop was working. But the subway reached only some parts of the city. Access to transportation, then, would circumscribe where the man lived and where he worked, or if he even worked at all. If people like him were precluded from working, then they would depend on welfare. If a society expected its disabled people not to work and instead need public assistance, would it even try to give them a decent education? Back at my office, I began writing my first story about disability as a rights issue.[29]

Shapiro eventually found the interesting and significant story he was looking for, but doing so was not a matter of unearthing more facts about the disability rights movement. Rather, it was a process of re-eval-

---

[29] Joseph Shapiro, *No Pity: People with Disabilities Forging a New Civil Rights Movement* 8–10 (New York, Times Books, 1993).

uating facts that were already before him. He grew to understand the logical connection between the story of one person being unable to cross the street and systemic problems of transportation, employment, education and social expectations for people with disabilities. Ultimately then, U.S. experiential writings point squarely, as do the British sociological studies, to the interaction between people with disabilities and those without as the place where (lack of) understanding of disability is socially created, defined and maintained.

U.S. accounts of disability that are less experiential or narrative, and more directly theoretical or oriented toward historiography, have tended to focus on specific institutional or policy aspects of disability, rather than offer broad structuralist critiques of capitalism.[30] As such, they may not be written with the express goal of exposing systemic prejudice and stereotype, although they usually acknowledge the presence of such.[31] In the last decade, U.S. scholarship on disability has also grown increasingly cross-disciplinary as academics from fields as diverse as philosophy, ethics, literary criticism, archaeology, and cultural anthropology have joined sociologists in examining disability as a formed and forming aspect of modern culture.[32] The resulting body of disability-related

---

30 *See* for example Stone, *supra* note 19, who examines how the administrative category of "disability" has been historically and politically created and controlled by the state for social security purposes; Michael L. Perlin, *The Hidden Prejudice: Mental Disability on Trial* (Washington, American Psychological Association, 2000), who offers a scathing discussion of how the U.S. legal system curtails and denies the rights of people with mental disabilities. One of the latest entrants in this line of scholarly inquiry critically reviews how social policies left over from the post-World War II rehabilitation era of disability continue to undermine current bureaucratic and legal interpretations of U.S. disability rights laws: *see* Ruth O'Brien, *Crippled Justice: The History of Modern Disability Policy in the Workplace* (Chicago, U. of Chicago Press, 2001).

31 Stone explains her position as follows: "[t]o argue that disability creates political privilege is not to deny that it also entails handicap, social stigma, dependence, isolation and economic disadvantage. The fact that the state creates a formal category for the disabled within its distributive policies and accords this category privileged status does not obviate the myriad ways in which the disabled suffer in both private relationships and treatment by public institutions." *Supra* note 19, at 4.

32 *See* for example Anita Silvers, "Defective Agents: Equality, Difference and the Tyranny of the Normal," *J. Soc. Philosophy, 25th Ann. Special Issue* 154 (1994)

work has provided rich and thought-provoking support for the claims of the social model of disability.

Certain fields, such as cultural anthropology, are particularly adept at illustrating how disability is a function of cultural and social understanding rather than a self-evident state of being, since the discipline must disassociate itself from medical or technical understandings of disability that are not by any means universally embraced or understood. The method of cultural juxtaposition requires anthropologists to "relate concepts of disability to notions about power and bodies, normality and order, individual capacity and social existence," and further demands the understanding that cultural concepts "are not just 'found in' cultural analysis. They are asserted by the media, the clergy, health personnel, and development agencies; they are negotiated by parents, represented in ritual, contested or ignored by people with impairments."[33]

Other seemingly more distant disciplines such as literary criticism or cultural studies add valuable insight by virtue of the fact that social assumptions and beliefs are in large part communicated through visual, literary and popular culture. Thus Rosemarie Garland Thomson examines the mid-19th- to 20th-century American "Freak Show," sentimental fiction and black women's liberatory writings to reveal the "critical gap between disabled figures as fashioned corporeal others whose bodies carry social meaning and actual people with atypical bodies in real-world social relations," because she recognizes that "representation informs the identity—and often the fate—of real people with extraor-

---

[and in numerous publications since on the topic of disability and social justice]; Hans S. Reinders, *The Future of the Disabled in Liberal Society: An Ethical Analysis* (Notre Dame, U. of Notre Dame, 2000); Lennard J. Davis, *Enforcing Normalcy: Disability, Deafness and the Body* (London, New York, Verso, 1995); Rosemarie Garland Thomson, *Extraordinary Bodies: Figuring Physical Disability in American Culture and Literature* (New York, Columbia U. Press, 1997); *Disability and Culture* (Benedicte Ingstad & Susan Reynolds Whyte eds., Berkeley, U. of California Press, 1995); *Madness, Disability and Social Exclusion: The Archaeology and Anthropology of "Difference,"* One World Archaeology, v. 7 (Jane Hubert ed., London, New York, Routledge, 2000).

33 Susan Reynolds Whyte & Benedicte Ingstad, "Disability and Culture: An Overview," *in Disability and Culture*, *supra* note 32, 3 at 25.

dinary bodies."[34] Other humanities scholars bring into question language itself, especially those discursive practices commonly used to describe the difference of disability. Lennard J. Davis provides a compelling portrait of how modern ideals of "normalcy" and the "normal" body are less a constant feature of the human condition than "a configuration that arises in a particular historical moment. It is part of a notion of progress, of industrialization, and of ideological consolidation of the power of the bourgeoisie."[35] From the appearance of words such as "norm," "average" and "abnormal" in the English language in the mid-19th century, through to the normalizing plot devices, character development and very structure of 19th- and 20th-century novels, the "hegemony of normalcy" extends its influence to "the very heart of cultural production."[36] Davis traces this path to show that "the 'problem' is not the person with disabilities; the problem is the way that normalcy is constructed to create the 'problem' of the disabled person."[37]

With the close scrutiny of administrative disability categories, and the addition of cross-disciplinary techniques, disability studies have grown increasingly sophisticated in tracing the often subtle ways in which cultural rules, norms, language, and social institutions create disability as different and lesser. Nonetheless, the first major insights of disability studies still hold. Even if one were bored by philosophy, disinclined to read anthropology or cultural studies texts, and preferred the comics over political editorials, the connection drawn by Shapiro outside his Washington hotel room is truly not that obscure. Do people without disabilities simply not notice or understand that accessibility is linked to social and economic opportunities, the lack of which leads to poverty, physical isolation and political powerlessness, with these in turn becoming a "naturalized" status quo for people with disabilities? When a persons with a wheelchair is halted by a single step at a public place or university lectures are given without sign language or transcripts for the Deaf, people with disabilities are substantively excluded. On the

---

34 Garland Thomson, *supra* note 32, at 15.

35 Davis, *supra* note 32, Ch. 2, "Constructing Normalcy."

36 *Id.* at 49.

37 *Id.* at 24.

other hand, if the implications of a built and technologic environment that excludes people with disabilities are truly "inescapable," as Anita Silvers maintains, why is it that "nondisabled people appear sincerely to regret these profoundly marginalizing outcomes, yet they do little to avoid them?"[38]

Furthermore, even if a non-disabled world is apathetic about the "incidental" (that is, non-intentioned) exclusion of people with disabilities, the current failure to take account of the subjective expression of individuals with disabilities requires at least some measure of active avoidance. Irrespective of theorizing, and as any chronicle of the disability civil rights movement shows, people with disabilities have been growing increasingly active and vocal about encountering inaccessibility every day in all aspects of their lives.[39] Obviously, people with various kinds and levels of disabilities are capable, willing and desirous of communicating their personal experiences, and the historical absence of records of the lives, feelings and experiences of people with disabilities is not an inevitable or "natural" consequence of impairment. Therefore, any continuing lack of these voices in mainstream social or political agendas cannot logically be attributable to the mere fact of disability, so much as to an assumption that people with disabilities have little to say and even less to share. This longstanding stereotype, like most stereotypes about people with disabilities, has long gone unquestioned in the non-disabled world, even though it has been factually disputed by people with disabilities time and again.

Various explanations have been advanced for the origin and persistence of stereotypes about people with disabilities in contemporary society. Barnes looks to history and the roots of Western culture in ancient Greek civilization's "obsession with bodily perfection, as evidenced in Greek myth, competitive sport and the practice of infanticide for children with impairments."[40] Others hypothesise a deeper, psychological

---

38 *Supra* note 19, at 50.

39 For fine examples of such chronicles see Shapiro, *supra* note 29, and James Charleton, *Nothing About Us Without Us* (Berkeley, U. of California Press, 1998).

40 *Supra* note 22, "Theories of Disability and the Origins of the Oppression of Disabled People in Western Society," at 52–56. Barnes also highlights the Judeao-

rationale for stereotypes in stating that for the nondisabled, people with disabilities are a threatening reminder of the ever-present possibility of accident, impairment, helplessness.[41] One author asserts that irrational prejudice against the mentally disabled occurs "because we fear the unknown, and we fear the possibility that *we* may become mentally ill. To make the world less indeterminate, we simplify via stereotypes that simultaneously demonize and infantilize. And we continue to irrationally conflate mental illness with dangerousness."[42] Other academics point out how the 19th century provided a particularly fertile breeding ground for stereotypes: "[a]s we locked up, isolated, and segregated people, the perception of their lives became one of speculation and mystery rather than based [sic] on fact and experience. As the curve of social isolation increased, so did misunderstanding."[43]

Disability scholars have addressed issues of stereotyping and discrimination, but the factor of prejudice is usually asserted without a similar degree of systematic theorization. From an experiential viewpoint, such theorization is unnecessary. What else could possibly account for the world's refusal to acknowledge or care that its institutions, social rules and cultural expressions ignore both the needs and capacities of people with disabilities? How can prejudice *not* be present when the mere fact of a disability or impairment cannot objectively explain per-

---

Christian religious tradition of judging human imperfections as signs of impurity, divine judgment and diabolical influence. He concludes rather pointedly that "prejudice, in whatever form it takes, is not an inevitable consequence of the human condition, it is the product of a particular form of social development associated with western capitalism." *Id.* at 57.

[41] Morris, *supra* note 28; Iris Marion Young, *Justice and the Politics of Difference* (Princeton, Princeton U. Press, 1990).

[42] Perlin, *supra* note 30, at 40.

[43] Herbert C. Covey, *Social Perceptions of People with Disabilities in History* 5 (Springfield, Il, Charles C. Thomas, 1998). Covey examines diverse historical influences on how people with disabilities have been socially perceived (for example, theories of "Social Darwinism," the physical uniformity demanded by industrialized processes, and so on), and provides a veritable catalogue of those perceptions, noting that "regardless if the perception is negative or positive, the perception nevertheless serves to separate and distinguish people with disabilities from those who lack them." *Id.* at 25.

vasive differences of treatment? The experience of a profound gap between what people with disabilities feel and believe their lives and their worth to be, and the way in which they are persistently excluded, assessed and portrayed—so similar in many ways to the experience described by Jews, Blacks, women, gay people—is held in common by victims of discrimination. Like those other victims, people with disabilities turn to prejudice as the root explanation for the misperception, damaging stereotyping and discrimination that marks their lives.[44]

Hunt expressed something of this feeling of affinity with other minorities when he wrote:

> Maybe it is invidious to compare our situation with that of racial minorities in any way. The injustice and brutality suffered by so many because of racial tension makes our troubles as disabled people look very small. But I think there is a connection somewhere, since all prejudice springs from the same roots.[45]

Attempts to compare the sufferings of people with disabilities and racial minorities might be of arguable worth,[46] but Hunt's general understanding of all prejudices sharing common roots remains essentially

---

[44] I do not mean to imply that people with disabilities have always universally recognised prejudice as such when it is directed against them. Collective action and writings provided forums in which people with disabilities could politically and socially enlighten themselves and others. Before this, the very invidiousness of socially sanctioned prejudice against impairment and disability meant that people with disabilities could grow up believing the stereotypes that society holds about them, even to the extent of emotionally, psychologically and/or physically distancing themselves from other people with disabilities and denying the role of disability in their own identity. Abraham Kaplan, in a classic essay on equality and anti-Semitism in particular, describes the result succinctly when he writes that the "[d]enial of identity leaves an emptiness within when it succeeds, and adds despair to self-contempt when it fails." "Equality," *in Hatred, Bigotry, and Prejudice: Definitions, Causes and Solutions* 81, 87 (Robert M. Baird & Stuart E. Rosenbaum eds., Amherst, NY, Prometheus Books, 1999).

[45] *Supra* note 20, at 6.

[46] It is also possible that Hunt at the time of writing was not fully aware of the extent to which people with disabilities are historically and presently subjected to abuse, from infanticide to eugenics, from extermination in Nazi death camps to

unchallenged in disability studies. In the 1960s, when Hunt wrote these words, he would have found virtually uniform agreement among scholars of intolerance and prejudice. This is no longer the case. For immediate victims of intolerance and discrimination, this academic splintering may seem of little moment, but anyone with a stake in how our society analyzes, judges, punishes, or combats the consequences of prejudice in general, and disability prejudice in particular, will find it worthwhile to further investigate the junction of prejudice and disability.

C. DISABILITY IN PREJUDICE STUDIES

Prejudice as an independent topic of scholarly investigation in the Western world came into its own after the Second World War. *Studies in Prejudice*, a five-volume series of social science enquiry into anti-Semitism, intolerance and intergroup conflict, was commissioned in the United States by the American Jewish Committee as a serious attempt to understand and avoid the forces that allowed the Holocaust to occur.[47] While experientially based literary and historical accounts from within the Black community as victims of prejudice were also being written during this period, these usually were not focussed on the broad subject of prejudice as a phenomenon in and of itself.[48] In the 1950s, rising social awareness of intolerance and violence in U.S. race relations provoked a corresponding increase in the academic theorization of prejudice as a seemingly inescapable ingredient in all human relations.

Gordon Allport's seminal *The Nature of Prejudice*[49] is the most widely quoted and classic English study of prejudice in the post-World War II era. Allport sought to provide a thorough review of scholarly work that had been undertaken to date, but even more importantly, a

present-day horrors of neglect and rape in institutionalised settings all over the world. *See supra* notes 7–8, *infra* notes 83–84.

47 *Studies in Prejudice* (Max Horkheimer & Samuel H. Flowerman eds., New York, American Jewish Committee: Harper & Bros., 1949–50).

48 *See* for example Ralph W. Ellison, *Invisible Man* (1952); James Baldwin, *Notes of a Native Son* (1955).

49 Gordon W. Allport, *The Nature of Prejudice* (Cambridge, MA, Addison-Wesley, 1954).

"framework" for the future investigation of prejudice in all its manifestations. Innumerable college texts have adopted not only Allport's definition of prejudice, usually formulated as "prejudice is an unjustified attitude, positive or negative, directed toward others because of their membership in a social category or group,"[50] but also his entire approach to studying the subject. Endemic in this approach is both a conceptual conviction that despite prejudice's various manifestations, "the basic causes and correlates are essentially identical,"[51] and a professional faith in the social sciences as a means of easing and solving the dilemma of intergroup conflict. Both themes are evident in the following:

> in recent years men in large numbers have become convinced that scientific intelligence may help us solve the conflict [of group rivalry and hatred]. . . . Men are saying, "Let us make an objective study of conflict in culture and industry, between people of different color and race; let us seek out the roots of prejudice and find concrete means for implementing men's affiliative values. Since the end of the Second World War universities in many lands have given new prominence to this approach under various academic names: *social sciences, human development, social psychology, human relations, social relations*. Though not yet securely christened, the infant science is thriving. . . .
>
> The present volume does not pretend to deal with the science of human relations as a whole. It aims merely to clarify one underlying issue—the nature of human prejudice. But this issue is basic, for without knowledge of the roots of hostility

---

[50] Allport never offers a general definition of prejudice in his study, instead using his introductory chapter to present myriad definitions before building a composite definition for ethnic prejudice as "an antipathy based upon a faulty and inflexible generalization. It may be felt or expressed. It may be directed toward a group as a whole, or toward an individual because he is a member of that group." *Id.* at 9. Nevertheless, the degree to which this opening chapter explores the elements of this definition have enabled subsequent authors to derive a general definition for prejudice that Allport would have endorsed. The one I give here is based upon my own reading of Allport and the simplified definition presented in Sampson, *supra* note 18.

[51] Allport, *id.* at xvii.

> we cannot hope to employ our intelligence effectively in controlling its destructiveness.[52]

Allport's belief in the transforming power of the social sciences probably strikes most contemporary readers as naive, but his understanding of the essentially singular nature of prejudice generally has remained entrenched in subsequent studies, albeit with increasing emphasis on the unlikelihood that the social sciences will ever succeed in finding one unified theory of prejudice.[53]

Allport himself used various "lenses"—historical, psychological, cultural, economic—to view the phenomenon of prejudice, and endorsed specific techniques ranging from field interviews to psychoanalysis. Nonetheless, results obtained from interview/questionnaire studies in particular led him to state that "[o]ne of the facts of which we are most certain is that people who reject one out-group will tend to reject other out-groups. If a person is anti-Jewish, he is likely to be anti-Catholic, anti-Negro, anti any out-group." This finding in turn fueled his conclusion "that prejudice tends to be a general trait in personality," a "generalized attitude."[54] In further support, he notes "[t]he fact that scapegoats of different breeds are so often harnessed together [in verbal condemnations] shows that it is the *totality* of prejudice that is important rather than specific accusations against single groups." In this regard, Allport built on the earlier work of Theodor Adorno and his fellow Marxist social theorists in their development of the "F-scale," a measure for tendencies and personality traits that exhibited an affinity with fascism (authoritarianism).[55] These concepts, of an "authoritarian personality," a "generalized attitude" behind prejudice, of ethnocentrism

---

52 *Id.* at xiv–xv. As may be inferred from this passage, sexism does not form a major component of Allport's study; to be fair, gender prejudices were not as commonly recognised in this era.

53 Sampson, *supra* note 18, at 11.

54 Allport, *supra* note 49, at 68–69. Throughout this section I have adopted the socio-psychological terms "in-group" and "out-group" as convenient ways to indicate respectively those with whom one identifies and those whom one sees as "other."

55 T.W. Adorno, E. Frenkel-Brunswik, D.J. Levinson & R.N. Sanford, *The Authoritarian Personality* (New York, Harper, 1950). In this and previous post-World War II work, Adorno attempted to combine the individually focussed psychological

in which hostility is more or less "naturally" directed towards anyone who falls outside of one's self-defined "in-group," all reinforce the understanding of prejudice as a unitary phenomenon.

In the last couple of decades, theories concerning prejudice have grown increasingly diverse in their approach, but these theories often continue to present the many manifestations of prejudice as rooted in a single thing, whether that thing is fear of the unknown, dislike of the unknown, competition for scarce resources, or hierarchical social structures.[56] Similarly, different disciplines advance theories that present prejudice in terms of evolution (socio-biological roots), group interactions (structural roots), individual tendencies (social-psychological roots), or the ways in which people communicate through symbols (roots in linguistics, rhetoric, discourse, and historical power relations),[57] with the implicit premise that any given theory is equally applicable to any particular manifestation of prejudice. After thoroughly reviewing and analyzing the strengths and weaknesses of numerous representative examples of prejudice studies from each of these four conceptual frameworks, Michael Hecht and John Baldwin propose "that intolerance can exist at various levels and be expressed in different ways. . . . we argue that although there may be an underlying, global, or unifying construction of prejudice, there also are various intolerances; even ethnic intolerances can be expressed differently toward one group than toward another."[58]

---

theories of Freud with a Marxist consciousness of how social structural conditions shape modern life and specifically modern ways of thought. In asserting the existence of a modern form of prejudice that tends to cover many out-groups, Adorno used the term "ethnocentrism," which "is based on a pervasive and rigid in-group-out-group distinction; it involves stereotyped negative imagery and hostile attitudes regarding out-groups, stereotyped positive imagery and submissive attitudes regarding in-groups, and a hierarchical authoritarian view of group interaction in which in-groups are rightly dominant, out-groups subordinate." *Id.* at 150.

56 Adopted from Michael Hecht's presentation of four central metaphors of prejudice: "*Introduction*," *in Communicating Prejudice* 3, (Michael L. Hecht ed., Thousand Oaks, CA, Sage, 1998).

57 John R. Baldwin, "Tolerance/Intolerance: A Multidisciplinary View of Prejudice," *in Communicating Prejudice*, *id.* 24 at 26–55.

58 "Layers and Holograms: A New Look at Prejudice," *in Communicating Prejudice*, *supra* note 56, 57 at 58.

A glance at the British and American disability writings reviewed in Part B of this article reveals a fairly fluid appropriation of various of these theoretical approaches. In other words, disability writers have not sharply distinguished between presenting disability prejudice as fear of difference and the unknown, as a consequence of capitalist ideology and an individualistic culture, or as the product of hegemonic cultural and representational norms. As might be expected in an emerging field of study that is prominently marked by strong narrative and personal accounts of actual experiences of disability, disability scholars have not felt compelled to maintain watertight compartments of prejudice theory. Nor, however, has any disability scholar explicitly rejected the implication that disability prejudice shares the same roots and course of development as other prejudices.

In fact, the adoption of terms like "disablism"[59] and "sanism"[60] advances an implicit premise that disability prejudice is a prejudice "like the others"—for example, prejudices such as anti-Semitism, racism, and sexism[61] that have gained earlier popular, academic and cultural recognition. The term "disablism" is useful in many ways. It instantly connotes a relationship of prejudice and social oppression, and by doing so serves as a rallying point for members of the disability community. "Isms" are publicly recognised as a civil rights issue requiring legal action and policy redress. On the other hand, the use of the term also necessarily invites comparison between victims of disability prejudice

---

59 "Disablism" has been used by such British disability scholars as Oliver, *supra* note 23, but is not widely used in U.S. disability studies.

60 This term is coined by Perlin, who uses it to describe an irrational prejudice against people with mental disabilities, purposefully evoking a kinship to other more recognised "isms" such as racism and sexism, although he also recognises that "sanism" is "frequently practiced (consciously and unconsciously) by individuals who regularly take 'liberal' or 'progressive' positions decrying similar biases and prejudices that involve sex, race, ethnicity, or sexual orientation." *Supra* note 30, at 21–22.

61 "Classism"—both the term and the prejudice it describes—seems to have fallen out of general Western consciousness, and interestingly, "homophobia" seems to have escaped following in the footsteps of previous prejudice monikers. "Ageism" may be a little more commonly encountered than disablism, but it is also not widely used in popular terminology.

and victims of other kinds of prejudice, as well as a search for conceptual correlation in the motives and actions of those who harbor disability prejudice and those who display other prejudices. Ultimately, I believe this process of comparison does a disservice to the unique social dynamics and evolution of disability prejudice, and obscures the operation and purpose of disability anti-discrimination measures. Without discounting the possibility of similarity to other prejudices, I agree with recent theoretical assertions that there are prejudices rather than prejudice, each with its own internal logic, historical subtleties and political issues.

Elisabeth Young-Bruehl, one of the strongest critics of the "unitary prejudice" idea, presents a multi-pronged and deeply theorised approach to prejudices, specifically anti-Semitism, racism, sexism and homophobia. In the remainder of this section, I would like to discuss aspects of her approach that could prove particularly relevant to our understanding of disability prejudice.

1. Prejudices in Act and in Interpretation

In *The Anatomy of Prejudices*,[62] Young-Bruehl begins by describing an incident wherein a number of white varsity wrestlers at her university were overheard discussing the rising number of young Asian-American wrestlers on the team. Their apparent apprehension over this fact was collectively and laughingly dispersed by mutual assurances that the new Asian team members would not "be much of a threat in the competition for girls, because they have such small penises. . . . condom manufacturers could make a killing if they designed a condom just for these small penises."[63] The gist of this locker room conversation was overheard and consequently reported by the campus newspaper, provoking a wide range of reactions from outrage to casual dismissal. Young-Bruehl describes the furor as follows:

> Like most publicized instances of prejudice, this one had two stages: one of word or deed, and one of interpretation. Prejudices manifested in slurs, acts of discrimination, attacks, are

62 Elisabeth Young-Bruehl, *The Anatomy of Prejudices* (Cambridge, MA, Harvard U. Press, 1996).

63 *Id.* at 3.

> followed by prejudices—not necessarily the same ones—manifested in rationalizations, self-serving descriptions, denials, commentaries, often ones designed to discredit the victims' truthfulness or belittle their pain. Prejudices have histories, and the second stage commonly involves a reference to history or an argument about the applicability of history: this episode is like or unlike that one in kind or degree or intention. Theoretical or interpretive prejudices or spins, which can, of course, serve rawer forms of prejudice, come into play. There are wars, and there are culture wars.

This insight has particular significance for disability prejudice, and indeed, any intolerance that has achieved public and legal recognition after the traditional "troika" of racism, sexism, classism. The economic exploitation and abuse of socially lower classes has led to various civil wars and revolutions in many cultures and nations when those classes sought better treatment. After World War II, the horrific revelations of the Holocaust were a brutal picture of ethnic intolerance. In the United States, Blacks were subjected to racial prejudice long after the abolition of slavery, exhibited in forms ranging from social and legal segregation to mob violence. No doubt, there are still rare individuals who actually deny these events, or look back upon them and "interpret" them as rational or at least justifiable actions taken by divinely appointed rulers, a politically oppressed nation, a superior race. For most people, however, these examples serve as unequivocally clear instances of prejudice in action. And they are models not only for the acts of prejudice themselves, but for our intellectual and emotional interpretation of acts of prejudice.

We recognise an act as one motivated by prejudice when it takes lives that we believe are innocent—that is—when victims have been targeted and acted against on the basis of differences that we know are either totally irrelevant or simply created in the imaginations/needs of the majority. We acknowledge prejudice in the actions of others and ourselves when we have sought utter exclusion, extermination or complete control, or perhaps when our reaction to an objectively discernable difference is utterly disproportionate or unreasoning. In any event, we want a deliberate *action* by which we can judge the motivation. Prejudice against people with disabilities has taken the form of "purposeful unequal treatment," but it has also included forms such as "discriminatory effects" from an inaccessible built environment, the "failure to make modifications," and subjection to judgments "based on characteristics that are beyond the control of such individuals and resulting from stereotypic assumptions not truly indicative of the individual ability of such individuals to participate in, and contribute to, society."[64] While the U.S. Congress has recognised these things as discrimination, and they are certainly experienced as such by people with disabilities, they lack the prototypical indicia of prejudice. "Average" able-bodied Americans may follow Davis' argument about the hegemony of normalcy, but they can do so without agreeing that prejudice is involved. They may feel sympathy and even empathy for people with disabilities, but they will not feel *culpable*. The dissemination of experiential minority writings and feminist theory may increase our appreciation for the subtlety of prejudices in their modern forms, but the bulk of that appreciation is still likely to be credited towards groups that have been traditionally subjected to the extremes of discrimination noted above.

2. Feminism, Consciousness Raising and "Victimhood"

The familiarity of academic references to "racism, sexism, classism" may give the impression that the history of prejudice is one that encompasses equal scholarly consideration of each element of the troika. In fact, this has not been the case, especially in the "melting pot" of the United States where racial tensions among peoples of colour have exploded so violently and recurrently since the 1960s. As Young-Bruehl observes: "[a]ntisemitism, the prejudice over which social psychology had its immediate postwar flourishing, has disappeared from '*the* social psychology of prejudice.' . . . [w]hile race prejudice has become Prejudice, sexism, like antisemitism has had its own books. But sexism has its own books without ever having been, historically, included in the

64 42 U.S.C.A. § 12101(a)(5) and (7). *See also* 134 Cong. Rec. S5106, S5108 (daily ed. Apr. 28, 1988) (statement of Sen. Weicker); 136 Cong. Rec. H2599, H2622 (daily ed. May 22, 1990) (statement of Rep. Hoyer); 136 Cong. Rec. H2421, H2440 (daily ed. May 17, 1990) (statement of Rep. Fish, to the effect that disability discrimination often "is not the malicious, violent, ugly discrimination experienced on account of one's race, national origin or religion").

Studies of Prejudice traditions."[65] The evolution of sexism, both as a term and as a socially and legally recognised prejudice, is of particular interest to disability studies because of certain parallels in the situation of women and people with disabilities as oppressed groups.

In reviewing the American feminist literature of the 1970s, Young-Bruehl remarks on "the emphasis on 'consciousness raising'":

> The first thing that the writers, most of them middle-class and educationally privileged, had to do was to convince themselves and other women that they were, indeed, oppressed and oppressed *as women*. They had to legitimate their status as victims, something that no victim of "racism"—the word on which "sexism" was modeled—ever had to do. But they specifically had to alter their consciousnesses, their minds, their thoughts; they had to resist as thinkers. Eventually, the designation "theorist" was appropriated, and "feminist theory" was born. This focus on thinking, on theory, was the answer to the central modality in which the oppression of women was felt by that generation of educated, middle-class, and predominantly urban and white feminists. . . . Victim groups must respond to their oppression first at the site where it most threatens their ability to respond . . . a group attacked for its mindlessness, which means body-onlyness, responds with consciousness raising.
>
> For privileged women to say, clearly and unequivocally, "we are oppressed," or "we are the victims of sexism," required analysis of sexism as a complex and multifaceted form of mind control and body control.
>
> . . . women in households, experiencing domination in the paternalistic mode, "mitigated by mutual obligations and reciprocal rights," did not see themselves as a group and did not perceive themselves as potentially political, as resisters. . . .

---

[65] Young-Bruehl, *supra* note 62, at 110. The sentences here quoted make embedded reference to John Duckitt's *The Social Psychology of Prejudice* (New York, Praeger, 1992), a bibliography of British and American social scientific studies of exclusively race prejudice, and to *Studies in Prejudice*, *supra* note 47.

> Consciousness raising was the necessary step to resistance for women, who had to make themselves into a group and learn solidarity.[66]

From the beginning, the disability rights movement faced the challenge of forging solidarity among widely heterogenous individuals who potentially shared nothing in common except for the fact of experiencing disability.[67] Not only does disability cut across every other minority identity, the difficulty of achieving solidarity was exacerbated by the need to reconcile the vested social and political interests of established groups that had historically organized according to particular disabilities (for example, blindness), as well as groups who did not consider themselves disabled at all (for example, the Deaf). Ultimately, the experience of discrimination is the commonality that unite people with disabilities, but defending themselves against this discrimination is a complex theoretical challenge. If the site where women are most threatened by oppression is the assumption of mindlessness, then the corresponding site for people with disabilities is helplessness. If privileged white women have to raise their own consciousness and that of others concerning their status as victims of prejudice, people with disabilities face a similar task, but with the added complication of simultaneously *refuting* their status as victims of disability, per se.

As a theoretical and practical exercise, this task has proven astonishingly difficult. The general public often responds with profound ambivalence to people with disabilities, seemingly motivated by a complex interaction of admiration and pity.[68] The most logical way to fight stereotypes of needy, childlike and dependent people with disabilities is to provide stories and images of people with disabilities as strong, independent and enjoying life to the full, but this not only contradicts

---

66 *Id.* at 116–17, 119.

67 For a very practical lesson in how solidarity can be achieved, *see* Patrisha Wright & Jane West, "When to Hold 'Em and When to Fold 'Em: Lessons Learned From Enacting The Americans with Disabilities Act," *infra* in this volume at Part IV.

68 1991 Louis Harris and Associates Survey, "Public Attitudes toward People with Disabilities," as cited in Silvers, *supra* note 19, at 50–51.

social expectations,[69] it may be perceived as a contradiction of the disability rights movement's claims concerning the effects of pervasive institutional and social prejudice.

Women are challenged to establish their oppression for being different while proving their capability with difference.[70] This is also a core challenge for people with disabilities, and for many, the way forward has been to challenge social and economic assumptions about what capability really means.[71] Once again though, such approaches are a departure from the traditional social and legal understanding of prejudice as it has been established through racism.[72] An employer who declines to hire an individual because of a disability that makes the

---

69 Furthermore, such positive depictions run into another stereotype peculiar to people with disabilities. In research conducted by Irwin Katz, R. Glenn Hass & Joan Bailey, "Attitudinal Ambivalence and Behavior toward People with Disabilities," *in Attitudes Toward Persons with Disabilities* (Harold Yuker ed., New York, Springer, 1988), paid subjects were asked to fill out surveys that were administered by individual researchers, some of whom used wheelchairs. In some cases, the researcher was efficient, positive and pleasant. In others, the researcher complained, was inefficient and acted unhappy. A second individual arrived after the surveys were done, explained that the first researcher had given incorrect instructions, and asked subjects to donate their time to redo the survey. The research found that subjects were three times as likely to donate their time when the nondisabled surveyor had been positive, but they were just as biased in favor of the depressed disabled surveyer. As a possible explanation for these unexpected results, Katz *et al.* hypothesised that people who encounter fulfilled persons with disabilities "devaluate the unfortunate persons because he or she ought to suffer but does not." *Id.* at 53.

70 For a classic text on this, and on the feminist distinction between gender (socially created) and sex (biological), *see* Simone de Beauvoir, *The Second Sex* (New York, Penguin, 1947, 1972).

71 The ADA's definition of a "qualified individual" [for employment] as someone who can perform the "essential functions" of the job is an example of the attempt to separate employment functions from the accretion of unjustified social expectations: 42 U.S.C.A §§ 12111(8), 12112(a).

72 The development of U.S. constitutional equal protection law, even in the prototypical area of racial discrimination, arguably reflects the impact of social ideas about what prejudice "really" is. The Supreme Court protects racial minorities from "disparate treatment" (intentional discrimination) by subjecting that treatment to a heightened form of judicial scrutiny under the Equal Protection Clause, but "disparate impact" (facially neutral treatment that causes disproportionate harm) does not trigger this higher level of protection: Washington v. Davis, 426 U.S. 229,

desired work environment particularly dangerous to the potential employee[73] simply is not prejudiced *in the same way* as someone who puts on a white hood and goes out to burn crosses on the lawns of Black neighbors. Therefore, we may conclude that the Black homeowners are victims of prejudice, while the individual seeking a job is a victim of his disability or bad luck. In any event, this entire discussion presumes that prejudice is intentional and cognitively controlled—at least enough so that once victims can intellectually or physically prove their capabilities, prejudice will go away or be suppressed. This is an oversimplification.

3. Ideologies of Desire

The "generalized attitude" approach to defining prejudice implies a certain level of cognition. If an individual "takes an attitude," it is because it is consistent with what she or he already knows, thinks, and feels about a subject.[74] This perception of prejudice may be due in part to an understanding that is rooted in the very general notion of ethnocentrism[75] as the rationale for modern prejudice. However, the theory of love of one's own group, of dislike or fear towards other groups, fails to explain how prejudices are manifested to such obviously varying degrees of violence, paternalism and justification, directed toward certain groups and not others at certain points in history, and resistant to social change. Young-Bruehl makes a distinction between ethnocentrism, which she defines more

---

238–48 (1976). The farther we get from such indicia of prejudice as intent, conscious but unreasonable justification and motivations of obvious stereotype, the less courts are willing to extend constitutional anti-discrimination protection.

73 Derived from the facts of an actual case recently decided by the U.S. Supreme Court: *Chevron v. Echazabal*, 122 S. Ct. 2045 (2002). Ct. 456 (Oct. 29, 2001) (No. 00-1406).

74 Perlin, *supra* note 30 expressly refutes this. This point is made another way by Ruth O'Brien, who writes of her own experience conducting research while sustaining a workplace injury (tendinitis): "I discovered that I could not guess how someone would respond to a request for an accommodation. I could never anticipate if someone would help, oftentimes generously offering more assistance than was necessary, or if someone would stand in my way. Self-proclaimed progressive people could react with as little understanding as those identifying with conservative causes, or vice versa." *Supra* note 30, at ix.

75 *See supra* note 55.

narrowly as "a form of prejudice that protects group identity in economic, social, and political terms" and the broader concept of "ideologies of desire":

> Ideologies of desire are, generally, backlashes against movements of equality; they are regressive prejudices that reinstate inequalities and distinctions when the force of movements for equality has been registered and (often unconsciously) rejected. . . . Prejudices institutionalize at deeper and more inchoate individual and social or political levels the differences between "us" and "them" that movements for equality address.
>
> . . . the era of state economies and world wars, of internationalism and what is now known as globalism, which gives all local conflicts larger contexts of interference, has been an era in which "us versus them" has been both enacted and rationalized, converted into ideology, in quite distinctive ways. . . . Progress on legal fronts has changed the contexts of prejudices. But the needs those prejudices serve stay very much the same. Sometimes the needs simply find a new target when their familiar ones become harder to hit because it [sic] is somewhat protected.[76]

Young-Bruehl goes on to develop a theory of three distinct types of modern ideological prejudices, each linked to a broad "character" type.[77] She links anti-Semitism with obsessional prejudice, racism with hysterical prejudice, and sexism with narcissistic prejudice. I raise Young-Bruehl's typology not necessarily to endorse her specific analysis, although I find it quite compelling, but to make the point that all of her prejudices operate both discretely and collectively against people with disabilities, even though distinctions between them are invariably subsumed within the general rubric of prejudice. I take this as evidence of the idiomatic difficulties of untangling disability prejudice, which intersects with such a wide variety of historical ethnocentrisms, modern fears and social expectations. This, in combination with the insidious under-

---

[76] Young-Bruehl, *supra* note 62, at 27, 30–31.

[77] Young-Bruehl's "character" is not a pathological or clinical designation, but simply a means of naming a configuration of certain psychological and sociological characteristics that provide fertile ground for one of the ideologies of desire. *Id.* at 32.

standing of prejudice as both unified and somehow "unchanging," is leaving disability prejudice in a place of exile—not "prejudice" as the law or general public expects it to be, but nonetheless extant and active against people with disabilities in hidden ways that are difficult to fight.

a. Narcissistic Prejudices

Young-Bruehl describes sexists as people:

> who cannot tolerate the idea that there exists people not like them, not—specifically—anatomically like them. Their prejudice has a narcissistic foundation, and it is, of the ideologies of desire, the most universal . . . narcissistic prejudices are prejudices of boundary establishment . . . On the other side of the narcissists' boundaries there is not a "them," a "not-us," but blank, a lack—or at the most, a profound mystery.[78]

The marks of difference in women, especially female sexuality and reproductive capacities, threaten male gender identity, and according to Young-Bruehl, the deepest counter to that anxiety is control over female difference. "Sexism is expressed in many ways, but its essential meaning is control over female sexuality and reproduction, and its essential purpose is to keep men from recognizing women in their difference or from succumbing to their fear of becoming women."

Young-Bruehl applies her analysis very specifically to sexism, but the threat to self-identity and desire for control that is the hallmark of narcissistically based prejudices are easily discernible in prejudices commonly exhibited against people with visible disabilities. Narcissistic prejudices recognise disability as difference and perceive a threat to their very identity as human beings. The way to assuage this fear is to linguistically and socially control access to what will be considered human. If narcissists cannot tolerate the thought of "people not like them," then upon being confronted with people not like them, they will refuse to acknowledge that they are being confronted with people at all.

Throughout history, societies "have believed that people with disabilities were closer to wild animals than humans"; have presented peo-

---

78 *Supra* note 62, at 35.

ple with mental illness "as being wildmen, savages, wildwomen, or animals"; "have thought of and labeled people with physical disabilities or deformities as monsters or monstrosities"; and "have viewed people with developmental disabilities as inhuman, subhuman, or biological throwbacks."[79] Women, even when given a narrowly circumscribed role by narcissists, still had to be recognised as necessary to the continuation of the human race (this remains essentially true despite recent developments in cloning and genetics); this was not true of people with disabilities as individuals or as a group. If "the disabled" were considered inhuman, then they did not even have to be acknowledged as "other," any more than one would consider wildlife an "other."

With the rise of Christianity, people with disabilities were perceived either as unclean and judged by God, in which case they were divinely separate from the rest of humanity who were created "in the image of God," or more "charitable" impulses prevailed and disabilities "were not specifically distinguished from other forms of misery or suffering"[80] that were common in the Middle Ages. Even if the more humane latter view prevailed, however, "the ethical and spiritual integration of difference did not accomplish social integration. The infirm were marginal, cared for by their families or by charitable patrons, without any social function or identity as a distinct group."[81] From a narcissistic point of view, if people with disabilities could no longer be denied their humanity, they could at least be avoided and controlled. Once it was no longer socially acceptable or common to call people with disabilities inhuman, the medical model of disability and its pervasive influence in rehabilitation medicine and social/unemployment welfare controlled the segregated category of "the disabled," in relation to both who was admitted and their treatment upon admittance.

The narcissist's deep need to deny and control the difference of the Other continues to evolve. Davis describes contemporary media portrayals of people with disabilities as follows:

---

[79] Covey, *supra* note 43, at 6–10.

[80] Susan Reynolds White, "Disability Between Discourse and Experience," *in Disability and Culture*, *supra* note 32, 267 at 269 (paraphrasing Henri-Jacques Stiker in *Corps Infirmes et Sociétés* (Paris, Aubier Montaigne, 1982) on the Western construction of disability).

[81] *Id.*

> Whether we are talking about AIDS, low-birth weight babies, special education issues, euthanasia, and the thousand other topics listed in the newspapers every day, the examination, discussion, anatomising of this form of "difference," is nothing less than a desperate attempt of people to consolidate their normality.[82]

Davis interprets this as the need of the nondisabled to single out an Other by which to define themselves. To my mind, Young-Bruehl's ideas present an equally plausible explanation: narcissistic prejudices drive those who have them to restrict the totality of the world to people who are as they are themselves. Those who persist, willingly or otherwise, in being Other are labelled, treated, rehabilitated, confined, and even abused and eliminated—whether outright,[83] through eugenics,[84] or by being offered the "choice" of assisted suicide.[85]

---

82 Lennard J. Davis, "The Rules of Normalcy: Politics and Disability in the USA [United States of Ability]," *in Disability, Divers-Ability and Legal Change*, *supra* note 25, 35 at 46.

83 For the Nazi regime, the murder of some 40,000 children with disabilities in 1940 was a practical confirmation of their logistical methods for mass extermination and the starting point to a pogrom targetting people with disabilities, Jews and Gypsies; the elimination of such peoples was justified by the Nazi belief in human inequality and their determination to "cleanse the gene pool of the German Nation." *See* Henry Friedlander, *The Origins of Nazi Genocide: From Euthanasia to the Final Solution* (Chapel Hill, U. of N. Carolina Press, 1995). *See also* Arthur L. Caplan, *When Medicine Went Mad: Bioethics and the Holocaust* (Totowa, N.J., Humana Press, 1992); Michael Burleigh, *Ethics and Extermination: Reflections on Nazi Genocide* (Cambridge, Cambridge U. Press, 1997).

84 The first U.S. physician to castrate a prison inmate as a check on the individual's masturbation and to control population growth offers this repellantly fascinating mix of pseudo-scientific and nationalistic rationales: "Idiots, imbeciles and degenerate criminals are prolific, and their defects are transmissible. Each person is a unit of the nation, and the nation is strong and pure and sane, or weak and corrupt and insane in the proportion that the mentally and physically healthy exceed the diseased, nor can any nation live if there is a reverse ratio. So we owe if not only to ourselves, but the future of our race and nation, to see that the defective and diseased do not multiply." *Cited in* P.L. Tyor & L.V. Bell, *Caring for the Retarded in America: A History* 102 (Westport, Greenwood Press, 1984)

85 Larry James McAfee is often held out as an example of how social perceptions about the less valuable life of a person with a disability influence public, medical and legal opinions about counselling and sanctioning individuals who express

b. Hysterical Prejudices

In distinction to sexism and the narcissistic prejudices, Young-Bruehl states that:

> Racism, by contrast, exemplifies hysterical prejudice, by which I mean a prejudice that a person uses unconsciously to appoint a group to act out in the world forbidden sexual and sexually aggressive desires that the person has repressed. . . . The victims are, like victims of the most common forms of classism, another hysterical prejudice, "lower."
>
> . . . The "others," either as domestic servants or slaves or as a fantasized part of the prejudiced person's household, are love and hate objects in the loving and hating of whom no bans on incest or on rivalry are violated; they are the safe—for the prejudiced person—objects of childhood passions. Ideally, the victims do not get destroyed completely or flushed away as the obsessional's victims do; they are needed alive, so that they can be loved like mammies, prostituted or raped like whores, sexually mutilated, beaten, deprived of their power, crippled, emasculated—and in all instances, kept in their places.[86]

Again, Young-Bruehl clearly characterises hysterical prejudices in the context of the historical reality of white racism as it has developed against Blacks in the United States. I am struck, however, by the parallels between her description and the prejudices exhibited against people with disabilities—developmental disabilities in particular. Historically, prejudices against Blacks, lower socio-economic classes and people with disabilities coalesced in the 19th century as people with developmental disabilities were "viewed as the product of degenerate families, which formed a major part of the lower economic strata. . . . 'degenerate' families spawned disease, disability, dependency, and social

---

suicidal wishes. McAfee became quadriplegic at the age of 30 and successfully won the legal right to assisted suicide, but he did not end his life after he received technological support and advocacy assistance towards living a productive, independent life. *See* Shapiro, *No Pity*, *supra* note 29, at 258–88 (Ch. 9).

[86] *Supra* note 62, at 34.

misfits . . . People with developmental disabilities were included in these groups of perceived racially inferior and hypersexual people."[87] Since people with developmental disabilities were assumed to have "lower moral intelligence, poor judgement, and subhuman characteristics, they were seen as sexual predators frequently wanting sex."[88] This cluster of stereotypes around people with developmental disabilities follows them and colours the way that they are perceived, treated and spoken about, even by those with whom they have prosaic daily contact, and even when they are clearly in a position of powerlessness.

Jane Hubert, in her paper on the effects of long-term segregation in mental institutions, writes of life in a locked hospital ward in Britain, where 20 adult men diagnosed with severe cognitive or developmental disabilities and "challenging behaviour" had lived most of their lives.[89] She describes how at the beginning of her project, before the field work in the ward had begun, "the female psychiatrist in charge described all the men in the ward as either perpetrators or victims of sexual abuse (or both), and added that the ward "smelled of sex." She then adds that:

> Subsequent experience in the ward did not bear out any of this: it smelled of faeces, and urine and drug-laden breath, but not of sex. What she was really suggesting was something quite different—that these men were sexually uncontrolled, polluted and polluting, a common fantasy about the ward. What this psychiatrist was saying could often be heard in the voices of other professionals, especially those who did not actually work directly with the men. There were clear undercurrents of fear, and prurience, in the way they spoke of them: fear of potentially uncontrollable sexual activity, of violence, ugliness, the unknown, and of the undefined power of people who are perceived as almost totally "other."[90]

---

[87] Covey, *supra* note 43, at 24.

[88] *Id.*

[89] Jane Hubert, "The Social, Individual and Moral Consequences of Physical Exclusion in Long-stay Institutions," *in Madness, Disability and Social Exclusion*, *supra* note 32, 196.

[90] *Id.* at 200–01.

Hubert further illustrates her point by describing her interactions with David, a resident who has lived in institutions for some 30 years since his first admittance as a child. David is "very tall" and at first sight is "both strange and threatening" as he "strides around the ward for most of the day, often roaring loudly." The most striking thing about David, however, is that he never has any clothes on. Even though the ward staff may tolerate degrees of undress from other residents, no one else is allowed to walk around without clothes. David is the exception because he simply tears up clothes when he is put in them. As Hubert notes rather dryly, "[i]n 'normal' society, we do not accept nudity in the everyday social environment." In the ward there are 19 other residents, various visiting health professionals, domestic staff, maintenance men, and so on, and approximately 40 male and female staff members who are trained to closely observe for and protect against sexual abuse towards or among the residents, "yet, sitting with the other residents, walking around among them, is a naked man." David is placed outside of the boundaries of normal adult social rules, but he is simultaneously ignored as an adult male even though he obviously is one. "To all intents and purposes his sexuality is denied. He is de-sexed and de-gendered." Hubert concludes that for David and the other men, "although their sexual dangerousness is often used as a justification for controlling them within a locked environment, at the same time, not only are they denied normal gender roles, but also their sexuality is mocked."[91]

Hubert's observations capture the hysterical prejudices that lie at the heart of modern society's interest in keeping people with developmental disabilities physically and socially isolated, ostensibly maintaining purity in the community while relegating the Other to an imagined sexual degeneracy that yet remains biddable, reportable, accessible. We can imagine institutions where *they* get to walk around without clothes, gesticulating obscenely and saying words that the rest of *us* blush to think. *They* are free to have sex and not consider the consequences or be subject to any moral, emotional or ethical constraints. Even as people with developmental disabilities are institutionalised and constricted medically and socially in ways that often strip away even the possibility of having significant intimate relationships, they function as fantasy figures for

---

[91] *Id.* at 202–03.

society at large—unfettered from constraints imposed on "the rest of us" by social mores and upstanding public morality.

For a final comment on hysterical prejudices in disability prejudice, I refer to Young-Bruehl's statement that "societies in which hysterical individuals are common and sexual repression or puritanism rife are societies split . . . committed to visions of equality and fairness, . . . at the same time, sexually and aggressively explosive."[92] I doubt that many would consider 21st century U.S. culture puritanical or sexually repressed, but I do propose that the hypocritical social "double vision" implicit in Young-Bruehl's statement is fairly found today with regard to people with disabilities in general. When it comes to the sexual identity and activity of people with physical disabilities, Western society *is* extremely limiting and repressed. Especially for women with physical disabilities, "identification with a disability is to be socialised in a way that brings one's competence in sexuality, procreation and nurturing into question."[93] At the same time, people with developmental disabilities are mythologized as promiscuous and prolific. The manner in which these two distinct stereotypes about people with disabilities interact, or rather fail to interact, reveals the impacted and entwined roots of disability and gender prejudices. The operation of all of this against a backdrop of civil rights and a commonly endorsed belief in sexual freedom enables us to see how society is deeply and hysterically prejudiced against people with disabilities.

---

92 *Supra* note 62, at 34–35.

93 Anita Silvers, "Double Consciousness, Triple Difference: Disability, Race, Gender and the Politics of Recognition," *in Disability, Divers-Ability and Legal Change*, *supra* note 25, 75 at 81. Tom Shakespeare points out how the assumption that people with disabilities are asexual contributes towards their disregard, which influences how "disabled people are infantilised, and denied the status of active subjects," leading in turn to the further undermining of their sexuality in modern societies where "sexual agency is considered the essential element of full adult personhood." Tom Shakespeare, "Power and Prejudice: Issues of Gender, Sexuality and Disability," *in Disability and Society*, *supra* note 22, 190 at 192. *See also* Tom Shakespeare, Kath Gillespie-Sells & Dominic Davies, *The Sexual Politics of Disability: Untold Desires* (London, Cassell, 1996).

c. Obsessional Prejudices

"Obsessional prejudices are the prejudices toward which people who are given to fixed ideas and ritualistic acts gravitate and through which they can behave sadistically without being conscious of their victims."[94] Young-Bruehl writes. This is her first category of prejudices, and she cites anti-Semitism, anti-Communism during the McCarthy era, and the more contemporary "Japan-bashing" by U.S. commercial interests as exemplars. She continues:

> The obsessional prejudices feature conspiracies of demonic enemies everywhere, omnipresent pollutants, filthy people, which the obsessionally prejudiced feel compelled to eliminate—wash away, flush away, fumigate, demolish. The obsessionally prejudiced attribute to their victims a special capacity for commercial or economic conspiracy and diabolical behind-the-scenes cleverness, and they both envy this capacity and, acting imitatively, turn the fruits of this cleverness (particularly in the domain of technology) on their victims. They imagine the conspirators as having the capacity to penetrate them, get into their bowels and their privacies.[95]

At first glance, it may seem that people with disabilities are not targets of Young-Bruehl's obsessional prejudices. While people with disabilities have been depicted as demonic and unclean, this is usually connected to narcissistic or hysterical forms of prejudices that respectively seek either elimination or control of the difference that is disability or maintenance of a prurient interest in the perceived sexual waywardness of people with certain disabilities. Since the very category of "the disabled" is a late historical development,[96] it is not surprising that conspiracy theories have not evolved against people with disabilities as a group. Nonetheless, I argue that such conspiracies are evolving right now. People with certain disabilities are facing the emergence of a mod-

---

94 *Supra* note 62, at 33.

95 *Id.* at 33–34.

96 *See supra* note 19.

ern, and possibly milder form of the obsessional prejudices. Ironically, the fact that these prejudices are emerging is attributable in part to the very success that has been enjoyed by people with disabilities in fighting social, political and economic discrimination caused by other kinds of prejudices.

I have already mentioned the existence of a negative media backlash[97] against the ADA, but running through the reports of excessive and nonsensical claims is a particular thread that attacks certain segments of people with disabilities as undeserving of the law's protection. Invariably they refer to the "real" intentions behind the law, and implicitly or explicitly allege that some people with (or without) disabilities are collectively taking advantage of loopholes or uncertainties in the ADA to gain economic and social advantages. In 1997, Joseph Perkins wrote that "President Bush . . . hardly could have imagined that of all the discrimination complaints filed under the law, most have come not from blind or deaf or wheelchair-bound Americans, but from folks claiming back problems (that's right)."[98] Almost two years later, a story appearing in the same paper indicated that "a decade after the landmark civil rights legislation was crafted to integrate disabled workers into the job market, a flood of workplace discrimination complaints has come not from employees who are blind or deaf or using wheelchairs, but from workers claiming psychological stress."[99] The sentiment behind these statements is clear: the ADA is for people who are blind or deaf or use wheelchairs. These are "real" victims and everyone else, regardless of whether they have faced discrimination or not, is merely illicitly taking economic advantage of the law. Identifying himself as a "supporter" of the law, Perkins nonetheless criticises its regulations "[t]hey do not merely provide workplace equality for our fellow citizens with mental disabilities. They give the mentally disabled workplace rights and entitlements that are far above those of not only non-disabled workers, but physically disabled workers as well."[100]

---

97 *See supra* note 14.

98 "ADA Well-intentioned, But Its Implementation Is Increasingly Unreasonable," *supra* note 14.

99 May, "Disability Act Being Redefined," *supra* note 14.

100 *Supra* note 14.

Other U.S. writers go one step farther, and intimate that even people with undisputed physical disabilities take advantage of the law and actually conspire—in league with the government—against American businesses and freedoms. The case of *PGA Tour, Inc. v. Martin*, which pitted a well-known non-profit professional sports association against a professional golfer with a circulatory disorder and a resulting malformed right leg, sparked a series of critical media responses from the first trial court summary decision in Martin's favor until the U.S. Supreme Court's final denial of the PGA's appeal.[101] Among the first of these criticisms was an editorial that commented "[t]o argue that walking the course is a mere detail, an expendable part of the game of professional golf, is absurd. To argue that Casey Martin derives no advantage from being able to ride and conserve energy while other competitors must expend theirs is to be dishonest."[102] Clearly the author takes issue not only with the court's opinion that walking is not essential to the game, he disputes the court's uncontested finding that Martin easily suffered as much or more fatigue, even riding a cart, than able-bodied competitors did walking the course. Such active disbelief, coupled with a general criticism of the "absurd and outrageous judicial overreach" that, for example, "endows [disabled Boston University students] almost with the status of a separate species" reveals a prejudice that has taken on an obsessional character. In the writer's overstated opinion, Martin's case is tragic because his golfing talent is "nullified by a disability," but somehow this same disability is entirely discounted when it comes to considering its impact on the fatigue and physical effort that walking 18-holes is supposed to impart. Treating unlike persons as if they are alike violates even a formal model of justice, but the writer seems to argue that this principle should not apply if the difference "is not my fault." This is the social model of disability at its worst, with the additional implicit assertion that any court or law that interferes with able-bodied society's right to set its own rules exactly and only as it wishes is engaged in some kind of dishonest subversion.

---

[101] 121 S. Ct. 1879 (2001), in which a majority of the court found that the essence of golf was shot-making, so that permitting Martin to use a golf court during the PGA's qualifying tournaments would not so "fundamentally alter the nature" of the tournament as to enable the PGA to deny such a modification.

[102] "A Judge Blows a Chip Shot," *supra* note 14.

This emerging "conspiracy aspect" of disability prejudice is even more apparent in a press release issued by the Libertarian Party after the initial *Martin* decision. According to Steve Dasbach, then-national Chairman of the Libertarian Party:

> The real issue isn't whether Martin should be allowed to use a golf cart . . . The issue isn't even whether Martin has gotten a bum deal from life—or whether it's a personal tragedy that he couldn't compete in a sport he loves. The real issue is: Who decides? Do professional sports associations have the right to set their own rules? Or does the federal government have the final decision-making power over every aspect of our lives—including professional sports. . . . If you think the government will stop with professional golf, you're probably protected by the ADA because of your chronic case of gullibility . . . The ADA is a bureaucratic disease that's getting worse every year—and the only question is which sport or industry will be the next victim.[103]

This recasting of one individual's request for a personal accommodation in pro golf into a government plot to interfere with "every aspect of our lives" exemplifies many aspects of obsessional prejudices. People with disabilities are assigned the role of Others who want to corrupt and disrupt the system, using and/or being used by a "big brother" federal government. Rather than propose outright destruction, which would be socially unacceptable, obsessional prejudices centered on disability propose a kind of social extermination in they forcefully attack those tools of social understanding, cultural education and civil laws that have enabled people with disabilities to achieve a new life of growing economic power and political self-identity. Holders of these prejudices applauded when the Supreme Court handed down its decision in *Toyota Motor Mfg. v. Williams*, further narrowing the field of those who are disabled enough to call on the equal protection promise of the ADA.[104]

---

103 "What's Next in the ADA-Protected World of Professional Sports?," *supra* note 14.

104 122 S. Ct. 681 (2002), in which the unanimous court declared that terms in the ADA related to the definition of disability "need to be interpreted strictly to create a demanding standard for qualifying as disabled . . . to be substantially limited

There are other unique facets to obsessional prejudices as they are beginning to be applied to people with disabilities. The obsessional fear that conspirators have "the capacity to penetrate them, get into their bowels and their privacies" is particularly acute when the category of disability is both extremely heterogenous and very fluid.[105] People with disabilities are not necessarily visibly distinct. Health conditions and symptoms are not necessarily medically static or identically incapacitating. The next-door neighbor could develop a back problem and suddenly turn into a claimant under the ADA, or your own widowed father-in-laws's lethargy and loneliness could be diagnosed as a clinical depression that requires accommodation in the workplace. Not only do we all face the possibility of getting a disability ourselves, a child with a disability can "issue forth" from one's own lions, intractably a part of one's own social group and identity. Amidst this reality, the prejudicial fear of omnipresent disability conspirators seeking and getting "special treatment" must loom especially large.

People with disabilities share this aspect of fluidity with the category of "homosexual" in which it is also "not clear who should be registered in it."[106] Young-Bruehl notes that "homosexuals pervade all 'racial' and most if not all ethnic population groups; the chances that a

---

in performing manual tasks, an individual must have an impairment that prevents or severely restricts the individual from doing activities that are of central importance to most people's daily lives. The impairment's impact must also be permanent or long-term." *Id.* at 690. The decision has been described as "a victory for employers," and one defense attorney in ADA cases stated that "Employers have always been skeptical of disabilities that arise or become apparent when someone clocks in and end when they clock out. Implicit in the Supreme Court's decision is their own skepticism on that point." *See* "Supreme Court Limits Disability Law" (Associated Press), Jan. 9, 2002 *at* http://my.aol.com/news/news_story.psp? type=1%cat=0100&id=0201082100551261.

[105] Numerous articles have discussed these and other difficult aspects inherent in the need to define "disability" for legal, social and/or administrative purposes. *See* for example Jerome E. Bickenbach, "Minority Rights or Universal Participation: The Politics of Disablement," *in Disability, Divers-Ability, and Legal Change*, *supra* note 25, 10; Aart Hendriks, *Different Definitions—Same Problem—One Way Out?*, *infra* in this volume at Part II; Stone, *supra* note 19.

[106] *Supra* note 62, at 141.

homophobe will be hating someone who is kin are very great." Further:

> the homosexual is a kind of fiction, because homosexual behavior occurs along a continuum, ranging from entertaining homoerotic fantasies to having a single experience or period of experience to exclusive preference. And at least some people can move back and forth on the continuum during their lifetime—from a homosexual preference in adolescence, for example, to heterosexuality in adulthood, or vice versa. Such complexities have led many people to say, simply, a homosexual is a person who identifies himself or herself as a homosexual.[107]

Until recently, homosexual self-identification has not led courts or the public to try and strictly control entrance to the category, though this issue may have been subsumed in the continuing battle among gay activists, religious communities, scientists, and social scientists over the origins of homosexuality.[108] People with disabilities have never been

---

[107] *Supra* note 62, at 142.

[108] One advantage that gay people presently enjoy in the continuing battle over definitional control is the fact that gay activists have succeeded for the most part in taking homosexuality out of the realm of psychiatric pathology. Gay "leadership realized that until the stigma of being diseased was removed, homosexuals would never be able 'to live in dignity' or to combat the older but still powerful form of prejudice against homosexuals prevalent in Jewish and Christian milieus." Young-Bruehl, *supra* note 62, at 141. People with disabilities have less room to maneuver in this regard since many physical, cognitive and developmental impairments require an ongoing relationship with the medical community to enable individuals to manage their lives; the medical/pathological aspects of disability cannot be completely severed. On the other hand, gay people are beginning to face the kind of categorical controls that people with disabilities have always had to deal with. As homosexuality is beginning to be associated with some social benefits, and perhaps losing some of its historical social stigma, homosexual self-identification is increasingly being questioned. In Fort Bragg, Captain David Donovan's four requests for discharge, made between 2000 and 2002, on the grounds of his self-disclosed bisexuality have been refused because "[t]here is insufficient evidence that any homosexual conduct has occurred. . . . The resignation does not disclose a homosexual act or marriage and does not contain a statement of homosexual conduct." Donovan's treatment is at odds with the Army's general "don't ask, don't tell" policy in which verbal admission of homosexuality may be grounds for discharge. The case is particularly odd since Donovan has served 17 years of active duty, is will-

given the privilege of self-identification. Stone attributes this to the fact that disability, "even in its early incarnations as more specific conditions, was seen to exist in both genuine and artificial forms. People could either be truly injured or feign injury. In the modern understanding of disability, deception has become part and parcel of the concept itself."[109] For Stone, "disability entails (or may entail) at least as much political privilege as it does social stigma. [That is, exemption from a work-based distributive system, military service, criminal liability, and so on] . . . the intense political interest in disability benefit programs in recent years can only be understood if we see that the fight is about privilege rather than handicap or stigma."[110] This is an excellent point, but it is not one which can or should account for the social tendency to concentrate on the political privilege aspect of disability to the *utter exclusion* of the stigma aspect of disability. There may well be people who fraudulently claim a disability to gain political or economic privileges, but this fact fails to fully explain the common perception that people will freely and eagerly choose to categorise themselves as disabled. I submit that obsessional prejudices play a part in this myth, strengthening a belief in the conspiratorial ability of target groups to "work the system" to their own advantage, and impeding the understanding or belief that there is such a thing as a social stigma attached to disability. Absent the measurable physical impact of a "real" medical condition, and at times even with such evidence, the obsessional character believes everyone claiming a disability to be tarred with the same scheming brush.

In this potent mix of stereotype, competitive fear and political paranoia, Gavin Langmuir's insight into what he saw as the dual nature of anti-Semitism is pointedly applicable:

---

ing to accept the standard "Other Than Honorable" discharge, and volunteers to recompense the government whatever it feels it is owed. *See* "Army Refuses Sex-Related Resignation" (Associated Press), *The Charlotte Observer*, posted Feb. 11, 2002 *at* http:// www.charlotte.com/mld/observer/2002/02/11/news/local2646775.htm; *see* also Hensala v. Dept. of the Air Force, 148 F. Supp. 2d 988 (N.D. Cal 2001) (Air Force entitled to seek financial recoupment for officer's medical training after latter's voluntary separation from Air Force on declaration of homosexuality).

[109] *Supra* note 19, at 28.

[110] *Id.*

> On the one hand, there are situation in which Jews, like any other major group, are confronted with realistic hostility, or with that well-nigh universal xenophobic hostility which uses the real conduct of some members of an outgroup to symbolize a social menace. On the other hand, there may still be situations in which Jewish existence is much more seriously endangered because real Jews have been irrationally converted in the minds of many into a symbol, "the Jews," a symbol whose meaning does not depend on the empirical characteristics of Jews yet justifies their total elimination from the earth.[111]

Langmuir identified the second type of prejudice described above as "antisemitism of 'chimerical character,' which paved the way to Auschwitz."[112] My impression is that as obsessional prejudices develop against people with disabilities, they will not necessarily be so cleanly reality-based or chimerical. One person may be prejudiced against people with back injuries because she had an acquaintance that purposefully and falsely exaggerated the extent of her disability to collect unemployment insurance. Others may be convinced without any evidence[113] that "the disabled" cost U.S. businesses millions of dollars, weaken the economy, control the federal government and courts, and take away the jobs of better-qualified Americans like themselves. "The disabled" become the symbol of the lazy, duplicitous, undeserving "Other" who threatens our most cherished rights and institutions from a privileged insider's position. Symbolic prejudice against people with disabilities may never reach the levels needed to initiate an explicit plan

---

[111] Gavin Langmuir, *Toward a Definition of Antisemitism* (Berkeley, U. of California Press, 1990), as quoted *in* Young-Bruehl, *supra* note 62, at 79.

[112] Young-Bruehl, *supra* note 62, at 77.

[113] Media articles that cite the most factually extreme ADA claims generally fail to mention that the claims are dismissed or never make it past a summary judgment level, nor do they mention actual ADA statistical information, such as the fact that at the trial level, defendants prevail in over 93 percent of reported ADA employment discrimination cases. Where defendants appeal, they succeed in 84 percent of the reported cases, and both pre-trial and pre-appellate settlement success rates are also extraordinarily low for ADA plaintiffs. *See* "The Americans with Disabilities Act: A Windfall for Defendants," *supra* note 14, at 99–100.

for their physical elimination, but the mere fact that such a prejudice is coalescing bears watching.

4. Disability Prejudices

For many, the malleability and self-identification of homosexuality as described above by Young-Bruehl, along with her attendant observation that "all the types of prejudice can appear in homophobic forms,"[114] may seem totally inapposite to the context of disability. If disability consists of a medical fact, a chronic, pathological and measurable deviance from the norm, then flexibility in categorization seems like mere wishful thinking on the part of disability advocates. If people are prejudiced against "the disabled" it is because they either attach unjustified consequences to the fact of, or unreasonably refuse to make the smallest accommodation for, the fact of the disability. As disability studies have established, however, disability is not confined to medical facts, and certainty is not inherent in the way that human beings adopt to the environment and live out their lives, or are socially and institutionally inhibited from doing so. Categorical certainty is artificially imposed for socially created reasons, such as the administrative imperative of benefits distribution. As Jerome Bickenbach puts it, the definitional boundaries drawn around "the disabled" are not "facts of the world—like gravity—but negotiable political and economic stances which, in a democratic setting, should always be open to challenge, debate and revision."[115]

In this contested arena of disability definition, Robert Burgdorf advances a vision of the ADA that has nothing to do with categorical certainty. As the drafter of the original bill that eventually became the ADA, Burgdorf describes a misconception that there are:

> two distinct groups in society—those with disabilities and those without—and that it's possible to have a list of all those who have disabilities . . . That's simply not reality . . . People vary across a whole spectrum of infinitely small gradations of abil-

---

[114] Young-Bruehl, *supra* note 62, at 137.

[115] *Supra* note 105, at 112.

> ity with regard to any given function. . . . The importance of any functional skill varies immensely according to the situation . . . The focus of the Act was—and should be—on eliminating employers' practices that make people unnecessarily different.
>
> What makes anyone "eligible" for protection under the ADA is the same thing makes any of us "eligible" for protection under the laws against age discrimination or under discrimination: We're "eligible" to use the law once we run into discrimination. . . . Where the courts have gone wrong is to try and first establish some "group" for whom the ADA offers protection. That's simply not how civil rights laws work in this country.[116]

In contradistinction to civil rights, most prejudices *do* work by identifying and establishing a target group. People with disabilities, especially in the United States, have worked hard to define and solidify their own collective social identity, and the effort has resulted in unprecedented gains in political and legal strength. At the same time, cultural awareness of people with disabilities *as* a group means that they are more easily targetted by modern narcissistic and hysterical prejudices. By refusing to allow nondisabled society to medically define disability or "norm-ally" define humanity, by resisting confinement in homes and institutions, and by fighting for equal opportunities in all facets of life, people with disabilities increasingly threaten the narcissist need to control difference and the hysterical need for "lower" love and hate objects. At the same time, the inherently dynamic and heterogenous nature of the disability community, with its tremendous variety of physical, social and racial characteristics, aggravates obsessional prejudices, which imagine people with disabilities everywhere gaining power in all ways. While Burgdorf's interpretation of the ADA makes perfect theoretical sense with regard to social justice and civil rights, they exacerbate the obsessive fear that there is no way for the nondisabled to fully guard against, control or exclude people with disabilities.

---

116 "The Disabilities Act Covers All of Us," interview with Robert L. Burgdorf, Jr., Jan. 14, 2002, *at* http://www.raggededgemagazine.com/extra/edgextraburgdorf.htm.

I have not delved into Young-Bruehl's framework for identifying ideologies of desire simply to enable academics to exhaustively catalogue disability prejudices. Neither am I trying to present a picture of unmitigated hopelessness where first, last and always, people with disabilities will face prejudice. First, cataloging disability prejudices is impossible given the gradations, combinations and dynamic nature of real life prejudice against people with disabilities. Prejudices develop as they are communicated, exhibited and repressed in various social and institutional settings, and these further dimensions of prejudice need to be investigated in their own right. Second, identifying and trying to understand the pervasive and subtle operation of various prejudices against people with disabilities is not to admit defeat in the face of prejudice. In fact, the more the social sciences and disability studies can combine their understanding of disability as an historically specific target of distinguishable prejudices, the greater the possibility of crafting effective long-term social strategies for containing these prejudices. My goal is simply to raise questions about how to best fight disability prejudices that do not have the same internal logic, meet different psychological needs, favor distinct means of institutional expression and propagation, and do not even apply equally to all people with disabilities. If different disability prejudices are distinctly motivated and expressed (that is, in laws, medical policies, popular culture and so on), there are practical and important implications for people with disabilities, collectively and as individuals, as well as for those who study disability and prejudice, and for our lawmakers and courts.

D. SOME CONSEQUENCES AND IMPLICATIONS OF DISABILITY PREJUDICES

At one point in her discussion of ideologies of desire, Young-Bruehl gives her opinion that:

> The needs manifested in the various types of ideological prejudices are, as the end of the twentieth century approaches, being challenged not so much by antiprejudice efforts and campaigns for tolerance and human rights as by peoples once victims and now more powerful, each in a different mode—by gaining inter-

> national standing, by gaining numerical strength, by appearing in public, and so forth.[117]

Young-Bruehl seems to imply that institutional actions of anti-prejudice, such as the enactment of laws and educational campaigns, lie at one end of a response spectrum while individual and collective actions of self-empowerment by victims of prejudice lie at the other. For people with disabilities, historically unrecognised as victims of prejudice, such a view of anti-prejudice action underestimates the vital connection between human rights campaigns and victims standing up for themselves in response to discrimination.

Since World War II, the existence of human rights has been recognised in international law, and to varying degrees, in most domestic legal systems. Putting aside the question of how effectively these laws are enforced, the very fact of their enactment has changed the political and social landscape of the world.[118] Working from basic Allportian con-

---

[117] *Supra* note 62, at 31.

[118] This precise point has been emphasised by post-modern philosophers who argue that it has rendered the foundational question of "what is human nature" outmoded and irrelevant. Richard Rorty borrows the term "human rights culture" from Eduardo Rabossi, an Argentinian jurist and philosopher. "Rabossi argues that philosophers should think of this culture as a new, welcome fact of the post-Holocaust world. . . . On Rabossi's view, philosophers . . . are wrong to argue that human rights cannot depend upon historical facts. 'My basic point,' Rabossi says, is that 'the world has changed, that the human rights phenomenon renders human rights foundationalism outmoded and irrelevant.'" Rorty then expands on this to argue that not only is it irrelevant whether human beings really *have* the rights enumerated in human rights instruments, but that "nothing relevant to moral choice separates human beings from animals except historically contingent facts of the world, cultural facts." *See* "Human Rights, Rationality, and Sentimentality," *in Hatred, Bigotry, and Prejudice*, *supra* note 44, 263 at 265–66, *citing* Eduardo Rabossi, "La teoria de los derechos humanos naturalizada," 5 *Revista del Centro de Estudios Constitucionales* (Madrid) 159 (1990). It seems to me that such a viewpoint only grants human rights to groups who have *already* been culturally recognised as victims of prejudice and discrimination. Further, Rorty's ultimate recommendation to repeat "long, sad, sentimental stories" to induce tolerance and even cherishing of powerless people "whose appearance or habits or beliefs at first seemed an insult to our own moral identity, our sense of the limits of permissible human variation," would only be effective advice where the prejudice in question

cepts of prejudice and discrimination, and recognizing how human rights are historically denied to others on the basis of certain recurring grounds, most of these national and international instruments make a ringing declaration along the lines that "human rights shall not be denied on the basis of," followed by a specific enumerated list that typically includes the grounds of race, ethnicity, national origin, and gender.

There was no doubt after the attempted genocide of World War II and the realities of racial segregation and violence all over the world that racial and ethnic minorities belonged to this new "human rights club," and women gained entrance with both increased political self-consciousness and overwhelming evidence that half of the world's population endured physical abuse, political oppression, and diminished economic and social opportunities with no common link other than their gender. Disability, on the other hand, was not initially admitted into the club; the diminished opportunities and isolation of people with disabilities was seen as an inevitable consequence of their individual conditions and an issue for charity, not a matter of human rights being denied. Until relatively recently, disability has never been specifically included as a prohibited ground for the denial of human rights.[119] Even now, the United Nations tends to frame disability matters as an agenda item of economic and social concern rather than a matter of "pure" human rights, which remains dominated by civil and political issues. Within this historical context, the achievement of unequivocal inclusion in international human rights instruments and law, and civil rights traditions wherever these exist, is an integral aspect of people with disabilities empowering themselves and believing that they are fully accepted and protected as human beings.

Obviously the importance of achieving "rights parity" is not unique to people with disabilities. Patricia Williams describes the feelings of Black Americans upon the enactment of racial anti-discrimination laws:

---

is obsessional, or perhaps narcissistic. Where the problem is an hysterical prejudice that needs to keep the Other in a lower place—perhaps through the very stereotypes being repeated (that is, the disabled person's need for charity and pity)—I fail to see how sentimental repetition will help. *Id.* at 277.

[119] *See supra* notes 5 and 7, *also* "Preface" and "Introduction" to this volume.

> "Rights" feel new in the mouths of most black people. It is still deliciously empowering to say. It is the magic wand of visibility and invisibility, of inclusion and exclusion, of power and no power. The concept of rights, both positive and negative, is the marker of our citizenship, our relation to others.[120]

Nonetheless, the achievement of international human rights recognition and civil rights laws has been especially rewarding for people with disabilities after modern society's long resistance to the idea that there was even such a thing as disability prejudice.

On a related point, people with disabilities have come to political and social self-consciousness at a certain point along the historical development of disability prejudices. Wherever the disability rights movement has made a mark, the medically oriented, charitable view of disability as an exclusive concern for rehabilitation and welfare has been there first, and tempered the most violent and intentional aspects of disability prejudice. That is, even where intentional physical and mental abuse, social segregation and euthanasia are still visited upon people with disabilities, these things co-exist and have generally been subsumed within another view "born out of the Christian tradition which emphasized charity towards the disadvantaged. Societies have gone to great lengths to pity and feel sorry for people with disabilities."[121] Of course, traditional charitable institutions carry their own oppressive ethos, "in which the helpers invariably occupy positions of power and authority within agencies, and the helped stand in circumstances subordinate to these."[122] But they do not look or sound like the Nazi regime or the Ku Klux Klan or invading armed forces, and the discrimination that traditional charities practice bears little overt resemblance to the discriminatory acts engaged in by members of the former groups, even though

---

[120] As cited *in* Melinda Jones & Lee Ann Basser Marks, "Law and the Social Construction of Disability," *in Disability, Divers-Ability and Legal Change*, *supra* note 25, 3 at 23.

[121] Covey, *supra* note 43, 11.

[122] Robert F. Drake, "A Critique of the Role of the Traditional Charities," *in Disability and Society*, *supra* note 22, 147 at 152.

the underlying prejudice typology (that is, obsessional, hysterical or narcissistic) may be the same.

My claim is that much of modern society, even though it has enacted laws that reflect the reality of disability prejudice, continues to demonstrate that it lacks an *interpretive* history for accepting and understanding disability as a target of prejudice. Throughout this and the prior section, I have discussed unique aspects of disability's history and social development that make recognizing disability prejudice so difficult. In such circumstances, the most natural tendency is to build on the strengths and insights of movements that have already gained recognition as victims of prejudice (that is, ethnic and racial minorities, women, gay people), and draw analogies to the barriers and prejudice that they face. The strength of these analogies is rooted in the common subjective experience of those who have been targets of discriminatory practice, but invariably this approach fails to fully investigate or account for the ways in which the prejudice behind any particular discriminatory act may be like or unlike any other. Similarly, the analogy approach runs into difficulty when dissimilarities between people with disabilities and other minority groups emerge. Bickenbach refers to these problems after he criticizes the ADA and the U.S. disability rights movement's minority group analysis for distracting from what he sees as the true problem of distributional injustice:

> None of this is to deny that the root cause of the distributional injustice are either attitudes that people have or economic forces that operate to sustain capitalist structures, and that either or both of these phenomena perversely justify the denial of opportunities to disabled persons. Nor is it to deny that the impact of these attitudes or economic forces is concentrated upon those who have, or are viewed as having, impairments or disabilities. But this does not entail that the process is that of discrimination, and the victims form a discrete and insular minority defined in part by their experiences of a common discriminatory response.[123]

---

[123] *Supra* note 105, at 110. Even Bickenbach, however, acknowledges that "[a]s a political strategy, the minority group analysis and civil rights approach are a

Of course, it should be remembered that prior to this time, people with disabilities had little or no legal recourse at all in the face of discrimination. Still, it is true that the foundational assumption behind the use of terms such as "disablism" and "sanism,"[124] and the collective identity building that is so important in a civil rights approach, leave little room for a nuanced understanding of disability prejudices as either manifold or divergent from other legally recognised prejudices. In their defense, disability advocates are usually too busy on the front lines, fighting to preserve legal and social gains that have finally given people with disabilities social options and economic opportunities, to construct detailed social theories. This preference for action and a theory that will lead to and support social change is also expressed by disability scholars:

> The social constructionist view sees the problem as being located within the minds of able-bodied people, whether individually (prejudice) or collectively, through the manifestation of hostile social attitudes and the enactment of social policies based upon a tragic view of disability. The social creationist view, however, sees the problem as located within the institutionalised practices of society.
>
> The important advance that the social creationist approach makes over the social constructionist one, therefore, is that it does not assume that the institutionalised practices of society are nothing more nor less than the sum total of individual and collective views of the people who comprise that society. To make the point again; ideas are not free-floating, they are themselves material forces. The point, however, is not to choose between these two views but to find a way of integrating them . . .[125]

---

proven success. They formed the basic political platform upon which disability rights movements around the world have been based. These movements can be credited with nearly every change in attitude and treatment of people with disabilities in the last two decades—from kerb cuts and accessible bathrooms, to programs to integrate developmentally disabled children into the public schools to protections of the rights of people in mental institutions." *Id.* at 105.

124 *See* notes 59–60 and accompanying text.

125 Oliver, *supra* note 23, at 83.

In countries with a common law tradition,[126] precedent and analogy are central to the interpretation of law. As soon as people with disabilities gained legal rights modelled on those of existing civil rights laws, disability discrimination had to fit within existing legal standards for statutory or constitutional discrimination.[127] The fact is, however, the applicability of precedent and analogy is decided by people, along with the contents—both conscious and unconscious—of their minds. I suggest that the fact that concepts such as prejudice, discrimination and equal treatment have been legally established on the basis of discrimination as it has been experienced historically by other minority groups means that there is another interpretive layer applied to people with disabilities before they even reach the substantive requirements of the law. On the one level, people with disabilities have to prove what is being done to them—discrimination in accordance with legal precedent. On another level, they must show that they are victims of prejudice *just like* other victims. That is, they are implicitly held to account for establishing that they *are* something—a blameless and targetted member of a discrete and insular minority, and that the actions complained of were *not* something—reasonably justifiable in any way. Such a reading would explain the following statement from the majority decision of the U.S. Supreme Court in a critical decision on the applicability to state governments of the ADA's Title I (employment) damage provisions:

> States are not required by the Fourteenth Amendment to make special accommodations for the disabled, so long as their actions towards such individuals are rational. They could quite hard headedly—and perhaps hardheartedly—hold to job qualification requirements which do not make allowance for the disabled. If special accommodations for the disabled are to be

[126] Essentially, most of the non-French speaking Western world.

[127] For instance, the standard of intent required for a violation of the U.S. Constitution's Equal Protection Clause is "'Discriminatory purpose' . . . [which] implies more than intent as volition or intent as awareness of consequences. It implies that the decisionmaker . . . selected or reaffirmed a particular course of action at least in part 'because of,' not merely 'in spite of,' its adverse effects upon an identifiable group." Personnel Administrator v. Feeney, 442 U.S. 256, 279 (1979).

required, they have to come from positive law and not through the Equal Protection Clause.[128]

This is a journey of some distance: from the theoretical conception that prejudice is a single phenomenon, through the accretion of a narrow public understanding of prejudice as intentional,[129] to the socially institutionalised and increasingly legally entrenched view that anti-discrimination law will only guard against prejudice that looks and acts a certain way. Ruth O'Brien traces some aspects of this journey as it has played out in the context of the ADA's employment provisions:

> On one hand, the legislation provides people with strong statutory rights. It ascribes much of the joblessness of people with disabilities to employment discrimination, not their inability to work. On the other hand, the legislation gave the federal courts the discretion to interpret these rights, knowing that the courts might make it difficult for people with disabilities to obtain them. And indeed, this is what has happened. The lower federal courts have followed the Supreme Court's notion that society's

---

[128] Board of Trustees of Univ. of Alabama v. Garrett, 121 S. Ct. 955, 959 (2000). This passage's clear implication that even purposeful or willfully neglectful discrimination against people with disabilities could be shielded under the auspice of "rational" actions seems to be rejected by the separate concurring opinion of Justices Kennedy and O'Conner, which stated that "[t]here can be little doubt, then that persons with mental or physical impairments are confronted with prejudice which can stem from indifference or insecurity as well as from malicious ill will. . . . citizens have an incentive, flowing from a legal duty, to develop a better understanding, a more decent perspective, for accepting persons with impairments or disabilities into the larger society." *Id.* at 968.

[129] This is an opinion that can often be seen in the media. One early editorial states "It is not hard to imagine that a good many businesses . . . with no *discriminatory intent* against the disabled, could be found in violation of various sections of the ADA" and "When the ADA was passed, it was meant to ensure that disabled Americans were given equal treatment under the law, not preferential treatment. In protecting the rights of the disabled, the rights of *innocent* employers and businesses should not be ignored." (Emphasis added) "Disabilities Act Unreasonable Law," *supra* note 14. This approach to the ADA also exhibits signs of obsessional prejudices.

> prejudicial attitudes about people with disabilities should not be highlighted. The Court's perception has been that these attitudes do not stop disabled people from securing employment. Rather, it is their actual physical or mental impairments that limit job performance and, therefore, their ability to find and maintain work.
>
> . . . Interpreting the employment provisions for the first time, the Supreme Court decided against disabled people, not because they could not perform a job, or their requests were unreasonable, or even that they caused an employer endue hardship. Instead, the Court held that they should not be protected under the ADA.[130]

Reflecting on how the federal courts have used the term "mitigation"[131] in the ADA to effectively assess the very identity of a person with a disability, O'Brien concludes that "[t]he federal courts have essentially stripped down the meaning of employment relations provisions to one based not upon rights but upon vulnerabilities and needs. People with disabilities must demonstrate that they have done all that can be done to mitigate their condition. If they cannot compensate . . . then and only then will the federal court rule that they have a disability and allow them to proceed to trial."[132] Such an interpretation of the ADA can only be explained by the courts' lingering perception that an accommodation under the ADA is equivalent to giving a plaintiff an unfair advantage unless the plaintiff can show that he is more needy than his co-workers—an interpretation that completely undermines the law's rights orientation.

---

130 *Supra* note 30, at 168.

131 The term relates to the ADA's definition of a disability, which requires an impairment that substantially limits one or more major life activities. A majority of the U.S. Supreme Court, in a trio of cases issued in 1999, found that any plaintiff with an impairment whose effect was sufficiently mitigated, either by artificial aids or his or her own compensatory abilities, fell out of the definitional requirement of the law. *See* Sutton v. United Air Lines, 527 U.S. 417 (1999); Murphy v. United Parcel Service, Inc., 527 U.S. 516 (1999); Albertsons Inc. v. Kirkingburg, 527 U.S. 555 (1999).

132 *Supra* note 30, at 217.

The federal courts' apparent inability to perceive the presence or effect of disability prejudices, and their resistance to recognising the ADA's full rights orientation, could be interpreted as signs of hysterical and obsessional prejudices in themselves, taking place within the very legal and social institutions that are appointed to protect the equal rights of people with disabilities. The fear that people with disabilities are receiving undeserved benefits under the ADA on the backs of innocent businesses, and the determination to cast protection under the ADA into a charitable mold,[133] bespeak a need to keep people with disabilities "in their place," and even deny them their legal existence under the ADA. This is not to assert that any or all of the members of the Supreme Court are personally "prejudiced" in the manner that we usually associate with that term, but merely to point out that the failure to deeply examine ourselves and the assumptions that influence our ability to perceive the presence of "prejudice" and "disability" will have an effect on every aspect of society, even those that are supposed to be enforcing disability rights. If, as Jones and Basser Marks claim, the success and value of law "depends on its ability to discipline behaviour via an ideology of normalisation," then the Supreme Court's failure to "normalise" disability in a way that fully recognises the oppressive presence of prejudices in the lives of people with disabilities is highly discouraging.[134]

If courts, the media, and other social and cultural institutions will not or cannot recognize disability prejudices for what they are because of the fundamental error that prejudice is monolithic and must look and operate a certain way, then what can we do about it? One thing legal scholars can do is direct their attention to those interstices of anti-discrimination law through which inconsistencies or social presuppositions in judicial reasoning can be glimpsed. Two recently published papers do precisely this. Christine Jolls examines the relationship between anti-discrimination and accommodation. Given the Supreme Court's ten-

---

[133] True charitable concepts at least operate across the board—that is, they would require assistance or employment to be given to all who need it. Even if interpreted as benefits legislation, the ADA would only provide a "truncated" charity since employers would still only be required to hire needy individuals who could actually perform the "essential functions" of the job.

[134] *Supra* note 25, at 4.

dency to view accommodation as an "irrational" and disproportionate requirement of the ADA while disparate impact is (still) within the purview of Congress's power under Section 5 of the 14th Amendment, Joll's finding that the two things are factually and operationally similar raises questions about the existence of deeper, non-economic reasons behind the courts' attempt to draw a sharp distinction between the two concepts.[135] Michelle Travis investigates how courts have tried to determine liability in employment discrimination when faced with a wide range of employer conduct. She alleges that "[j]udges either decide that an employer's conduct is 'close enough' to a prototypic form of discrimination to be treated similarly, thereby triggering full liability, or they decide that the employer's conduct is 'too far away' from prototypic discrimination claims to be covered by the statute, thereby resulting in no liability at all."[136] Travis proposes a "limited remedies" approach that would take account of, and impose sanctions for, intermediate states of employer discrimination. These topics and others concerned with employer cognition,[137] carry the potential for opening up a dialogue into the nature of discrimination, the prejudices that motivate it, the role of law, and the almost instinctive, socially shaped assumptions that every judge brings to the bench when considering anti-discrimination laws.

---

[135] Christine Jolls, "Antidiscrimination and Accommodation," 115 *Harv. L. Rev.* 642 (2001).

[136] Michelle A. Travis, "Perceived Disabilities, Social Cognition, and 'Innocent Mistakes'" 55 *Vand. L. Rev.* 481, 482–3 (2002).

[137] *See* for example: David Benjamin Oppenheimer, "Negligent Discrimination," 141 *U. Pa. L. Rev.* 899 (1993) (noting studies that show "that most discrimination . . . is the result of unintended and unconscious stereotyping"); Linda Hamilton Kreiger, "The Content of Our Categories: A Cognitive Bias Approach to Discrimination and Equal Employment Opportunity," 47 *Stan. L. Rev.* 1161 (1995) (arguing that "a broad class of discriminatory employment decisions result not from discriminatory motivation, but from normal cognitive processes and strategies that tend to bias intergroup perception and judgement"); Judith Olans Brown *et al.*, "Some Thoughts About Social Perception and Employment Discrimination Law: A Modest Proposal for Reopening the Judicial Dialogue," 46 *Emory L.J.* 1487 (1997) (noting a large body of scholarship "showing the inevitability of bias; racism occurs through unconscious cognitive processes"). As might be expect, most studies in this area focus on the more established discrimination categories rather than directly on disability discrimination.

Prejudice and disability scholars also need to work together in this area. When Young-Bruehl published her study of prejudice in 1996, she lamented the fact that both sexism and homophobia had yet to gain recognition as prejudices in official social scientific texts. Instead, each area had developed its own independent base of theoretical and experiential literature, while social scientific studies of prejudice confined themselves to either studying prejudice broadly as ethnocentrism or examining racism as the prototypical prejudice.[138] In the six years since, the situation has not radically altered. Recently published college texts with titles like *Dealing With Differences: An Introduction to the Social Psychology of Prejudice*[139] essentially equate prejudice with ethnocentrism, perhaps paying some lip service along the way to the role of feminism and homophobia in intergroup conflict. Cross-disciplinary anthologies with titles like *Hatred, Bigotry, and Prejudice*[140] and *Communicating Prejudice*[141] now habitually include contributing articles that focus on sexism and homophobia, but disability and disablism often are not even found in the index, much less included as an actual paper topic. Young-Bruehl's *The Anatomy of Prejudice* contains only the briefest, passing mention of disability as a target of prejudice. If the social sciences will not bring its investigative tools to bear on the multiplicity and complexity of all modern prejudices, institutions such as the media and courts are even less likely to question their own outdated or incomplete understandings of disability and prejudice in general. For its part, disability studies can add a more deeply theorised understanding of prejudice's roots and contexts to its already rich experientially based consideration of disability prejudice. In a modern society constantly confronted with the most extreme results of violent intolerance and prejudice, a principled and clear exposition of how disability prejudice can be both like and unlike other prejudices operating in the world may ulti-

---

[138] *Supra* note 62, at 114–15.

[139] Sampson, *supra* note 18.

[140] Baird & Rosenbaum, *supra* note 44.

[141] Hecht, *supra* note 56. As editor, Hecht does express regret over the "isms" that are not considered in the collection, but aside from offering his regret, offers no explanation for the omissions.

mately have as much value for the disability movement as the consciousness-raising revelations of the original social model of disability.

For those who would rather be active in the trenches, the reality of different disability prejudices gives disability advocates the challenge and opportunity of building even more effective cross-disability coalitions and cross-minority affiliations. This picture of prejudice also helps us to understand why having the experience of being victimised by prejudice immunises us from neither holding prejudices ourselves, especially those that are based on a different need and logic than the ones with which we are most familiar, nor holding different prejudices to varying degrees. While the resistance and complex adaptability of Young-Bruehl's ideologies of desire are certainly intimidating, they serve as a very potent reminder that even the strongest laws still require a constant campaign of social and cultural education to be effective. As Jones and Basser Marks emphasise, "even if there existed a perfect regime of human rights, a system of formal law promoting and empowering people with disabilities, this is only going to be a small part of what is necessary to bring about true equality for people with disabilities."[142] Fighting disability prejudices is a dynamic process. Social and cultural attitudes are never static, prejudices shape and are shaped by history and social conditions, and even the laws change. If individual attitudes and social perceptions are flexible enough to be changed by the habits engendered by law, a belief inherent in the social rational for civil rights and anti-discrimination laws, then they are also flexible enough to be molded into new and far less obvious patterns of prejudice and discrimination once individual and institutional resistance to law comes into play.

Minority groups who are aware of the various types of modern prejudices and their distinct psycho-social tendencies are able to shape educational and organised social and legal responses to more effectively combat the prejudices that victimise them. Since disability is capable of being targetted by any of the three typologies of desire advanced by Young-Bruehl, disability advocates must understand the myriad ways that disability prejudices can surface.[143] For example, hysterical preju-

---

142 *Supra* note 120, at 4.

143 The following discussion is based on my interpretation, and application to

dices may endorse legal regulations that help keep people with developmental disabilities in institutionalised environments, or resist legislative measures that would help people with disabilities gain economic parity and high-quality community services. The Other is thereby kept in an officially sanctioned and "cared for" position while still available to be an actual or imagined sexual figure. Obsessional prejudices will tend to avoid enmeshing themselves too much in official government activity because of their fear of government conspiracies, but they will publicly rail and campaign against civil rights and other laws that would be viewed as giving unfair advantage and power to the disabled Other. Narcissistic prejudices can be very subtle, proactively undermining the educational and social initiatives of the disability community on the simple argument that private spheres—the very spheres in which a medical, personal tragedy model of disability is often socially constructed and maintained—should remain private. Efforts to paint assisted suicide and the euthanasia of infants with disabilities as purely private matters between an individual and/or a family and their doctors serve as examples of actions that can be motivated by narcissistic prejudice.

E. CONCLUSION

Most individuals feel that they have encountered negative perceptions, been judged as different and less worthy, at some point in their lives because of an irrelevant characteristic, trait or personal choice. The experience of discrimination is, in this way, truly universal. Similarly, virtually everyone can probably recall holding a "view of things in which one's own group is the center of everything and all others are scaled and rated with reference to it,"[144] especially if the "group" in question can range from being others of our gender to our circle of friends in high school. When discrimination and prejudice are expanded to embrace such general desires as feeling left out or wanting to belong,

---

the context of disability, of some connections that Young-Bruehl traces between her prejudices typology and different kinds of social/political/legal actions: *see supra* note 62, at 541–47.

[144] This very broad definition of ethnocentrism was adopted by M.B. Brewer & D.T. Campbell, *Ethnocentrism And Intergroup Attitudes: East African Evidence* (New York, John Wiley, 1976), *as cited in* Baldwin, *Tolerance/Intolerance supra* note 57, at 44.

the terms lose their usefulness as either social scientific concepts or part of the experienced reality of socially oppressed groups.

My point here is not merely one of definition. In the above, broadly drawn notion of prejudice as the motivation behind leaving others out, prejudice not only appears universal, but eternal as well, something that has plagued humanity since the origins of social organization. It is a very short step from here to conceive of prejudice as a single phenomenon rooted in human nature, one that thrives under the same conditions, uses the same internal logic, and proceeds along the same continuum of development from simple avoidance to extermination, no matter which outgroup is targetted. In this article, I have argued that such a notion of prejudice completely fails to capture the historical specificity and virulence of modern disability prejudices. Further, the pervasive influence of such an all-inclusive conception of prejudice has hampered not only social scientific investigation into disability *as* a grounds of prejudice, but has impeded public and judicial perception of disability prejudice and discrimination, even with the enactment of anti-discrimination laws. However much nuance is added by disability studies' exploration of, and debate over, the various social and psychological factors that motivate disability prejudice, the unified theory of prejudice continues to unduly influence the ways that courts interpret laws and other international instruments.

People with disabilities have encountered particular difficulty under the notion that prejudice is a single phenomenon because disability least fits the social and legal mold set by earlier recognised victims of prejudice. If prejudice is only ethnocentrism brought to an extreme, then the easiest way for minority groups such as Blacks and Jews to counter prejudice is to demonstrate the potential for assimilation despite difference. Even when everyone agrees that assimilation is undesired, unnecessary, unfair, foolish, wasteful, politically impossible, and so on, the *potential* for assimilation can still be recognised and proven. This approach may be somewhat less applicable to women, but it is wholly inapplicable for people with disabilities. Hence the court's lingering difficulties with accepting disability prejudice, because ultimately, people with disabilities cannot be assimilated into the social, economic and physical environment as it stands now; the latter must be adapted for the former. The need for adaption stands at the crux of current legal and social objections to the use of law to combat disability prejudice. If prejudice is one single human problem, then no single minority group should need something that others do not. This is the point where disability studies and prejudice studies can join forces, and effectively demonstrate the unique nature of disability prejudices *as* a prejudice.

In all of this, the underlying challenge will be to move beyond being sheerly defensive, and towards a vision of a genuinely inclusive society where prejudices are not only barely kept in check in their worst excesses, but specifically recognised and intelligently denounced in all their manifestations. For this to happen, individuals and society as a whole must advocate not only for a bare tolerance of difference, but for a celebration of diversity, intrinsic worth and human ability in all its forms. Given the "uncomfortable, subversive position from which [people with disabilities] act as a living reproach to any scale of values that puts attributes or possessions before the person,"[145] people with disabilities have a particularly important and leading role to play in developing such a radically transformed world. Will this vision be achieved simply through the enactment of national and international anti-discrimination laws? Not likely. But the more important question for people with disabilities today is whether this vision could ever be achieved without such laws. Clearly, the answer is no.

---

145 Hunt, *supra* note 20, at 10.

Different Definition—Same Problems—One Way Out?

*Aart C. Hendriks**

A. INTRODUCTION

The principle of non-discrimination is to a certain extent the corollary of equality. Non-discrimination reflects the idea that no one should be subjected to unfair or less favorable treatment because of personal characteristics that in a given context are irrelevant. This principle constitutes a fundamental human right ("the right to be free from discrimination") and is deeply rooted in contemporary international and national law (McKean 1971).

Non-discrimination law is particularly concerned with redressing structural disadvantage and counterbalancing the underlying power inequalities in society, as a result of which people with some personal characteristics encounter more difficulties in enjoying equal rights and opportunities than others. As with other human rights, the main function of non-discrimination law is to challenge power relations in society with a view to protecting non-dominant groups and strengthening their societal position (Goldschmidt 1997). Non-discrimination law therefore typically seeks to offer protection against unfair or unfavorable treatment on grounds known to correlate with disadvantage, exclusion and the denial of equal opportunities. Having a long history of discrimination is an important factor in determining whether and to what

---

* Aart C. Hendriks, LL.M., M.Pol.Sc., Ph.D. is Secretary of the Programme on Health Law Evaluation, Health Research and Development Council *(ZON)*, The Hague, The Netherlands and member of the Advisory Board of the Dutch Council of People with Disabilities *(Gehandicaptenraad)*. The views expressed in this article are strictly personal and do not necessarily reflect those of *ZON* or the *Gehandicaptenraad*. The author would like to express his sincere thanks to Prof. Dr. Theresia Degener and Dr. Rikki Holtmaat for their thought provoking comments on an earlier draft of this article. All mistakes remain, however, the sole responsibility of the author.

extent a ground is covered by non-discrimination law (*Massachusetts Bd. of Retirement v. Murgia*, 1976).

Around the world, there is a longstanding practice of excluding people with disabilities from mainstream society and subjecting them to all forms of inhuman and degrading treatment (Wolfensberger 1981; Degener 1995). In fact, people with disabilities were (and still are) often perceived as social outcasts and dangers to society. This was painfully reflected in the opinion of U.S. Supreme Court Justice Oliver Wendell Holmes when upholding the forced sterilization of a woman with mental disabilities:

> [T]hree generations of imbeciles are enough (*Buck v. Bell*, 1927 at 207).

People with disabilities therefore doubtless are constituent among those groups of non-dominant people most in need of and entitled to legal protection against discrimination.

Against this background it is rather surprising, if not disappointing, to note that only a few countries have enacted legislation that offers adequate protection against discrimination on grounds of disability. In the majority of countries, the law continues to condone, endorse and perpetuate disability discrimination by "protecting" the rest of society from people with disabilities through segregation.[1]

International human rights law has so far been unable to rectify this flaw in national law. There are only a few treaties which offer protection against disability discrimination, mostly inadequately by way of an open-ended "or other status" criterion (*infra* Section G.2). The fact that disability discrimination is condemned by a large number of declarations, resolutions and recommendations adopted by all kinds of international organizations and conferences cannot fully compensate for this, since these other instruments—different from treaties—are not legally binding.[2] This also holds true with respect to the *United Nations* (UN)

---

1 Many countries have, for example, immigration laws imposing arbitrary entrance and/or residence restrictions on people with disabilities.

2 The foundations of (binding) international law can be found both in treaty

Standard Rules on the Equalization of Opportunities for People with Disabilities (Standard Rules),[3] by far the most important and comprehensive international instrument guaranteeing the rights of people with disabilities. Due to the vigorous opposition of some UN member states—notably the United States—this text was deprived of the status of a treaty, to become an "international instrument of a different type,"[4] which is a euphemism for a non-binding instrument.

The 21st century promises to become the century of legal change. It is expected that both the international and national legal landscape with respect to disability discrimination will soon undergo a metamorphosis. Numerous international organizations and countries have committed themselves to expanding the scope of existing non-discrimination treaties and acts to include the ground of disability, or to introduce comprehensive disability specific non-discrimination codes or provisions. Many international organizations and countries have drawn inspiration from the Americans with Disabilities Act (ADA),[5] from the successes *and* shortcomings of which one can hopefully learn.[6]

---

law, international customary law and the general principles of law. Non-binding instruments sometimes reflect emerging international customary law standards.

3 General Assembly Resolution 48/96, U.N. GAOR, 48th Sess., Supp. No. 49, U.N. Doc. A/48/49 (20 Dec 1993).

4 Resolution 1990/26 on Human Rights and Disability (24 May 1990), U.N. ESCOR 1990, Sess. 1, Supp. No. 1, U.N. Doc. E/1990/69 (1991).

5 42 U.S.C.A. §§ 12101–12213. The ADA was signed into law by—then—U.S. President Bush on July 26, 1990.

6 *Cf.* the analysis of the—then—UN Secretary General Boutros Boutros-Ghali: "The enactment of specific legislation to guarantee equality and eliminate discriminatory practices is essential, even where constitutional or general legal provisions exist. . . . In line with the recommendation of the Programme of Action, some countries have made efforts to adopt specific disability legislation that protects the rights of disabled persons, e.g., Australia, China, Kuwait, the United States of America. That country's Americans with Disabilities Act (ADA) is considered a breakthrough" (Secretary-General 1992, p. 11, § 38). *See also* Resolution B3-0580/93 of the European Parliament: "3. Calls on the Commission to set up a forum consisting of disabled persons from the Member States, charged with the task of: (. . .)—investigating the possibility of introducing anti-discrimination laws based on the US model;" (European Parliament 1993).

The reason why these commitments are not always translated into concrete action often has to do with the difficulties legislatures encounter when seeking to define the term disability. The definitional question is a crucially important aspect of non-discrimination law, since the meaning attached to the term "disability" determines whether an individual is a member of the protected class or not, and can thus file a complaint in case of an alleged violation of his or her right not to be discriminated against. The definition of disability in the ADA, and the (restrictive) way this is currently being interpreted by U.S. courts, has given rise to great controversy, and raises the fundamental question of how to define disability as a prohibitive ground for discrimination.

I will begin this article with a comparison of various theoretical approaches to disability, as these models underlie present and future disability definitions (Section B). I will subsequently review a number of disability definitions, focussing on international and national non-discrimination law (Section C). I submit that all these definitions raise similar "demarcation problems," that is to say, they draw an arbitrary line between people who are protected by the law and those who are not protected, a line which can easily be contested (Section D). This raises the question whether it is really necessary to define the concept of disability for the sake of non-discrimination law, when we are concerned about people being subjected to unfair or less favorable treatment because of human attributes relating to independent functioning and societal participation (Section E). I will subsequently argue that, at least with respect to non-discrimination law, it is better to use the neutral and inclusive term "capabilities" instead of the polarized and exclusive term "disability" (Section F). Thereafter, the application of non-discrimination law, and the choice of the focus of comparison, will be examined in greater detail (Section G). I conclude by suggesting that we can do without a definition of disability if we are to introduce legislation aimed at eliminating disability discrimination and promoting equal opportunities for people with disabilities, although we should always remain aware of those most vulnerable to disadvantage, exclusion and inequality as persons entitled to the highest level of protection (Section H).

B. THEORETICAL APPROACHES TO DISABILITY

Over the course of the last few decades, there has been an enormous discussion on how to define disability and related terminological issues (Zola 1993). This followed attempts by medical professionals to design, along the lines of the International Classification of Diseases (ICD), a one-dimensional taxonomy stipulating the impact of disease or disorder on the individuals concerned. These efforts resulted, in 1980, in the adoption by the World Health Organization (WHO) of the International Classification of Impairments, Disabilities and Handicaps (ICIDH). This classification has had an immense impact on the medical community and policy makers, but was never accepted by its "users," those being people with disabilities themselves.

1. Locating the Problems of Disability

The discussion of how to define disability has largely been a discussion of where to locate the problem(s) of disability. In this discussion two opposing views—or "pathologies" (Rioux 1997)—can be distinguished (Waddington 1995a).

a. Individual Models

Disability is traditionally defined as an observable physical, mental, sensory or psychological deviation from normality caused by disease, trauma or another health condition. As a result of these medically defined conditions, a person with disabilities experiences functional limitations, some of which can be prevented by medical interventions or compensated for by way of aids or rehabilitation, while others result in permanent restrictions of life activities. For these reasons the individual model is often called the medical or biomedical model.

All individual models have in common the fact that they situate the problems of disability in the person concerned while paying little or no attention to his or her physical and social environment. In other words, a disability is perceived as an individual attribute, and all problems relating to disability stem from individual functional limitations.

These models heavily rely on medical research. The medical sciences are seen as an objective tool for explaining the genesis of deviation from normality and for understanding the functional limitations thought to be inherent in people with disabilities. Medical research is subsequently applied towards eliminating the disability by developing methods of intervention to bridge the gap between the norm and the deviation, or, if such cannot be achieved, to rehabilitating the person concerned to the greatest extent possible or comparatively calculating the loss of "normal" functional capacities.

The individual (and medical) approach to disability underlies almost all medical taxonomies, including the ICIDH (WHO 1980). The latter classification builds on a threefold distinction (impairments, disabilities and handicaps) among what are perceived as impacts from disease or disorder. The medical view is also prominent in the frequently used concepts of quality adjusted life years (QALYs) and disability-adjusted life years (DALYs). A QALY is a unit that quantifies a health situation by correcting the number of life years through a judgment of the quality of life (Van Busschbach 1994), while a DALY is a unit that measures the burden of disease by combining (a) losses from premature death, defined as the difference between actual age at death and life expectancy at that age in a low mortality population, and (b) loss of healthy life resulting from disability (World Bank 1993).

In the literature, various other forms of individual models have been distinguished. One of these is the economic model of disability, which equates disabilities with human harm resulting in a loss of earning capacities (Klosse 1989). These losses can be compensated for either by remedying the injuries—by way of offering rehabilitation and/or by adopting the work or work environment—or by bridging the income gap through welfare support and payments.

Other variations of the individual approach to disability include administrative models that relate to specific areas of life, philanthropic models that are the models presented by charities, and lay models of disability, which determine how the public at large thinks of people with disabilities (French 1994).

b. Social Models

The social approaches to disability evolved out of dissatisfaction with the individual models, which were allegedly based upon able-bodied assumptions of normality. The social models are, instead, centred around the idea that disability can be seen as a social construct. That is to say, society creates disability by accepting an idealised norm as given and by measuring deviation therefrom. The "social constructionists" therefore reject the causal relationship between individual impairment and disability put forward by the individual models, and contend that disabilities are products of the failure of the physical and social environment to take into account the needs of particular individuals or groups (Oliver 1985; Rebell 1986; Abberley 1986; Liachowitz 1988; Oliver 1990).

The social model focuses on the interaction between people with functional limitations and broader social and economic forces, paying special attention to the question of how institutions, organisations and processes that constitute society compound the functional limitation by constructing social and economic processes that fail to take impairment into adequate account. The disadvantage, exclusion and inequality many people with disabilities experience are therefore not taken for granted, but perceived as a form of injustice which requires a legal and political response.

The social models are reflected in the definitions of disability that are advocated by the international disability movement, such as the famous definition of the Union of the Physically Impaired Against Segregation, that was later on also adopted by Disabled Peoples' International (DPI):

> [D]isability [is a] disadvantage or restriction of activity caused by a contemporary social organisation which takes no or little account of people who have physical impairments and thus excludes them from participation in the mainstream of social activities. Physical disability is therefore a particular form of social oppression. (UPIAS 1976).

In 1994, on the occasion of the European Day of Disabled Persons, a new definition was presented that also clearly builds on the social concept of disability. This definition reads as follows:

> A Disabled Person is an individual in their (sic) own right placed in a disabling situation, brought about by environmental, economic and social barriers that the person, because of their (sic) impairment(s), cannot overcome in the same way as other persons. These barriers are all too often reinforced by the marginalising attitudes of society.
>
> It is up to society to eliminate, reduce or compensate for these barriers in order to allow each individual to enjoy full citizenship, respecting the rights and duties of each individual (Waddington 1995b).

The minority-group model of disability is closely related to the social model of disability. It argues that people with disabilities are a suppressed minority and that discrimination is the major obstacle to them, inhibiting independent functioning and societal participation. In this respect, Barnes even speaks about "disablism" to indicate the similarities between discrimination on the basis of disability, race, sex and other recognized grounds (Barnes 1991). Another eloquent proponent of this view is Hahn, who has written extensively on the minority-group approach (Hahn 1985; Hahn 1986).

2. Factors Relating to Independent Functioning and Societal Participation

Over the course of the last few years, various scholars have argued that the problems related to disability cannot be solely attributed either to the individual or to the environment, as proponents of the individual and social approaches respectively tend to claim, but are much more complex and require a deeper understanding of the various intrinsic and extrinsic factors determining (and hindering) the independent functioning and societal participation of individuals (Groce & Zola 1993; Pinder 1995). Some authors find the social model almost as determinist as the individual model, since its underlying idea is that disability automatically results in disadvantage. Others contend that social models proved to be a very powerful device for demanding social change by identifying society as the main problem for people with disabilities, but that the models said little about people with disabilities themselves. The minority-group model, on the other hand, is also criticized for running the risk of reinforcing separations instead of breaking down walls of exclusion (Shakespeare 1999). It is also maintained that the minority-group model is based upon a forced analogy between racial minorities and disabled people that breaks down at many instances (Bickenbach 1999).

In response to this criticism, some social constructionists have adapted their model (e.g., Priestly 1998). For others, this has been reason to try to develop a new, multi-dimensional model that integrates the individual and social models and focuses on societal participation. Valuable research was carried out by the social anthropologist Fougeyrollas, who studied the determinants of societal participation. He proposes distinguishing between intrinsic factors belonging to the person, extrinsic factors belonging to the environment, and factors relating to the specific life situation (Fougeyrollas 1998). Another important thinker and so-called "universalist" is Bickenbach who, building on the work of the late Zola, asks for policies that respect difference and widen the range of normality (Bickenbach 1999).

Criticism of the individual *and* social models has also deeply influenced the revision process of the ICIDH, which should lead to the adoption of the ICIDH-II later in the year 2000 (Halbertsma 1995; Bickenbach *et al.* 1999). The forthcoming classification, which focuses on functioning and disability as an important factor of health, covers disturbances at bodily, individual and societal levels. Functioning and disability are umbrella terms that cover three dimensions: body functions and structure; activities at the individual level; and participation in society.

C. A REVIEW OF DISABILITY DEFINITIONS

After this examination of theoretical models, it is time to see how disability has been defined in non-discrimination legislation in the United States and some other countries known to have laws prohibiting discrimination on grounds of disability.

From the definitions included in Appendix B, it can be learned that various legislatures have tried to give a very detailed description of the term "disability" as a prohibitive ground for discrimination (Australia, Ireland, New Zealand, South Africa, the U.K., and the U.S.), whereas others contented themselves with a basic delineation of disability (Canada/HRA & EEA, OAS, Sweden and the UN, see also Commission 2000) or have not even endeavored to define the ground at all (Canada/Charter, Finland and Germany, *see also* Council 1996).

The detailed definitions are all centered around the term "impairment" (New Zealand, South Africa, the U.K., and the U.S.) or otherwise worded "conditions" that affect a person's bodily or mental functions (Australia and Ireland). These definitions are therefore mainly based on an individual model of disability, even though it is also recognized—at least in some cases—that a disability may only come to light in the interaction between an individual and his or her environment. It remains, however, indispensable for someone allegedly being discriminated against on the basis of disability to provide at least *prima facie* proof of an impairment (past, present, future, or perceived) or similar condition, in order to be recognized as a member of the protected class.

The more basic definitions contain a few characterizations which are deemed to be inherent to disability. All these characteristics focus on "impairment" (Canada and OAS) or "functional limitations" (Sweden and the UN). It can therefore be maintained that the basic definitions also situate the main problem of disability in the persons concerned. An alleged victim of disability discrimination accordingly has to prove that he or she has an impairment of a physical, mental, sensory, or psychological nature, as a precondition for being covered by a non-discrimination law.[7] If the plaintiff fails to meet this test, than he or she is not covered by the law and cannot derive protection from it.

It is maintained here that even those non-discrimination laws that do not contain a definition of disability predominantly adhere to an individual model of disability. This follows from the fact that disability is placed among other prohibitive grounds for discrimination that are all

---

[7] In some countries, like Australia, the law also protects family members (e.g., the mother of a disabled child) against disability discrimination.

personal characteristics of an individual or a group. This is rather clear from Article 6 of the Finnish Constitution which describes the listed grounds as "reason[s] that concern his or her person." It therefore seems logical that the ground of disability is to be understood in an analogous way.

This tripartite classification is, admittedly, a very rough and imprecise categorization of approaches to disability definitions, and does not even include non-discrimination provisions where disability is or might by covered by other descriptive grounds, such as personal or social conditions and circumstances (Italy and Spain). The mentioned definitions contain many more particularities on the basis of which distinctions can be made. Some of them refer, for example, to the effect of an impairment on "activities" (OAS, the U.K. and the U.S.) whereas others equal disabilities with functional limitations (OAS, Sweden and the UN). There are also definitions which explicitly include people with a history of disability (Australia, Canada/HRA, Ireland, and the U.S.), a perceived or imputed disability (Australia, Ireland, South Africa, and the U.S.), and/or a future disability or genetic predisposition (Australia, Ireland, New Zealand, South Africa, and Sweden), whereas other confine themselves to covering only present or actual disabilities (the U.K.).

Reference should also be made to the Indian Constitution. The non-discrimination provision (Article 15) does not refer to disability as a prohibitive ground for discrimination, but it is—according to the second paragraph—forbidden to subject a citizen to a disability. The Indian Constitution thus employs a radically different concept of disability, in the sense of an externally imposed disadvantage. In the Indian perception, disability is not an independent prohibitive ground for discrimination but a disadvantage placed on a person which leads to discrimination on another ground. However, it would be wrong to conclude from this that India has adopted a social model of disability.

D. APPRAISAL

From the above discussion, it becomes clear that a wide variety of approaches to disability definition are applied around the world. Nonetheless, they all seem to have in common the fact that they are individually centered, that is to say, they attribute the problems associated with disability to personal characteristics, at least to a certain extent. They therefore mainly embrace an individual model of disability.

The more detailed definitions have in common the fact that they all seek to describe comprehensively and exhaustively the members of the protected class. The advantage of this approach is that it becomes optimally clear, both for potential plaintiffs and defendants, who qualifies as a person with disabilities and who does not. The disadvantage of this approach, however, is that these definitions are rather inflexible and preclude new evolutions from taking place, or at least from being recognized by the law.

The basic descriptions of disabilities may be imprecise, as legislatures confined themselves to giving a few basic characterizations of disability, but they allow for more flexibility and for the incorporation in law of developments in medical and social sciences or society at large. Even more flexibility is offered by an open definition, as may become clear from a judgment of the European Court of Human Rights with respect to the meaning of the term "persons of unsound mind" as laid down in Article 5 para. 1(e) of the European Convention on Human Rights (ECHR). In the *Winterwerp* case the Court held:

> The Convention does not state what is to be understood by the words "persons of unsound mind." This term is not one that can be given a definitive interpretation: as was pointed out by the Commission, the [Dutch] Government and the applicant, it is a term whose meaning is continually evolving as research in psychiatry progresses, an increasing flexibility in treatment develops and society's attitude to mental illness changes, in particular so that a greater understanding of the problems of mental patients is becoming more wide-spread (*Winterwerp*, 1979 at ¶ 37).

For people coming from the United States and other common law (inspired) countries where detailed legal definitions are the norm, it may be surprising to see that there are jurisdictions where the law does not articulate who is a "person with disabilities." Such persons might have the opinion that the absence of a definition would make it difficult, if not impossible, to determine who is qualified for the protection of the law and who is not (Gutow 1998). The experience in countries with basic definitions and open grounds shows, however, that "demarcation problems" in these countries are not necessarily greater than in others (Disability Rights Task Force 1999).

All countries with disability non-discrimination legislation, no matter what type of disability definition or which approach to disability they apply, are confronted with demarcation problems. These problems have given rise to an extensive body of jurisprudence. From this body it becomes abundantly clear that it is rather unpredictable, bordering on arbitrariness, whether a person is covered by a given non-discrimination law or not (for the United Stats, *see e.g.*, *Southeastern Community College v. Davis*, 1979; *Bragdon v. Abbott*, 1998; *Sutton v. United Airlines*, 1999; *Murphy v. United Parcel Service*, 1999; *Albertsons, Inc. v. Kirkingburg*, 1999). It is not only this sense of arbitrariness that raises concern, but also the sheer fact that plaintiffs first have to "prove" that they are a member of a protected class. This latter requirement sometimes necessitates the provision of extensive medical evidence to demonstrate that a plaintiff is disabled in the eyes of the law before courts will recognize his or her standing to bring the case. This is a particularly difficult requirement to meet in a case where a person does not have a medical condition that constitutes a disability, but is nevertheless treated—and discriminated against—as if he or she were disabled, because of fears or prejudices related to a medical condition wrongly assumed to be contagious. Various authors have expressed severe criticism of this demarcation problem under the ADA. According to the Canadian scholar Bickenbach, an inordinate amount of time and energy is spent nowadays on determining whether the individual plaintiff qualifies as a member of a group to whom the ADA applies (Bickenbach 1999). As Mayerson has stated, establishing whether a plaintiff has a disability has become a threshold determination in any ADA case (Mayerson 1997).

The typical response to problems with the scope of disability definitions is to call for their enlargement, to make sure that more people who were wrongly excluded will be covered in the future (Disability Rights Task Force 1999). There are also authors who, along the lines of the social models of disability, argue that more attention should be paid to socially constructed limitations (Parmet & Jackson 1997).

E. DO WE NEED A DEFINITION OF DISABILITY AFTER ALL?

Given the demarcation problems which will likely always exist, one could also ask oneself whether, in legislation that seeks to eliminate disability discrimination and promote equal opportunities for people with disabilities, a definition of disability is needed at all. This depends, it seems, on the meaning of discrimination as a principle of human rights law and the way this has been codified in international and national law.

At the beginning of this article, it was argued that the principle of non-discrimination reflects the idea that no one should be subjected to unfair or less favorable treatment because of personal characteristics. This interpretation is also inherent in the definition of discrimination given by the Human Rights Committee, a UN organ of independent experts established to supervise the implementation of the International Covenant on Civil and Political Rights:

> [A]ny distinction, exclusion, restriction or preference which is based on any ground such as race, colour, sex, language, religion, political or other opinion, national or social origin, property, birth or other status, and which has the purpose or effect of nullifying or impairing the recognition or enjoyment or exercise by all persons, on an equal footing, of all rights and freedoms (Human Rights Committee 1990).

The term "discrimination" therefore has a pejorative connotation[8] and is in several jurisdictions linked to the concept of disadvantage. Discrimination is to be distinguished from (fair) "differentiation" (Skogly 1992; *Darby v. Sweden*, 1990), that is to say, a form of differ-

---

[8] Many therefore recommend avoiding the term "positive discrimination" for describing measures that are taken to remove inequalities and to ameliorate the position of members of disadvantaged groups. These affirmative action measures, or forms of preferential treatment, are taken to rebut (the consequences of) past discrimination, and do not constitute a form of discrimination in themselves, unless such measures lead to a violation of the right of others not to be discriminated against (*Adarand Constructors, Inc. v. Peña*, 1995; *Kalanke*, 1995; *Abrahamsson & Anderson*, 2000).

ent treatment for which there is an objective and reasonable justification.[9] Furthermore, discrimination is inextricably linked to redressing structural disadvantage and counterbalancing underlying power inequalities in society, as a result of which people with some personal characteristics encounter more difficulties in enjoying equal rights and opportunities than others. The mere fact that a differentiation is unfair does not automatically constitute discrimination. The term discrimination should be reserved for unfair or less favorable treatment because of *particular* personal characteristics.

Another reason not to confound discrimination with differentiation is that discrimination[10] also takes place if differently situated persons are, without an objective and reasonable justification, treated the same instead of differently, in proportion to the unalikeness of their situation (Hendriks 1995; *Thlimmenos*, 2000). Neglecting difference can be as detrimental as overemphasizing inter-human variation.

It is, in this respect, important to note that not every human attribute qualifies as a prohibitive ground for discrimination. The principle of non-discrimination primarily seeks to prevent the unfair or less favorable treatment of people because of immutable characteristics that are either inherent or uncontrollable (such as sex and race), or characteristics which only can be changed or suppressed at the detriment of one's identity (such as religion, political opinion and sexual preference) (*Frontiero v. Richardson*, 1973).[11] Or, in brief, "grounds relating to personal characteristics of the individual or group" (*Andrews v. Law Society of British Columbia*, 1989).[12] Making wrongful differentiations on these

---

9 *Cf. Abdulaziz, Cabales and Balkandali*, 1985, § 72: "a difference of treatment is discriminatory if it has 'no objective and reasonable justification,' that is, if it does not pursue a 'legitimate aim' or if there is not a 'reasonable relationship of proportionality between the means employed and the aim sought to be realised'."

10 Non-discrimination law itself is, unfortunately, not always very consistent in this respect. See Ramcharan 1981 and *Belgian Linguistic Case*, 1968.

11 Notably Brennan J. at 686.

12 According to Canadian Supreme Court Justice McIntyre, "discrimination may be described as a distinction, whether intentional or not but based on grounds relating to personal characteristics of the individual or group, which has the effect of imposing burdens, obligations, or disadvantages, on such individual or group not imposed on others, or which withholds or limits access to opportunities, bene-

grounds impairs the equality of human beings. This is also the reason why only a selective number of human attributes, and not all forms of inter-human variation (including e.g., talents, hair color, voice, memory), are considered as grounds for non-discrimination.

Prohibitive grounds for discrimination are, as becomes clear from the discussion above, always seen as human attributes. This has been motivated by the fact that non-discrimination law is traditionally concerned with persons who, because of individual or group characteristics, are being discriminated against by others. Protected classes are therefore always defined on the basis of personal characteristics, and not on the basis of environmental factors. This approach is at odds with social models of disability which locate the origin of disability problems in the human environment.

It is also important to note that prohibitive grounds for discrimination are generally formulated in an inclusive way, that is to say, in a manner that covers all human beings and not just the group disproportionately affected by discrimination.[13] This explains why such neutral terms are used as "sex," covering both men and women; "race," which includes people of every race, skin color, form of descent, and type of national or ethnic origin;[14] "religion," which covers people of every denomination as well as non-believers; "age," a neutral criterion including both young and elderly people, etc. The criterion "disability" is inconsistent with these grounds, since disability is not a generally applicable human characteristic, but rather a group characteristic that separates people with disabilities from their able-bodied peers. This is a highly problematic approach, if only because ability-disability is a continuum, with very few people finding themselves at the extreme points of the spectrum. Every point of demarcation (and definition of disability) is therefore inherently arbitrary. This does not mean that the term "disability" should be taken out of all laws and programs altogether; this exclusive term can still be very useful for defining those entitled to pref-

---

fits, and advantages available to other members of society." *Andrews v. Law Society of British Columbia*, [1989] 1 S.C.R. 143, 174.

13 CEDAW is an exception.

14 *Cf.* Article 1 § 1 CERD.

erential treatment, social security, welfare, and other support and facility measures, but it is less appropriate for non-discrimination law.

The symmetric way of describing prohibitive grounds for discrimination bears in it the risk of concealing structural patterns of discrimination, misrepresenting social problems to which non-discrimination law purports to respond, and ignoring different needs and justified distinctions between people. This approach has therefore also been heavily criticized. In order to reduce the risks inherent in a symmetric approach, it is important to acknowledge that women, racial, religious, national and sexual minorities, and people with disabilities run the risk of experiencing forms of disadvantage, exclusion and barriers to societal integration that their counterparts (men, dominant racial, religious, national and sexual groups, and able-bodied persons) may never face during their life. Able-bodied persons will, for example, never be excluded from the bulk of social activities, nor will they ever feel as embarrassed and humiliated by the way in which able-bodied people and institutions react to people with disabilities. Non-discrimination laws and measures should therefore, despite a neutral formulation of prohibitive grounds for discrimination, primarily be tailored to eliminating discrimination against members of non-dominant groups, thus taking into account disadvantage, exclusion and the denial of equal opportunities (asymmetric approach).

F. FROM DISABILITIES TO CAPABILITIES

1. Rationale

The concept of discrimination is, by definition, relational or comparative. This follows from the Aristotelian notion of equality according to which "things that are alike should be treated alike and things that are unalike should be treated unalike in proportion to their unalikeness." (Aristotle 1980). A person can therefore only be found to be discriminated against in relation to or in comparison with some other person who serves as a standard. Or, to say it briefly, discrimination entails comparison (Banton 1999).

The same holds true with respect to the term disability. The term has no independent meaning without any form of comparison. This comparative aspect is embedded in the prefix "dis" which indicates that a person does not have the same physical, mental, sensory, or psychological abilities as those that are deemed normal. In other words, the term disabled denotes making a negative distinction between people on the basis of their abilities, or capacities, with able-bodied persons implicitly serving as a focus of comparison.

Disability discrimination can, however, take many forms and also includes, at least in my view, making unjustified distinctions between disabled persons. For example, making adaptations for deaf people but not for blind people, or the other way around. In such cases, the counterpart to whom one is compared is someone who is also, but differently, (dis)abled. This forms an additional reason to avoid the term "disability" in non-discrimination law, since its use may automatically result in comparisons being made between disabled and non-disabled persons, and thus preclude courts from comparing people with different "types" of disabilities.

It is therefore argued here that the inclusive term "capabilities," a short-hand, catch-all expression for those human attributes essential for independent functioning and societal participation, is a better term to be used in non-discrimination law than disability. Capacities is a neutral and inclusive term, covering both able-bodied and disabled persons, and does not suggest that a disability discrimination claim can only be grounded on a comparison made between a disabled person and a similarly situated non-disabled counterpart.

2. Interpretation

It is important to interpret the attributes covered by the term capabilities broadly. These should not only include a person's—literal—abilities, but also all those attributes which determine a person's functioning and participation, notably a person's physical, mental, sensory and psychological condition. These attributes are not only a precondition for how certain abilities can be exercised, but may also be the very root-cause of (dis)ability discrimination. In this respect it should be remembered that many people are being discriminated against because of prejudices or other value judgments about their physical, mental, sensory and psychological condition. These judgments, such as fear of contamination or disgust, may be unrelated to any actual loss in a person's ability to function and participate, but they are as disabling in their effect.

3. Application

How can disability discrimination be established when the protected class of persons is not confined to people with disabilities, but when the law prohibits the unfair and less favorable treatment of any person because of capabilities? And how does the notion of capabilities relate to the duty to provide effective accommodation (also known as "reasonable accommodation" and "reasonable adjustment")?

Before answering these questions, it should be recalled that the primary objective of non-discrimination law is not the prohibition of differentiation, but the elimination of disadvantage, exclusion, and the denial of equal opportunities, particularly for non-dominant groups. Secondly, discrimination only takes place when a prohibited ground for discrimination is used as a selection or exclusion criterion in situations where the ground is irrelevant or where it is possible to provide an effective accommodation which, for unjustified reasons, is being denied. Not hiring a blind person as a taxi driver does not therefore constitute discrimination, since "vision," at least with respect to driving a car, is a relevant capability on the basis of which an employer can—and maybe should—differentiate. The same could hold true with respect to a university who turns down the application of a student with a learning disability. For university study, "intelligence"—leaving aside the issues raised by its definition and measurement—is a relevant capability which justifies differentiation. The situation would be different if a university were to decide to exclude wheelchair users, left handed, blind and deaf students. Mobility, left or right handedness, vision and hearing are capabilities which, in general, are irrelevant selection criteria for universities. A university applying one of these capabilities as a selection criterion therefore runs the risk of being found guilty of disability or capabilities discrimination. In other words, capabilities can only serve as selection criterion when they are directly and closely related to the function(s) to be performed.

These examples should be distinguished from cases where a landlord prefers someone with dark hair over a blond person as a tenant, or someone who is tall and thin over a small and obese person. Hair color, length and weight are not capabilities, although these human characteristics may, in some instances, reflect a certain condition. Differentiation on these grounds therefore, at least generally, does not constitute disability or capabilities discrimination. This is not to say that it is necessarily fair to distinguish on these grounds. It should be reminded, however, that non-discrimination is not the equivalent of fairness, but is a right in itself with its own background, aims and taxonomy.

In cases where a person, on the basis of a capability which is directly and closely related to the function(s) to be performed, is at risk of being excluded due to incapacity, then the provider of goods of services should, at least in my view, examine whether the lack of a necessary ability can be compensated for by an effective accommodation. This affirmative duty placed on providers of goods and services, as well as schools, employers, landlords and others, is meant to take away disadvantage and secure equal opportunities, notably for members of groups prone to discrimination. For the latter reason, it is submitted here that the justification for not making such an adaptation or modification should depend on the recipient at issue. In a case where the person concerned pertains to a group that has a history of disadvantage, exclusion and denial of equal opportunities, such as wheelchair users, then the provider of goods and services should furnish more evidence that the necessary adaptation or modification is unreasonable (i.e., constitutes an "undue hardship") than in a case where the potential recipient with a "wrong" capability—e.g., the person is "only" short sighted—is not otherwise disadvantaged and belongs to the dominant societal group.

G. WHY "CAPABILITIES" SHOULD BE EXPLICITLY RECOGNISED AS A PROHIBITIVE GROUND FOR NON-DISCRIMINATION

1. Introduction

While I need not articulate the precise meaning of non-discrimination as a principle of law and as a legal right, for the purposes of this article, it is important nonetheless to assess the implications of being or not being covered by an enumerated ground in non-discrimination law, and to have a closer look at the way in which non-discrimination provisions are being applied by courts and quasi-judicial bodies. In doing so, I will largely confine myself to international human rights treaties and their provisions prohibiting discrimination.

2. Grounds for Non-Discrimination

Some people might say that there is no need to discuss the incorporation of "capabilities" as a forbidden ground for discrimination in non-discrimination law, since the law now prohibits all forms of discrimination[15] and thereby also includes disability or capabilities discrimination. This assertion is, however, only partially true.

Many instruments contain an exhaustive list of prohibitive grounds for discrimination.[16] Classifications made on non-enumerated grounds cannot be challenged under such instruments,[17] unless an apparently neutral provision, criterion or practice factually disadvantages a substantially higher proportion of people belonging to a prohibited ground for discrimination than their counterparts. The term "indirect discrimination," also known as "disparate impact," has been coined to refer to these latter situations.

Non-discrimination instruments containing a non-exhaustive list of prohibitive grounds for discriminations do not necessarily offer the required level of protection against disability or capabilities discrimination (Hendriks 1999; Hendriks 2000). These instruments typically

---

15 *Cf.* Art. 24 ACHR. *See, e.g., also* Article 33 § 2 of the Constitution of China: "All citizens of the People's Republic of China are equal before the law"; Article 91 of the Constitution of Latvia: "All human beings in Latvia shall be equal before the law and the courts. Human rights shall be realised without discrimination of any kind"; and Article 32 of the Polish Constitution: "(1) All persons shall be equal before the law. All persons shall have the right to equal treatment by public authorities. (2) No one shall be discriminated against in political, social or economic life for any reason whatsoever."

16 *See, e.g.*, Article 1 § 2 UN Charter; Article E ESC (revised) and Articles 13 and 141 EC Treaty.

17 *Cf. Grant*, 1998, where the Court of Justice held that the plaintiff had not been treated unequally on grounds of her sex but because of her sexual orientation, and that EC law did not prohibit discrimination on the basis of sexual orientation.

contain a—seemingly illustrative—non-exhaustive list of forbidden grounds for discrimination, that is supplemented by the open-ended criterion "or other status."[18] Since disability or capabilities is usually not listed in these instruments, protection against disability or capabilities discrimination is dependent on the way courts and (quasi-)judicial bodies interpret and apply the criterion "other ground." From the case law it becomes clear that courts and (quasi-)judicial bodies make a sharp distinction between listed grounds on the one hand and non-listed on the other. Listed grounds are assumed to correspond with suspect classifications, that is to say, classifications which immediately raise the suspicion of discrimination. This implies that it is commonly sufficient for a plaintiff to deliver *prima facie* proof of discriminatory acts, after which the court will shift the *onus* of proving non-discrimination on to the defendant. In the case of a discrimination complaint based on a non-listed ground,[19] courts and (quasi-)judicial bodies commonly require the plaintiff to bear the entire burden of proof, and tend to apply a high standard of scrutiny that effectively leaves defendants with a large margin of discretion to decide what constitutes a justified differentiation. In these cases the plaintiff has to prove that the distinction made by the defendant did not serve a legitimate goal, that the relationship between the goal and the means was disproportionate or that the differentiation was otherwise unreasonable, and that the differentiation did not fall within the margin of discretion of the defendant. It is only in exceptional cases that these discrimination complaints yield success in court.[20]

---

[18] *See, e.g.*, Article 2 UDHR; Article 2 § 2 ICESCR; Articles 2 and 26 ICCPR; Article 14 ECHR; Article 2 ACHPR and Protocol No. 12 to the ECHR.

[19] Courts and (quasi-)judicial bodies in charge of the supervision of non-discrimination treaties and provisions usually require plaintiffs to indicate on which ground they allegedly have been discriminated against. Not all grounds are recognised as deserving protection against discrimination. *Cf. Debreczeny v. The Netherlands*, 1995.

[20] In some cases, however, courts consider a non-listed ground to be part of a listed ground. *Cf. Broeks v. the Netherlands*, 1987 (differentiation on the basis of breadwinnership constitutes discrimination on the basis of sex), *Dekker v. Stichting Vormingscentrum voor Jong Volwassen Plus*, 1990 (differentiation on pregnancy constitutes discrimination on the basis of sex) and *Toonen v. Australia*, 1994 (differentiation on the basis of sexual orientation constitutes discrimination on the basis of sex).

From the discussion above, I conclude that the protection non-discrimination law offers to people with disabilities is to a large extent dependent on the explicit recognition of capabilities as an enumerated prohibitive ground for discrimination. There is therefore every reason to campaign for the incorporation of "capabilities" or any similar inclusive term in non-discrimination instruments.

3. (Defining) the Focus of Comparison

Non-discrimination instruments usually do not indicate with whom comparisons should be made in order to establish "distinction, exclusion, restriction or preference" (Human Rights Committee 1990).

From the case law of international courts and (quasi-)judicial bodies it can be learned that a comparison usually takes place on an individual level. A comparison is made with a similarly situated counterpart, that is to say someone who is different from the plaintiff with respect to the invoked non-discrimination ground, but the same or similar with respect to all other relevant features. It is usually evident who should serve as a focus of comparison. There have, however, also been instances where this is not the case. For example, should the way a pregnant woman is treated be compared with the way a man or the way a non-pregnant woman is treated (*Bliss v. Attorney General of Canada*, 1976)? Can a gay man who is being harassed by his male colleagues be the victim of sex discrimination, or does sex discrimination only offer protection against harassment from people of the opposite sex (*Oncale v. Sundowner Offshore Services Incorporated*, 1998)? And should the way a member of a religious minority is treated be compared with the way a member of another religious minority is treated, or with a representative member of the dominant religious group, or maybe even with a non-believer? Nonetheless, in general it is not difficult to identify an appropriate counterpart, particularly not if the courts relate the concept of discrimination to the elimination of disadvantage and exclusion and the promotion of equal opportunities. Here it should once more be recalled that discrimination is a pejorative term and not the same as differentiation. In defining the focus of comparison, attention should also be paid to the function of non-discrimination law, which is to redress structural disadvantage and to counterbalance the underlying power inequalities in society with a view to protecting members of non-dominant groups and strengthening their societal position.

The test applied is slightly different in the case of a plaintiff arguing that discrimination is the result of the application of a seemingly neutral provision, criterion or practice, which disadvantages a substantially higher proportion of people on a forbidden ground for discrimination (*cf. Griggs v. Duke Power Company*, 1971; *Jenkins*, 1981; *Bilka Kaufhaus*, 1986; *Danmark v. Danfoss*, 1989). Establishing indirect discrimination—or "disparate impact"—entails making a group-based comparison and requires that the adverse impact on one's own group can be demonstrated.

The lesson we can learn from this for the elimination of disability or capabilities discrimination is—as said before—that we should not automatically subdivide humanity into disabled and able-bodied persons, wherever this line of demarcation is to be drawn. This particularly holds true with respect to alleged instances of indirect discrimination. Measures or practices that have a significantly negative effect on a particular group of people with disabilities, let us say wheelchair users, do not necessarily have to affect all people with disabilities,[21] and perhaps not even all wheelchair users.[22] I would still argue that in such cases, adversely affected persons should be able to challenge a contested measure or practice in court, something that would probably not be possible if a non-discrimination law that availed itself of the term "disability" only allowed for a comparison between disabled and able-bodied persons. The latter problem can be prevented by using the inclusive term capabilities instead of the exclusive term disabilities as a prohibitive ground for discrimination. The term capabilities allows for optimal flexibility with respect to the choice of the focus of comparison and the definition of affected groups, while acknowledging the disadvantage, exclusion and barriers to societal integration which all people with disabilities face, be it to different degrees.

---

[21] There are, in fact, few measures and practices I can think of that would be discriminative towards all people with disabilities.

[22] Some wheelchair users can stand and walk for short distances, while others cannot stand at all unaided. Measures and practices affecting wheelchair users can therefore affect them differently.

H. FINAL REMARKS

The conclusion of this article is that there is an urgent need to offer people with disabilities full protection against discrimination by expanding the scope of international and national non-discrimination law. This should not be done, as one might expect, by adding the exclusive ground of "disability," but by using instead the neutral and inclusive term "capabilities" or a similar term indicating that we are talking about "an infinitely various but universal feature of the human condition" (Bickenbach 1999). There is no need to define this term,[23] as long as it is clear that it covers all human attributes essential for independent functioning and societal participation, including a person's physical, mental, sensory and psychological condition.

My plea to refer to "capabilities" should not allow us to close our eyes to the structural disadvantage, exclusion and barriers to societal integration which people with disabilities face in an able-bodied dominated world. It is therefore important for non-discrimination laws to be applied in an asymmetric way[24] to promote real equality. That is to say, our goal should be substantive equality, a notion of equality that is concerned with the construction of equal social conditions that take differences into account, and not just formal equality, a notion of equality that restricts itself to prohibiting the less favorable treatment of individuals who are similarly situated (Vierdag 1973; Loenen 1995; Borgetto 1999). An asymmetric interpretation of non-discrimination law with respect to the term capabilities presupposes that the law recognizes structural and historical disadvantages, and that it is particularly concerned with the protection of non-dominant groups and the strengthening of their societal position.

---

23 This is in line with the European Commission's draft Council directive on equal treatment in employment and occupation (Commission 2000), which—although still referring to the term "disability"—does not define "disability." This decision was welcomed by Joke Swiebel, who served as rapporteur of the European Parliament's Committee on Citizens' Freedoms and Rights, Justice and Home Affairs (Swiebel 2000).

24 In this respect, Article 3 § 3 of the German Constitution is quite unique now that it applies the prohibition of discrimination in an asymmetric way, however only with respect to disability and not with regard to the other grounds.

At the same time, we should remain aware of the fact that not all inequality problems will automatically cease to exist after the incorporation of "capabilities" as a prohibitive ground for discrimination in international or national non-discrimination law, or even after the introduction of special laws prohibiting discrimination on grounds of "capabilities." Many of the disadvantages encountered by people with disabilities are more the result of distributive justice problems, and not so much caused by discriminatory measures or practices (Bickenbach 1999). Continuous priority should therefore be given to the respect, the protection and the realisation of social human rights, such as those laid down in the International Covenant of Economic, Social and Cultural Rights, and not only to the promotion of political and civil rights, because "[a]ll human rights are universal, indivisible and interdependent and interrelated" (Vienna 1993).

Appendix A

List of Abbreviations

ACHPR	African Charter on Human and Peoples' Rights (1986)
ACHR	American Convention on Human Rights (1978)
CEDAW	Convention on the Elimination of All Forms of Discrimination Against Women (1979)
CERD	International Convention on the Elimination of All Forms of Racial Discrimination (1965)
CFR	Code of Federal Regulations
DALY	disability-adjusted life years
DPI	Disabled Peoples' International
EC Treaty	Treaty establishing the European Community (1957, as revised)
ECHR	European Convention on Human Rights (1950)
ECOSOC	Economic and Social Council of the UN
ESC	European Social Charter (1961; revised in 1986)
ICCPR	International Covenant on Civil and Political Rights (1966)
ICD	International Classification of Diseases
ICESCR	International Covenant on Economic, Social and Cultural Rights (1966)
ICIDH	International Classification of Impairments, Disabilities and Handicaps
OAS	Organisation of American States
QALY	quality adjusted life years
UDHR	Universal Declaration of Human Rights (1948)
UPIAS	Union of the Physically Impaired Against Segregation
UN Charter	United Nations Charter (1945)
U.K.	United Kingdom
U.S.	United States of America
WHO	World Health Organization

Appendix B

References to and Definitions of Disability in Legal Texts

AUSTRALIA

Disability Discrimination Act 1992

Section 4—Interpretation

(1) In this Act, unless the contrary intention appears:

. . .

"disability," in relation to a person, means:

(a) total or partial loss of the person's bodily or mental functions; or

(b) total or partial loss of a part of the body; or

(c) the presence in the body of organisms causing disease or illness; or

(d) the presence in the body of organisms capable of causing disease or illness; or

(e) the malfunction, malformation or disfigurement of a part of the person's body; or

(f) a disorder or malfunction that results in the person learning differently from a person without the disorder or malfunction; or

(g) a disorder, illness or disease that affects a person's thought processes, perception of reality, emotions or judgment or that results in disturbed behaviour;

and includes a disability that:

(h) presently exists; or

(i) previously existed but no longer exists; or

(j) may exist in the future; or

(k) is imputed to a person.

CANADA

Canadian Charter of Rights and Freedoms (1982)

Section 15—Equality rights

1. Every individual is equal before and under the law and has the right to the equal protection and equal benefit of the law without discrimination and, in particular, without discrimination based on race, national or ethnic origin, colour, religion, sex, age or mental or physical disability.
2. Subsection (1) does not preclude any law, program or activity that has as its object the amelioration of conditions of disadvantaged individuals or groups including those that are disadvantaged because of race, national or ethnic origin, colour, religion, sex, age or mental or physical disability.

Canadian Human Rights Act (1985)

Section 3—Prohibited grounds for discrimination

1. For all purposes of this Act, the prohibited grounds of discrimination are race, national or ethnic origin, colour, religion, age, sex, sexual orientation, marital status, family status, disability and conviction for which a pardon has been granted.
2. Where the ground of discrimination is pregnancy or child-birth, the discrimination shall be deemed to be on the ground of sex.

Section 25—Definitions

In this Act,

. . .

"disability" means any previous or existing mental or physical disability and includes disfigurement and previous or existing dependence on alcohol or a drug.

Employment Equity Act (1995)

Section 2—Purpose of Act

The purpose of this Act is to achieve equality in the workplace so that no person shall be denied employment opportunities or benefits for reasons unrelated to ability and, in the fulfilment of that goal, to correct the conditions of disadvantage in employment experienced by women, aboriginal peoples, persons with disabilities and members of visible minorities by giving effect to the principle that employment equity means more than treating persons in the same way but also requires special measures and the accommodation of differences.

Section 3—Definitions

In this Act,

. . .

"persons with disabilities" means persons who have a long-term or recurring physical, mental, sensory, psychiatric or learning impairment and who

(a) consider themselves to be disadvantaged in employment by reason of that impairment, or

(b) believe that a employer or potential employer is likely to consider them to be disadvantaged in employment by reason of that impairment,

and includes persons whose functional limitations owing to their impairment have been accommodated in their current job or workplace;

. . .

European Communities/European Union

European Commission

People with disabilities do not constitute a homogeneous group and there is a broad range of disabilities and issues. Disabilities may be apparent or hidden, severe or mild, singular or multiple, chronic or intermittent. Types of disabilities include mobility/agility, mental/cognitive, hearing, speaking, and visual impairments (Commission 2000 at 4).

"people with disabilities" is taken to include any person with an impairment of a physical, sensory, mental, or intellectual nature who faces obstacles to participation on equal and equally effective terms with all others in all aspects of life of the community (Commission 1996)

FINLAND

Constitution 2000

Section 6—Equality

Everyone is equal before the law.

No one shall, without an acceptable reason, be treated differently from other persons on the ground of sex, age, origin, language, religion, conviction, opinion, health, disability or other reason that concerns his or her person.

Children shall be treated equally and as individuals and they shall be allowed to influence matters pertaining to themselves to a degree corresponding to their level of development.

Equality of the sexes is promoted in societal activity and working life, especially in the determination of pay and the other terms of employment, as provided in more detail by an Act.

GERMANY

Constitution (1949)

Article 3—Gleichheit vor dem Gesetz [Equality]

(1) Alle Menschen sind vor dem Gesetz gleich [All humans are equal before the law].

(2) Männer und Frauen sind gleichberechtigt. Der Staat fördert die tatsächliche Durchsetzung der Gleichberechtigung von Frauen und Männern und wirkt auf die Beseitigung bestehender Nachteile hin [Men and women are equal. The State supports the effective realisation of equality of women and men and works towards abolishing present disadvantages].

(3) Niemand darf wegen seines Geschlechtes, seiner Abstammung, seiner Rasse, siener Sprache, seiner Heimat und Herkunft, seines Glaubens, seiner religiösen oder politischen Anschauungen benachteiligt oder bevorzugt werden. Niemand darf wegen seiner Behinderung benachteiligt werden [No one may be favoured or disadvantaged because of his sex, his parentage, his race, his language, his homeland and origin, his faith, or his religious or political opinions. No one may be disadvantaged because of his handicap].

INDIA

Constitution 1950

Article 14 Equality before law

The State shall not deny to any person equality before the law or the equal protection of the laws within the territory of India.

Article 15 Prohibition of discrimination on grounds of religion, race, caste, sex or place of birth

(1) The State shall not discriminate against any citizen on grounds only of religion, race, caste, sex, place of birth or any of them.

(2) No citizen shall, on ground only of religion, race, caste, sex, place of birth or any of them, be subject to any disability, liability, restriction or condition with regard to —

(a) access to shops, public restaurants, hotels and places of public entertainment; or

(b) the use of wells, tanks, bathing ghats, roads and places of public resort maintained whole or partly out of State funds or dedicated to the use of [the] general public.

(3) Nothing in this article shall prevent the State from making any special provision for women and children.

(4) Nothing in this article or in clause (2) or article 29 shall prevent the State from making any special provision for the advancement of any socially and educationally backward classes of citizens or for the Scheduled Castes and the Scheduled Tribes.

IRELAND

Employment Equality Act, Act No. 21 of 1998

Section 2—Interpretation

(1) In this Act, unless the context otherwise requires-

. . .

"disability" means—

(a) the total or partial absence of a person's bodily or mental functions, including the absence of a part of a person's body,

(b) the presence in the body of organisms causing, or likely to cause, chronic disease or illness,

(c) the malfunctioning, malformation or disfigurement of a part of a person's body,

(d) a condition or malfunction which results in a person learning differently from a person without the condition or malfunction, or

(e) a condition, illness or disease which affects a person's thought process, perception of reality, emotions or judgement or which results in disturbed behaviour,

and shall be taken to include a disability which exists at present, or which previously existed but no longer exists, or which may exist in the future or which is imputed to a person.

. . .

Equal Status Act, Act No. 8 of 2000

Part 1—Preliminary

. . .

2(1) In this Act, unless the context otherwise requires—

. . .

"disability" means—

(a) the total or partial absence of a person's bodily or mental functions, including the absence of a part of a person's body,

(b) the presence in the body of organisms causing, or likely to cause, chronic disease or illness,

(c) the malfunctioning, malformation or disfigurement of a part of a person's body,

(d) a condition or malfunction which results in a person learning differently from a person without the condition or malfunction, or

(e) a condition, illness or disease which affects a person's thought process, perception of reality, emotions or judgement or which results in disturbed behaviour;

. . .

ITALY

Constitution 2000

Article 3 [Equality]

(1) All citizens possess an equal social status and are equal before the law, without distinction as to sex, race, language, religion, political opinions, and personal or social conditions.

(2) It is the duty of the Republic to remove all economic and social obstacles which, by limiting the freedom and equality of citizens, prevent the full development of the individual and the participation of all workers in the political, economic, and social organization of the country.

NEW ZEALAND

Bill of Rights Act 1990

Section 19 Freedom from Discrimination

(1) Everyone has the right to freedom from discrimination on the grounds of discrimination in the Human Rights Act 1993.

(2) Measures taken in good faith for the purpose of assisting or advancing persons or groups of persons disadvantaged because of discrimination that is unlawful by virtue of Part II of the Human Rights Act 1993 do not constitute discrimination.

Human Rights Act 1993*

Section 21 Prohibited grounds of discrimination.

(1) For the purposes of this Act, the prohibited grounds of discrimination are:

. . .

(h) disability, which means:

(i) physical disability or impairment;

(ii) physical illness;

(iii) psychiatric illness;

---

* On the basis of a description of the act through <www.hrc.co.nz>. The present author was, unfortunately, unable to retrieve a full copy of the act.

(iv) intellectual or psychological disability or impairment;
(v) any other loss or abnormality of psychological, physiological, or anatomical structure or function;
(vi) reliance on a guide dog, wheelchair or other remedial means;
(vii) the presence in the body of organisms capable of causing illness;

ORGANISATION OF AMERICAN STATES

The Inter-American Convention on the Elimination of All Forms of Discrimination against People with Disabilities (1999)

Article 1

For the purpose of this Convention, the following terms are defined:
Disability
The term "disability" means a physical, mental, or sensory impairment, whether permanent or temporary, that limits the capacity to perform one or more essential activities of daily life, and which can be caused or aggravated by the economic and social environment.

SPAIN

Constitution 1978

Article 14

(1) Los españoles son iguales ante la ley, sin que pueda prevalecer discriminación alguna por razón de nacimiento, raza, sexo, religión, opinión o cualquir otra condición o circunstancia personal o social [Spaniards are equal before the law, without any distinction because of birth, race, sex, religion, opinion or any other personal or social condition or circumstances].

SOUTH AFRICA

Employment Equity Act (Act No. 55 of 1998)

Section 1—Definitions

In this Act, unless the context otherwise indicates—

. . .

"people with disabilities" means people who have long-term or recurring physical or mental impairment which substantially limits their prospects of entry into, or advancement in, employment;

Promotion of Equality and Prevention of Unfair Discrimination Act (Act No. 4 of 2000)

Section 1—Definitions

In this Act, unless the context indicates otherwise—

. . .

(viii) "discrimination" means any act or omission, including policy, law, rule, practice, condition or situation which directly or indirectly—

(a) imposes burdens, obligations or disadvantage on; or

(b) withholds benefits, opportunities or advantages from,

any person on one or more of the prohibited grounds;

(xiv) "HIV/AIDS status" includes actual or perceived presence in a person's body of the Human Immunodeficiency Virus (HIV) or symptoms of Acquired Immune Deficiency Syndrome (AIDS), as well as adverse assumptions based on this status;

(xxii) "prohibited grounds" are—

(*a*) race, gender, sex, pregnancy, marital status, ethnic or social origin, colour, sexual orientation, age, disability, religion, conscience, belief, culture, language and birth; or

b) any other ground where discrimination based on that other ground—

(i) causes or perpetuates systemic disadvantage;

(ii) undermines human dignity; or

(iii) adversely affects the equal enjoyment of a person's rights and freedoms in a serious manner that is comparable to discrimination on a ground in paragraph (*a*);

SWEDEN

Lag (1999:132) om förbud mot diskriminering i arbetslivet av personer med funktionshinder

Lagens ändamål

1 Denna lag har til ändamål att motverka diskriminering i arbetslivet av personer med funtionshinder [The aim of this act is to eliminate discrimination at work of persons with functional limitations].

2 Med funktionshinder avses varaktiga fysiska, psychiska eller begåvningsmässiga begränsningar av en persons funktionsförmåga som till fjöld av en skada eller en sjukdom fanns vid födelsen, har uppstått därefter eller kan förväntas uppstå [Functional limitations are substantial physical, mental or intellectual restrictions of a person's functional capacities as a result of an injury or disease at birth, which have manifested themselves afterwards or which may occur in the future].

UNITED KINGDOM

Disability Discrimination Act 1995 (1995 c. 50)

Section 1—Meaning of "disability" and "disabled person"

(1) Subject to the provisions of Schedule 1, a person has a disability for the purposes of this Act if he has a physical or mental impairment which has a substantial and long-term adverse effect on his ability to carry out normal day-to-day activities.

(2) In this Act "disabled person" means a person who has a disability.

Section 2—Past disabilities

(1) The provisions of this Part and Parts II and III apply in relation to a person who has had a disability as they apply in relation to a person who has that disability.

(2) Those provisions are subject to the modifications made by Schedule 2.

. . .

UNITED NATIONS

Standard Rules on the Equalization of Opportunities for People with Disabilities (1993)

17. The term "disability" summarizes a great number of different functional limitations occurring in any population in any country of the world. People may be disabled by physical, intellectual or sensory impairment, medical conditions or mental illness. Such impairments, conditions or illnesses may be permanent or transitory in nature.

UNITED STATES

Americans with Disabilities Act (1990) [42 U.S.C.]

Section 12102 [Sec. 3—Definitions]

As used in this chapter:

. . .

(2) Disability—The term "disability" means, with respect to an individual—

(A) a physical or mental impairment that substantially limits one or more of the major life activities of such individual.

(B) a record of such an impairment; or

(C) being regarded as having such an impairment.

Section 12211 [Sec. 511—Definitions]

(a) Homosexuality and bisexuality—For purposes of the definition of "disability" in section 12102(2) of this title, homosexuality and bisexuality are not impairments and as such are not disabilities under this chapter.

(b) Certain conditions—Under this chapter, the term "disability" shall not include—

(1) transvestism, transsexualism, pedophilia, exhibitionism, voyeurism, gender identity disorders not resulting from physical impairments, or other sexual behavior disorders;

(2) compulsive gambling, kleptomania, or pyromania; or

(c) psychoactive substance use disorders resulting from current illegal use of drugs.

Equal Employment Opportunity Commission—Regulations to implement the equal employment provisions of the Americans with Disabilities Act

29 CFR § 1630.2 Definitions.

(h) Physical or mental impairment means:

(1) Any physiological disorder, or condition, cosmetic disfigurement, or anatomical loss affecting one or more of the following body systems: neurological, musculoskeletal, special sense organs, respiratory (including speech organs), cardiovascular, reproductive, digestive, genito-urinary, hemic and lymphatic, skin, and endocrine; or

(2) Any mental or psychological disorder, such as mental retardation, organic brain syndrome, emotional or mental illness, and specific learning disabilities.

Appendix C

References

I DOCTRINE

Abberley, P. (1987). "The Concept of Oppression and the Development of a Social Theory of Disability." *Disability, Handicap & Society*, 2 (1), 5–19.

Aristotle (1980). *The Nicomachean Ethics*. Oxford / New York: Oxford University Press (translated by D. Ross and revised by J. L. Ackrill & J. O. Urmson). Series: *The World's Classics*.

Banton, M. (1999). "Discrimination Entails Comparison." *In* T. Loenen & P. R. Rodrigues (Eds), *Non-Discrimination Law: Comparative Perspectives: A Case for Anti-discrimination Legislation* (pp. 107–117). The Hague / London / Boston: Kluwer Law International.

Barnes, C. (1991). *Disabled People in Britain and Discrimination*. London: C. Hurst & Company.

Bickenbach, J. E. (1999). "Minority Rights or Universal Participation: The Politics of Disablement." *In* M. Jones & L. A. Basser Marks (Eds), *Disability, Divers-ability & Legal Change* (pp. 101–116). The Hague / Boston / London: Martinus Nijhoff Publishers. Series: *International Studies in Human Rights, v. 56*.

Bickenbach, J. E., Chatterji, S., Badley, E. M. & Üstün, T. B. (1999). "Models of Disablement, Universalism and the International Classification of Disabilities and Handicaps." *Social Science & Medicine*, 48, 1173–1187.

Borgetto, M. (1999). "Équité, égalité des chances et politique de lutte contre les exclusions" [Equity, Equal Opportunities and Policy to Fight Exclusions]. *Droit Social* [Social Law], 61 (3), 221–29.

Busschbach, J. J. van (1994). *De validiteit van QALY's* [The Validity of QALYs]. Arnhem: Gouda Quint.

Commission (1996). *Communication of the Commission on Equality of Opportunity for People with Disabilities—A New European Community Disability Strategy—Draft Resolution of the Council and of Representatives of the Governments of the Member States*

Meeting Within the Council on Equality of Opportunity for People with Disabilities (presented by the Commission), COM(96) 406 final. Brussels: Commission of the European Communities.

Commission (1999). *Proposal for a Council Directive Establishing a General Framework for Equal Treatment in Employment and Occupation*, COM(99) 565 final. Brussels: Commission of the European Communities.

Commission (2000). *Communication from the Commission to the Council, the European Parliament, the Economic and Social Committee and the Committee of the Regions—Towards a Barrier Free Europe for People with Disabilities*, COM(2000) 284 final. Brussels: Commission of the European Communities.

Council (1996). Resolution of the Council and of the Representatives of the Governments of the Member States Meeting Within the Council of 20 December 1996 on Equality of Opportunities for People with Disabilities. *Official Journal*, No. C 1997 12/1–2.

Degener, Th. (1995). "Disabled Persons and Human Rights: The Legal Framework." *In* Th. Degener & Y. Koster-Dreese (Eds), *Human Rights and Disabled Persons: Essays and Relevant Human Rights Instruments* (pp. 9–39). Dordrecht / Boston / London: Martinus Nijhoff Publishers.

Disability Rights Task Force (1999). *From Exclusion to Inclusion: A Report of the Disability Rights Task Force on Civil Rights for Disabled People*. London: Disability Rights Task Force.

European Parliament (1993). Resolution B3-0580/93 on the Upsurge of Violence Against Handicapped Persons. *Official Journal*, No. C 150/270, 31 May 1993.

French, S. (1994). "What is Disability?" *In* S. French (Ed.), *On Equal Terms: Working with Disabled People* (pp. 3–11). Oxford: Butterworth & Heinemann.

Fougeyrollas, P. (1998). "La classification québecoise du processus du handicap et la révision de la CIDIH" [The Quebec Classification of the Handicap Creation Process and the Revision of the ICIDH]. *Handicaps et Inadaptations*, 79/80, 85–103.

Goldschmidt J. E. (1997). "Het gelijkheidsbeginsel. Gelijk zijn en het gelijke krijgen is twee" [The Principle of Equality. Being Equal and Being Treated as an Equal are Two]. *Justitiële Verkenningen*, 23 (9), 8–19.

Groce, N. E. & Zola, I. K. (1993). "Multiculturalism, Chronic Illness, and Disability." *Pediatrics* 91 (5), 1048–55.

Gutow, B. (1998), "Survey of Rights of Workers with Disabilities: Comparison of the United States with the European Community." *New York International Law Review*, 11, 101–130.

Hahn, H. (1985). "Toward a Politics of Disability: Definitions, Disciplines, and Policies." *The Social Science Journal*, 22 (4), 87–105.

Hahn, H. (1986). "Public Support for Rehabilitation Programmes: the Analysis of US Disability Policy." *Disability, Handicap & Society*, 1 (2), 121–138.

Halbertsma, J. (1995). "The ICIDH: Health Problems in a Medical and Social Perspective." *Disability and Rehabilitation*, 17 (3/4), 128–134.

Hendriks, A. C. (1995), "Disabled Persons and their Right to Equal Treatment: Allowing Differentiation While Ending Discrimination." *Health and Human Rights*, 1 (2), 152–173.

Hendriks, A. C. (1999). "From Social (In)Security to Equal Employment Opportunities—a Report from the Netherlands." *In* M. Jones & L. A. Basser Marks (Eds), *Disability, Divers-ability & Legal Change* (pp. 153–69). The Hague / Boston / London: Martinus Nijhoff Publishers.

Hendriks, A. C. (2000). *Gelijke toegang tot de arbeid voor gehandicapten* [Equal Access to Employment for People with Disabilities]. Deventer: Kluwer.

Human Rights Committee (1990). *General Comment 18/37 Non-discrimination*. U.N. GAOR, 45th Sess., Supp. No. 40, U.N. Doc. A/45/40, pp. 173–175.

Klosse, S. (1989). *Menselijke schade: vergoeden of herstellen?* [Human Harm: Compensating or Repairing]. Antwerpen / Apeldoorn: Maklu.

Liachowitz, C. H. (1988). *Disability as a Social Construct: Legislative Roots*. Philadelphia, PA: University of Pennsylvania Press.

Loenen, T. (1995). "Substantive Equality as a Right to Inclusion: Dilemmas and Limits in Law." *Rechtsfilosofie en Rechtstheorie* [Philosophy of Law and Theory of Law], 24 (3), 194–203.

Mayerson, A. B. (1997). "Restoring Regard for the 'Regarded as' Prong: Giving Effect to Congressional Intent." *Villanova Law Review*, 42 (2), 587–612.

McKean, W. A. (1971). "The Meaning of Discrimination in International and Municipal Law." *The British Year Book of International Law 1970* (pp. 177–92). London: Royal Institute of International Affairs.

Oliver, M. (1985). "Discrimination, Disability and Social Policy." *In* M. Brenton & C. Jones (Eds.), *The Year Book of Social Policy* (pp. 74–97). London: Routledge and Kegan Paul.

Oliver, M. (1990). *The Politics of Disablement.* London: Macmillan 1990.

Parmet, W. E. & Jackson, D. J. (1997). "No Longer Disabled: The Legal Impact of the New Social Construction of HIV." *American Journal of Law & Medicine*, 23 (1), 7–43.

Pinder, R. (1995). "Bringing Back the Body Without the Blame?—The Experience of Ill and Disabled People at Work." *Sociology of Health & Illness*, 17 (5), 605–631.

Priestly, M. (1998). "Constructions and Creations: Idealism, Materialism and Disability Theory." *Disability & Society*, 13 (1), 75–94.

Ramcharan, B. G. (1981). "Equality and Non-discrimination." *In* L. Henkin (Ed.), *The International Bill of Rights: The Covenant on Civil and Political Rights* (pp. 246–69). New York: Columbia University Press.

Rebell, M. A. (1986). "Structural Discrimination and the Rights of the Disabled." *Georgetown Law Journal*, 74 (5), 1435–89.

Rioux, M. H. (1997). "Disability: The Place of Judgement in a World of Fact." *Journal of Intellectual Disability Research*, 41 (2), 102–11.

Secretary-General (1992). *Social Development: Questions Relating to the World Social Situation and to Youth, Ageing, Disabled Persons and the Family; Implementation of the World Programme of Action concerning Disabled Persons and the United Nations Decade of Disabled Persons*, U.N. Doc. A/47/415 (11 September 1992).

Shakespeare, T. (1999). "What is a Disabled Person?" *In* M. Jones & L.A. Basser Marks (Eds), *Disability, Divers-ability & Legal Change* (pp. 25–34). The Hague / Boston / London: Martinus Nijhoff Publishers.

Skogly, S. (1992). "Article 2." *In* A. Eide *et al.* (Eds.), *The Universal Declaration of Human Rights. A Commentary* (pp. 57–72). Oslo: Scandinavian University Press.

Swiebel, J. (2000). *Working Document on the Proposal for a Council Directive Establishing a General Framework for Equal Treatment in Employment and Occupation.* Brussels: European Parliament/ Committee on Citizens' Freedoms and Rights, Justice and Home Affairs, PE 285.927 (6 June 2000).

UPIAS (1976). *Fundamental Principles of Disability*. London: Union of Physically Impaired Against Segregation.

Vienna (1993). *Vienna Declaration and Programme of Action. Final Document of the World Conference on Human Rights* (Vienna, 14–25 June 1993). U.N. Doc. A/CONF.157/23.

Vierdag, E. W. (1973). *The Concept of Discrimination in International Law*. The Hague: Martinus Nijhoff Publishers.

Waddington, L. (1995a). *Disability, Employment and the European Community*. Antwerp: Maklu *et al.* [under the auspices of METRO —Institute for Transnational Legal Research at the University of Limburg, Maastricht].

Waddington, L. (1995b). "Working Towards a European Definition of Disability." *European Journal of Health Law*, 2 (3), 255–260.

WHO (1980). *International Classification of Impairments, Disabilities, and Handicaps: A Manual of Classification Relating to the Consequences of Disease*. Geneva: World Health Organization.

Wolfensberger, W. (1981). "The Extermination of Handicapped People in World War II Germany." *Mental Retardation*, 19 (1), 1–7.

World Bank (1993). *World Development Report 1993: Investing in Health*. Oxford: Oxford University Press.

Zola, I. K. (1993). "Self, Identity and the Naming Question: Reflections on the Language of Disability." *Social Science & Medicine*, 36 (2), 167–73.

II CASE LAW

Court of Justice of the EC [http://www.europa.eu.int/cj/en]

Case 96/80 *Jenkins v. Kinsgate* [1981] *E.C.R.*, p. 911

Case 170/84 *Bilka Kaufhaus v. Weber von Hartz* [1986] *E.C.R.*, p. 1607

Case 109/88 *Danmark v. Danfoss* [1989] *E.C.R.*, p. 3199

Case C-177/88 *Dekker v. Stichting Vormingscentrum voor Jong Volwassen Plus* [1990] *E.C.R.*, p. I-3941

Case C-450/93 *Kalanke v. Bremen* [1995] *E.C.R.*, p. I-3051

Case C-249/96 *Grant v. South-West Trains Ltd.* [1998] *E.C.R.*, p. I-621

Case C-407/98 *Abrahamsson & Anderson v. Fogelqvist* [2000] E.C.R., p. I-5539

European Court of Human Rights [http://www.echr.coe.int/]

Belgian Linguistic Case (23 July 1968), *A*-6

Winterwerp v. The Netherlands (24 October 1979), *A*-33

Abdulaziz, Cabales and Balkandali v. The United Kingdom (28 May 1985), *A*-94

Darby v. Sweden (23 October 1990), *A*-187

Thlimmenos v. Greece (6 April 2000), not published yet [www.dhcour.coe.int/hudoc]

Human Rights Committee

Broeks v. The Netherlands (Views adopted on 9 April 1987), Communication No. 172/1984, U.N. GAOR, 42nd Sess., Supp. No. 40, at 139, U.N. Doc. A/42/40 (1987)

Toonen v. Australia (Views adopted on 31 March 1994), Communication No. 488/1992, U.N. GAOR, 49th Sess., Supp. No. 40, Vol. II, at 226, U.N. Doc. A/49/40 (1992)

Debreczeny v. The Netherlands (Views adopted on 3 April 1995), Communication No. 500/1992, U.N. GAOR, 50th Sess., Supp. No. 40, Vol. II, at 59, U.N. Doc. A/50/40 (1999)

Supreme Court of Canada

Bliss v. Attorney General of Canada, [1979] 1 S.C.R. 183

Andrews v. Law Society of British Columbia, [1989] 1 S.C.R. 143

United States Supreme Court

Buck v. Bell, 274 U.S. 200 (1927)

Griggs v. Duke Power Company Co., 401 U.S. 424 (1971)

Frontiero v. Richardson, 411 U.S. 677 (1973)

Massachusetts Bd. of Retirement v. Murgia, 427 U.S. 307 (1976)

Southeastern Community College v. Davis, 442 U.S. 397 (1979)

Adarand Constructors, Inc. v. Peña, 515 U.S. 200 (1995)

Oncale v. Sundowner Offshore Services, Inc., 118 S.Ct. 998 (1998)

Bragdon v. Abbott, 524 U.S. 624 (1998)

Sutton v. United Airlines, Inc., 119 S.Ct. 2139 (1999)

Murphy v. United Parcel Service, Inc., 119 S.Ct. 2133 (1999)

Albertsons, Inc. v. Kirkingburg, 119 S.Ct. 2162 (1999)

Tensions and Coherence in Disability Policy: The Uneasy Relationship Between Social Welfare and Civil Rights Models of Disability in American, European and International Employment Law

Lisa Waddington and Matthew Diller***

A. INTRODUCTION

For a number of years disability activists in both North America and many parts of Western Europe have argued for a re-evaluation of the concept of disability and the thinking behind disability policy.[1] They have sought a re-conceptualization of the notion of disability, based on both a recognition of the role which physical and attitudinal barriers play in excluding people with disabilities (a key tenant of the civil rights model of disability), and a rejection of the assumption that medical

---

* Associate Professor in Law, Maastricht University, The Netherlands and Legal Adviser to the European Disability Forum. This article was written in a personal capacity. Work on this article was commenced in Maastricht and completed at the University of British Columbia, Vancouver, Canada. Lisa Waddington would like to thank the Faculty of Law at the University of British Columbia for hosting her during her sabbatical and the Human Rights Research School of Maastricht University for providing financial support for the duration of the sabbatical. Both authors are very grateful to DREDF for having taken the initiative in organising the conference "Principles to Practice" and to the financial backers of the Conference. We are particularly grateful to the conference participants whose helpful comments were of immense assistance in completing the article.

** Professor, Fordham University School of Law.

1 We recognize that similar advocacy efforts have been and are taking place in many other parts of the world, but numerous factors have influenced us to focus this paper on the geographic areas mentioned.

impairments automatically result in disadvantage and exclusion (an assumption inherent in the social welfare model of disability). In many cases the key demand of disability activists has been the adoption of disability anti-discrimination legislation, and these campaigns have not been without success.[2] The adoption of disability anti-discrimination legislation also reflects the acceptance by policy makers of the civil rights model of disability.

However, this recognition of the civil rights model has not resulted in a complete overhaul of disability policy. Instead newer policy instruments, inspired by the civil rights model, have been added to existing and older instruments, such as the long-established social security schemes, segregated education and housing programs, and employment quotas which were originally inspired by the social welfare model. As a result, disability-related instruments which ostensibly have the same goals, such as promoting employment or education, have completely different starting points and send out conflicting messages about the abilities of people with disabilities. This problem is compounded by the fact that, in some cases, the disability activists and policy makers who support a civil rights model of disability and anti-discrimination legislation also support the extension and strengthening of some elements of disability policy, such as social security schemes and employment quotas, that traditionally have been motivated by a social welfare model of disability.

The purpose of this article is to examine the relationship between the social welfare and civil rights models in disability policy, and to consider whether the tension between the two models can be resolved or lessened, and indeed, to what extent the tension is problematic. We also consider whether, in the alternative, a new conception of disability policy is needed which can achieve coherence amongst existing practices and instruments that are incompatible when viewed in terms of the established models. In making this examination we shall confine ourselves to the area of employment; however, these tensions and issues are

---

2 One thinks of the campaigns to secure the adoption of the Americans with Disabilities Act of 1990, the inclusion of a general non-discrimination clause within the revised Treaty of the European Community (the Amsterdam Treaty), and the adoption of the British Disability Discrimination Act 1995.

also evident in many other areas of disability policy and our conclusions are also relevant for these areas.

Following a brief outline of the two established models, we discuss existing situations through case studies focussing on the United States and Western Europe. In addition we consider whether the tension between the two models can also be identified at the international level. After this analysis we reflect on whether support for people with disabilities, such as affirmative action policies, can be reconciled with the civil rights model. We conclude by considering whether an alternative understanding of disability and disability policy could achieve the coherence which is currently lacking.

B. THE SOCIAL WELFARE AND CIVIL RIGHTS MODELS OF DISABILITY POLICY

On both sides of the Atlantic, countries have struggled to deal with the dilemmas clustered around the intersection of work and disability. At root, the choice is one between a strategy of exclusion, that views disability as both an excuse from the obligation to work and a ground for denying employment, or a strategy of inclusion, that creates an expectation that people with disabilities continue in the workforce and a requirement that employers accept them. Because neither one of these polarities fully captures the complexity of societal views about disability and work, neither offers a complete and satisfying response. Not surprisingly, both the United States and the nations of Western Europe have dealt with the problem through a series of policies that frequently fail to add up to a coherent whole. More often than not, both employers and people with disabilities are given mixed signals concerning the expectations that society places on them. In various ways, people with disabilities are told they should work, but are simultaneously encouraged to stay home or shunted into segregated work settings. Employers are instructed to provide jobs, and yet are excused from doing so.

Nonetheless, there are commonalities among these mixed signals. These commonalities stem from the fact that the basic ways of viewing disability transcend national borders. In both Europe and the United States, the medical model, which conceives of disability as a medical defect in the individual, has had an enormous influence on policy. In both regions, a civil rights model, which focuses on the societal response to disability, has gained strength and influence in recent years. Moreover, on both sides of the Atlantic the two models have established an uneasy coexistence.[3] However, because of differences in social and cultural contexts, the particular policies which emerge from these models are sometimes quite different. This section identifies the social welfare and civil rights models that form the core assumptions upon which disability policy is based, and examines the tensions between the two models.

1. Models of Disability Policy

Disability policies are rooted in core assumptions about the nature of disabilities and the obligations of both individuals and society. These core assumptions can be grouped into a number of distinct models that inform and animate particular policies. In this article, we will focus on two of these models: the social welfare model and the civil rights model.

a. The Social Welfare Model

Under the social welfare model, disability is seen as a defect in an individual that renders him or her unable to work or function in society in a conventional way. In this approach, social institutions such as employment and public services are designed to meet the needs of the non-disabled. Rather than adapting these institutions to accommodate disabilities, people with disabilities are directed toward a separate parallel track that provides income and services apart from the institutions that serve the non-disabled majority. In the area of employment, people with disabilities are either pensioned off, or placed in segregated jobs for the disabled. This two track approach can also be seen in education, transportation and other areas.

The social welfare model has proven dominant because it poses no threat to mainstream institutions. It permits society to establish public services and social institutions without regard for people with disabilities, since it adopts the premise that medical limitations will inevitably

---

[3] This trend is also notable in parts of Africa, Australia, South America, and Asia.

render people with disabilities unable to participate. The exclusion of people with disabilities is thus accepted as an inevitable natural consequence of medical realities.

At the same time, people with disabilities are not completely ignored. Instead, policies and programs are developed to address what the non-disabled perceive as basic needs. People with disabilities may be offered income support such as public assistance or pensions, housing, schooling, and even special jobs. This parallel track is an essential component of the social welfare model, because it justifies the failure to include people with disabilities in mainstream institutions. It allows society to exclude people with disabilities with a clear conscience. Nonetheless, the social welfare model is not necessarily or inherently begrudging or miserly. Indeed, non-disabled people may view the parallel set of institutions that serve the disabled as generous and desirable.

In the end, regardless of its justifications or how people feel about it, the social welfare model must place heavy emphasis on sorting and labelling. It inevitably relies on mechanisms to determine which track any given individual should be directed to. In the context of income support and pension programs, individuals screened out of the disability category are expected to become part of the labor force, while those found to be "disabled" are exempted from work. Definitions of disability in these programs define the nature and extent of the social obligation to work.[4] Seen in this light, they are part and parcel of a nation's policies concerning labor and employment.

In general, the more generous the package offered to people with disabilities, the more stringent and exacting the screening mechanism. When the disability track is seen as generous, fears arise that people will seek to exploit the status of disability.[5] Generosity therefore brings with it a certain suspicion or a fear that people will pose as disabled in order to gain certain benefits.

---

[4] Matthew Diller, "Entitlement & Exclusion: The Role of Disability in the Social Welfare System," 44 *UCLA L. Rev*. 361, 386–92 (1996).

[5] *Id*. at 393–94. When benefits are provided on harsh and punitive terms, these concerns may be more muted and the boundaries of the disability category may be less zealously guarded. *Id*.

The social welfare model inevitably comes to rely on some notion of the truly disabled, the idea that there is in fact an identifiable category of people that can be treated apart from the mainstream of society.[6] In situations in which separate treatment is viewed as advantageous, enormous energy and resources may be spent in identifying the truly disabled and protecting the category from perceived malingerers and shirkers. This sorting process is most often viewed as an inquiry into medical fact rather than a moral or social judgment. This approach stems from and reinforces the idea that disability is a discrete medically determined status.

The sorting process is always problematic. There is no clear way of disaggregating the impact of a medical impairment from the other characteristics of an individual.[7] The impact of an impairment inevitably varies depending on the age, education and work experience of an individual, as well as economic and other conditions in the area or region where the individual resides. Deciding which of these factors to take into account and how to do so requires making a series of judgments about employment policy and the labor market which are distinct from, and yet inherent in, evaluating the impact of a medical impairment.

b. The Civil Rights Model

The civil rights model rejects the premise that social exclusion is an inevitable consequence of disability. Under this view, people with disabilities have historically been excluded from social institutions because those institutions have failed to adapt to the needs of the disabled, even as they routinely adapt to the needs of others. Proponents of the civil rights model posit that this failure to accommodate flows from both conscious and unconscious aversions to people with disabilities. Seen in this light, the problem is one of discrimination, rather than the need to address the inherent medical limitations imposed by disability.[8] Under

---

6 *See* Deborah A. Stone, *The Disabled State* (Philadelphia, PA.: Temple University Press, 1984).

7 Diller, *supra* note 4, at 388 (discussing the problematic role of causation in definitions of disability).

8 *See* Joseph Shapiro, *No Pity: People with Disabilities Forging a New Civil Rights Movement* (New York: Times Books, 1993).

the civil rights model, the goal of disability policy is to reform mainstream social institutions to include people with disabilities, rather than to maintain a parallel track.[9] Moreover, as the non-disabled majority gain increasing contact with people with disabilities, prejudice may abate and the necessity for legal intervention may diminish.

2. Tensions Between the Two Models

The mere description of these two models makes evident the tension between them. The two models stem from extremely different assumptions and tend toward conflicting objectives.[10] The social welfare model views disability as a medically determined status. In contrast, under the civil rights model, the limitations relating to medical conditions are the result of an interaction between the condition itself and the social context that gives significance to the condition. Accordingly, under the civil rights model, there is no objectively fixed status of disability.

A number of consequences flow from this disparity in assumptions. First, the social welfare model is built on the idea of separation, while the civil rights model focuses on inclusion. The civil rights model is directed at abolishing separate institutions for people with disabilities, and integrating the latter into the social mainstream. As the social welfare model removes people from the mainstream, the civil rights model seeks to return them. Second, the emphasis on labeling and sorting that characterizes the social welfare model emphasizes the inabilities of people with disabilities, rather than their areas of competence and capability. Mechanisms designed to identify the truly disabled require individuals to validate their status as disabled by proving various functional inabilities. Indeed, it compels people with disabilities to confess their inabilities in order to gain entry to the separate disability track. This process thereby reinforces stereotypes about the incompetence of people with disabilities. In contrast, the civil rights model emphasizes the capabilities of people with disabilities, and reluctantly accepts the

---

9 *See* Richard K. Scotch, *From Good Will to Civil Rights: Transforming Federal Disability Policy* (Philadelphia, PA.: Temple University Press, 1984).

10 *See* Matthew Diller, "Dissonant Disability Policies: The Tensions Between the Americans with Disabilities Act and Federal Disability Benefit Programs," 76 *Texas L. Rev.* 1003 (1998).

conclusion that an individual cannot perform a given task only after examining whether the task itself can be re-structured.[11]

In these ways the two models work at cross purposes. Support for those institutions based on the social welfare model can be seen as undercutting efforts to advance the civil rights model. Moreover, the civil rights model can be seen as a threat to institutions which provide benefits to people with disabilities through a separate track.

This discussion suggests that the social welfare and civil rights models cannot coexist. And yet, many nations have policies and programs based on both of these models, and in some instances, on a mixture of the two. A number of views can be advanced to attempt to reconcile these divergent policies and programs, or at least to blunt their contradictions. Two of these approaches are outlined here.

First, the coexistence of both models can be rationalized on the ground that the two models serve different people. Under this view, a subcategory of people with disabilities are seen as conforming to the assumptions of the social welfare model, while others are seen through the lens of the civil rights model. Some individuals are classified as severely disabled and tracked into a separate social welfare system while others are viewed as less impaired and encouraged to join the social mainstream. Given the broad and amorphous nature of disability, this solution has a certain appeal as it acknowledges the heterogeneous nature of disability. It depends, however, on some method of sorting individuals into these two subcategories. There is no clear way of drawing such a line, absent reliance on the social welfare model's medical approach. Moreover, this approach still involves establishing a category of people with disabilities that is segregated into a separate track. Thus, at root it relies on the outlook of the social welfare approach.

Second, people with disabilities can be given the option of choosing for themselves whether to avail themselves of civil rights policies or social welfare programs. The advantage of this approach is that it does not require formal tracking into one system or another. Moreover, it acknowledges the individual nature of disability and accords respect for the autonomy of those most affected. The question is whether soci-

---

11 *Id.*

eties will accept this approach, as it accords people with disabilities a range of choices that are not provided to others. Most members of society are subject to a social obligation to work, rather than an option.

In practice it is therefore very difficult to reconcile the two divergent models of disability. For this reason it is not surprising to find that there has frequently been no attempt to develop a logical and coherent policy. Newer policy instruments, such as anti-discrimination laws that are based on the civil rights model of disability, have been added to existing policy instruments inspired by the social welfare model. In this way numerous layers are developed in an ad hoc approach to policy development. Rarely do policy makers have the time or the inclination to take a step back and consider the coherence and logic of disability policy.

C. DISABILITY POLICY IN PRACTICE—AN EXAMINATION OF THE TENSION BETWEEN THE SOCIAL WELFARE MODEL AND THE CIVIL RIGHTS MODEL AT THE NATIONAL LEVEL

It has been noted above that disability policy is frequently based on a confused and conflicting set of assumptions and beliefs. In this section, and the following one, we will examine how the tension between the social welfare model and the civil rights model of disability manifests itself in specific national and international policies. In particular, we consider the strained relationships between anti-discrimination legislation and social security provisions in the United States, and between anti-discrimination legislation and employment quotas in Europe.

1. United States Case Study: The Relationship between Anti-discrimination Legislation and Social Security Provisions

The experience of the United States sharply illustrates the tensions between the social welfare and civil rights approaches to disability. Since the 1950s, the largest and most well-funded programs dealing with disability have been the pension programs of the Social Security Act. Beginning in 1956, the Social Security Disability Insurance (SSDI)

Program has provided income support to workers who demonstrate that they are unable to work due to medical impairments.[12] In 1972, SSDI was joined by the Supplemental Security Income (SSI) program which provides monthly payments to the disabled poor who do not have sufficient work records to qualify for SSDI.[13] With the enactment of the Americans with Disabilities Act of 1990 (ADA), civil rights protections were added to these public pension programs as a basic part of U.S. disability policy. The ADA prohibits employers from discriminating against people with disabilities in hiring, promotion and other aspects of employment.

At the time the ADA was enacted, scant attention was paid to the relationship between these two approaches. To the extent the issue was considered, it was simply assumed that the ADA's emphasis on employment would reduce expenditures on income support. As the ADA took effect, however, it became clear that the interaction between the ADA and the disability benefit programs was far more complex, and in many ways, quite troubling.

a. The Social Security Act

The disability benefit programs of the Social Security Act view disability as analogous to old age—a condition that calls for long-term or permanent excuse from any obligation to work and acts as a justification for social support. The proposal to add a disability program to the Act in the 1950s was highly contentious. Proponents argued that disability benefits constitute a form of early retirement for those whose health has broken down prematurely. As a result, eligibility for SSDI and SSI is predicated upon a finding that an applicant is unable to engage in substantial gainful activity by reason of any medically determinable physical or mental impairment which can be expected to last for a continuous

---

[12] For histories of SSDI, *see* Edward Berkowitz, *Disabled Policy: America's Programs for the Handicapped* (Cambridge; New York: Cambridge University Press, 1987); Matthew Diller, UCLA, *supra* note 4; Stone, *supra* note 6.

[13] SSDI is only available to individuals with a substantial work record who become disabled within five years of when they stop working. It thus envisions disability as an acquired status. The SSDI program has no means test.

period of not less than 12 months.[14] The law further states that an individual can only be found to meet this standard if he or she is not only unable to do his previous work but cannot, considering the individual's age, education and work experience, engage in any other kind of work which exists in the national economy.[15] In essence, benefits are available only to those who are incapable of performing both their past jobs and other jobs for which they would otherwise be qualified.

The Social Security Administration (SSA) administers these requirements through an elaborate process. Individuals must present extensive medical and often testimonial evidence about their impairments and functional limitations. In many cases, the process of establishing eligibility takes years. Because of the strict eligibility requirements and the administrative obstacles, a determination of eligibility for disability benefits is difficult to obtain.

Over the years, Congress has enacted a number of provisions intended to encourage disability benefit recipients to return to work, such as creating a trial work period in which an individual can work without jeopardizing his or her benefits. However, these provisions have had little impact to date. It is not surprising that after requiring applicants to go through a torturous process to get benefits, few of those who succeed would risk the attempt to turn around and reenter the work force. President Clinton recently signed into law the Ticket to Work and Work Incentives Improvement Act of 1999, which expands the availability of health coverage and employment services for disability benefit recipients who seek to return to the work force. The impact of this new law is not yet clear.[16]

The disability benefit programs of the Social Security Act are rooted in the social welfare model. They are based on the assumption that the disabled are incapable of work and should be supported outside of the mainstream market economy. They are also predicated on the idea that disability is an objective medically determinable status, and rely on an elaborate sorting procedure to screen people into and out of the dis-

---

14 42 U.S.C. § 423(d).

15 42 U.S.C. § 423(d)(2)(A).

16 The new law is discussed further *infra.*, at the end of section E.1.

ability category. Although the expansion of programs and services to encourage and help benefits recipients return to the work force reflects an attempt to shift the social welfare paradigm, no transformation has yet taken place.

b. The Americans With Disabilities Act

Title I of the ADA prohibits employers from discriminating against people with disabilities. The Act defines discrimination as the denial of equal jobs or benefits to a qualified individual because of a known disability. It also establishes that the failure to provide reasonable accommodations for the known physical or mental limitations of an individual with a disability is a form of discrimination, unless an employer can show that the accommodation would impose an undue burden. The principal enforcement mechanism of the ADA is the civil law suit. In order to establish a case, an ADA plaintiff must demonstrate, among other things, that he or she is qualified for the job, meaning that he or she can—with or without accommodations—perform the essential functions of the job in question. Finally, the ADA defines disability as a physical or mental impairment that substantially limits one or more of the major life activities of the individual. This definition has been interpreted by the courts as a threshold requirement for protection under the Act—every plaintiff must show that he or she falls within this definition.[17] The ADA is based on the premise that discrimination is the central problem confronting people with disabilities in the area of employment. The preamble of the ADA states that "society has tended to isolate and segregate individuals with disabilities, and, despite some improvements, such forms of discrimination against people with disabilities continue to be a serious and pervasive social problem."[18] The Act only permits the conclusion that a person is unqualified for a job due to a disability after both the essential job functions and the possibility of altering the job to accommodate the disability have been examined.

---

17 The ADA prohibits discrimination against individuals perceived as disabled as well as those who satisfy the actual definition of disability.

18 42 U.S.C. § 12101(a)(2).

As this description makes clear, the ADA is principally based on a civil rights model of disability policy. It seeks to integrate people with disabilities into the social mainstream and to break down barriers erected by prejudice.

c. Tensions Between the ADA and the Disability Benefit Programs

In the years following the ADA's enactment, it became clear that there were significant tensions between the civil rights approach of the ADA and the social welfare programs of the Social Security Act. Viewed together, the two policies send mixed messages about disability to the general public. Moreover, these tensions create dilemmas for people with disabilities.

The ADA promotes the idea that people with disabilities should be included in the workforce and should be viewed similarly to non-disabled workers. Underpinning this approach is the premise that people with disabilities are not that different from everyone else, and therefore do not need separate parallel social institutions. The ADA is based on the idea that the principal employment barriers faced by people with disabilities are misperception and stereotypes. The analysis which the law requires employers to undertake is designed to overcome these barriers.

At the same time, the disability benefit programs emphasize the differences between people with disabilities and the non-disabled, and suggest that medical screening can effectively sort people into two different categories. The disability benefit programs encourage people with disabilities and the non-disabled public to focus on all the things that disabled people cannot do, while the ADA seeks to shift the focus to their capabilities. Moreover, the disability benefit programs can be seen as excusing employers from the obligation to hire or retain people with disabilities, because they can reject or terminate disabled applicants with the assurance that the government will provide for them.

Two examples may illuminate the problems that result from these tensions.

In administering the disability benefit programs, the Social Security Administration uses a list of impairments, defined in clinical terms, that are considered disabling *per se*. Claimants whose conditions satisfy the terms of this Listing are automatically presumed unable to work, and therefore qualify for benefits.[19] Any private employer who used such a list in categorizing individuals as unable to work, however, would undoubtedly run afoul of the ADA, since the list does not reflect the individualized consideration of functional limitations that the ADA requires. On the one hand, the Listing is an archetype of the medical model: it is based on and perpetuates the assumption that decisions about an individual's employability can be based on clinical test results. On the other hand, the Listing makes it much easier for some people with disabilities to obtain benefits. Since claims can be allowed, but not denied, based on the Listing, it has the effect of expanding eligibility for the benefit programs. In addition, the Listing provides elements of predictability and consistency to the benefit application process. Thus, disability advocates in the early 1990s filed a class action lawsuit against the Social Security Administration because the agency had issued a narrow and under-inclusive Listing in relation to HIV infection. The plaintiffs claimed that the absence of a better listing caused delays and unpredictability in the benefit application process for people with AIDS and related diseases.

As this discussion suggests, the Listing confronts disability advocates with a dilemma. If the goal is to sweep away outdated assumptions about disability and to emphasize the abilities, rather than the limitations, of people with disabilities, the Listing is a ripe target for attack. On the other hand, the Listing undeniably helps many people, by creating an expedited and reliable means of getting benefits into the hands of people who need them.

A second example presents another variant on this same conundrum. With increasing frequency over the past five years, employers have sought to defend ADA cases by arguing that plaintiffs should not be able to sue under the ADA once they have sought and received disability benefits. Employers have argued that since eligibility for bene-

---

[19] The List is set out in Part 404, Subpart P, App. 1 of the Social Security Act regulations: 20 C.F.R. § 404.1520. Claimants who do not meet the terms of a Listing are not automatically denied benefits. Rather SSA then evaluates the impact of the individuals functional limitations in light of his or her age, education and work experience.

fits is based on claiming the inability to work, benefits recipients should not be permitted to argue that they are qualified for their former jobs. Although many courts initially accepted this line of argument and held that benefit recipients were estopped from bringing or maintaining ADA cases, this reasoning was rejected by the U.S. Supreme Court in 1999.[20] The Court pointed out that under the terms of the two laws, an individual can be qualified for a job under the ADA, even though he or she satisfies the definition of disability under the Social Security Act. This overlap is possible for a number of reasons, the most significant of which is the fact that the SSA does not take into account the employer's obligation to provide accommodations under the ADA.

In holding that benefit applicants are not automatically barred from bringing ADA cases, however, the Supreme Court, did not foreclose the possibility that statements made during the benefit application process could be brought back to haunt ADA plaintiffs. The plaintiff can be required to explain why he or she could claim the inability to work on an application for benefits, and yet still be qualified for the job in question. The employer is still permitted to wave the benefits application in front of a jury, and may argue that the plaintiff is simply exploiting his or her disability and lying about the impact of his or her impairments.

In both of these instances, people with disabilities may be perceived as trying to have their cake and eat it too. In one form or another, the question inevitably arises that if the goal of civil rights legislation is to ensure a place for people with disabilities in the social mainstream, then why should society maintain a separate track that gives people with disabilities benefits that are not accorded to others? If the ADA embodies the idea that people with disabilities can participate in the mainstream labor market, then why should they not be required to do so? If the premises of the civil rights model are accepted, is there any room left for social welfare programs in a coherent overall disability policy?

These questions go to the heart of the tension between the two models of disability, and reveal why this problem is of more than merely academic interest. They are considered in more detail in the conclusion to this article.

---

20 *See* Cleveland v. Policy Management Systems Corp., 526 U.S. 795 (1999).

2. European Case Study: The Relationship Between Anti-Discrimination Legislation and Employment Quotas

a. European Employment Quotas

An examination of European disability employment policy reveals similar tensions. For the greater part of the previous century, quotas, whereby employers are encouraged or obliged to employ persons with a disability as a set percentage of their total workforce, were the main plank of disability employment policy in Western Europe.[21] Notwithstanding recent interest in disability (employment) anti-discrimination legislation in Europe, quotas continue to be seen as the key tool for securing the employment of people with disabilities in many countries.

The early quota systems had their origins in the post-First World War period, and only covered disabled veterans. These quotas were based on the idea that society owed a duty to those who had been disabled while serving their country, and by the end of 1923 Germany, Austria, Italy, Poland, and France had all adopted such systems.[22] In contrast, some countries shied away from imposing an employment obligation on employers, and instead sought to encourage employers to voluntarily take on disabled veterans.[23] The high unemployment levels among disabled veterans during the inter-war years, and the lack of success of the voluntary approach, led most European countries to turn to the obligation-based quota system in the post-Second World War period. These second generation quotas were eventually extended to cover the disabled civilian population. A consequence of this extension was that the concept of a *quid pro quo* societal duty, which had existed when the systems were exclusively targeted at veterans, was lost, and the new quotas became part of overall national social-welfare policy. Today ten of the fifteen Member States of the European Union have some form of

---

21 The Scandinavian countries form an exception to this general rule.

22 Madhav R. Kulkarni, *Quota Systems and the Employment of the Handicapped. Experiences in Three Countries* 10 (Michigan State University, University Center for Institutional Rehabilitation, undated).

23 This was the approach adopted in the United Kingdom.

quota system,[24] and quotas can also be found in many European countries which are at present not members of the Union.[25] All quota systems direct employers to hire disabled workers as a set percentage of their work force, but within this general framework there is a great deal of scope for variety, and for this reason one cannot speak of a uniform European quota system. Instead European quota systems can be divided into the following three basic models:

i. Legislative Recommendation

Under this approach, employers are not obliged to employ a set percentage of workers with disabilities, but it is recommended that they do so.[26] Such quotas are voluntary and the legislation does not provide for the imposition of sanctions in the event of employers failing to meet the quota.

Not surprisingly experience suggests that a voluntary quota, which imposes no legal obligation upon employers and provides for no sanctions, has little impact on the numbers of people with disabilities in open employment.[27]

---

[24] Portugal, the United Kingdom and the three Scandinavian Member States do not have a quota system.

[25] Such as Poland, *see* Law on Employment and Vocational Rehabilitation of Disabled People (consolidated text) (Dz. U. No 46, item 201) published in *Disability: Problems and Solutions*, Bulletin: Special Edition 1994 Centre for Europe Warsaw University, Information and Documentation Unit on the Council of Europe 8.

[26] For an example see the Dutch Handicapped Workers Employment Act of 1986 (*WAGW*). This Act has now been replaced by the Law on the (Re)Integration of the Work Disabled (*REA*). One could argue that the REA provides for an indirect quota, since employers whose workforce consists of at least 5 percent of employees with a disability are exempted from paying certain social security premiums.

[27] For further information *see* Waddington's commentary on the Dutch Handicapped Workers Employment Act of 1986 (WAGW), *in* "Legislating to Employ People with Disabilities: The European and American Way," 1(4) *Maastricht J. Eur. & Comp. Law* 367 (1994).

ii. Legislative Obligation But No Effective Sanction

A second approach does rely on legislation to oblige employers to employ a quota of people with disabilities; however this obligation is either not backed up with any effective sanction or the sanction is not actually enforced. This model is typified by the quota system adopted in Britain after the Second World War under the Disabled Persons (Employment) Act (DPEA) of 1944. In Britain this form of quota was not successful in promoting the employment of disabled people, and each year progressively fewer employers met their quota obligation. There were a number of reasons for the failure of the British quota system, but it is submitted that the most important one was the unwillingness or inability of successive governments to enforce the quota through strict policing of the granting of exemption permits and prosecuting errant employers.

Evidence from Britain clearly shows that it is insufficient to simply legislate an obligation on employers to employ people with disabilities. The bare imposition of a quota system does little more than rely on the goodwill of employers, and does not greatly increase employment opportunities for covered individuals in the open labor market. The quota was finally abolished in Britain on December 2, 1996, when the employment provisions of the new disability anti-discrimination law, the Disability Discrimination Act of 1995, came into force.

iii. Legislative Obligation Backed Up By Sanction (Levy-Grant System)

Under this model, employers are obliged to either meet their quota target or pay a fine or levy, which usually goes into a fund to support the employment of people with disabilities. Germany provides one of the earliest examples of such a system, and its quota has since served as a model for other countries, such as France.

Such quotas are based on the principle that all employers above a certain size should contribute to the economic integration of workers with a severe disability. Ideally this integration should occur through the actual provision of employment for such workers, but where this is not the case, a contribution should be made via the levy procedure.

The German quota system has undoubtedly made a greater contribution to promoting the employment of people with disabilities than either of the two systems described above. However in recent years the German quota has become progressively less effective, and has proved itself incapable of maintaining the targeted level of employment for workers with a severe disability during periods of economic recession. Economic difficulties combined with a relatively low levy seem to make payment a more attractive option for employers than taking the perceived risk of hiring a worker with a severe disability.

b. European Anti-Discrimination Legislation

The adoption of disability anti-discrimination legislation (in the field of employment) is a fairly recent phenomenon in Europe. Today three European countries have some form of civil law designed to combat disability discrimination (the United Kingdom,[28] Sweden[29] and Ireland[30]). A number of other countries are considering adopting such legislation. In addition some national constitutions have been amended in recent years to specifically include a reference to disability in an equality clause (Germany, Finland[31] and Austria). Of most significance from a continental perspective is a recently adopted European Community Directive designed to combat employment discrimination on a number of grounds,[32] including disability. As a result of the Directive, all European Union Member States are obliged to adopt employment anti-discrimination legislation specifically addressing disability by the end of 2006 at the latest. This legislation must cover direct and indirect discrimination, as well as discrimination in the form of harassment. In addition the legislation must impose an obligation to make reasonable accommodations for people with disabilities, unless the making of such an accommodation would impose a "disproportionate burden" on the employer.

---

28 The Disability Discrimination Act 1995, 1995, ch. 50.

29 Law prohibiting Discrimination in Working Life on Grounds of Disability 1999, SFS 1999:132.

30 Employment Equity Act 1998 and Equal Status Bill (revised) 1998.

31 FIN. CONST. (731/1999), ch. II, s. 6.

32 *Council Directive 2000/78/EC of 27 November 2000 Establishing a General*

c. Tensions Between Employment Quotas and Anti-Discrimination Legislation

European quota systems are clearly inspired by the social-welfare model of disability, since medical limitations are seen as the explanation for an individual's inability to obtain employment in a conventional manner. By creating quotas, States have sought to establish an alternative labor market which is only open to those people who are labeled as disabled, albeit those finding work via this route (should) work side by side with their non-disabled counterparts. Such quotas are based on the following assumptions:

(1) people with disabilities are able to work in the open labor market;
(2) employers should hire a set percentage of people with a disability; and
(3) a large number of people with disabilities are neither able to compete for jobs with their non-disabled counterparts on an equal basis nor win jobs on their own merit, thus rendering legislative intervention necessary.

The quota system therefore sends out mixed and confusing messages to both employers and people with disabilities. On the one hand employers and people with disabilities are told the latter's employment in the open labor market is desirable and achievable, while on the other hand, they are told that workers with a disability cannot compete for jobs in a truly open labor market. In short, the message sent out is that most workers with a disability are less valuable economically and less productive, and that, if such workers are to be integrated in the (semi-) open labor market, employers need to be obliged to hire them. Given this inherent contradiction it is not surprising that European quota systems have in fact made little direct contribution to the employment of people with disabilities.

In contrast, European anti-discrimination laws, like their American counterpart (from which, in many cases, inspiration was drawn during

---

Framework for Equal Treatment in Employment and Occupation, O.J. 2000, L 303, p. 16.

the drafting processes), are inspired by the civil rights model of disability, and are based on the assumption that people with disabilities are able to compete for and win jobs on their own merit, as long as they are provided with equal opportunities. This recent addition to the European legislative arsenal of tools designed to promote the employment of people with disabilities therefore raises an interesting question: Can anti-discrimination legislation, inspired by the civil rights model of disability, exist side by side with quota systems, inspired by a social-welfare model of disability, or do the two approaches inevitably undermine and contradict each other in the European context?

In fact the question is not so pressing as it may seem at first sight, or at least not at present. Of the three European countries which currently have disability employment anti-discrimination legislation: Sweden has never had a quota system; Ireland's quota system is confined to the public sector and largely ignored; and the United Kingdom abolished its ineffective quota at the same time as it adopted anti-discrimination legislation. However, the British decision to abolish the quota was not inspired by the desire for a theoretically coherent set of policy instruments, but rather by pragmatic reasons: the quota was seen as ineffective and there was no will on the part of the government to enforce the quota law. The adoption of the Disability Discrimination Act of 1995 in Britain provided a good political opportunity to abolish the old system. Many disability activists in fact argued for the simultaneous adoption of anti-discrimination legislation and the retention and effective enforcement of the quota scheme.

However, the Community anti-discrimination Directive referred to above will result in the adoption and implementation of disability anti-discrimination legislation in all European Community Member States. This will lead to an ineluctable clash between social welfare quotas and civil rights anti-discrimination legislation in those countries, such as Germany and France, where there is a strong commitment to the levy-grant quota system. At a theoretical level, it seems that the only way to resolve the tension between anti-discrimination legislation and quotas in Europe is to direct the instruments at two discrete groups. In such a scenario, anti-discrimination legislation would be targeted at people who can compete for and obtain jobs on their merit in a situation of equality of opportunity, while quotas would be targeted at people who are capable of working in the open labor market, but require more than a non-discriminatory environment in order to obtain that employment. In practice, as we have seen, it is impossible to separate people with disabilities into two such groups, quite apart from the question of whether this would be desirable. It therefore seems that as long as disability policy is conceived in terms of the social welfare or civil rights models, tensions between the two types of policy instruments will be inevitable, at least in those European countries that have a well-established levy-grant form of quota.

Ironically, in practice the two approaches may actually complement each other in some respects—at least with regard to the financing of the adaptions or accommodations needed in order to employ some people with disabilities, a condition which is usually required by disability anti-discrimination legislation. Money raised through the charging of levies on employers who do not meet their quota obligations could be used to finance "expensive" accommodations, thus reducing the number of cases in which employers would be able to argue that the employment of a particular individual would result in their assumption of a disproportionate burden because of the cost of the accommodation required. This point is considered in the recently adopted Community Directive which provides that the making of a reasonable accommodation for a person with a disability will not amount to a disproportionate burden where that burden is "sufficiently remedied by measures existing within the framework of the disability policy in the Member State concerned."[33] The resulting relationship between the civil rights and social welfare models may therefore be uneasy, but it may also have some positive elements.

D. DISABILITY POLICY IN PRACTICE—THE TENSION BETWEEN THE SOCIAL WELFARE MODEL AND THE CIVIL RIGHTS MODEL AT THE INTERNATIONAL LEVEL

The previous section revealed the extent to which elements of both American and European national policies designed to promote the employment of people with disabilities are based on conflicting and con-

---

33 *Id.* at Article 5.

tradictory models of disability. In this section we will examine if such contradictions also present themselves in some of the key international human rights instruments which address employment (and disability). Until relatively recently, international human rights texts generally adopted one of two approaches towards disability: universal instruments, such as the International Covenant on Economic, Social and Cultural Rights of 1966, tended not to specifically mention people with disabilities, whilst specialist instruments, such as the UN Declaration on the Rights of Mentally Retarded Persons (1971) and the Declaration on the Rights of Disabled Persons (1975), were specifically targeted at people with disabilities.[34] As we have seen above, this development of separate instruments, and even at times a separate parallel approach for people with disabilities, was also reflected in policies created at the national level in Europe and America.

However, the last decade has seen notable changes in disability policy at the international level. This has resulted in the development of new disability-specific instruments, such as the United Nations Standard Rules on the Equalization of Opportunities for Persons with Disabilities, which are clearly based on the civil rights model of disability, and the re-interpretation of at least one long-standing universal instrument which does not specifically mention disability: the International Covenant on Economic, Social and Cultural Rights of 1966.

In the following section we note how key universal human rights instruments (focussed on or applicable to employment) have traditionally failed to specifically mention people with disabilities, even as a parallel set of instruments targeting people with disabilities have developed. We will consider why the international community has adopted this approach for so long and note recent changes. In conclusion we will reflect on whether international instruments are less troubled than their

---

34 Such targeted instruments were naturally also directed towards other groups (*See*, e.g., International Convention on the Elimination of All Forms of Racial Discrimination (1965) and the Convention on the Elimination of All Forms of Discrimination against Women (1979))—however, these other groups tended to also receive attention in universal instruments (for example, in the general non-discrimination / equality articles contained in the instruments), and the targeted instruments which were directed at them tended to have a higher legal status than the Declarations, Resolutions and Recommendations which addressed disability.

national counterparts by the tension between the social welfare and civil rights models of disability.

1. Universal Instruments

A number of important universal human rights instruments specifically address employment. For example, the Universal Declaration of Human Rights adopted by the UN General Assembly in December 1948 provides for the right to work, as well as a number of other related rights (Article 23). Furthermore, according to Article 2(1) of the Declaration:

> Everyone is entitled to all the rights and freedoms set forth in this Declaration, without distinction of any kind, such as race, colour, sex, language, religion, political or other opinion, national or social origin, property, birth or other social status.

Clearly no specific mention is made of disability in this clause, nor indeed, elsewhere in the Declaration.

A further key international human rights instrument covering *inter alia* employment is the International Covenant on Economic, Social and Cultural Rights of 1966 (ICESCR). The Covenant does not refer to people with disabilities and, most notably, disability is again not mentioned in the anti-discrimination provision contained in Article 2(2). Various other employment related rights are covered, including the "right to work, which includes the right of everyone to the opportunity to gain his living by work which he freely chooses or accepts. . . ." (Article 6(1)). States are to implement this right through steps such as "technical and vocational guidance and training programmes, policies and techniques to achieve steady economic, social and cultural development. . . ." (Article 6(2)). In addition states are to recognize "the right of everyone to the enjoyment of just and favourable conditions of work," including the equal opportunity for everyone to be promoted in his employment to an appropriate higher level, subject to no considerations other than those of seniority and competence" (Article 7, 7(c)).

It has always been clear that the norms contained in the UN Declaration and ICESCR apply to all individuals, including people with disabilities. However, as Philip Alston has noted with regard to the ICE-

SCR: "The relevant norms were in fact interpreted and applied for many years in a way which tended to overlook or even entirely ignore [disabled persons]." Alston continues:

> Indeed, there was often an unstated assumption that in the case of persons with disabilities a significant range of otherwise applicable human rights was for some reason mysteriously suspended or rendered inapplicable.[35]

Given that the Covenant was adopted in 1966, and finally came into force in 1976, it is not altogether surprising that the state parties failed to specifically address the situation of people with disabilities. As noted above, both national and international policy makers rarely attempted to integrate people with disabilities into mainstream policies at this time, and failed to recognize the role which discrimination played in excluding this group.

Numerous general instruments concerning employment policy and employment discrimination have also been adopted under the auspices of the International Labour Organization (ILO). These include Convention 111 on Discrimination (Employment and Occupation) (1958), Convention 122 on Employment Policy (1964), and two Recommendations on Employment Policy (Recommendation 122 (1964) and Recommendation 169 (1984)). Like the ICESCR, none of these instruments specifically refer to people with disabilities, and disability is not included in the (at times) closed list of grounds covered in specific anti-discrimination clauses.[36] At the same time as the ILO adopted these general instruments which failed to refer explicitly to persons with disabilities, they adopted a number of Conventions and Recommendations which specifically targeted this group (see below). This again reflected a segregated approach to policy making.

---

[35] Philip Alston, "Disability and the International Covenant on Economic, Social and Cultural Rights," *in Human Rights and Disabled Persons: Essays and Relevant Human Rights Instruments* 94, 98 (Theresia Degener & Yolan Koster-Dreese eds., Dordrecht; Boston; London: Martinus Nijhoff Publishers, 1995).

[36] See for example, Article 1(a) of ILO Convention 111 Discrimination (Employment and Occupation), though Article 1(b) indicates that individual Member States can determine for themselves whether additional distinctions, exclusions or preferences may constitute discrimination within their own state.

2. Targeted Instruments

As noted above, the general neglect, or at least separate treatment, of people with disabilities in universal human rights texts was paralleled by a tendency to adopt specialized and targeted instruments dealing only with disability. One early such document was Recommendation 99 of the ILO on Vocational Rehabilitation (Disabled) (1955). This Recommendation is very much based on the social welfare model of disability. The preamble to the Recommendation notes that there are many and varied problems concerning those who suffer disability, and the rehabilitation of such persons is essential in order that they be restored to the fullest possible physical, mental, social, vocational, and economic usefulness of which they are capable. The emphasis is therefore on adapting the individual with a disability, rather than on seeking the elimination of disability discrimination and the barriers which hamper the participation of people with disabilities. Even though integrated employment and training are the preferred options under the Recommendation, the role of specialized guidance services (Article 3), training provisions (Article 8), placement services (Article 10), and sheltered employment (Article 32 to 35) is also emphasized.

Two other international texts which focus exclusively on persons with disabilities are the UN Declaration on the Rights of Mentally Retarded Persons (1971) and the UN Declaration on the Rights of Disabled Persons (1975). The latter Declaration, even though it contains a definition of disability that is based on the social welfare model (any disadvantages are identified as being caused by the "deficiency . . . in . . . physical or mental capabilities": Article 1), also emphasizes the need to both respect the human rights of people with disabilities (Articles 3 and 4) and to protect disabled persons "against all exploitation, all regulations and all treatment of a discriminatory, abusive or degrading nature" (Article 10).

3. Reassessing Universal Instruments

In the 1970s and 1980s the disability civil rights movement brought pressure to bear on some national policy makers. This was particularly the case in the United States; and by the 1990s a similar movement could clearly be identified in many parts of Europe. This pressure was also felt in the corridors of the United Nations, and on March 12, 1984 the UN Commission on Human Rights adopted a resolution[37] recommending that the Sub-Commission on Prevention of Discrimination and Protection of Minorities appoint a Special Rapporteur to report on the connection between disability and serious violations of human rights and fundamental freedoms. The report by Leandro Despouy,[38] which was published in 1993, revealed the extent to which the human rights of people with disabilities, including employment related rights, were being overlooked and abused, and greatly increased the international community's awareness of its previous neglect of this group.

In relation to the ICESCR, the most significant result of this new awareness of the rights of people with disabilities was the General Comment[39] on People with Disabilities, adopted in 1994 by the Committee on Economic, Social and Cultural Rights. The General Comment emphasizes *inter alia* the applicability of the employment provisions of the Covenant, noting for example that the right to the opportunity to gain a living by work which is freely chosen or accepted (stated in Article 6(1)) "is not realized where the only real opportunity open to disabled workers is to work in so-called 'sheltered' facilities under substandard conditions" (Para. 21). Significantly the General Comment also notes the role which discrimination and physical barriers, such as inaccessible transportation and work places, play in excluding people with disabilities, and calls on governments to take action to remove such barriers and reasonably accommodate the needs of disabled workers (Para.22).

The General Comment also notes the absence of a specific reference to disability in the Covenant, which is attributed to a previous lack of awareness of the need to protect and promote the human rights of per-

---

37 Resolution 1984/31, U.N. ESCOR 1984, Supp. No. 4, at 67, U.N. Doc. E/1984/14-E/CN.4/1984/77 (1984).

38 Leandro Despouy, *Human Rights and Disabled Persons*, Human Rights Study Series 6 (New York: United Nations, 1993).

39 *Report on the Tenth and Eleventh Sessions*, U.N. ESCOR, 1995, Supp. 2 [according to U.N. Doc. E/1995/22/Corr.1-E/C.12/1994/20/Corr.1 of 14 July 1995], at 99, U.N. Doc. E/1995/22-E/C.12/1994/20 (1995).

sons with disabilities through general as well as specially designed laws, policies and programs. This reflects the newer approach to disability policy at the international level which has been inspired by the civil rights model.

4. Developing New Targeted Instruments

In 1983, influenced by the UN International Year of Disabled Persons (1981) and the recognition that rehabilitation policy had advanced, the ILO adopted Convention 159 on Vocational Rehabilitation and Employment (Disabled Persons). It is clear from the Convention that the ILO had considerably advanced its understanding of disability since 1955, when Recommendation 99 on Vocational Rehabilitation had been adopted. The newer Convention encouraged States to ensure that "appropriate vocational rehabilitation measures are made available to all categories of disabled persons," and promoted "employment opportunities for disabled persons in the open labour market" (Article 3). The Convention emphasized that policy "shall be based on the principle of equal opportunity" (Article 4). This emphasis on equality is not found in the earlier ILO Recommendation.

Undoubtedly the most far-reaching and modern international instrument targeted at people with disabilities is the United Nations Standard Rules on the Equalization of Opportunities for Persons with Disabilities, adopted by the General Assembly of the United Nations in 1993. The Rules were conceived as a substitute for a binding international treaty,[40]

---

[40] In 1987, The 3rd Committee of the General Assembly considered the recommendations that had been made by the "Global Meeting of Experts to Review the Implementation of the World Programme of Action Concerning Disabled Persons at the Mid-Point of the United Nations Decade of Disabled Persons." Among the recommendations was a proposal for an international convention on the elimination of all forms of discrimination against disabled persons. The Italian delegate raised and supported the possibility of such a convention (U.N. Doc. A/C.3/42/SR.16 (1987)), but numerous objections to such a convention were raised in subsequent meetings by various countries (e.g., the U.K. and Japan were concerned about financial implications, while Germany and the Nordic countries believed that the rights of disabled persons were protected by existing universal human rights documents such as the ICESCR—*see* U.N. Docs. A/C.3/42/SR.17 to A/C.3/ 42/SR/19). Eventually, the 3rd Committee adopted a resolution on disabled

and aim to set the standard for national (and international) disability policy and laws.[41] The Standard Rules are very much based on a rights-based approach to disability, and address the role which discrimination, in its many forms, plays in disadvantaging people with disabilities. The Rules are critical of the way in which the terms "disability" and "handicap" have been used in the past, stating that "[t]he terminology reflects a medical and diagnostic approach, which ignored the imperfections and deficiencies of the surrounding society."[42] One of the areas targeted in the Standard Rules for equal participation is employment (Rule 7). This Rule provides that:

> 1. Laws and regulations in the employment field must not discriminate against persons with disabilities and must not raise obstacles to their employment
>
> 2. States should actively support the integration of persons with disabilities into open employment. . . .
>
> 3. States' action programmes should include:
> (a) Measures to design and adapt workplaces and premises in such a way that they become accessible to persons with different disabilities; . . .
>
> 7. The aim should always be for persons with disabilities to obtain employment in the open labour market. For persons with disabilities whose needs cannot be met in open employment, small units of sheltered or supported employment may be an alternative. . . .

---

persons that did not recommend the drafting or implementation of a binding convention on eliminating discrimination against disabled persons (U.N. Doc. A/C.3/42/L.25). The possibility of a convention was raised again by Sweden in 1989, and once again failed to garner sufficient support, but this later initiative did lead to the eventual establishment of the Rules. *See also* Theresia Degener, "Disabled Persons and Human Rights: The Legal Framework," *in Human Rights and Disabled Persons, supra* note 35, 9 at 12.

41 Note however Preamble 14 to the Introduction of the Standard Rules which states that "[a]lthough the Rules are not compulsory, they can become international customary rules when they are applied by a great number of States with the intention of respecting a rule in international law."

42 Introduction, Preamble 19.

This relatively modern instrument of disability policy therefore places a significant emphasis on the equal rights of people with disabilities and fully embraces the rights-based concept of disability.

5. The Influence of the Social Welfare and Civil Rights Models of Disability at the International Level

The failure to refer to disability in (earlier) universal human rights texts, and the use of weaker non-binding instruments for those measures which targeted people with disabilities, is evidence that the international community believed that people with disabilities were not a group that was particularly vulnerable to human rights abuses. While policy makers could not have doubted that people with disabilities were disadvantaged, this was attributed to the existence of physical or mental impairments (i.e., in accordance with a social welfare model of disability), and not seen as the result of discrimination and inadequate respect for human rights (i.e., in accordance with a civil rights based model of disability). In light of pressure from disability NGOs and some State parties, as well as the authoritative Despouy Report, the international community has revised its outdated view of disability and increasingly come to accept the civil rights model of disability. However, this has not resulted in the re-drafting of long established universal instruments such as the ICESCR. Given the difficulty of reaching agreement on such universal texts in the first place, and the familiarity and recognition which such instruments have now achieved, such re-drafting could not be expected. Instead, through General Comments and other texts and statements used in the interpretation of universal instruments, the international community has made it clear that such instruments are to be interpreted as applying to people with disabilities. This kind of interpretive re-direction has been possible because these instruments have never expressly intended to exclude people with disabilities, and have usually purported to be universal, for example, through the inclusion of non-discrimination/equality clauses which emphasize that the relevant rights are to be enjoyed by all. By facilitating a "re-interpretation" of the instruments, universality has become more of a reality.

Newer disability-specific instruments have also updated and effectively revised the standards which the international community are expected to meet. Older instruments, inspired by a medical and social welfare model of disability, have not been repealed, but on the whole, they have not been perceived as contradicting the newer approach. The older instruments often contain fairly general requirements, and—in the case of employment measures—have the broad aim of promoting employment for people with disabilities. Since newer instruments share this general goal, they can be seen as simply reflecting a greater understanding of, and further developing solutions for, the problems which were raised and addressed in earlier texts.

These comments suggest that although tension can be identified between the social welfare and civil rights models of disability in international instruments, these tensions have not proved to be as problematic as they have been at the national level. This is partly because of the proclaimed universality of many instruments, which is open-ended enough to allow for the recent emphasis on the equal rights of people with disabilities, but also because of the general (and at times vague) nature of many of the provisions contained in international instruments. Furthermore such instruments, unlike the national provisions examined earlier, are addressed to signatory states rather than individuals (such as people with disabilities or employers). As a result, those who are actually responsible for making decisions concerning the employment of people with disabilities at the grass roots level are unlikely to (directly) receive any mixed messages sent out by international instruments.

E. RECONCILING SUPPORT FOR PEOPLE WITH DISABILITIES WITH THE CIVIL RIGHTS MODEL

In the previous sections we have seen how certain measures ostensibly designed to promote the employment of people with disabilities, and that are based on the social welfare model of disability, sit uneasily with anti-discrimination legislation inspired by the civil rights model. In this section and the conclusion, we will consider whether all forms of employment-related support targeted exclusively at people with disabilities raise the tension described above, or whether some forms of support can be reconciled with the civil rights model. In doing so we will consider the justification for such targeted intervention. We will also draw inspiration from measures directed at other groups which have been traditionally disadvantaged in the labor market, such as women and ethnic minorities, for whom the civil rights model has long been accepted.

Before turning to these issues, we consider one possible solution which would obviate the need to reconcile the two approaches: outright abolition of the social welfare model and the programs inspired by it. Such an approach has the great advantage of achieving immediate coherence and consistency. It simply casts aside the outdated social welfare model and its manifestations. However, such a solution could only be based on an analysis that reduces disability policy to a binary choice between the two approaches; it fails to address many of the problems faced by people with disabilities and overlooks the complexity and nuance of societal views of disability.

Civil rights legislation, by itself, is not an adequate response to the issues raised by disability. It provides only a limited solution for many people with disabilities. First, although civil rights legislation prohibits discrimination, discrimination nonetheless persists. Discrimination is too ingrained to be dispelled by the simple passage of legislation. Moreover, individual litigation is a time consuming, anxiety producing, and costly means of redress. Civil suits by individual victims of discrimination cannot be expected to solve the problem.

Second, civil rights legislation is limited in scope. The duty to provide accommodations to people with disabilities is qualified by the proviso that employers need not provide accommodations that impose undue or disproportionate burdens. Thus, even if all employers complied with disability anti-discrimination legislation, many workers could still be rejected or terminated based on their disabilities. Furthermore the possibility exists that courts will adopt a narrow interpretation of the concept of "disability," and so exclude many people from the scope of protection of any legislation. This has occurred with regard to the Americans with Disabilities Act, which has been interpreted so as to exclude many individuals whose medical impairment has formed the basis for an adverse employment decision. In *Sutton v. United Airlines*,[43] the U.S. Supreme Court emphasized that the ADA defines disability as

---

43 119 S. Ct. 2139 (1999).

a substantial limitation on the ability to perform a major life activity; consequently they endorsed the view that some impairments which would prompt employers to refuse to hire individuals for jobs that they seek, may nonetheless be considered insubstantial for the purposes of the ADA. The recently adopted European Directive allows Member States to introduce their own definition of disability when adopting national anti-discrimination law, and it is quite possible that narrow definitions or interpretations will be developed in at least some Member States once the Directive is implemented.

Third, anti-discrimination legislation focuses on discrimination by the employer based on a particular trait or characteristic of the job applicant, in this case his or her disability. It does not address other aspects of the employment decision, even though these aspects may be related to disability, either causally or as correlates.[44] Decisions which at first sight may appear to be motivated by non-discriminatory factors, such as rejections based on inadequate training, qualifications or work experience, and which would not be open to challenge under anti-discrimination legislation, may in fact hide patterns of earlier discriminatory treatment which denied individuals with a disability the opportunity to gain the relevant skills. Employers therefore remain free to reject applicants with disabilities as lacking in skills or experience, even though these deficits may be connected with historical unfair treatment connected to an individual's disability.

There is also a further negative consequence of disability policy inspired by the civil rights model. Since this model focuses exclusively on removing discrimination which has come to be associated with disability, it provides no grounds for continuing to provide preferential treatment to people with a disability who, even in the ideal non-discriminatory environment created by the transformation of this model

---

44 *See* Frederick C. Collignon, "The Role of Reasonable Accommodation in Employing Disabled Persons in Private Industry," *in Disability and the Labor Market: Economic Problems, Policies, and Programs* 196, 232 (Monroe Berkowitz & M. Anne Hill, eds., Ithaca, New York: ILR Press, 1986): Noting that "the principal correlates of failure in job finding for disabled individuals have fairly consistently turned out to be lack of past work experience and characteristics other than the type or severity of the disability itself such as the individual's youth, poor education, or minority or female status."

into policy and fact, might be unable to take up employment. One probable and logical consequence would be that unemployed people with disabilities would receive the same financial support as unemployed non-disabled people. The result would be even more poverty amongst a group that is often subject to heavy medical expenses, little choice with regard to insurance, and various other economic disadvantages.

Given the continuing need for programs based on the social welfare model, the central challenge is to derive common principles that can form the basis of both civil rights and social welfare protections. Two such possibilities are discussed below.

1. Broadening Notions of Equality

One possible means of reconciling preexisting social welfare programs with the civil rights model is to reconceive such programs as part of a comprehensive civil rights policy. Such a reconception could be effected by broadening the concept of equality underpinning the civil rights model, so that it embraces key aspects of social welfare programs as well. While not wishing to venture too far into an investigation of the concept of equality, one can argue that anti-discrimination legislation is typically based on a narrow notion of equality of opportunity. This notion assumes that all job applicants have had an equal chance to prepare themselves before applying for the job, and that once all elements of discrimination are removed from the recruitment process, the best and most qualified person will be appointed. To use the well known analogy to a foot race, all competitors have an equal opportunity to prepare for and win the race. If one accepts this view, then no additional intervention is permitted to advantage any particular competitor, and the mission of civil rights law is simply to remove the element of discrimination from the calculus, so that members of disadvantaged groups receive the same treatment as others.

However, alternative views of equality, which are perhaps more realistic from the point of view of the situation of people with disabilities, also exist. Indeed, civil rights legislation that embraces the concept of reasonable accommodation draws on the idea that some adjustments in the workplace may be necessary in order to place people with disabilities on an equal footing. These requirements constitute a recognition that treating people the same does not always constitute equal treatment.[45] Reasonable accommodation requirements, however, reflect only a small expansion of the traditional civil rights model. Such requirements only compel employers to treat a disabled employee differently if the departure from what they would otherwise do does not impose a significant burden or hardship. In a sense, the requirement mandates little more than a somewhat deeper consideration of whether an individual can really perform the critical functions of a job, thereby preventing employers from relying on reflexive judgments based on stereotypes and preconceived notions.

A broader understanding of equality which would allow for further intervention therefore seems necessary. Some of the problems and tensions identified in this article might be capable of resolution if a broader notion of equality were accepted. This could take into account the history of disadvantage, and the lack of education, training and work experience that can be its result for some people with disabilities. These deficits hamper many individuals even when employers do not discriminate based on disability, and even when employers reasonably accommodate the impact of medical impairments.

Moreover, people with disabilities may encounter barriers to many public services and institutions that others in the labor market take advantage of routinely. For example, they may have limited access to housing and transportation, two vital prerequisites to work. Similarly, a broader notion of equality might recognize that reasonable accommodation requirements do not place many people with disabilities on an equal footing because the requirements fail to recognize or respond to the full range of restrictions caused by a physical of mental impairment, some of which may be very difficult or impossible to fully accommodate. The very concept of "reasonable accommodations" actually allows social institutions and structures to continue to be based on some fictional non-disabled "norm," as long as minimal adaptions are made where necessary for specific individuals with a disability.

A notion of equality that takes into account the full range of disadvantages experienced by many people with disabilities would, of neces-

---

45 *See* Matthew Diller, "Judicial Backlash, The ADA & the Civil Rights Model," 21 *Berkeley J. Employment & Labor* 19 (2000).

sity, call for policies that extend far beyond traditional civil rights legislation and the notion of reasonable accommodation. Under this vision of equality, many advantages provided to people with disabilities appear not as a form of publicly mandated charity, but as pieces of a larger policy intended to move toward equality. Thus, benefits such as job training, income supplements and affirmative action requirements, may all be thought of as tools for overcoming or redressing the full range of disadvantages experienced by people with disabilities.

In Europe, such employment advantages are common vehicles for helping disadvantaged groups, and are not necessarily seen as problematic. European Community law specifically allows Member States to adopt certain forms of positive action to promote the employment of disadvantaged groups.[46] Canadian law goes even further. Under the Canadian Human Rights Act courts can order employers to adopt positive action programs in order to address systemic patterns of discrimination[47] and the Canadian Supreme Court has noted:

> The goal [of the Canadian Human Rights Act] is not to compensate past victims or even to provide new opportunities for specific individuals who have been unfairly refused jobs or promotion in the past, although some such individuals may be beneficiaries of an employment equity scheme. Rather, an employment equity program is an attempt to ensure that future applicants and workers from the affected group will not face the same insidious barriers that blocked their forebears. . . .

---

[46] *See* Article 2(4) of *Council Directive 76/207/EC of 9 February 1976 on the Implementation of the Principle of Equal Treatment for Men and Women as Regards Access to Employment, Vocational Training and Promotion, and Working Conditions*, O.J. 1976, L39, p. 40; Article 7 of the Framework Employment Directive, *supra* note 32; and Article 5 of *Council Directive 2000/43/EC of 29 June 2000 Implementing the Principle of Equal Treatment Between Persons Irrespective of Racial or Ethnic Origin*, O.J. 2000, L 80, p. 22. The latter Article for example reads: "With a view to ensuring full equality in practice, the principle of equal treatment shall not prevent any Member State from maintaining or adopting specific measures to prevent or compensate for disadvantages linked to racial or ethnic origin."

[47] *See* Canadian National Railway Co. v. Canada (Canadian Human Rights Commission), [1987] 1 S.C.R. 1114.

> When the theoretical roots of employment equity programs are exposed, it is readily apparent that, in attempting to combat systemic discrimination, it is essential to look to the past patterns of discrimination and to destroy those patterns in order to prevent the same type of discrimination in the future.[48]

Even quota systems could be reconceived to fit within the civil rights model of disability as long as the latter is based on a broadened concept of equality. Some American commentators,[49] for example, have argued for the adoption of numerical employment targets alongside the Americans with Disabilities Act. They argue that anti-discrimination legislation alone is insufficient to replace a long history of disadvantage and exclusion that has frequently resulted in educational and social deprivations that have long term effects on employment possibilities. Positive or affirmative action is therefore required in order to address the disadvantaged position of at least some people with disabilities on the labor market.[50] Seen in this light, quotas could be rendered compatible with the civil rights model of disability.

However, given the history and development of European quota policies, the task of reshaping them into civil rights instruments appears daunting. They have come to stand for the proposition that (some) workers with a disability are inferior and are unable to compete for jobs in the open labor market. Given the long-standing European experience, it is questionable if quota systems can be successfully re-envisioned as instruments of civil rights policy.

---

48 *Id.* at 1143, 1145.

49 Mark Weber, "Beyond the Americans with Disabilities Act: A National Employment Policy for People with Disabilities," 46 *Buff. L. Rev.* 123 (1998). Weber argues for remedial affirmative action to overcome discrimination in the form of employment targets. He also argues for more rigid quotas modeled on European models, but does not view the quotas as a remedy for discrimination.

50 Many of the arguments used to support affirmative action as a means of overcoming racial discrimination in the United States are readily applicable to the issue of disability. *See* Christopher Edley, *Not All Black and White: Affirmative Action, Race and American Values* (New York: Hill & Wang, 1996); Charles Lawrence & Mari Matsuda, *We Won't Go Back: Making the Case for Affirmative Action* (Boston: Houghton Mifflin, 1997).

In contrast with Europe, broader visions of equality have proven extremely controversial in the U.S. The debate over affirmative action for racial minorities shows the deep ambivalence that Americans have toward broad views of equality. Indeed, even the reasonable accommodation requirement of the Americans with Disabilities Act has been harshly criticized as transforming a civil rights measure into a mandated benefits program.[51] Under this view, the reasonable accommodation requirement is seen as a social welfare program for people with disabilities whose costs have been foisted on employers. This perception may, in fact, contribute to the narrow and begrudging interpretations of the Act that have dominated in the courts.[52]

Nonetheless, recent policy initiatives in the United States have sought to draw connections between the disability benefit programs of the Social Security Act and policies designed to integrate people with disabilities into the work force. The recently enacted American Ticket to Work and Work Incentives Improvement Act of 1999 links older social welfare programs with the more recent legislative emphasis on inclusion in the work force. It can be seen as an effort to co-opt preexisting components of the social welfare approach into the newer civil rights based model.

2. A New Synthesis—A Model of Social Justice

Just as broad notions of equality may defuse the tension between civil rights and social welfare based disability policies, broader thinking about social welfare also may permit a reconciliation of the two approaches. The traditional social welfare model relies on disability as a means of sorting individuals into categories based on judgments about their ability and obligation to work. The implicit purpose of this sorting is to compel people that are found to be not disabled to remain in the work force. At heart, the social welfare model rests on a deep rooted

---

51 *See, e.g.*, Sherwin Rosen, "Disability Accommodation and the Labor Market," *in Disability and Work: Incentives, Rights, and Opportunities* 18, 29 (Carolyn Weaver, ed., Washington, D.C.; Lanham, MD: AEI Press; Distributed by University Press of America, 1991).

52 *See* Diller, *Berkeley*, *supra* note 45.

suspicion of the poor. Those found to be not disabled are excluded from the social welfare model, often harshly, as a means of enforcing the general obligation to work.

Re-examination of this basic assumption could have a major impact on disability policy. Absent this suspicion of the poor, social welfare policies could be reconceived to accord the poor both reasonable income assistance and a range of supports to help achieve entry and success in the job market. A different system could replace the idea of social welfare with a concept of social and economic rights. Under this framework, the benefits provided to people with disabilities would appear as simply one form of recognizing the right of each individual to economic security and full participation in society.[53] In such a system, the process of sorting people into and out of the disability category would be much less important as meaningful assistance would be available in either event. The provision of various forms of assistance to people with disabilities would not appear exceptional, as all individuals who face barriers to full economic and social participation in society would have a positive claim for assistance in overcoming such barriers. In sum, a system based on a broader notion of social justice that stressed the right of each individual to a basic income and opportunity for economic success would move social policy beyond the basic dichotomy between social welfare and civil rights based policies. Policies associated with the social welfare approach, such as income support programs, and those associated with the civil rights model, such as nondiscrimination legislation, would be complementary components of a larger set of economic and social rights that are grounded on principles of respect for human dignity.

F. CONCLUSION

In many countries disability policies have been layered on top of each other. As new ways of thinking about disability have gained ascendence, new policies have been adopted, frequently without the replacement or

---

[53] *See* Carlos Ball, "Autonomy, Justice and Disability," 47 *UCLA L. Rev*. 599, 644–48 (2000): arguing that fundamental respect for human autonomy requires the provision of assistance to people with disabilities.

revision of preexisting approaches. The result is a confusing jumble of policies and instruments that often have failed to add up to a coherent whole. Further, this layering stems in part from the fact that the new policies do not fully address the needs met by the earlier policies and programs.

More specifically, in a number of countries anti-discrimination policies based on a civil rights model of disability have been superimposed on preexisting income support and quota policies that are grounded on a social welfare view. The social welfare and civil rights models are based on very different, and in some respects conflicting, views about the difficulties that people with disabilities face in the labor market. The civil rights model, however, is too limited and restricted by itself to address all of the issues related to disability. Indeed, even with anti-discrimination laws in place, people with disabilities will continue to face distinct barriers that will make it far too early to simply close down all preexisting programs based on the social welfare model. Reconciling policies based on the social welfare model with those based on the civil right model is therefore a central challenge in disability policy today.

We suggest two possible means of achieving this aim. First, by broadening the notion of equality beyond the scope of many non-discrimination requirements, policies traditionally viewed in social welfare terms may be recast as aspects of civil rights policy. Second, the problem could be addressed by abandoning many of the premises of the social welfare model in favor of a social justice model that emphasizes the rights of each individual to participate fully in the economic and social mainstream of society. In such a system all individuals would be entitled to assistance to overcome barriers to equal participation, and any benefits accorded to people with disabilities would not appear as unusual or extraordinary. Such an approach would remove the emphasis on sorting and labeling that currently dominates the social welfare model and fuels many of its conflicts with the civil rights approach.

Part III:
Focus on the Operation of Laws

The ADA and Models of Equality

Arlene B. Mayerson and Silvia Yee***

The drafters of the Americans with Disabilities Act are facing the difficulty of reconciling the Act's language—which envisions the achievement of equal opportunity and emphasizes the need for affirmative steps to eliminate barriers to inclusion and participation for persons with disabilities—with the limits of the formal equality model applied in the United States Supreme Court's interpretation of the Fourteenth Amendment. This article discusses the shortcomings of the Supreme Court's traditional equal protection doctrine, and its requirement for discriminatory intent or improper motive, when applied in the context of persons with disabilities. After briefly examining the contrasting material equality model that has come to prevail in international disability antidiscrimination law, the article focuses on Canadian constitutional equality provisions and jurisprudence. The Supreme Court of Canada explicitly rejected the limits of the American formal equality model when first interpreting the Canadian Charter of Rights and Freedoms, and the difference in result for persons with disabilities is evident in the Court's recent 1997 decision, *Eldridge v. British Columbia (Attorney General)*. While the Canadian approach bears its own anomalies of reasoning, it clearly recognizes something that the

---

* Directing Attorney, Disability Rights Education and Defense Fund, Inc. (DREDF); B.S. 1971, Boston University; J.D. 1977, Boalt School of Law; L.L.M. 1978, Georgetown University School of Law. Arlene Mayerson authored the portions of the article dealing with the American historical analysis of the drafting of the ADA as well as the model of equality under which the ADA was drafted in the United States. Any first person references in these portions of the article refer to Arlene Mayerson and not Silvia Yee.

** L.B. 1989; B.Mus. 1995; M.A. 1997, University of Alberta; Ph.D graduate studies, University of California-Berkeley, 1997–2000. Silvia Yee authored the international and Canadian law portions of this article.

American approach has so far failed to admit: that the "same" treatment can perpetuate exclusion, discrimination, and inequality for persons with disabilities.

A. INTRODUCTION

The Americans with Disabilities Act (ADA) has been a hallmark around the world encouraging the development of disability civil rights in international forums and in countries everywhere. The ADA is being studied and used as a model internationally. Many foreign activists have come here to talk to many of us, and American disability activists have been invited to speak to activists and governmental policy makers around the world.

Any history or analysis of the ADA always begins with its underpinnings in the American civil rights tradition. This tradition is seen as a major advantage in achieving the passage and enforcement of the ADA. There can be no doubt that this civil rights tradition was used as a strong moral imperative in advocating for a comprehensive civil rights statute for people with disabilities. Throughout the committee reports and floor statements, the statement was continually made that the ADA simply would complete the path taken in the 1964 Civil Rights Act,[1] which prohibited discrimination on the basis of race, color, and national origin,[2] and later, gender.[3] People with disabilities are referred to as the largest minority group, as they are still lacking basic civil rights protections. The findings of the ADA emphasize the civil rights nature of the ADA, even adopting verbatim the Supreme Court's description of racial minorities.

> [I]ndividuals with disabilities are a discrete and insular minority who have been faced with restrictions and limitations, sub-

1 42 U.S.C. § 12101(a)(4) (1994); 136 Cong. Rec. H2639 (daily ed. May 22, 1990) (statement of Rep. Dellums); 135 Cong. Rec. S4979-2 (daily ed. May 9, 1989) (statements of Sen. Harkin and Sen. Riegle); 136 Cong. Rec. H2425–27 (daily ed. May 17, 1990) (statement of Rep. Hoyer).

2 42 U.S.C. § 2000d (1994).

3 *E.g.*, Education Amendments of 1974, 20 U.S.C. § 1681(a) (1994).

> jected to a history of purposeful unequal treatment, and relegated to a position of political powerlessness in our society, based on characteristics that are beyond the control of such individuals and resulting from stereotypic assumptions not truly indicative of the individual ability of such individuals to participate in, and contribute to, society.[4]

There can be no doubt that the previous civil rights achievements and precepts were fundamental and necessary ingredients to successful passage of the ADA. This tradition also accounts for the enforcement infrastructure on which ADA enforcement depends.[5] However, ten years later we are also starting to encounter the limits of that tradition in achieving the true goals of the ADA, inclusion and participation.

As drafters of the ADA, we[6] never discussed theories of equality. Using the rhetoric of traditional civil rights, which focuses on equal treatment, we incorporated non-discrimination provisions from Section 504 implementing regulations that assured that different treatment would be provided when necessary to achieve equal opportunity.[7] We were insistent that reasonable accommodation *was not* affirmative action but simply part and parcel of meaningful non-discrimination. Unlike the women's movement, which has been hotly debating the wisdom of ever veering from the equal treatment paradigm,[8] the disability movement

---

4 Americans with Disabilities Act, 42 U.S.C. § 12101(7) (1994); United States v. Carolene Prods. Co., 304 U.S. 144, 152 n. 4 (1938) (stating that "discrete and insular minorities" may not be properly protected by the political process).

5 *See* 42 U.S.C. § 12117 (1994) (incorporating Title VII remedies, 42 U.S.C. § 2000(e)(4)–(9) (1994), for employment discrimination); 42 U.S.C. § 12133 (1994) (incorporating remedies of Section 504 of the Rehabilitation Act, 29 U.S.C. § 794 (1994)); 29 U.S.C. § 794(a) (1994) (incorporating remedies of Title VII of the Civil Rights Act of 1964, 42 U.S.C. § 2000(e)(4)–(9) (1994)).

6 The first person references regarding the drafting of the ADA refer to Arlene Mayerson and the other ADA drafters and do not include Silvia Yee, the co-author of this article.

7 29 U.S.C. § 794 (1994); 28 C.F.R. § 42 (1978).

8 *See generally, e.g.*, Catherine A. MacKinnon, *Feminism Unmodified: Discourses on Life and Law* 32 (Cambridge, MA: Harvard U. Press, 1987); Joan Williams, *Unbending Gender: Why Family and Work Conflict and What to Do About*

has known from the outset that for people with disabilities, a civil rights statute based solely on equal treatment would fall far short of achieving the goals of inclusion and participation.

In other words, we conceptualized equal protection as equal opportunity, which by necessity required affirmative steps to eliminate barriers to participation. We had every reason to be confident. Unfortunately, recent Supreme Court decisions are forcing us to confront head-on the limitations of traditional equal protection doctrine. Recent cases have held that suits against states can be brought only if the legislation is a valid exercise of Congress's authority under Section 5 of the 14th Amendment.[9] Cases challenging the constitutionality of the ADA as applied to states have forced ADA lawyers to make the hybrid ADA model fit traditional doctrine. As one of the authors of the brief on behalf of respondents in the cases currently before the Supreme Court,[10] I have found the process tortured and tormenting.

My original idea was to share this process with the international community as they struggle to formulate non-discrimination principles. The prospect of starting from scratch, or at least not being bound by the peculiarities of American 14th Amendment jurisprudence became more and more appealing. What I found in starting to do some international research is that there is a very rich dialogue in the international arena about approaches to equality. While the United States is hailed as a fore-

---

It (New York: Oxford U. Press, 1999); Katharine T. Bartlett, "Tradition, Change, and the Idea of Progress in Feminist Legal Thought," 1995 *Wis. L. Rev.* 303 (1995); Martha Albertson Fineman, "Feminist Theory in Law: The Difference It Makes," 2 *Colum. J. Gender & L.* 1 (1992); Herma Hill Kay, "Equality and Difference: The Case of Pregnancy," 1 *Berkeley Women's L.J.* 1 (1985); Christine A. Littleton, "Reconstructing Sexual Equality," 75 *Cal. L. Rev.* 1279 (1987); Wendy Webster Williams, "The Equality Crisis: Some Reflection on Culture, Courts, and Feminism," 7 *Wom. Rts. L. Rep.* 175 (1982). Christine A. Littleton provides a relatively recent overview of "women and the law" texts and casebooks in "Whose Law Is This Anyway?," 95 *Mich. L. Rev.* 1560 (1997).

9 *See, e.g.*, City of Boerne v. Flores, 521 U.S. 507 (1997).

10 Univ. of Ala. Bd. of Trs. v. Garrett, No. 99-1240 (U.S. argued Oct. 11, 2000), *cert. granted*, 68 U.S.L.W. 3654 (U.S. Apr. 17, 2000). After this article was completed, the *Garrett* case was decided. *See* 531 U.S. 356 (2000).

runner in disability rights because of the ADA, the narrow equality underpinnings of the Constitution threaten a major setback.

In this article, we will first set forth two models of non-discrimination, formal and material non-discrimination. We will then discuss 14th Amendment jurisprudence as an example of formal non-discrimination, and some international developments as examples of material non-discrimination, eventually focusing on Canadian jurisprudence which directly confronts and contradicts the American model.

Under formal equality, the law treats similarly situated persons the same. The underpinnings of this paradigm is that goods should be distributed according to merit and all individuals are able to compete equally if treated equally. Under material equality, sometimes called substantial or genuine equality, the focus is not on being treated equally but on being treated as an equal.[11] The concept of material equality acknowledges the importance of individual and group differences and takes into account both personal and environmental barriers that inhibit societal participation. Therefore, barriers that deny or limit an individual's right to be an equal member of society should be eliminated.

B. THE U.S. MODEL OF EQUALITY

A good starting point for understanding how disability fits into traditional equal protection doctrine is the Supreme Court's discussion in *Cleburne v. Cleburne Living Center, Inc.*[12] *Cleburne* involved a challenge to a zoning ordinance that excluded group homes for individuals with developmental disabilities. The Supreme Court, for the first time, discussed the proper level of review to be accorded people with mental retardation under the Constitution. Key to the Court's decision that classifications based on disability should *not* get heightened scrutiny under the 14th Amendment was the Court's belief that people with disabilities are not similarly situated to people without disabilities and may require "special treatment." The Court stated: "The Equal Protection Clause of the Fourteenth Amendment commands that no State shall 'deny to any

---

11 *See infra* notes 33, 40 and accompanying text.

12 473 U.S. 432 (1985).

person within its jurisdiction the equal protection of the laws,' which is essentially a direction that all persons similarly situated should be treated alike."[13] In the Court's mind, being different or needing something different distinguishes people with disabilities from racial minorities and women. The fact that disability may sometimes be a valid basis for legislative distinctions justifies the Court's refusal to carefully examine the use of disability as a legislative proxy. So long as a state acts rationally, the Court will not second-guess state decisions about people with disabilities. Rationality requires minimal justification.[14]

Since the neighbors in *Cleburne* were not acting rationally, but rather based on irrational prejudice, the Court ruled in favor of the group home—the result: equal treatment to others who were not subject to the zoning ordinance restrictions.[15] For purposes of zoning, the Court saw the residents who were mentally retarded and their neighbors as similarly situated.[16]

So what happens in the analysis when the reasonable accommodation and barrier-removal provisions of the ADA are involved? How does the Court's decision to grant only rational-basis review to disability-based classifications affect the validity of these provisions? These are the issues we have been struggling with in preparing to defend the ADA's constitutionality before the U.S. Supreme Court.

Recent Supreme Court cases have established a test for 14th Amendment legislation, which shows that Congress's principle concern was remedying constitutional violations as defined by the Court. The Court recognizes that Congress is not limited under Section 5[17] to sim-

---

13 *Id.* at 439 (citing Plyler v. Doe, 457 U.S. 202, 216 (1982)).

14 Race-based distinctions require the state to have a compelling state interest, which as a practical matter is virtually impossible. U.S. v. Carolene Prods. Co., 304 U.S. 144 (1938).

15 *See Cleburne*, 473 U.S. at 448. Among the users allowed by the zoning ordinance were fraternity and sorority houses and nursing homes. *Id.* at 436 n. 3.

16 473 U.S. at 448.

17 The 14th Amendment provides in pertinent part:

> Section 1: No state shall . . . deny to any person within its jurisdiction the equal protection of the laws.

ply codifying Supreme Court rulings, but may enact legislation "both to remedy and to deter violation[s] of rights guaranteed [by the 14th Amendment] by prohibiting a somewhat broader swath of conduct, including that which is not itself forbidden by the Amendment's text."[18] The appropriate size of the swath is defined through "congruence and proportionality."[19] I call it the jelly donut rule. The bigger the jelly center (constitutional violations), the bigger the donut (swath) can be.

Our task has now become the daunting one of fitting the ADA into this framework. There are two steps: (1) defining what is unconstitutional conduct, and (2) determining what is a proportionate response to remedy or deter such conduct. In the first step, we are confronted with the role of intent or improper motive as developed in the race and gender cases, most notably *Washington v. Davis*[20] and *Massachusetts v. Feeney*.[21] In these cases, the Court held that legislation that is neutral on its face will not be violative of the 14th Amendment without a showing of discriminatory purpose. The Court held that the state must be found to have "selected or reaffirmed a particular course of action at least in part 'because of,' not merely 'in spite of,' its adverse affects upon an identifiable group."[22] In other words, foreseeable consequences are not enough. If the racial distinction is explicit, heightened scrutiny assumes an intent to discriminate because race is assumed irrelevant to any legitimate classification.

So, I and the other brief writers on the ADA constitutional cases are reevaluating the ADA and its history from this perspective. We assume

---

> . . .
>
> Section 5: The Congress shall have the power to enforce, by appropriate legislation, the provisions of this article.

U.S. Const. amend. XIV, §§ 2, 5.

18 Kimel v. Fla. Bd. of Regents, 120 S. Ct. 631, 644 (2000) (to be published at 528 U.S. 62 (2000)) (footnote omitted) (citing City of Boerne v. Flores, 521 U.S. 507, 518 (1997)).

19 *Id.* at 645.

20 426 U.S. 229 (1976).

21 442 U.S. 256 (1979).

22 *Id.* at 279.

that some actions by states indisputably fall into the unconstitutional core (the jelly center). Such actions that fall into this core are all of the by-products of the eugenics era—institutionalization, forced sterilization, and prohibitions on the right to marry.[23] Other actions, like the denial of the right to vote based on broad disqualifiers or denials by state employers based on demonstrated bias, may fit the core.[24] Rejections from employment opportunities based on discomfort and negative attitudes should be considered unconstitutional.

What about Congress's concerns about lack of accessible transportation, access to buildings, and reasonable accommodation? This is where I have found the arguments excruciating. For 20 years, I have been involved in a concerted effort to explain the nature of discrimination against people with disabilities as involving not just intent or malice, but also benign neglect, thoughtlessness, and oversight. I co-counseled in *Alexander v. Choate*[25] and hailed the part of the decision that recognized that discrimination against people with disabilities includes barriers to participation, whether erected by design or neglect. The court accepted that:

> [M]uch of the conduct that Congress sought to alter in passing the Rehabilitation Act would be difficult if not impossible to reach were the Act construed to proscribe only conduct fueled by a discriminatory intent. . . . [S]tatements [by Congress regarding overcoming barriers to participation] would ring hollow if the resulting legislation could not rectify the harms resulting from action that discriminated by effect as well as by design.[26]

---

[23] For a review of this history, *see generally* Timothy M. Cook, "The Americans with Disabilities Act: The Move to Integration," 64 *Temp. L. Rev.* 393 (1991).

[24] A federal report issued in 1989 showed that eighty-two percent of the state officials polled found that negative attitudes and misconceptions about the abilities of people with disabilities had either a strong or moderate impact on state employment of persons with disabilities. *See* Advisory Commission on Intergovernmental Relations (ACIR), *Disability Rights Mandates, Federal and State Compliance with Employment Protections & Architectural Barrier Removal* 72 (Apr. 1989).

[25] 469 U.S. 287 (1985).

[26] *Id.* at 296–97.

This portion of *Alexander* is now a liability. The constitutional framework for 14th Amendment equal protection, as defined by the recent cases, forces us to argue that the ADA was primarily concerned with intentional, discriminatory conduct or with deterring or remedying such conduct.

Disability policy makers and activists are perplexed. Wasn't our whole effort in the ADA to establish a model of non-discrimination that ensured equal opportunity not simply equal treatment? And isn't it obvious that equal opportunity requires access and accommodations? Why isn't that what we tell the Supreme Court?

So now we are confronted with the real problem. We must justify a material equality statute in formal equality terms. We must show that the ADA's requirements to remove barriers and provide accommodations were really Congress's attempt to deter future intentional discrimination or remedy past intentional discrimination. I think the remedy argument works fairly well. The state established, perpetuated, and reinforced negative and demeaning views of people with disabilities by state-sanctioned isolation and segregation. Since people with disabilities were cast as outsiders, remedial measures need to be taken to bring them back into society. Likewise, Congress can decide that increased interaction is the best remedy to negative stereotyping.[27]

---

[27] As the respondents point out:

> Attorney General Thornburgh, testifying in support of the ADA, declared: "Attitudes can only be reshaped gradually. One of the keys to this reshaping is to increase contact between and among people with disabilities and their non-disabled peers." The US Commission on Civil Rights told Congress that "[s]tudies suggest that increased positive interaction with handicapped people reduces fears and discomfort and leads to better acceptance of handicapped people." . . . Representative Collins made the same point, noting that "only by breaking down barriers between people can we dispel the negative attitudes and myths," and predicting that employers would not apply false stereotypes if they saw the capabilities of persons with disabilities. Senator Durenburger stated that the ADA will "remove the shades many of us wear, focusing on people's abilities rather than their disabilities." . . .

Brief for Respondents at 48, Bd. of Trs. of the Univ. of Ala. v. Garrett (U.S. filed Aug. 11, 2000) (No. 99-1240).

The deterrence argument, which some believe will be more important to the Court, is harder to make fit. Under this theory, the affirmative provisions of the ADA must be justified as deterring future unconstitutional, i.e., intentionally discriminatory, conduct. The classic example of this is upholding as constitutional the Voting Rights Act provisions striking down literacy tests. Because the history of animus was so great toward nonwhites in voting, the chances of the literacy test being a ruse to disguise continued animus was great. Therefore, the Court found that the ban on literacy tests was an attempt by Congress to deter outright discrimination in voting.[28]

Making this argument for access or reasonable accommodation is possible, but forced. The real reason for these provisions was the recognition that equal opportunity could not be achieved without them. No one cared about the reason for the barrier—it was considered irrelevant. No one imagined that we would need to argue that Congress needed to have access requirements in order to ensure that a state was not using an architectural barrier as an excuse for purposeful exclusion that was really based on animus.

Is it really impossible to argue that equal protection in the 14th Amendment means equal opportunity and that a disability equal protection statute must have access provisions in order to have any meaning *whatsoever?* Can we argue that disability discrimination should be taken on its own terms and that the equal treatment approach developed in the race and gender context just does not work? While the types of prejudice, bias, and paternalism faced by racial minorities and women are similar to that experienced by people with disabilities, the remedies are necessarily different. This is easiest to see in the area of architectural access. If equal treatment is designed to promote meritocracy, then architectural and communication access is necessary for a person who is blind, deaf, or in a wheelchair to compete on his/her merits. The consensus of brief writers in support of the ADA is that such a direct argu-

---

[28] Katzenbach v. Morgan, 384 U.S. 641, 653–54 (1966) (showing that the literacy test ban "was merely legislation aimed at the elimination of an invidious discrimination in establishing voter qualifications"); South Carolina v. Katzenbach, 383 U.S. 301, 309 (1966) (stating that the law was enacted in response to "an insidious and pervasive evil").

ment would meet with disfavor by the conservative majority of the Court. So we are forced to explain the obvious need for accommodation to ensure participation as a deterrent for unconstitutional conduct.

The problem with arguing that access is required to ensure that prejudice is not the real motive for exclusion (i.e., deterrence) is that access can often cost money, which means there is an equally, and maybe more, credible reason for failure to remove barriers. Under the rational basis test, this fiscal reason could very well pass muster.[29]

This worst case scenario is unfortunately a reality in the Seventh Circuit. In *Erickson v. Board of Governors*,[30] the Seventh Circuit court held that Title I of the ADA is not a proper exercise of Congress's Section 5 authority because it makes "rational" employer decisions unlawful. Here is the example:

> Consider this from the perspective of a university such as our defendant. A would-be professor who is not in the top 1% of the population in mental acuity is not apt to be a good teacher and scholar. Likewise it is rational for a university to favor someone with good vision over someone who requires the assistance of a reader. The sighted person can master more of the academic literature (reading is much faster than listening), improving his chance to be a productive scholar, and also is less expensive (because the university need not pay for the reader). An academic institution that prefers to use a given budget to hire a sighted scholar plus a graduate teaching assistant, rather than a blind scholar plus a reader, has complied with its constitutional obligation to avoid irrational action. But it has *not* complied with the ADA, which requires accommodation at any cost less than "undue hardship."[31]

---

29 The issue of cost is problematic. If society were built to be inclusive, there would be no extra costs involved in access. Therefore, viewing access as costly creates a hierarchy where nonaccessible is "normal" and "access" abnormal.

30 207 F.3d 945 (7th Cir. 2000).

31 *Id.* at 949.

The Seventh Circuit states that because the ADA requires employers to "accommodate rather than disregard disabilities"[32] it runs counter to the 14th Amendment. Congress's authority to create meaningful equal protection remedies for people with disabilities will soon be decided by the Supreme Court. If Congress is given its due, all of the provisions of the ADA are justified as remedies for historic exclusion and segregation. If the Supreme Court decides that even the remedial and deterrent authority of Congress is limited to a strict equal treatment/intent model of nondiscrimination, the ADA would be rendered meaningless. The world awaits the answer.

C. EQUALITY IN INTERNATIONAL LAW

In contrast to American jurisprudence and its deep roots in classical liberal thought, international law over the past few decades has increasingly taken its cue from the fundamental human rights assumption "that all human beings are equal in respect of their dignity, irrespective of individual or social variations. Each person is thus entitled to equal membership of society, and there is a corresponding duty on the part of the state to secure this aspiration."[33] The resulting model of equality rejects the idea of setting social and cultural standards according to the needs of a "normal" majority, and extends the idea of equality beyond equal treatment towards equal outcome. By logical implication, such a model of equality rejects both the idea of establishing laws that achieve equality only for certain "similarly situated" persons, and an ideal that rigidly refuses to make any kind of differentiation between individuals, since the needs of *all* human beings—with their myriad differences—have to be considered.

Numerous United Nations (UN) and state officials have raised this last issue more explicitly in discussions about non-discrimination pro-

---

32 *Id.* at 950.

33 Aart Hendriks, "The Significance of Equality and Non-Discrimination," *in Human Rights and Disabled Persons: Essays and Relevant Human Rights Instruments* 40, 46 (Theresia Degener & Yolan Koster-Dreese eds., Dordrecht; Boston; London: Martinus Nijhoff Pub., 1995) [hereinafter H.R. and D.P.] (citing J. Donald C. Galloway, "Three Models of (In) Equality," 38 *McGill L.J.* 64, 83 (1993)).

visions in the International Covenant on Civil and Political Rights (ICCPR)[34] and the International Covenant on Economic, Social, and Cultural Rights (ICESCR),[35] the two covenants which—together with the Universal Declaration of Human Rights[36]—form the backbone of the UN's Human Rights Bill.[37] For instance, the UN Human Rights Committee has stated that:

> [T]he term "discrimination" as used in the Covenant [ICCPR] should be understood to imply any distinction, exclusion, restriction or preference which is based on any ground such as race, colour, sex, language, religion, political or other opinion, national or social origin, property, birth or other status, and which has the purpose or effect of nullifying or impairing the recognition or enjoyment or exercise by all persons, on an equal footing, of all rights and freedoms.[38]

Clearly the notion of discrimination in international human rights law extends beyond the limits of formal equality, since discrimination encompasses not only making an unjustified distinction, but includes acts that have "the purpose *or effect of nullifying or impairing* the recognition or enjoyment or exercise by all persons, on an equal footing, of all rights and freedoms."[39] It is not the intention behind an act that is

---

[34] Dec. 19, 1966, 6 I.L.M. 368, 999 U.N.T.S. 171.

[35] Dec. 16, 1966, 993 U.N.T.S. 3.

[36] G.A. Res. 217A, U.N. GAOR, 3rd Sess., Supp. No. 1, U.N. Doc. A/810 (1948).

[37] The ICCPR and the ICESCR both have the status of a treaty, which means that they are considered binding and carry the obligation of domestic legal implementation for signing states; their status for nonsigning states is more uncertain—for example, the United States has not ratified the ICESCR. The Universal Declaration is not a treaty, but has been extremely influential on the constitutional enactments and human rights policies of numerous states and has achieved a certain status in international law as an interpretive tool at least.

[38] 1 *Report of the Human Rights Committee*, General Comment No. 18(37) (nondiscrimination), U.N. GAOR, 45th Sess., Supp. No. 40, at 174, ¶ 7, U.N. Doc. A/45/40 (1990).

[39] *Id.* (emphasis added).

important, but its consequence for people. The UN Committee on Economic, Social, and Cultural Rights has gone further, and made a specific reference to disability in stating that "[f]or the purpose of the Covenant [ICESCR], 'disability-based discrimination' may be defined as including any distinction, exclusion, restriction or preference, or denial of reasonable accommodation based on disability which has the effect of nullifying or impairing the recognition, enjoyment or exercise of economic, social or cultural rights."[40] The unambiguous reference to "reasonable accommodation" clearly moves beyond the U.S. constitutional adherence to formal equality and embraces material equality.

Ironically, this broad conception of equality comes from an international law movement that has traditionally dealt with disabled persons as a health and welfare issue rather than a human rights issue; even now, the United Nations concept of minorities focuses on ethnic, linguistic and religious identifiers rather than characteristics of physical or mental disability.[41] The particular contribution of disability activists in the United States since the 1960s has been to insist on viewing disability as a civil rights issue, and the example of their approach to legal reform has undoubtedly helped international disability organizations "to demand civil rights rather than goodwill."[42] The battle for disability organizations in the arena of international law, then, has not usually been over an appropriate model of equality, but gaining explicit recognition *within* the broad umbrella of human rights law. The advantage, once such recognition was achieved, was that international human rights already tended towards a material and substantive model of equality, rather than a formal model.

The question must then be asked—has this recognition been achieved? The UN Decade of Disabled Persons, initiated in 1982, marked a period of real change and increased visibility for international

---

40 *General Comment No. 5 (1994) on Persons with Disabilities*, U.N. ESCOR, Report on the 10th and 11th Sessions, Supp. No. 2 [according to U.N. Doc. E/1995/22/Corr.1–E/C.12/1994/20/Corr.1], at 102, ¶ 15, U.N. Doc. E/1995/22–E/C.12/1994/20 (1995).

41 Theresia Degener, "Disabled Persons and Human Rights: The Legal Framework," *in* H.R. AND D.P., supra note 33, at 13.

42 *Id.* at 10.

disability activism. The UN's second World Conference on Human Rights, which took place June 25, 1993, explicitly links persons with disabilities to a human rights model of material equality by reconfirming:

> that all human rights and fundamental freedoms are universal and thus unreservedly include persons with disabilities . . . [and] calls on all Governments, where necessary, to adopt or adjust legislation to ensure access to these [life, welfare, education, work, living independently, and active participation in all aspects of society] and other rights for disabled persons.[43]

The decade culminated in the drafting of the Standard Rules on the Equalization of Opportunities for Persons with Disabilities (StRE),[44] which were adopted by the UN General Assembly on December 20, 1993,[45] and intended as a basic international standard for future state programs, laws and policies on disability. The merging of the civil rights approach of disability activists and the material equality notions of international human rights is evident in the StRE's introduction, which strongly emphasizes both equality of opportunity and integration:

> The term "equalization of opportunities" means the process through which the various systems of society and environment, such as services, activities, information and documentation, are made available to all, particularly to persons with disabilities. The principle of equal rights implies that the needs of each and every individual are of equal importance, that those needs must be made the basis for the planning of societies and that all resources must be employed in such a way as to ensure that

---

[43] United Nations, Vienna Declaration and Programme of Action, *Reports of the World Conference*, at Title II, ¶ 63, U.N. Doc.A/CONF.157/23 (1993).

[44] G.A. Res. 48/96, U.N. GAOR, 48th Sess., Supp. No. 49, U.N. Doc. A/48/49 (1994).

[45] The StRE are nonbinding U.N. instruments because they cannot be signed and ratified by individual nation-states. On the other hand, whatever force the Rules have is at least immediate since they came into force when adopted by the General Assembly and could eventually attain binding force in international law, if enough states apply them with the intention of establishing an "international customary rule."

every individual has equal opportunity for participation. Persons with disabilities are members of society and have the right to remain within their local communities. They should receive the support they need within the ordinary structures of education, health, employment and social services.[46]

Even though the UN Comments and Declarations, the ICCPR and the ICESCR, and the Rules are important steps towards the achievement of material equality for persons with disabilities, the lack of a binding covenant on disability antidiscrimination is still a tremendous problem in international law.[47] Ultimately, the StRE encapsulates both the strengths and the weaknesses of advancing disability rights in the arena of international law: as long as the Rules address disability as a civil rights issue, they do so within a clear context of material equality and social responsibility for reasonable accommodation, but the Rules themselves remain nonbinding and lack domestic enforcement mechanisms.

D. CANADIAN JUDICIAL MODEL OF EQUALITY

In other countries around the world, we can see that a number of nations that have had the opportunity to draft constitutional discrimination provisions more recently than the United States have also had the chance to learn from that country's painful and convoluted struggle to define the reach and limits of the 14th Amendment. The equality provisions of the Canadian Charter of Rights and Freedoms (Charter) have left the

---

46 *Standard Rules for the Equalization of Opportunities for Persons with Disabilities*, G.A. Res. 48/96, *supra* note 44, at 204, ¶¶ 24–26.

47 Further, the 22 Rules are biased towards economic, social and cultural rights, rather than civil and political rights. So, for instance, human rights violations, such as the forced sterilization of women with disabilities, are simply not discussed. This odd oversight likely reflects the fact that the Rules were drafted under the auspices of the UN's Commission for Social Development, instead of the Commission on Human Rights or the Sub-Commission on Prevention of Discrimination and Protection of Minorities; in any event, the StRE does explicitly refer to numerous UN instruments in its preamble—including the ICCPR—and should therefore be interpreted in light of these additional pronouncements. For a fuller exposition on the StRE and other UN instruments relevant to persons with disabilities, *see* Degener, *supra* note 41.

Canadian judiciary with the difficult task of interpreting the applicability of formal and substantive models of equality. In this regard, Canadian jurisprudence is particularly useful for the purposes of this article as the Supreme Court of Canada (SCC) has expressly considered and rejected the analytical route taken in the United States equal protection jurisprudence.[48]

Section 15 of the Canadian Charter reads as follows:

> 15(1) Every individual is equal before and under the law and has the right to the equal protection and equal benefit of the law without discrimination and, in particular, without discrimination based on race, national or ethnic origin, colour, religion, sex, age or mental or physical disability.
>
> (2) Subsection (1) does not preclude any law, program or activity that has as its object the amelioration of conditions of disadvantaged individuals or groups including those that are disadvantaged because of race, national or ethnic origin, colour, religion, sex, age or mental or physical disability.[49]

Section 15 first came into effect in 1985, three years after the Charter was enacted, and the first Section 15 case did not come before the SCC until 1989. In 1997, the court reiterated how, from the very beginning of its Section 15 jurisprudence, it "has staked out a different path than the United States Supreme Court, which requires a discriminatory intent in order to ground an equal protection claim under the Fourteenth Amendment of the Constitution."[50] In its first Section 15 decision, the court had refused to restrict itself to using the "similarly situated" test, and recognized:

---

48 For a useful examination of the equality models embraced by the courts of other countries, *see generally Non-Discrimination Law: Comparative Perspectives* (Titia Loenen & Peter R. Rodrigues eds., Dordrecht; Boston; London: Martinus Nijhoff Pub., 1999).

49 Can. Const. (Constitution Act, 1982) pt. I (Canadian Charter of Rights and Freedoms), § 15.

50 Eldridge v. British Columbia (Attorney General), [1997] 151 D.L.R. (4th) 577, 616 (Can.).

> that every difference in treatment between individuals under the law will not necessarily result in inequality and, as well, that identical treatment may frequently produce inequality . . . [t]o approach the ideal of full equality before and under the law . . . the main consideration must be the impact of the law on the individual or the group concerned.[51]

Section 15(1)'s specific wording of equality "before and under the law" and the "equal protection and equal benefit of the law" has been referred to as the "four equalities," and has been interpreted as a deliberate attempt to avoid the shortcomings of the prior Canadian Bill of Rights, which lacked constitutional force and only ensured "equality before the law."[52] In cases from the 1970s, the SCC had interpreted this latter phrase in the Canadian Bill of Rights as providing only a very narrow form of formal equality, "requiring that laws be applied in an even-handed manner but leaving the content and effect of the law itself immune to judicial scrutiny."[53] The expansion of the equality language in Section 15 was at the very least a signal that the Charter should be interpreted as giving individuals more than a mere guarantee of strictly formal equality. In addition, Section 15(2)'s explicit reference to the "amelioration" of existing conditions of discrimination could be taken as another signal that the Charter endorsed a more substantive model of equality. Finally, Section 15's open-ended list of what constitutes a prohibited ground of discrimination would come to be taken as yet another interpretive tool for a judiciary searching for guidelines and limiting principles in a new era of discrimination protection; the court would come to see social, political, and economic *disadvantage* as the critical factor common to the enumerated grounds and other "analogous" kinds of discrimination prohibited by Section 15.[54]

---

[51] Andrews v. L. Soc'y of B.C., [1989] 1 S.C.R. 143, 164–65 (Can.).

[52] S.C. 1969, c. 44 (Can.), (now R.S.C. 1985, app. III).

[53] Béatrice Vizkelety, "Adverse Effect Discrimination in Canada: Crossing the Rubicon from Formal to Substantive Equality," *in Non-Discrimination Law: Comparative Perspectives*, *supra* note 48, at 223–24.

[54] R. v. Turpin, [1989] 1 S.C.R. 1296 (Can.), in which the SCC held that

Another crucial tool of interpretation available to the SCC in its Section 15 interpretation is Section 1 of the Charter, which the court has expressly noted as a limiting provision unavailable to the United States Supreme Court under their 14th Amendment.[55] Section 1 applies to the entire Charter and states that "The *Canadian Charter of Rights and Freedoms* guarantees the rights and freedoms set out in it subject only to such reasonable limits prescribed by law as can be demonstrably justified in a free and democratic society."

Since the SCC's 1986 foundational decision on Section 1 in *R. v. Oakes*,[56] the government has borne the onus of establishing that: (a) the objective behind the impugned legislation or action is of sufficient importance to justify a Charter infringement; and (b) the means chosen to achieve this objective are reasonable and justified. This second part of the test includes three parts: (i) is there a *rational connection* between the objective and the means? (ii) is there *minimal impairment* of the Charter right? and (iii) does the objective have a *proportionality of effects?* The relationship between Section 1 and Section 15 of the Charter was brought up again recently by the SCC when it referred to the government's duty to take positive action as being limited by the human rights principle of reasonable accommodation and "undue hardship." Speaking for a unanimous court, Justice La Forest wrote, "In my view, in § 15(1) cases this principle is best addressed as a component of the § 1 analysis. Reasonable accommodation, in this context, is generally equivalent to the concept of 'reasonable limits.' It should not be employed to restrict the ambit of § 15(1)."[57]

Section 15 was not violated by a law that allowed a distinction in the mode of trial between persons in Alberta and those in the rest of Canada accused of certain offenses; since the statutory distinction did not result in actual disadvantage, the plaintiffs were not a group analogous to a Section 15 enumerated group within the meaning of the Charter. The use of the "analogous grounds" principal as a concept has been hailed by some as a means of directing equality rights towards those groups in society which are most in need of protection. *See* Vizkelety, *supra* note 53, at 26–27. *But see, e.g.*, David Beatty, "The Canadian Conception of Equality," 46 *U. Toronto L.J.* 349 (1996) (criticizing the distinction as unnecessary and categorical).

[55] Andrews v. L. Soc'y of B.C., [1989] 1 S.C.R. 143, 177–78.

[56] [1986] 26 D.L.R. (4th) 200 (Can.).

[57] Having said this, there is still a trio of SCC cases from 1995 which threw

Within this interpretive context, we can now look closely at *Eldridge v. British Columbia (Attorney General)*,[58] one of the SCC's most recent decisions on Section 15 and a pivotal case on disability rights in Canadian law. The plaintiffs in *Eldridge* first brought their case before the British Columbia (B.C.) Supreme Court because the province did not provide medical interpretation services to deaf patients. Robin Eldridge had been unable to communicate with her physician, and John and Linda Warren had undergone the ordeal of giving premature birth to their twins without being able to fully comprehend what their doctors and nurses were telling them. The plaintiffs framed their action under Section 15 of the Charter, claiming that provincial hospitals legislation discriminated against the deaf by failing to provide for sign language interpretive services when effective communication was an inherent and necessary component of the delivery of medical services. Both the provincial trial judge and appellate court majority[59] rejected

---

serious doubt on this view of the interaction of Section 1 and Section 15. In *Miron v. Trudel*, [1995] 2 S.C.R. 418 (Can.), the concept of a "functional values" test for Section 15 was set forth in the dissenting opinion of four of the justices. The functional-values test essentially posited an additional step for Section 15 analysis: claimants under Section 15 would need to not only establish that (i) a distinction had been made, and (ii) the distinction resulted in discrimination, i.e., a burden or disadvantage, but also that (iii) the distinction had been based on a personal characteristic that was *irrelevant* to the functional values underlying the legislation. *Miron* itself dealt with a claim that the Ontario Insurance Act violated Section 15 by defining the term "spouse" in relation to married couples, thereby excluding unmarried common law spouses. The majority found that Section 15 had been violated, but the minority considered the institution of marriage as a "functional value" underlying the Act that was both relevant to legitimate legislative aims and clearly related to the grounds of the distinction. Even though the functional-values test was never relied on by a clear majority of the SCC in any case of the trilogy, which also included *Egan v. Canada*, [1995] 2 S.C.R. 513 (Can.), and *Thibaudeau v. Canada*, [1995] 2 S.C.R. 627 (Can.), enough references were made to the test that considerable confusion was sown among Canadian courts until the most recent Section 15 cases from 1997. For a critique of the "functional values" test and the dangers it poses, *see, e.g.*, David Beatty, "Canadian Constitutional Law in a Nutshell," 36 *Alberta L. Rev*. 605, 618 (1998).

58 [1997] 151 D.L.R. (4th) 577 (Can.).

59 J. A. Lambert of the British Columbia Court of Appeals found that Section 15 had been violated, but he found the violation justified under Section 1 of the

their claim, finding that the need for deaf persons to pay for interpreters arose from the fact of the disability and was not an effect of the B.C. Hospital Insurance Act[60] or the Medical and Health Care Services Act.[61]

The appeal to the SCC was allowed. The court began its Section 15(1) analysis[62] by stressing the Section's "two distinct but related purposes." First, the Section "expresses a commitment—deeply ingrained in our social, political and legal culture—to the equal worth and human dignity of all persons." Second, "it instantiates a desire to rectify and prevent discrimination against particular groups 'suffering social, political and legal disadvantage in our society.'"[63] The decision continues by taking judicial notice of the "unfortunate truth that the history of disabled persons in Canada is largely one of exclusion and marginalization. Persons with disabilities have too often been excluded from the labour force, denied access to opportunities for social interaction and advancement, subjected to invidious stereotyping and relegated to institutions." By beginning their Section 15(1) analysis in this way, the SCC sends a strong message that equality in the Charter is not just a tool for formally comparing faceless citizens in an abstract manner, but a legitimate ideal that has a particular and dynamic role to play in the lives of individuals and groups that suffer real disadvantage in Canadian society.

Charter, basing his decision on the SCC's own dictum that the *Oakes* Section 1 test should be applied flexibly and with deference when reviewing the elected government's allocation of scarce resources between different needs and groups. Since it was accepted that the province's medical plan did not have to be comprehensive (for example dental services, wheelchairs, and transportation were not covered), Lambert accepted the government's decision not to cover sign-language interpreters.

60 R.S.B.C. 1979, c. 180 (Can.).

61 S.B.C. 1992, c. 76 (Can.).

62 The lengthy first portion of the decision dealt with the particular issue of whether, in the facts of the case, private hospitals fell under the ambit of the Charter. The approach eventually taken by the court has important implications in an era marked by the political attractiveness of government downsizing and privatization, but this ground of the decision is obviously beyond the scope of this paper. For a more in-depth analysis of the legal reasoning on this point, see Margot Young, "Change at the Margins: *Eldridge v. British Columbia (A.G.)* and *Vriend v. Alberta*," 10 *Canadian J. of Women and the L.* 244 (1998).

63 Eldridge, [1997] D.L.R. (4th) at 612.

In the end, the court unanimously found that the province could not satisfy Section 15 simply by providing deaf persons with health care services strictly identical to those received by hearing persons. They accepted that effective communication is an indispensable part of medical services, and that Section 15 placed the province under an obligation to ensure that deaf persons could effectively communicate with health care providers so as to receive equal advantage from their health care benefits under the Provincial Hospital Act. As a result, even though the two statutes in and of themselves did not violate Section 15, the province's failure to ensure the "equal benefit of the law" to persons with disabilities was a violation of the Charter. The court unmistakably endorsed a substantive model of equality when it wrote:

> Section 15(1) expressly states, after all, that every individual is "equal before and under the law and has the right to the equal protection *and* equal benefit of the law without discrimination. . . ." The provision makes no distinction between laws that impose unequal burdens and those that deny equal benefits. If we accept the concept of adverse effect discrimination, it seems inevitable, at least at the s. 15(1) stage of analysis, that the government will be required to take special measures to ensure that disadvantaged groups are able to benefit equally from government services.[64]

Furthermore, Section 1 did not save this violation of Section 15, despite the delicate and difficult balance invoked by legislative decisions regarding the budgetary allocation of health-care dollars within the province, because the province did not establish that a *total* denial of medical interpretation services for the deaf constituted a *minimal* impairment of their rights. As La Forest stated for the court:

> Given the central place of good health in the quality of life of all persons in our society, the provision of substandard medical services to the deaf necessarily diminishes the overall quality of their lives. The government has simply not demonstrated that this unpropitious state of affairs must be tolerated in order to

64 *Id.* at 623 (emphasis added).

> achieve the objective of limiting health care expenditures. Stated differently, the government has not made a "reasonable accommodation" of the appellants' disability. In the language of this Courts' [sic] human rights jurisprudence, it has not accommodated the appellants' needs to the point of "undue hardship."[65]

By interpreting Section 15 in a way that recognizes that certain groups may *need* a benefit in order to enjoy equality, *Eldridge* at least opens the possibility that governments are constitutionally required to take positive and substantive steps to ensure that persons with disabilities and other groups who experience discrimination receive the "equal protection and equal benefit" of the law. Also, Section 15 will provide protection even where the law itself is not making a distinction between individuals, but is merely being applied in a way that allows a distinction to exist.[66]

---

65 *Id.* at 631.

66 However, despite encouraging comments in *dicta*, the Supreme Court of Canada has continued to leave the issue of positive obligations under Section 15 open, thereby implying that the government must take account of the realities of social discrimination when they act, but need not redress the fact of that discrimination themselves. In *Vriend v. Alberta*, [1998] 1 S.C.R. 493 (Can.), the most recent SCC decision on Section 15, the Court dealt with the failure to include sexual preference as a ground for protection from discrimination under Alberta's Individual Rights Protection Act, R.S.A. 1980, c. I-2 (Can.). The case arose when the lead plaintiff was dismissed from a Christian college for being a practicing homosexual. The court unanimously decided that the provincial legislation violated Section 15 of the Charter, but the court was careful to state that:

> It is also unnecessary to consider whether a government could properly be subjected to a challenge under section 15 of the *Charter* for failing to act *at all*, in contrast to a case such as this where it acted in an underinclusive manner. . . . It has not yet been necessary to decide in other contexts whether the *Charter* might impose positive obligations on the legislatures or on Parliament such that a failure to legislate could be challenged under the *Charter*. Nonetheless, the possibility has been considered and left open in some cases. . . . [I]t is neither necessary nor appropriate to consider that broad issue in this case.

Vriend, [1998] 1 S.C.R. at ¶¶ 63–64.

While *Eldridge* does not require the government to enact non-discrimination legislation, the decision likely has already influenced Canadian legislation, given the 1998 amendments to the Canadian Human Rights Act,[67] which now requires employers to positively accommodate special needs short of undue hardship.

Eldridge has been applauded by numerous scholars and constitutional authorities. In his analysis of *Eldridge*, Bruce Porter notes that "[u]nder the emerging framework in *Eldridge*, the violation occurs, essentially, with the unmet need, not with any particular statute."[68] On a broader, doctrinal level, Dianne Pothier praises the court's willingness to delve deeper than the kind of analysis that prevailed in the lower courts, where sign language was viewed as just another discrete service that was ancillary to medical care, such as transportation to a hospital or doctor's office. In other words, both the trial judge and a majority of the appellate court placed emphasis on the fact that the province had the discretion to fill its basket of basic medical care with various services, and as long as this basket was equally available to able-bodied persons and persons with disabilities, there was no discrimination. The problem is that such an analysis fails to address the entrenched and unspoken assumption that there is only one "proper" way to receive these services—that is, via spoken communication—and if that means is not

---

Even though the court refused to decide whether Section 15 could require the government to take positive actions, the decision at least clearly indicated that government actions had to take account of existing social realities. Lesbians and gay men faced social discrimination where heterosexual persons did not, and "[i]t is not necessary to find that the legislation creates the discrimination existing in society in order to determine that it creates a potentially discriminatory distinction." *Id.* at ¶ 84. The Ontario Court of Appeals in *Ferrell v. Ontario (Attorney General)*, [1998] 168 D.L.R. (4th) 1 (Can.), reviewed much of the SCC's pronouncements on this point and expanded in some length on its own *dicta* opinion that Section 15(1) did *not* impose a duty of positive action on the government. The appellants in *Ferrell* filed a further leave to appeal to the SCC, which was denied on Dec. 6, 1999, 179 D.L.R. (4th) vii (Can.).

67 R.S.C. 1998, c. H-6 (Can.).

68 Bruce Porter, "Beyond Andrews: Substantive Equality and Positive Obligations After *Eldridge* and *Vriend*," 9 *Const. F.* 71, 78 (1998).

available, for whatever reason, then rectification of the situation is merely "ancillary" to basic health care. In Pothier's words:

> All patients require communication with their health care providers; hearing patients can do so directly, without charge, whereas deaf patients, assuming the health care provider does not know sign language, require an intermediary. . . . The Supreme Court of Canada's rejection of the characterization of sign language as an ancillary service is thus a rejection of an analysis that privileges able-bodied methods.[69]

The Canadian Supreme Court has explicitly rejected the United States Supreme Court's adherence to formal equality and embraced a substantive model of equality in which the adverse effects of discrimination will be regarded as potentially violative of Section 15, even without any evidence of invidious motivation or malicious intent. With *Eldridge*, the court has acknowledged that true equality may require the government to take special measures to ensure that disadvantaged groups can fully enjoy and participate in the benefits afforded by law.[70]

---

69 Dianne Pothier, *"Eldridge v. British Columbia (Attorney General):* How the Deaf Were Heard in the Supreme Court of Canada," 9 *Nat'l J. of Const. L.* 263, 268–69 (1998). Both Pothier and other authors remain wary of just how far *Eldridge* may be taken as a rejection of able-bodied norms in the face of severe disabilities given the SCC's slightly earlier decision in *Eaton v. Brant (County) Board of Education,* [1997] 142 D.L.R. (4th) 385, in which the court upheld a school board's decision to place a child with cerebral palsy in a special placement class over the parents' objections. *See also generally* Isabel Grant and Judith Mosoff, "Hearing Claims of Inequality: *Eldridge v. British Columbia (Attorney General),"* 10 *Canadian J. of Women and the L.* 229 (1998); Margot Young, "Sameness/Difference: A Tale of Two Girls," 4 *Rev. of Const. Studies* 150 (1997).

70 Nonetheless, the Canadian picture is not entirely rosy. While Eldridge and Vriend are encouraging, commentators have pointed out that they were both "easy" cases to decide factually and politically. *See generally* Margot Young, "Change at the Margins," *supra* note 62. Also, the "functional values" test, if applied as a threshold requirement of Section 15, has the potential to weaken or even negate the most liberating aspects of recognizing adverse discrimination. Through the back door, judicial focus would switch to legislative intentions and the objective relevance of disability for government actions and away from the real effects of inequal-

E. CONCLUSION

If the facts of *Eldridge* had been brought before the United States Supreme Court on 14th Amendment constitutional grounds, as opposed to the ADA,[71] it is questionable whether the plaintiffs would have prevailed. The health care legislation was facially neutral, and clearly enacted for a substantive general purpose, not "because of" its discriminatory effect upon persons with a disability. The most narrow application of formal equality perpetuates the exclusion of persons with disability by refusing to recognize that the "same" treatment can itself be discriminatory. In contrast, a material equality approach deals with the real-life consequences of "neutral" actions and requires accommodation when necessary to achieve equality.

Equal protection is violated when a person with a disability does not have equal access to the service that the government provides. The cases currently pending in the United States Supreme Court will determine whether the 14th Amendment is a vehicle for achieving equality or just one more barrier in the road to equal citizenship for people with disabilities.

---

ity experienced by persons with disabilities. Furthermore, neither decision went so far as to actually endorse the idea that Section 15 could be used to *require* governments to enact social change by taking positive actions in an area where none had been taken in the past.

[71] We note that it is questionable whether the Canadian federal government has the jurisdiction to enact legislation as sweeping in its application to private business as the ADA, given the Canadian Constitution's division of subjects between federal and provincial legislative spheres, and the long judicial history of constitutional interpretation. For example, the Employment Equity Act, R.S.C. 1985, c. 44 (Can.), holds both the federal government and federally registered businesses to a standard of reasonable accommodation in the employment of persons with disabilities and extends that requirement to provincial businesses that seek federal contracts, but does not directly apply to all private Canadian businesses. This is where issues concerning the ambit of the Charter's direct reach become critical. Similarly, it is arguable whether the SCC would find it unconstitutional if one province were to enact ADA-like legislation, while another Canadian province failed to do so.

The Right to Community Integration for People with Disabilities Under United States and International Law

Eric Rosenthal and Arlene Kanter[1]

A. INTRODUCTION

In many countries of the world today, people with disabilities are deprived of their rights and liberties, excluded from society, and blamed for many of society's most unsolvable problems, such as crime and homelessness. People with disabilities, particularly people with mental disabilities, may be involuntarily locked away in institutions, subjected to abuse and neglect, and deprived of their right to live as equal citizens in the community.[2] Governments that perpetuate such mistreatment are rarely subject to international scrutiny or recrimination. Although some

---

1 Eric Rosenthal, Executive Director, Mental Disability Rights International (MDRI), <http://www.mdri.org/>, 1156 15th St. N.W., Washington, D.C., U.S.A. 20005 and Arlene Kanter, Professor of Law and Director of Clinical Legal Education, Syracuse University College of Law, Syracuse, N.Y., U.S.A. 13244–1030. Please contact the authors at eric.rosenthal@erols.com and kantera@law.syr.edu, respectively. The authors wish to thank Professor Donna Arzt, Director of the Global Law and Practice Center of Syracuse University College of Law, for sharing her expertise and comments on a previous draft, and Mary Dispenza (SU COL '02) for her indispensable research assistance.

2 The term "people with mental disabilities" refers to people who have been diagnosed with developmental disabilities, intellectual disabilities, or mental illness, or who are perceived as having such mental disabilities. Although there is no internationally accepted definition of the term "disability," the Standard Rules of 1993 define "disability" as "summariz[ing] a great number of different functional limitations occurring in any population. . . . People may be disabled by physical, intellectual or sensory impairment, medical conditions or mental illness. Such impairments, conditions or illnesses may be permanent or transitory in nature." Introduction, ¶ 17, of the Standard Rules on the Equalization of Opportunities for Persons with Disabilities, G.A. Res. 48/96, U.N. GAOR., 48th Sess., Supp. No. 48, Annex at 202–11, U.N. Doc. A/Res/48/49 (1993) [hereinafter Standard Rules].

international laws that prohibit mistreatment and discrimination against people with disabilities have been adopted, no specific binding international human rights convention exists to protect explicitly the right of people with disabilities to live in the community or to be free from indeterminate institutionalization. Yet, there is a growing recognition that recent interpretations of United States law, as well as international human rights law, provide support for the right of an individual with a disability to live and receive any necessary treatment in the community, rather than in an institution.[3]

In *Olmstead v. L.C. ex rel. Zimring*, ("*Olmstead*") the United States Supreme Court held that it is discrimination to deny people with disabilities services in the most integrated setting appropriate.[4] Accordingly, the Court found that individuals with mental disabilities are entitled to live in the community, whenever appropriate, and to receive treatment there, rather than in institutions.[5] The Court reached its conclusion by relying on the non-discrimination provisions of the Americans with Disabilities Act of 1990.[6] The Court's reasoning, that institutionalization of people with disabilities who are capable of living in the community may constitute unlawful discrimination under the Americans with Disabilities Act (ADA), may serve as a model for a similar recognition under international human rights law. In fact, the United Nations Committee on Economic, Social, and Cultural Rights recently adopted General Comment 5[7] which provides a new and bold interpretation of

---

[3] This chapter seeks to highlight the most relevant binding and non-binding international laws and documents relevant to establishing a claim for community integration and against unnecessary institutionalization as discrimination under international law; it does not and could not include all relevant international documents, reports or comments.

[4] 527 U.S. 581 (1999).

[5] *Id.*

[6] 42 U.S.C. § 12101 *et seq.* (2001).

[7] *General Comment No. 5 (1994) on Persons with Disabilities, Report on the Tenth and Eleventh Sessions*, U.N. ESCOR 1995, Supp. No. 2 [according to U.N. Doc. E/1995/22/Corr.1–E/C.12/1994/20/Corr.1], at 102, ¶ 15, U.N. Doc. E/1995/22–E/C.12/1994/20 (1995) [hereinafter General Comment 5].

the right to protection against discrimination under the International Convention on Economic, Social, and Cultural Rights by implying a right to community integration within the anti-discrimination provision of the Covenant.[8]

Indeed, if the reasoning of the United States Supreme Court in *Olmstead* were to be used as a guide in interpreting the non-discrimination provisions of such international covenants as the International Covenant on Civil and Political Rights and the International Covenant on Economic, Social and Cultural Rights, it would have a major impact on the lives of people with disabilities who are unnecessarily confined in institutions throughout the world today. Although no specific international covenant exists on the rights and treatment of people with disabilities, recent international human rights laws, documents and interpretations may establish the right of people with disabilities to live in the community and to be free from institutionalization.

The first section of this article discusses the decision of the United States Supreme Court in *Olmstead*, in which the Supreme Court upholds a right to community integration for people with mental disabilities as a form of discrimination protection provided under Title II of the Americans with Disabilities Act. The second section of this article discusses existing international human rights laws and interpretations, including specific provisions addressing the right of individuals with disabilities to community integration and the rights of those detained in institutions. The article concludes by suggesting that the Supreme Court's reasoning in *Olmstead*, together with existing international human rights laws and interpretations, provides support for the right of people with disabilities to be free from indeterminate institutionalization and to live in the community as a form of protection from discrimination under international law.

---

8 For background on the development of General Comment 5, *see* Philip Alston, "Disability and the International Covenant on Economic, Social and Cultural Rights," *in Human Rights and Disabled Persons* 94–105 (Theresia Degener & Yolan Koster-Dreese eds., Dordrecht; Boston; London: Martinus Nijhoff Publishers, 1995) [hereinafter Degener & Koster-Dreese].

B. *OLMSTEAD* AND THE EMERGING RIGHT TO COMMUNITY INTEGRATION

In the United States, federal statutes and case law have established limits on the extent to which people with disabilities, and mental disabilities, in particular, may be institutionalized against their will.[9] Following the horrors of World War II, advocates for social security and rehabilitation sought to expand services for people with disabilities in the community, away from segregated institutions. As a result, in 1954, the United States Congress passed the country's first broad-based rehabilitation legislation, the Vocational Rehabilitation Amendments, which expanded rehabilitation programs available to people with a variety of disabilities.[10] Two decades later, in the midst of the civil rights movement, Congress passed the Rehabilitation Act of 1973, which prohibits discrimination against people with disabilities in federal programs, as part of the larger movement to achieve community integration and inclusion of people with disabilities in society.[11]

In 1990, when the United States Congress passed the Americans with Disabilities Act ("ADA"), it recognized the long history of mistreatment to which people with disabilities had been subjected. As the preamble of the ADA states, "individuals with disabilities are a discrete and insular minority who have been faced with restrictions and limitations, subjected to a history of purposeful unequal treatment, and relegated to a position of political powerlessness . . . based on characteristics that are beyond the control of such individuals and resulting from stereotypic assumptions not truly indicative of the individual ability of such individuals to participate in, and contribute to, society."[12] Accordingly, the ADA prohibits discrimination in a range of areas including employ-

---

[9] *See, e.g.*, O'Connor v. Donaldson, 422 U.S. 563 (1975); Youngberg v. Romeo, 457 U.S. 307 (1982); Olmstead v. L.C. *ex rel.* Zimring, 527 U.S. 581 (1999).

[10] The current Vocational Rehabilitation Act is codified at 29 U.S.C. §§ 701–796 (2001). The history of the Vocational Rehabilitation Act is detailed in S. Rep. No. 93–318 (1973), *reprinted in* 1973 U.S.C.C.A.N. 2076.

[11] 29 U.S.C. § 794 (1976).

[12] 42 U.S.C. § 12101(a)(7) (2001).

ment, public life, transportation, telecommunications, and public accommodations.[13] The law recognizes that the "[n]ation's proper goals regarding individuals with disabilities are to assure equality of opportunity, full participation, independent living, and economic self-sufficiency for such individuals."[14]

When Congress passed the ADA in 1990, by a large majority and with bipartisan support,[15] it recognized that its predecessor law, the Rehabilitation Act, had not been sufficient to eradicate discrimination against people with disabilities. As Congress declared in the introduction to the ADA, "despite some improvements, . . . discrimination against individuals with disabilities continue[s] to be a serious and pervasive social problem."[16]

Indeed, throughout history and throughout the world, societies have promoted or acquiesced in discrimination against people with disabilities.[17] Discrimination has taken the form of preventing qualified applicants with disabilities from obtaining or retaining employment, failing to make public transportation accessible or provide access to public places, and isolating people labeled mentally ill or developmentally disabled in institutions, often subjected to forced labor, deprived of liberty without due process, and stripped of their dignity as well.

Undoubtedly, one of the most egregious forms of discrimination is the involuntary segregation of people in institutions. When it enacted the ADA, Congress acknowledged that segregation and isolation of individuals with disabilities continues even today. Although people with disabilities have made progress towards equality and inclusion in workplaces, neighborhoods and recreational activities, many individu-

---

13 42 U.S.C. § 12101 *et seq.* (2001).

14 42 U.S.C. § 12101(a)(8) (2001).

15 The ADA was enacted amidst widespread support. It passed the House by a vote of 377–28 and the Senate by a vote of 91–6. *See* 2 Bonnie Tucker & Bruce Goldstein, *Legal Rights of Persons with Disabilities: An Analysis of Federal Law* 21 (Supp. 1996) (1992) (Horsham, PA.: LRP Publications, 1992).

16 42 U.S.C. § 12101(a)(2) (2001).

17 *See, e.g.*, Arlene Kanter & Kristin Dadey, "The Right to Asylum for People with Disabilities," 73 *Temple L. Rev.* 1117, 1137–39 (2000).

als with disabilities remain isolated in their own neighborhoods, or even worse, segregated in institutions. In short, even with the passage of the ADA, men, women and children labeled as disabled remain confined in institutions, often even after the state's own professionals determine that such individuals are capable of living in the community, with or without support.

Despite acknowledgment of the continued segregation of people with disabilities in institutions, the ADA, considered the "Emancipation Proclamation" for people with disabilities, does not mention involuntary institutionalization. Yet, Title II of the ADA does prohibit discrimination in the provision of public services, including mental health services.[18] Thus, based on this anti-discrimination language of Title II, the United States Supreme Court in *Olmstead*[19] concluded that undue institutionalization may constitute illegal discrimination against individuals who are capable of living in the community, and receiving mental health services in the community, rather than in institutions.

Title II of the ADA states that "no qualified individual with a disability shall, by reason of such disability, be excluded from participation in or be denied the benefits of the services, programs, or activities of a public entity, or be subjected to discrimination by any such entity."[20] The Department of Justice regulations that implement this anti-discrimination provision mandate that "[a] public entity shall administer services, programs, and activities in the most integrated setting appropriate to the needs of qualified individuals with disabilities."[21] The law's implementing regulations also provide that "a public entity shall make reasonable modifications in policies, practices, or procedures . . . unless the public entity can demonstrate that making the modifications would fundamentally alter the nature of the services, program, or activity."[22]

---

[18] Title II of the ADA states that "no qualified individual with a disability shall, by reason of such disability, be excluded from participation in or be denied the benefits of the services, programs, or activities of a public entity, or be subjected to discrimination by any such entity." 42 U.S.C. § 12132 (2001).

[19] 527 U.S. 581 (1999).

[20] 42 U.S.C. § 12132 (2001).

[21] 28 C.F.R. § 35.130(d) (2001).

[22] 28 C.F.R § 35.130(b)(7) (2001).

In *Olmstead*, the United States Supreme Court was asked to interpret the scope and coverage of Title II of the ADA with regard to the permissibility of continued institutionalization. The case involved a woman, known as L.C., who was labeled with mild mental retardation and schizophrenia, and who sued the state of Georgia, claiming that Title II of the ADA protects her right to be free from discrimination in the receipt of services. She sought to receive whatever treatment she might need in the community, rather than confined in a state psychiatric hospital.[23] Soon after her case was filed, another patient in the state institution, known as E.W., intervened to join in the case with an identical claim.[24]

The State of Georgia argued that it was not discriminating against these women by confining them in the state's psychiatric hospital. Rather, Georgia claimed that it had not provided services in the community to these women because it lacked the funds for such placements and that, in any event, such placements would "fundamentally alter" its mental health system. The district court held that Georgia's action violated Title II of the ADA.[25] The Court of Appeals for the 11th Circuit affirmed the decision, and remanded the case to the district court to determine whether the alleged additional expense to Georgia resulting from community placement would fundamentally alter the state's mental health program.[26] On remand, the district court found that the cost of providing placement in the community for these two women would not be excessive in relation to the State of Georgia's overall mental health budget.[27]

The United States Supreme Court began its analysis of the case with an overview of the relevant federal legislation which protects the right of individuals with disabilities to community integration, including the 1975 Developmentally Disabled Assistance and Bill of Rights Act (DD Act) and Section 504 of the Rehabilitation Act. The DD Act uses hor-

---

23 527 U.S. 581, 594 (1999).

24 *Id.*

25 *Id.*

26 *Id.* at 595.

27 *Id.* at 595–96.

tatory language to indicate that states "should" provide to individuals with developmental disabilities the right to receive treatment in the setting least restrictive to the individual's personal liberty.[28] Section 504 of the Rehabilitation Act of 1973 uses stronger mandatory language to proscribe discrimination against people with disabilities. It states that "[n]o otherwise qualified individual with a disability in the United States . . . *shall*, solely by reason of her or his disability, be excluded from participation in, be denied the benefits of, or be subjected to discrimination under any program or activity receiving Federal financial assistance."[29]

The Supreme Court then reviewed the legislative history of the ADA, which devotes considerable attention to the law's potential for inclusion of people with disabilities in the community.[30] The House Report on the ADA, for example, recognizes the importance of integrating individuals with disabilities into the community when it states that "[t]he ADA is a comprehensive piece of civil rights legislation which promises a new future: a future of inclusion and integration, and the end of exclusion and segregation."[31] Indeed, the ADA remains consistent with the overriding principle of deinstitutionalization, which is that individuals with mental disabilities are entitled to as much independence as possible and to receive treatment in appropriate settings.

Evidence of the ADA's applicability to institutionalization is found also in the Act's implementing regulations, which state specifically that a public entity shall administer services, programs and activities in the most integrated setting appropriate to the needs of qualified individuals with disabilities.[32] Accordingly, a public entity is required to make reasonable modifications in policies, practices or procedures when necessary to avoid discrimination on the basis of disability, unless the entity

---

[28] Id at 599.

[29] Id. at 599–600, *quoting* 29 U.S.C. § 794 (1976).

[30] *See, e.g.*, H.R. Rep. No. 101-485(III), at 26 (1990), *reprinted in* 1990 U.S.C.C.A.N. 445, 448–89.

[31] *See e.g.*, H.R. Rep. No. 101-485(III), at 26 (1990), *reprinted in* 1990 U.S.C.C.A.N. 445, 489.

[32] 28 C.F.R. § 35.130(d) (2001).

can demonstrate that it fits within the provided defense because the modifications would "fundamentally alter the service, program or activity."[33]

Based on this language, a majority of the United States Supreme Court held that continued confinement of people with mental disabilities in institutions may constitute prohibited discrimination. In an opinion written by Justice Ginsberg, the Court concluded that Title II of the ADA requires states to provide community placement in lieu of institutional placement so long as three conditions are met. These conditions are first, that the state's treatment professionals determine that such placement is appropriate; second, that the individual does not oppose the placement; and third, that the state can reasonably accommodate the placement without fundamentally altering its program, given the state's resources and the needs of other individuals with mental disabilities.[34] Although individuals with disabilities have long sought legal protections against institutionalization as a form of discrimination, it was not until the Supreme Court's decision in *Olmstead* that unnecessary institutionalization was found to constitute illegal discrimination under the Americans with Disabilities Act.

The Supreme Court rejected the state's claim that the plaintiffs did not experience discrimination "by reason of" their disabilities.[35] Instead, the Court held that the undue segregation of individuals with mental dis-

---

[33] 28 C.F.R. § 35.130(b)(7) (2001). It is noteworthy that Title II of the ADA does not include the same defenses available to employers as available, for example, under Title I. Under Title I, an employer is relieved of the obligation to provide accommodations to an employee with a disability if such accommodations would constitute an "undue hardship" for the employer. But the undue hardship defense with respect to costs was not included in Title II, perhaps because Congress felt that the benefits of integration outweighed the hardships that may result from additional costs. *See* Joanne Karger, "'Don't Tread on the ADA:' *Olmstead v. L.C. ex rel. Zimring* and the Future of Community Integration for Individuals With Mental Disabilities," 40 *B.C. L. Rev.* 1221, 1240 (1999), (*citing* Timothy M. Cook, "The Americans with Disabilities Act: The Move to Integration," 64 *Temp. L. Rev.* 393, 430–31 (1991)).

[34] 527 U.S. 581, 587 (1999).

[35] *Id.* (opinion by Justice Ginsberg) (Justices Stevens and Kennedy issued separate concurring opinions). *See id.* at 607.

abilities in institutions constitutes discrimination in this case.[36] The Court reasoned that undue institutionalization is discriminatory because it results in dissimilar treatment settings for individuals with mental disabilities vis-a-vis individuals without mental disabilities. It requires people with mental disabilities to forego life in the community and to remain confined to institutions in order to receive needed medical health treatment, unlike people without mental disabilities, who may receive medical treatment in the community.[37] The Court considered this dissimilar treatment of institutionalized individuals in comparison to those without mental disabilities, who do not have to relinquish participation in community life to receive medical services, as illegal discrimination under Title II of the ADA.[38]

But the Court found discrimination for another reason as well. The Court explained that the unnecessary institutionalization of an individual with a disability constitutes dissimilar treatment or discrimination because such confinement itself perpetuates unwarranted assumptions that the individual is incapable of participating in community life.[39] Moreover, this unnecessary confinement diminishes the individual's ability to have a social life and family relations, to receive an education, or to become economically independent through employment. Thus, undue institutionalization is discriminatory not only because it treats people with and without disabilities differently in terms of their access to mental health treatment, but also because it perpetuates negative stereotypes of people with mental disabilities as "incapable or unworthy of participating in community life," and deprives them of "everyday life activities" such as "family relations, social contacts, work options, economic independence, educational advancement, and cultural enrichment."[40]

---

36 *Id.* at 597.

37 *Id.* at 601.

38 *Id.*

39 *Id.*

40 *Id.* at 600–01. However, in Justice Ginsberg's opinion, states could satisfy the mandate of Title II if the states had waiting lists for placing qualified patients in community treatment settings, and if the waiting lists for such settings "moved at a reasonable pace not controlled by the State's endeavors to keep its institutions fully populated." *Id.* at 606.

Accordingly, the Supreme Court held that the unjustified isolation of the plaintiffs, L.C. and E.W., in state institutions constitutes prohibited discrimination under Title II of the ADA.[41]

The rights established under *Olmstead*, however, are not absolute. Although *Olmstead* endorses the well-established principle that individuals who receive community treatment benefit more than people who are confined in institutions,[42] it nonetheless allows the state to present as a defense the argument that the cost of community treatment is prohibitive. Such a defense, based on cost factors alone, seems highly inappropriate given the liberty interests at stake. The potential for abuse and the lack of rights afforded people confined in institutions is a human rights issue, and cannot and should not be relegated to a cost-benefit analysis.

However, even considering cost factors, little data exists to support a state's argument that it is more costly to provide programs and treatment in the community than to institutionalize someone considered in need of treatment within the United States today. Indeed, studies now suggest that community-based treatment for many people with mental disabilities in the United States is less costly than institutionalization, and that treatment is usually more effective in a community setting as well. For example, in a review of 14 studies in which individuals were

---

41 *Id.* at 597. In addition to affirming the 11th Circuit's decision, the Supreme Court remanded the case to the district court with instructions to reexamine the factors that may be considered in evaluating the state's claim that providing community placement would "fundamentally alter" the state's mental health system. The Supreme Court rejected the 11th Circuit's original approach, which held that the lower court's simple cost comparison was unworkable and unduly restrictive for defending states. *Id.* at 603–06. The Court noted that undue hardship includes more than cost; therefore, the fundamental alteration defense requires a case-by-case inquiry of factors such as the overall size and type of programs. *See also* Helen L. v. DiDario, 46 F.3d 325 (3d Cir. 1995), *cert. denied* Pennsylvania Secretary of Public Welfare v. Idell S., 516 U.S. 813 (1995); Kathleen S. v. Department of Public Welfare of Com. of Pa., 10 F. Supp. 2d 460 (E.D. Pa. 1998); Williams v. Wasserman, 937 F. Supp. 524 (D. Md. 1996) (cases involving the right to community placement under Title II of the ADA).

42 *See* Brief of Amici Curiae American Association on Mental Retardation *et al.*, 1999 WL 143937, at *15, Olmstead v. L.C. *ex rel.* Zimring, 527 U.S. 581 (1999).

placed randomly in institutional settings and community-based settings, researchers Kiesler and Sibulkin determined that "the most general conclusion one can draw from [these studies] is that alternative [community] care is more effective and less costly than mental hospitalization."[43] The study goes on to say that "regardless of the outpatient setting used, the outcome indices by which their effectiveness is measured, for the patient population using them, alternative care programs have universally provided more positive results more cheaply than institutionalization."[44] In other countries, however, the cost effectiveness argument may be less relevant since so few resources are placed in institutions in the first instance. Therefore, arguing for moving such resources from the institution to the community will not ensure the development of quality community-based programs. Instead, additional resources will be needed to develop and sustain new community-based programs in certain areas in the United States, as well as in other countries.[45]

But even more troubling than the state's efforts to confine people in institutions on the basis of the cost of treatment, is the *Olmstead* Court's decision to grant nearly unfettered discretion to mental health professionals.[46] *Olmstead* upholds the right of an individual with a mental dis-

---

[43] Charles A. Kiesler & Amy E. Sibulkin, *Mental Hospitalization: Myths and Facts About a National Crisis* 274 (Newbury Park: Sage Publications, 1987). Further, in 1982, Charles A. Kiesler reviewed ten research studies, all comparing treatment in the institutions with treatment provided outside of institutions. The results of this study indicated that it was not only less expensive to treat individuals with disabilities in the community as opposed to institutions, but that it was also better for and in the best interests of all involved. The study found that in general those in community based settings spent more time in independent settings with friends and social groups, had a higher level of self-esteem, showed fewer symptoms of their illness, and had greater medication and treatment compliance. *Id.* at 158. The review of these studies went on to conclude that those receiving treatment in the community were able to function better than those who remained in institutions. *Id.* at 164–65.

[44] *Id.* at 274.

[45] *See* MDRI, *Human Rights and Mental Health: Mexico* (Washington, DC: MDRI, 2000).

[46] It also presents treating professionals with a direct conflict of interest by which they are expected to authorize the release of the very people who provide the basis for their own livelihood as professional service providers within the hospital

ability to live in the community, but only when such placement is considered appropriate to the individual's needs, as judged by a treating professional. The treating professional, not the individual with a mental disability (who must be presumed to be competent unless found otherwise), is given the right to decide what treatment is provided, whether such treatment is voluntary or coercive, where such treatment will take place, and, in the end, where the person receiving treatment may live, who they will see, and what they will do each day.[47] By endorsing professional discretion in this way, the *Olmstead* Court abandons its full commitment to the non-discrimination principles of the ADA, which requires society to treat all individuals—including those seeking mental health treatment—as people who are capable of independent judgment with the right to dignity, equality, and self-determination.[48]

Nonetheless, the *Olmstead* decision remains a powerful statement that the ADA prohibits unjustified institutionalization as discrimination. The decision acknowledges the long overdue benefits of community living for those who have been deprived of the opportunity to have ordinary life experiences by prolonged involuntary institutionalization. *Olmstead* recognizes not only the right to community integration for

---

setting. *See also* Susan Stefan, "Leaving Civil Rights to the 'Experts': From Deference to Abdication Under the Professional Judgment Standard," 102 *Yale L.J.* 639 (1992).

47 527 U.S. 581, 607, 610 (Justice Kennedy, concurring).

48 In his *Olmstead* dissent, Justice Thomas, joined by Justices Rehnquist and Scalia, disagreed that unnecessary institutionalization constitutes discrimination under Title II of the ADA. According to the dissenting opinion, temporary exclusion from community-based treatment does not amount to discrimination, and plaintiffs failed to prove that the state discriminated against them on the basis of their disabilities. First, the dissenters disagreed with the majority's conclusion that discrimination can occur when there is disparate treatment of members of the same protected class. *Id.* at 616 (Thomas dissent). According to the dissent, a finding of discrimination under the ADA requires a comparison of the plaintiffs, who are mentally disabled, with non-disabled individuals, not a comparison between plaintiffs and other disabled people. The dissent points to Section 504 of the Rehabilitation Act and its case law to support the proposition that "Section 504 required merely 'the evenhanded treatment of handicapped persons' relative to those persons who do not have disabilities." Justice Thomas, dissenting at 619, *quoting* Southeastern Community College v. Davis, 442 U.S. 397, 410 (1979).

individuals with disabilities in the United States, but also the potential, at least, for an end to involuntary institutionalization. It is the first decision by the United States Supreme Court, or likely any high court of any country, which concludes that undue institutionalization may constitute unlawful discrimination. As such, even with its limitations, the *Olmstead* decision promises to spur further efforts to establish the right to community integration and inclusion for all people with disabilities, both through the United States legal system and under international law, which we will now address.

C. THE PROHIBITION OF DISCRIMINATION UNDER INTERNATIONAL HUMAN RIGHTS LAWS

No binding United Nations convention exists which guarantees the right of people with disabilities to receive treatment in the community rather than in institutions.[49] Similarly, no international convention currently exists which mandates, by its terms, that people with disabilities are entitled to be integrated into the community. But international laws and instruments prohibiting discrimination generally have been interpreted recently to apply to people with disabilities. Before examining selected international instruments which prohibit discrimination against people with disabilities, we must first examine the general body of relevant international human rights laws.

There are two primary sources of binding international human rights laws: international conventions or treaties, and customary international law. International conventions or treaties are considered "hard law." The UN Charter is perhaps the most important treaty since it establishes the framework for the United Nations and requires member states to pro-

---

[49] The Inter-American Convention on the Elimination of All Forms of Discrimination Against Persons with Disabilities requires states parties "[t]o adopt the legislative, social, educational, labor-related, or any other measures needed to eliminate discrimination against persons with disabilities and to promote their full integration into society." The Convention has just recently entered into force: AG/RES. 1608 (XXIX-0/99), 29th Sess. of the General Assembly; *opened for signature* June 7, 1999, *entered into force* Sept. 14, 2001 [not published]. For the full text, visit the official Inter-American Commission on Human Rights web site <http://www. cidh.org> (visited Jan. 19, 2002).

mote universal respect for human rights.[50] Other examples of such "hard law" include the two core United Nations human rights conventions, the International Covenant of Civil and Political Rights (ICCPR)[51] and the International Convention on Economic, Social and Cultural Rights (ICESCR).[52] Together with the Universal Declaration on Human Rights,[53] these Covenants[54] make up what is known as the "International Bill of Rights."[55] Both the ICCPR and the ICESCR were drafted to protect people against discrimination on the basis of "race, colour, sex, language, religion, . . . or other status," but neither convention specifies that discrimination on the basis of disability is unlawful.[56] This omission is somewhat ironic since these instruments were drafted largely in response to the atrocities of the Holocaust in which Jews as well as people with

---

[50] U.N. Charter, 59 Stat. 1031; *opened for signature* June 26, 1945, *entered into force* Oct. 24, 1945; *at* http://www.un.org/aboutun/charter/index.html, at arts. 55–56.

[51] The International Covenant on Civil and Political Rights, G.A. Res. 2200A (XXI), U.N. GAOR, 21st Sess., Supp. No. 16, at 52, U.N. Doc. A/6316 (1966); *opened for signature* Dec. 16, 1966, *entered into force* Mar. 23, 1976, 999 & 1057 U.N.T.S. 171 & 407 respectively; *at* http://www.unhchr.ch/html/menu3/b/a_ccpr.htm (visited Jan. 19, 2002) [hereinafter "ICCPR"].

[52] The International Covenant on Economic, Social and Cultural Rights, G.A. Res. 2200A (XXI), U.N. GAOR, 21st Sess., Supp. No. 16, at 49, U.N. Doc. A/6316 (1966); *opened for signature* Dec. 16, 1966, *entered into force* Jan. 3, 1976, 993 U.N.T.S. 3; *at* http://www.unhchr.ch.html/menu3/b/a_cescr.htm (visited Jan. 19, 2002) [hereinafter "ICESCR"].

[53] The Universal Declaration of Human Rights, G.A. Res. 217 A(III), U.N. Doc. A/810, at 71 (1948), provides a framework for the international recognition of human rights. *See* Richard B. Bilder, "An Overview of International Human Rights Law," *in Guide to International Human Rights Practice* 3, 7 (Hurst Hannum ed., 2d ed., Philadelphia: Univ. of Pennsylvania Press, 1992).

[54] ICCPR, *supra* note 51, at art. 26.

[55] *See generally The International Bill of Rights: The Covenant on Civil and Political Rights* (Louis Henkin ed., New York: Columbia Univ. Press, 1981).

[56] Article 2 of the ICCPR requires state parties to the covenant "to respect and ensure to all individuals . . . the rights recognized in the present Covenant, without distinction of any kind, such as race, colour, sex, language, religion, political or other opinion, national or social origin, property, birth or other status." ICCPR, *supra* note 51, at art. 2, ¶ 1. *See also* ICESCR, *supra* note 52 at art. 2, ¶ 2.

disabilities were singled out for extermination,[57] giving doctors in concentration camps the kind of unfettered medical discretion that made it possible to subject people to horrific and deadly medical research studies.[58] Indeed, it was many years before the international community recognized that people with disabilities also should be protected from discrimination in these covenants.

In recent years, a number of conventions have been adopted to address the rights of particular populations, including the Convention on the Rights of the Child,[59] the Convention on the Elimination of All Forms of Discrimination Against Women,[60] the Convention Concerning Discrimination in Respect of Employment and Occupation,[61] the

---

[57] *See* Robert N. Proctor, *Racial Hygiene Medicine Under the Nazis* (Cambridge, Mass.: Harvard Univ. Press, 1988). *See also The Nazi Doctors and the Nuremberg Code: Human Rights in Human Experimentation* (George J. Annas & Michael A. Grodin eds., New York: Oxford Univ. Press, 1992); Arthur L. Caplan, *When Medicine Went Mad: Bioethics and the Holocaust* (Totowa, N.J.: Humana Press, 1992); Michael Berenbaum & Abraham Peck, *The Holocaust and History: The Known, the Unknown, the Disputed, and the Reexamined* (Bloomington: Indiana Univ. Press, 1998); Henry Friedlander, *The Origins of Nazi Genocide: From Euthanasia to the Final Solution* (Chapel Hill: Univ. of N. Carolina Press, 1995); James Glass, *Life Unworthy of Life: Racial Phobia and Mass Murder in Hitler's Germany* (New York: Basic Books, 1997).

[58] The fact that the drafters of the international human rights covenants were thinking about the abuse of medical authority that had occurred in Nazi concentration camps is revealed in one of the most specific provisions of the ICCPR, which prohibits the use of human subjects in scientific experiments without their consent. Article 7 of the ICCPR states that "[n]o one shall be subjected to torture or to cruel, inhuman or degrading treatment or punishment. In particular, no one shall be subjected without his free consent to medical or scientific experimentation." ICCPR, *supra* note 51, at art. 7.

[59] G.A. Res. 44/25, U.N. GAOR, 44th Sess., Supp. No. 49, Annex, at 167, U.N. Doc. A/44/49 (1989); *opened for signature* Nov. 20, 1989, *entered into force* Sept. 2, 1990; *at* http://www.unhchr.ch/html/menu3/b/k2crc.htm (visited Jan. 19, 2002).

[60] G.A. Res. 34/180, U.N. GAOR, 34th Sess., Supp. No. 46, at 193, U.N. Doc. A/34/46; *opened for signature* Dec. 18, 1979, *entered into force* Sept. 3, 1981; *at* http://www.unhchr.ch/html/menu3/b/e1cedaw.htm.

[61] Convention Concerning Discrimination in Respect of Employment and Occupation, Convention No. 111 (1958), *opened for signature* June 25, 1958 by

Convention Against Torture and Other Cruel, Inhuman or Degrading Treatment or Punishment,[62] the Convention Concerning Indigenous and Tribal Peoples in Independent Countries,[63] as well as more general conventions such as the Convention Relating to the Status of Refugees,[64] and the Convention on the Prevention and Punishment of the Crime of Genocide.[65]

These human rights conventions create obligations on governments to promote or enforce individual rights. Yet such conventions will become sources of rights to individuals within a given country generally only if they are incorporated into a state's own domestic laws.[66] Thus, one of the primary ways in which governments may implement

---

the General Conference of the International Labour Organization at its 42nd Session, *entered into force* June 25, 1960, *at* http://www.unhchr.ch/html/ menu3/ b/d_ilo111.htm; Convention Concerning Vocational Rehabilitation and Employment (Disabled Persons), Convention No 159 (1983), *opened for signature* June 20, 1983 by ILO Sess. 69, *entered into force* June 20, 1985; Convention Concerning Vocational Guidance and Vocational Training in the Development of Human Resources, Convention No. 142 (1975), *opened for signature* June 23, 1975 by ILO Sess. 60, *entered into force* July 19, 1977, cited in Degener & Koster-Dreese, *supra* note 8. All of the International Labour Organization (ILO) Conventions may be found in English *at* http://www.ilolex.ilo.ch:1567/english/ convdisp1.htm.

62 G.A. Res. 39/46, 39 U.N. GAOR, 39th Sess., Supp. No. 51, Annex, at 197, U.N. Doc. A/39/51 (1984); *opened for signature* Dec. 10, 1984, *entered into force* June 26, 1987; *at* http://www.unhchr.ch/html/menu3/b/h_cat39.htm (visited Jan. 19, 2002).

63 ILO Convention No. 169, *opened for signature* June 27, 1989, *entered into force* Sept. 5, 1991 (1989); reprinted in 28 *Int'l Legal Materials* 1382 (1989); and *at* http://www.ilolex.ilo.ch:1567/english/convdisp1.htm.

64 U.N. Conference of Plenopotentiaries on the Status of Refugees and Stateless Persons convened under G.A. Res. 429(V), *opened for signature* July 28, 1951, *entered into force* Apr. 22, 1954, 189 U.N.T.S. 150; *at* http://www.unhchr.ch/html/menu3/b/o_c_ref.htm.

65 G.A. Res. 260A(III), *opened for signature* Dec. 9, 1948, *entered into force* Jan. 12, 1951, 78 U.N.T.S. 277; *at* http://www.unhchr.ch/html/menu3/b/p_genoci.htm.

66 *See Guide to International Human Rights Practice* (Hurst Hannum ed., 3d. ed., Ardsley, NY: Transnational, 1999).

their obligations under international law is through the enactment of domestic legislation. However, conventions must be ratified by a given nation in order for that government to be bound under international law.[67] Despite the complexities of treaty ratification in various countries, according to one source there are now over 100 state parties to each of the ICCPR and ICESCR, the Genocide Convention, the Torture Convention and the Convention Relating to Refugees; more than 150 state parties to the Convention on the Elimination of All Forms of Discrimination against Women; and over 185 parties to the Convention on the Rights of the Child.[68]

One of the most important features of international human rights conventions is their use as human rights monitoring instruments. Most conventions have mandatory reporting requirements that require states to report on a regular basis about their compliance with their obligations under the convention. Non-governmental organizations can both critique government reports and issue reports of their own. The reporting and public education functions of international human rights conventions are especially important to particularly vulnerable populations, such as people with disabilities confined in institutions, since they are necessarily cut off from public view.[69]

---

[67] *Id.* Rules governing the interpretation of treaties are contained in arts. 31–33 of the Vienna Convention on the Law of Treaties, *opened for signature* May 23, 1969, *entered into force* Jan. 27, 1980, 1155 U.N.T.S. 331; *at* http://www.un.org/law/ilc/ texts/treatfra.htm.

[68] *Id.* at 9. The United States has ratified very few conventions related to human rights, including the Convention on Civil and Political Rights, the Convention on the Status of Refugees, and the Convention on the Prevention and Punishment of the Crime of Genocide. *Id.* at Appendix E. However, the United States is a signatory to additional conventions, such as the Convention on Economic, Social and Cultural Rights, which was signed by President Carter. And, as a signatory, the United States, according to the Vienna Convention which governs the interpretation of treaties, is obligated to "refrain from acts which would defeat the object and purpose of [the] treaty. . ." *Id.* at art. 18, Vienna Convention on the Law of Treaties.

[69] *See* Eric Rosenthal & Clarence Sundram, *The Role of International Human Rights in Domestic Mental Health Legislation*, paper submitted to the World Health Organization, March 2002. Currently available *at* http://bazelon.org/legal/resources/internationallaw.pdf.

International human rights conventions also establish a legal basis for the international scrutiny of practices that would otherwise be considered matters of domestic social policy that are protected by principles of state sovereignty. By providing a legal basis for international scrutiny, international human rights laws may be used as tools, for example to ensure that conditions in closed institutions are documented, seen, assessed, and judged by the world community. Once a common practice of international human rights abuses against institutionalized people with disabilities is recognized as unlawful discrimination, the hope is that the government that allows such practices will be held accountable.[70]

In addition to international conventions, regional treaties have been drafted and adopted to protect human rights. Examples of such regional conventions include the American Convention on Human Rights (1969),[71] the Inter-American Convention to Prevent and Punish Torture,[72] the Inter-American Convention on the Prevention, Punishment and Eradication of Violence against Women,[73] the European Convention on Human Rights and Fundamental Freedoms (1950),[74] the European

---

70 *Id.*

71 *Opened for signature* Nov. 22, 1969, *entered into force* July 18, 1978, O.A.S. Treaty Series No. 36, 1144 U.N.T.S. 123; *reprinted in Basic Documents Pertaining to Human Rights in the Inter-American System*, OEA/Ser.L.V/II.82 doc. 6 rev.1, at 25 (1992).

72 *Opened for signature* Dec. 9, 1985, *entered into force* Feb. 28, 1987, O.A.S. Treaty Series No. 67.

73 *Opened for signature* June 9, 1994, *entered into force* Mar. 5, 1995 [not published]. For more information regarding the Inter-American Convention to Prevent and Punish Torture and the Inter-American Convention on the Prevention, Punishment and Eradication of Violence against Women, visit the official Inter-American Commission on Human Rights' web site: <http://www.cidh.org> (visited Jan. 19, 2002).

74 *Opened for signature* Nov. 4, 1950, *entered into force* Sept. 3, 1953, E.T.S. No. 005. For more information regarding the European Convention on Human Rights and Fundamental Freedoms, visit the official Council of Europe web site: <http://www.coe.int> (visited Jan. 19, 2002).

Social Charter,[75] the African Charter,[76] and, more recently, the Charter of Fundamental Rights of the European Union.[77]

Individuals can bring complaints against governments in commissions or courts established under these regional conventions, which may then settle the disputes or issue binding decisions on the government parties. In fact, a body of case law on the rights of people with mental disabilities under the European Convention of Human Rights has developed.[78] And the first case involving the rights of a person with a mental disability was recently decided under the American Convention on Human Rights.[79] Cases decided under these regional conventions may be useful in the interpretation of similar protections in other conventions, but they remain binding only within the human rights system created by the respective convention.

In addition to international conventions and regional conventions, a body of international customary law has developed that also establishes additional human rights and protections. Certain customs and principles have become so widely accepted that they have become binding as customary international law. To establish an international custom, the party must show a widespread practice by states of confirming to

---

75 *Opened for signature* Oct. 18, 1961, *entered into force* Feb. 26, 1965, 529 U.N.T.S. 89.

76 The African [Banjul] Charter On Human and Peoples' Rights, OAU Doc. CAB/LEG/67/3 rev. 5; *opened for signature* June 27, 1981, *entered into force* Oct. 21, 1986, 21 I.L.M. 58 (1982).

77 O.J. 2000, C 364, 1; *at* http://ue.eu.int/df/docs/en/CharteEN.pdf. For an overview of the European system of human rights and its application to people with disabilities, *see* Lawrence O. Gostin, "Human Rights of Persons with Mental Disabilities: The European Convention on Human Rights," 23 *Int'l J. L & Psychiatry* 125 (2000).

78 *See* Gostin, *id.; see also* Margaret G. Wachenfeld, *The Human Rights of the Mentally Ill in Europe* (Copenhagen: Danish Center for Human Rights, 1992); T.W. Harding, "The Application of the European Convention of Human Rights to the Field of Psychiatry," 12 *Int'l J. L. Psychiatry* 245 (1989).

79 *The Case of Victor Rosario Congo, Annual Report of the Inter-American Commission on Human Rights*, Report 63/99, Case 11.427, Ecuador, OEA/Ser.L/V/II.102 Doc. 6 rev. Apr. 13, 1999 [hereinafter *The Case of Victor Rosario Congo*].

the alleged rule, together with evidence that states have followed this practice because they believe that they are under an obligation to do so.[80] As such, customary human rights law may be found binding on all states without regard for whether a particular state has consented.[81]

Non-binding human rights resolutions that are widely accepted as binding can, over the years, come to be understood as customary international law. The Universal Declaration of Human Rights (UDHR) is an example of a non-binding General Assembly Resolution that has become binding as customary law since its enactment in 1948. The principle that "[a]ll human beings are born free and equal in dignity and rights" is enshrined in Article 1 of the Universal Declaration of Human

---

[80] Hannum, *Guide to International Human Rights Practice*, *supra* note 66, at 10.

[81] *Id.* Although establishing the existence of a customary rule of law may be difficult, the United States Court of Appeals for the Second Circuit, in *Filartiga v. Pena-Irala*, 630 F.2d 876 (2d Cir. 1980), recognized the existence of a customary law against torture, even before the U.N. Convention Against Torture and Other Cruel, Inhuman or Degrading Treatment or Punishment was adopted in 1984, and ratified by the United States years later. In this case, the court of appeals for the Second Circuit held that a Paraguay citizen could be sued in federal court for torturing and killing a man in retaliation for his political beliefs. The Court of Appeals recognized that even in the absence of an international convention against torture, international customary law supported a claim against torture. As the court wrote, "[i]n light of the universal condemnation of torture in numerous international agreements, and the renunciation of torture as an instrument of official policy by virtually all of the nations of the world (in principle if not in practice), we find that an act of torture committed by a state official against one held in detention violates established norms of the international law of human rights, and hence the law of nations." *Id.* at 880. The court goes on to quote the U.S. Supreme Court which recognized in *The Paquete Habana*, 175 U.S. 677 (1900), that "where there is no treaty and no controlling executive or legislative act or judicial decision, resort must be had to the customs and usages of civilized nations, and, as evidence of these, to the works of jurists and commentators who by years of labor, research and experience, have made themselves peculiarly well acquainted with the subjects of which they treat. Such works are resorted to by judicial tribunals, not for the speculations of their authors concerning what the law ought to be, but for trustworthy evidence of what the law really is." *Id.* at 700. Modern international sources confirm the propriety of this approach. *See* The Statute of the International Court of Justice, June 26, 1945, 59 Stat. 1055, arts. 38 & 59 at 1060 (1945).

Rights. Indeed, the Declaration establishes human rights law as "a common standard of achievement for all peoples and all nations."[82]

Despite what appears to be a proliferation of human rights conventions and documents, particularly since World War II, no binding United Nations convention has been adopted to specifically prohibit discrimination against people with disabilities. In fact, a draft *Convention on the Elimination of Discrimination Against Disabled Persons* was rejected by the United Nations in 1987.[83] Despite this disappointing development, there is new hope for a United Nations disability rights convention. On November 28, 2001, the Third Committee of the UN General Assembly adopted a resolution creating an Ad Hoc Committee "to consider proposals for a comprehensive and integral international convention to protect and promote the rights of persons with disabilities."[84] The first Ad Hoc Committee meeting is scheduled to take place in August 2002.

---

[82] *Supra* note 53, at preamble.

[83] In 1987, the 3rd Committee of the General Assembly considered the recommendations that had been made by the "Global Meeting of Experts to Review the Implementation of the World Programme of Action Concerning Disabled Persons at the Mid-Point of the United Nations Decade of Disabled Persons." Among the recommendations was a proposal for an international convention on the elimination of all forms of discrimination against disabled persons. The Italian delegate raised and supported the possibility of such a convention (U.N. Doc. A/C.3/42/SR.16 (1987)), but numerous objections to such a convention were raised in subsequent meetings by various countries (e.g., the U.K. and Japan were concerned about financial implications, while Germany and the Nordic countries believed that the rights of disabled persons were protected by existing universal human rights documents such as the ICESCR—*see* U.N. Docs. A/C.3/42/SR.17 to A/C.3/42/ SR/19). Eventually, the 3rd Committee adopted a resolution on disabled persons that did not recommend the drafting or implementation of a binding convention on eliminating discrimination against disabled persons (U.N. Doc. A/C.3/42/L.25). The possibility of a convention was raised again by Sweden in 1989, and once again failed to garner sufficient support, but this later initiative did lead to the eventual establishment of the Standard Rules, *supra* note 2.

[84] *Comprehensive and integral international convention to promote and protect the rights and dignity of persons with disabilities*, G.A. Res. 56/119b, U.N. GAOR 3rd Comm., 56 Sess., ¶ 1, U.N. Doc. A/C.3/56/L67/Rev.1 (2001).

The process of drafting a new United Nations convention can be long and complicated, and it is not yet certain that the UN will adopt a draft convention and send it to countries for ratification. Until such time as a convention is adopted and enters into force through widespread ratification, the most important binding protections under international human rights law are created by the broad language of the mainstream human rights conventions, such as the ICCPR, the ICESCR, and the Convention on the Rights of the Child (CRC). The main tools for interpreting these conventions are the General Comments of treaty-based Committees established by these specific conventions to assist with their interpretation, as well as non-binding UN General Assembly resolutions on mental and physical disability rights.[85] These instruments and their use are described further in Section D below. In recent years, a growing body of international declarations, standards and interpretations on covenants has emerged to protect certain rights of individuals with disabilities, including the right to be free from discrimination generally, and the right to be free from institutionalization as a form of discrimination.

D. INTERNATIONAL HUMAN RIGHTS LAWS' PROTECTIONS FOR PEOPLE WITH DISABILITIES

The UN General Assembly's Declaration on The Rights of Mentally Retarded Persons protects people with intellectual or developmental disabilities from discrimination as it recognizes that "to the maximum degree of feasibility, [they will be accorded] the same rights as other human beings" which cannot be restricted without due process that "must contain proper legal standards against every form of abuse."[86] Despite its outdated use of the term mental retardation, as opposed to the more appropriate and current term, intellectual or developmental disability, this Declaration established the international community's first formal recognition of the rights of people with intellectual or developmental disabilities.

---

85 Rosenthal & Sundram, *supra* note 69.

86 G.A. Res. 2856 (XXVI), U.N. GAOR, 26th Sess., Supp. No. 29, ¶¶ 1,7 at 93, U.N. Doc. A/8429 (1971); *at* http://www.unhchr.ch/html/menu3/b/m_mental.htm.

Further, in 1975, the UN General Assembly adopted the Declaration on the Rights of Disabled Persons. This Declaration seeks to extend the reach of the non-discrimination provisions of existing international conventions to people with disabilities.[87] For example, The Declaration on the Rights of Disabled Persons recognizes specifically the right of people with disabilities to equality, when it states that people with disabilities have "the inherent right to human dignity . . . and the same fundamental rights as their fellow-citizens of the same age, which implies first and foremost the right to enjoy a decent life, as normal and full as possible."[88]

In the 1990s, as part of its commitment to the *International Decade of Disabled Persons*, the United Nations appointed two Special Rapporteurs to report on the abhorrent and inhumane conditions in which many people with disabilities have been forced to live throughout the world.[89] According to the Despouy Report, published in 1991, the human rights of persons with disabilities are grossly violated throughout the world.[90] Institutionalization of persons with disabilities, institutional abuse (including the misuse of drugs), and forced sterilization were among a litany of the practices that Despouy identified as serious violations of international law and human rights.[91] Despouy reported that no "cultural factor could justify or excuse such acts, which [many] regard as being contrary to binding Human Rights standards

---

87 Declaration on the Rights of Disabled Persons, G.A. Res. 3447 (XXX), U.N. GAOR, 30th Sess., Supp. No. 34, at 88, U.N. Doc. A/10034 (1975); *at* http://www.unhchr.ch/html/menu3/b/72.htm.

88 *Id.* at ¶ 3.

89 Leandro Despouy, U.N. Centre for Human Rights & U.N. Sub-Commission on Prevention of Discrimination and Protection of Minorities, *Human Rights and Disabled Persons*, U.N. Doc. No. E/CN.4/Sub.2/1991/31, U.N. Sales No. E.92.XIV.4 (1993) [hereinafter Despouy Report]; United Nations, Sub-Commission on Prevention of Discrimination and Protection of Minorities, *Principles, Guidelines and Guarantees for the Protection of Persons Detained on Grounds of Mental Ill-Health or Suffering from Mental Disorder; Report by the Special Rapporteur: Erica-Irene A. Daes*, U.N. Doc. E/CN.4/Sub.2/1983/17/Rev.1, U.N. Sales No. E.85.XIV.9 (1997) [hereinafter Daes Report].

90 Despouy Report, *supra* note 89 at ¶ 174.

91 *Id.*

prohibiting torture and other cruel, inhuman and degrading treatment or punishment."[92] In addition, Special Rapporteur Daes specifically reported on the inhumane conditions of people with mental disabilities.[93] According to her report, psychiatric patients are held against their will and used "as guinea pigs for new scientific experiments."[94]

The United Nations has continued to direct international attention to the plight of people with disabilities.[95] In 1991, the United Nations General Assembly adopted the Principles for the Protection of Persons with Mental Illness and for the Improvement of Mental Health Care (the MI Principles).[96] Although the MI Principles are a non-binding resolution of the United Nations General Assembly, they can be and have been used as a guide to the interpretation of related provisions of international human rights conventions.[97] These MI Principles have been recognized as "the most complete standards for the protection of the rights of person with mental disabilities at the international level."[98] They "represent the

---

[92] *Id.*

[93] Daes Report, *supra* note 89.

[94] *Id.* at ¶ 225.

[95] Leslie Bennetts, "The Disabled Seek Public Awareness," *N.Y. Times*, Nov. 1, 1981, at 65. (The year 1991 was the International Year of the Disabled Persons which had as its primary purpose the changing of public attitudes and the creation of awareness.)

[96] *See Principles for the Protection of Persons with Mental Illness and for the Improvement of Mental Health Care*, G.A. Res. 119, U.N. G.A.O.R., 46th Sess., Supp. No. 49, Annex at 188, U.N. Doc. A/46/49 (1992) [hereinafter the MI Principles].

[97] Eric Rosenthal & Leonard S. Rubenstein, "International Human Rights Advocacy under the 'Principles for the Protection of Persons with Mental Illness,'" 16 *Int'l J. L. & Psychiatry* 257 (1993) (describing the use of the MI Principles as a guide to the interpretation of related provisions of human rights conventions). The Inter-American Commission on Human Rights adopted this analysis in the case of *Victor Rosario Congo*, the first case on the rights of a person with mental illness under the American Convention. *The Case of Victor Rosario Congo, supra* note 79, at ¶ 54. *See infra*, notes 195–208 and accompanying text. General Comment 5, *supra* note 7, also recognizes the importance of the MI Principles and uses it as a guide to the requirements of certain provisions of the ICESCR.

[98] *The Case of Victor Rosario Congo, supra* note 79, at ¶ 54. In this case, the

minimum United Nations standards for the protection of fundamental freedoms and human and legal rights of persons with mental illness."[99]

In particular, the MI Principles provide the minimum standard of practice for the delivery of mental health services, including standards for treatment and living conditions within psychiatric institutions, and protections against arbitrary detention in such facilities.[100] The MI Principles apply broadly to persons with mental illness, whether or not they are in psychiatric facilities; and they apply to all persons admitted to a mental health facility, whether or not they are diagnosed as mentally ill.

The United Nations took another significant step in 1993 when the World Conference on Human Rights met in Vienna, and reiterated that people with mental and physical disabilities are protected by international human rights law and that governments must establish domestic legislation to realize these rights. In what has come to be known as the "Vienna Declaration," the World Conference declared that "all human rights and fundamental freedoms are universal and thus unreservedly include persons with disabilities."[101] Pursuant to the recommendations of the 1993 World Conference on Human Rights, the United Nations General Assembly adopted a resolution the same year entitled the

---

Inter-American Commission recognized the importance of the MI Principles, as it stated "[t]hese Principles serve as a guide to States in the design and/or reform of mental health systems and are of utmost utility in evaluating the practice of existing systems. *Mental Health Principle 23* establishes that each State must adopt the legislative, judicial, administrative, educational, and other measures that may be necessary to implement them." *Id.* at n.8, *citing* Rosenthal & Rubenstein, *supra* note 97.

[99] U.N. ESCOR, U.N. Commission on Human Rights, *Report of the Working Group on the Principles for the Protection of Persons with Mental Illness and for the Improvement of Mental Health Care*, UN Doc. E/CN.4/1991/39 (prepared by Henry Steel) (1991). Leandro Despouy, Special Rapporteur on Human Rights and Disability, reaffirmed this viewpoint in Human Rights and Disabled persons, *supra* note 89.

[100] MI Principles, *supra* note 96, Principles 15–18.

[101] Vienna Declaration and Programme of Action, U.N. Doc. A/CONF.157/23, ¶ 63 (1993).

"Standard Rules on Equalization of Opportunities for Persons with Disabilities" ("Standard Rules").[102]

The Standard Rules do not have the binding effect of a Convention, but they were adopted to ensure "positive and full inclusion of persons with disabilities in all aspects of society."[103] To achieve this, the Standard Rules establish citizen participation by people with disabilities as an internationally recognized human right. To realize this right, governments "are under an obligation" to provide opportunities for people with disabilities, and organizations made up of people with disabilities, to be involved in drafting new legislation on matters that affect them.[104] Further, the Standard Rules call on every country to engage in a national planning process to bring legislation, policies, and programs into conformity with international human rights standards.[105] This process has

---

[102] "Unlike a Convention [the Standard Rules] are legally non-binding because they cannot be signed and ratified by Member States." Theresia Degener, "Disabled Persons and Human Rights: The Legal Framework. *in* Degener & Koster-Dreese, *supra* note 8, 9 at 12. Although they are not binding, they "can attain binding character as 'international customary rules when they are applied by a great number of States with the intention of respecting a rule in international law.' Until then, they serve as a 'strong moral and political commitment on behalf of States to take action for the equalization of opportunities.'" *Id.* at 12–13, *quoting* U.N. Doc. A/48/96 [G.A. Res. 48/96 (1993)].

[103] Degener, *id.* at 12, *quoting* U.N. Doc. A/48/95 [G.A. Res. 48/95 (1993)].

[104] Standard Rule 15(1) states in full:

> National legislation, embodying the rights and obligations of citizens, should include the rights and obligations of persons with disabilities. States are under an obligation to enable persons with disabilities to exercise their rights, including their human, civil and political rights, on an equal basis with other citizens. States must ensure that organizations of persons with disabilities are involved in the development of national legislation concerning the rights of persons with disabilities, as well as in the ongoing evaluation of that legislation. Standard Rules, *supra* note 2.

[105] "States should involve organizations of persons with disabilities in all decision-making relating to plans and programmes concerning persons with disabilities or affecting their economic and social status." *Id.* at Rule 14. The term "organizations of persons with disabilities" refers to organizations made up of and controlled by people with disabilities themselves. The role of such organizations in government is described further in Rule 18. Rule 15 provides additional guidance to governments in the legislative reform process, recommending that existing leg-

been hailed as a call to states to "create a legal basis for measures to achieve full participation and equality for persons with disabilities."[106] Accordingly, on December 3, 1996, the International Day of Disabled Persons, then-UN Secretary-General Boutros Boutros-Ghali proclaimed that persons with disabilities should enjoy their civil, political, social and cultural rights on an equal basis with other people.[107]

While the MI Principles and the Standard Rules provide detailed guidance to legislators as to the requirements of international human rights law, the fundamental obligations of governments remain dictated by the international human rights conventions. Human rights conventions require governments to report regularly on the legislation they adopt and the policies they establish to implement the provisions of conventions. Until recently, few governments have reported on the steps taken to ensure realization of the rights of people with mental or physical disabilities.

Yet one of the most important sources of interpretation of human rights conventions are the guidelines, known as General Comments, produced by human rights oversight bodies (also referred to as treaty-based committees) to guide governments in the preparation of their official reports. General Comments are non-binding, but they represent the official interpretation of the convention. Although these human rights oversight bodies have adopted very few General Comments on the rights of people with mental disabilities, the Comments that have been adopted are significant in their scope and language.

---

islation be reviewed to incorporate disability rights principles and that specialized new legislation be adopted where necessary. *See* Rule 15 (2–4). The United Nations established a monitoring mechanism "to further the effective implementation of the rules" (*id.* at Part IV, "Monitoring Mechanism" ¶ 1) and authorized the establishment of a Special Rapporteur to report to the UN Commission on Social Development regarding the implementation of the Standard Rules, *id.*, Part IV, ¶ 2. The current Special Rapporteur on Disability is Bengt Lindqvist of Sweden.

106 Bengt Lindqvist, "Standard Rules in the Disability Field—A New United Nations Instrument," Address at *Beyond Normalization—Towards One Society for All,* International United Nations Conference (June 1–3,1994), *in* Degener & Koster-Dreese, *supra* note 8, 63 at 66–67.

107 "United Nations Chief Stresses Equal Rights for Disabled," *Xinhua News Agency*, Dec. 3, 1996 *available in* LEXIS, News Library, News Group File.

The most significant Comment to date on the rights of people with disabilities was adopted in 1994 by the Committee on Economic, Social, and Cultural Rights. General Comment 5,[108] as it is known, details the application of the International Covenant on Economic, Social, and Cultural Rights with regard to people with mental and physical disabilities.[109] As part of General Comment 5, the Committee recognized the MI Principles, the Standard Rules, and the UN's Guidelines for National Coordinating Committees as instruments established by the international community for "ensuring the full range of human rights for persons with disabilities."[110] General Comment 5 singles out the Standard Rules as "a particularly valuable reference guide in identifying more precisely the relevant obligations of States parties under the Covenant."[111]

In 2000, the Committee on Economic, Social, and Cultural Rights elaborated further on the right of all people to the highest attainable standard of health.[112] In General Comment 14, the Committee specified the general and specific legal obligations of states in implementing Article 12 of the ICESCR.

The Committee on the Elimination of All Forms of Discrimination Against Women has also issued General Comments, including a recommendation pertaining to the rights of women with disabilities, in particular.[113] This recommendation calls on governments to improve their reporting on the enforcement of the rights of women with disabilities

---

108 General Comment 5, *supra* note 7.

109 For background on the development of General Comment 5, *supra* note 7, *see* Alston, *supra* note 8, at 100–02.

110 General Comment 5, *supra* note 7, at ¶ 7.

111 *Id.*

112 Regarding this, *see* CESCR *General Comment 14(2000) The Right to the Highest Attainable Standard of Health (Article 12 of the International Covenant on Economic, Social and Cultural Rights)*, U.N. Doc. E/C.12/2000/4 (2000) [hereinafter General Comment 14]. This document can be viewed at the official United Nations' web site, <http://www.un.org> (visited Jan. 19, 2002) under the Office for the High Commissioner of Human Rights.

113 CEDAW, *General Recommendation No. 18 Disabled Women*, U.N. Doc. A/46/38 (1991).

under the Convention on the Elimination of All Forms of Discrimination Against Women.[114]

The UN Human Rights Committee, established to monitor the International Covenant on Civil and Political Rights (the ICCPR) has yet to issue a General Comment specifically on the rights of people with mental disabilities. However, its General Comment 18 reiterates the broadness of the ICCPR's prohibition of discrimination.[115]

Further, as part of the World Program of Action Concerning Disabled Persons in the 1980s, the UN General Assembly called on all "State parties to the International Covenants on Human Rights [to] pay due attention, in their reports, to the application of the Covenants to the situation of disabled persons."[116] Then, finally, in April 2000, the United Nations Human Rights Commission adopted Resolution 2000/51 which "urges governments to cover fully the question of the human rights of persons with disabilities in complying with reporting obligations under the relevant United Nations instruments."[117]

Resolution 2000/51 refers to the Standard Rules as a guide to the interpretation of anti-discrimination provisions in international human rights conventions. As the Resolution states, "any violation of the fundamental principle of equality or any discrimination or other negative differential treatment of persons with disabilities inconsistent with the

---

[114] *Id.*

[115] CCPR, *General Comment 18 Non-Discrimination*, U.N. Doc. A/45/40 (1990) [hereinafter General Comment 18]. Portions of General Comment 18 (placed with those articles of the ICCPR on which they comment) are also found in United Nations Office of the High Commissioner for Human Rights, *Manual on Human Rights Reporting* 252 [reproducing ¶ 7 of General Comment 18] (Geneva: United Nations, 1997), Sales No. GV.E.97.0.16 (1997) [hereinafter UN Manual]. The manual can be found *at* http://www.unhchr.ch/pdf/manual_hrr.pdf

[116] World Programme of Action Concerning Disabled Persons ¶ 165, U.N. Doc. A/37/351/Add.1, Annex, 19–58; adopted by the U.N. General Assembly at its 37th Sess., 9th mtg., U.N. Doc. A/RES/37/52 (Dec. 3, 1982). The UN General Assembly specifically called on countries to report on the enforcement of the rights of people with disabilities under the ICCPR and the ICESCR.

[117] U.N. Commission on Human Rights, Resolution 2000/51, 56th Sess, U.N. Doc. E/CN.4/RES/2000/51, ¶ 11.

Standard Rules on the Equalization of Opportunities for Persons with Disabilities is an infringement of the human rights of persons with disabilities."[118] In addition, the Commission called on *all* human rights treaty monitoring bodies to monitor the compliance of state parties with regard to the rights of people with disabilities.[119] The Commission also called on non-governmental organizations (NGOs) to report violations to the Committee on Economic, Social, and Cultural Rights and to the Office of the High Commissioner on Human Rights.[120] Finally, the Commission wrote that it "[i]nvites the United Nations High Commissioner for Human Rights, in cooperation with the Special Rapporteur on Disability of the Commission for Social Development, to examine measures to strengthen the protection and monitoring of the human rights of persons with disabilities and to solicit input and proposals from interested parties," including a panel of experts to be convened by the Special Rapporteur.[121] Although the UN High Commissioner and the Special Rapporteur do not have the authority to establish binding interpretations of the human rights conventions, they can, in consultation with a panel of experts, issue reports that propose new interpretations of conventions to be adopted by treaty monitoring bodies.

It is important to note that the United Nations Committee on Economic, Social and Cultural Rights has made clear that the protection against discrimination on the basis of "other status" under Article 2(2) of the ICESCR "clearly applies to discrimination on the grounds of disability."[122] Further, in the context of health care, the Committee

---

[118] *Id.* at ¶ 1.

[119] The Commission "[i]invites all the human rights treaty monitoring bodies to respond positively to its invitation to monitor the compliance of States with their commitments under the relevant human rights instruments in order to ensure full enjoyment of those rights by persons with disabilities, and urges Governments to cover fully the question of the human rights of persons with disabilities in complying with reporting obligations under the relevant United Nations human rights instruments." *Id.* at ¶ 11.

[120] *Id.* at ¶ 7.

[121] *Id.* at ¶ 30.

[122] General Comment 5, *supra* note 7, at ¶ 5.

on Economic, Social and Cultural Rights has emphasized a positive right to gain access to health services.[123]

Some conventions, such as the European Convention, protect only against discrimination in the exercise of rights guaranteed under the convention itself.[124] Article 26 of the ICCPR, on the other hand, protects against discrimination in any area of law.[125] The UN Human Rights Committee, established by the ICCPR to assist in the interpretation of the convention, defines discrimination as "any distinction, exclusion, restriction or preference . . . which has the purpose or effect of nullifying or impairing the recognition, enjoyment or exercise by all persons, on an equal footing, of all rights and freedoms."[126] The Committee on Economic, Social and Cultural Rights also recognizes that "[i]n order to remedy past and present discrimination, and to deter future discrimination, comprehensive anti-discrimination legislation in relation to disability would seem to be indispensable in virtually all States parties."[127] Thus, protections against discrimination under international law extend beyond outlawing laws that explicitly or purposefully exclude or deny opportunities to people with disabilities. Legislation that has the *effect*

---

123 As part of the right to access health services, the principle of non-discrimination means that "health facilities, goods and services must be accessible to all, especially the most vulnerable or marginalized sections of the population, in law and in fact, without discrimination on any of the prohibited grounds." CESCR General Comment 14, *supra* note 112, at ¶ 12(b).

124 Article 14 of the European Convention provides that "[t]he enjoyment of the rights and freedoms *set forth in this Convention* shall be secured without discrimination on any ground." *Supra* note 74 (emphasis added). Article 2(1) of the ICCPR and article 2(2) of the ICESCR have similar protections.

125 UN Manual, *supra* note 115, at 255.

126 CCPR General Comment 18, *supra* note 115, at ¶ 7 Note that the MI Principles, *supra* note 96, incorporate almost the exact words of this definition of discrimination into Principle 1(4). This is one indication that the drafters of the MI Principles intended Principle 1 to help interpret Article 26 of the ICCPR. General Comment 5 of the UN Committee on Economic, Social, and Cultural Rights uses almost the same definition, but also includes language that creates even broader rights, such as the right to reasonable accommodation. General Comment 5, *supra* note 7 at ¶ 15.

127 General Comment 5, *id.* ¶ 16.

of denying rights and freedoms is prohibited as discrimination as well.[128] As the UN Committee on Economic, Social, and Cultural Rights has observed, the problem of discrimination goes well beyond that of intentions.

> Both *de jure* and *de facto* discrimination against persons with disabilities have a long history and take various forms. They range from invidious discrimination, such as the denial of educational opportunities, to more "subtle" forms of discrimination, such as segregation and isolation achieved through the imposition of physical and social barriers. . . . The effects of disability-based discrimination have been particularly severe in the fields of education, employment, housing, transport, cultural life, and access to public places and services.[129]

The United Nations General Assembly has taken such statements under consideration through the work of the Ad Hoc Committee that is currently considering proposals for a Convention on the Rights of People with Disabilities.[130] Thus, even if a Convention on the Rights of People with Disabilities is not adopted in the near future, the recent adoption of Resolution 2000/51 by the United Nations Commission on Human Rights, together with Committee comments, such as General Comment 5 of ICESCR, the Standard Rules, and the MI Principles, may provide the basis for protections against discrimination for people with disabilities under international law.

1. The Right to Community Integration Under International Human Rights Law

In addition to the general anti-discrimination provisions of international law that may be applied to people with disabilities, failing to provide opportunities for people with disabilities to live in the community, rather

---

[128] *Id.* ¶ 15.

[129] *Id.*

[130] G.A. Res., 56th Sess. [on the report of the 3rd Committee (A/56/583/Add.2)], U.N. Doc. A/RES/56/168 (2001). *See supra* note 84, for a citation to the resolution as first considered by the Third Committee of the UN General Assembly on November 28, 2001 (the resolution text was unchanged).

than in institutions, may violate a broad array of recognized human rights. Drawing on the reasoning used by a majority of the United States Supreme Court in *Olmstead*, governments that provide services to people with disabilities exclusively in institutions, without providing meaningful alternatives in the community, may be found to violate international human rights law by providing services in a discriminatory manner.

Of course, in many countries, the absence of community alternatives to institutions leads to unnecessary and exclusive reliance on institutions to provide care and treatment to people with all sorts of different disabilities. Admission to such institutions is often necessitated on the absence of alternatives, rather than based on the appropriateness of treatment of a specific clinical diagnosis in a specific institution. And once inside the institution, the same lack of community alternatives results in continued incarceration, often long after the condition of the person with a disability has stabilized sufficiently to enable the person to return to the community, with appropriate supports and services if necessary.[131]

While it is true that the right to community integration as a human right, grounded in the principles of non-discrimination, has yet to be recognized explicitly under general international human rights covenants, the right to community integration has gained some recognition over the past 20 years in various human rights documents. References to community integration are found in Article 23 of the Convention on the Rights of the Child,[132] and in instruments and documents of the UN General Assembly such as the Declaration on the Rights of Mentally

---

[131] Of course, the doctrine of least restrictive alternatives is meaningless unless community alternatives are developed. As General Comment 14 to the ICESCR recognizes, states must take steps that are "deliberate, concrete and targeted towards the full realization of the right to health." *Supra* note 112, ¶ 30.

[132] Article 23 of the CRC has many important provisions that provide the only convention-based recognition of a right to community integration. *Supra* note 59. These provisions provide a right to services to support and promote community integration, however, they are not linked with anti-discrimination principles. In contrast, the Inter-American Convention on the Elimination of Discrimination Against Persons with Disabilities does link the right to community integration with anti-discrimination principles, *see supra* note 49.

Retarded Persons,[133] the 1991 Principles for the Protection of Persons with Mental Illness,[134] the 1993 Standard Rules on Equalization of Opportunities for Persons with Disabilities,[135] and General Comment 5 to the International Convention on Economic, Social and Cultural Rights,[136] as well as in the Charter of Fundamental Rights of the European Union.[137] Further, and perhaps most significantly, on December 19, 2001, the United Nations General Assembly adopted a resolution calling for the creation of an Ad Hoc Committee "to consider proposals for a comprehensive and integral international convention to promote and protect the rights and dignity of persons with disabilities."[138] This recent action by the UN Assembly is certainly the clearest indication of the "increas[ed] interest of the international community in the promotion and protection of the rights and dignity of persons with disabilities."[139]

For children with disabilities, support for the right to community integration is found under Article 23 of the Convention on the Rights of the Child (CRC). Generally the CRC provides important, detailed protections for children with mental and physical disabilities, including the right to education, services and support in the community. It also provides a model of the kind of rights an international disability rights convention could provide—or the kind of rights that could be guaranteed under existing international conventions if they were supplemented with detailed General Comments.

---

133 *Supra* note 86.

134 *See* MI Principles, *supra* note 96.

135 *Supra* note 2.

136 *Supra* note 7.

137 *Supra* note 77. This Charter recognizes specifically the "right of persons with disabilities to benefit from measures designed to ensure their independence, social and occupation integration and participation in the life of the community." Charter of Fundamental Rights of the European Union, Article 26. For an overview of the European system of human rights and its application to people with disabilities, *see* Gostin, *supra* note 77.

138 *Supra* note 130, ¶ 1.

139 *Id.* at preamble.

Article 23(2) of the CRC also seeks to ensure that every child with a disability has "effective access to and receives education, training, health care services, rehabilitation services, preparation for employment and recreation opportunities. . . ." The same article requires services mandated under the convention to be provided to disabled children "in a manner conducive to the child's achieving the fullest possible social integration and individual development." Throughout the CRC, there are detailed provisions for the protection of the family, and recognition that the family is the "natural environment for the growth and well-being of all its members and . . . should be afforded the necessary protection and assistance so that it can fully assume its responsibilities within the community."[140]

Arguably, the requirement for the "fullest possible social integration" for the vast majority of children with disabilities, combined with protection of the right of children to a family, means that services themselves must be provided in a family-like environment in the community and *not* in orphanages or institutions. The CRC unfortunately does not state the logical outcome of the protections it provides, which would require a fundamental alteration of many countries' social care systems, but the Convention does provide sufficient detail to assess human rights protections within social service systems as a whole. In addition, it provides guidance to policy makers, human rights activists, and international development agencies about the need to emphasize community-based alternatives in any structured response to the human rights problem in institutions.

In addition to the CRC, the Declaration on the Rights of Mentally Retarded Persons recognizes a right to community integration and inclusion by establishing that "[w]henever possible, the mentally retarded person should live with his own family or with foster parents and participate in different forms of community life."[141] However, the MR Declaration contemplates the restriction or denial of the right to be free from institutionalization if it should "become necessary," a vague standard that could easily be clarified in domestic legislation. Yet this stan-

---

[140] *Supra* note 59, at Preamble.

[141] *Supra* note 86, at ¶ 4. *See also* Harding, *supra* note 78.

dard may evolve into a mandate for community integration as more and more countries develop community-based services and support systems that permit the full social inclusion of people with even the most severe intellectual disabilities. In societies where most or all people with intellectual disabilities live in the community, it should rarely, if ever, be necessary to place a person in an institution.

Similarly, the 1975 Declaration on the Rights of Disabled Persons recognizes a right to community integration when it states that disabled persons "have the right to live with their families or with foster parents and to participate in all social, creative or recreational activities."[142] The Declaration goes on to state that even if some sort of residential support is required, "the environment and living conditions therein shall be as close as possible to those of the normal life of a person of his or her age."[143] The UN Declaration on the Rights of Disabled Persons also recognizes the importance of social integration when it states that "[d]isabled persons are entitled to the measures designed to enable them to become as self-reliant as possible."[144]

A third declaration, the Vienna Declaration, endorses not only the right of people with disabilities to community integration but also their right to equality. As the Vienna Declaration provides:

> The World Conference on Human Rights reaffirms that all human rights and fundamental freedoms are universal and thus unreservedly include persons with disabilities. Every person is born equal and has the same right to life and welfare, education and work, living independently and active participation in all aspects of society. . . . The World Conference on Human Rights calls on Governments, where necessary, to adopt or adjust legislation to ensure access to these [life, welfare, education, work, living independently and active participation in all aspects of society] and other rights for disabled persons.

---

142 *Supra* note 87, at ¶ 9.

143 *Id.*

144 *Id.* at ¶ 5.

> . . . Persons with disabilities should be guaranteed equal opportunity through the elimination of all socially determined barriers, be they physical, financial, social or psychological, which exclude or restrict full participation in society.[145]

The right to community integration is also addressed specifically in the 1991 Principles for the Protection of Persons with Mental Illness.[146] These Principles recognize explicitly the right of every person with a mental illness "to live and work, as far as possible, in the community"[147] and, if treatment is necessary, "the right to be treated and cared for, as far as possible, in the community in which he or she lives."[148] This preference for community living is reinforced by the duty to treat persons with mental illness in the least restrictive setting in their own community and to preserve and enhance their autonomy.[149]

The MI Principles explicitly prohibit discrimination on the grounds of mental illness by defining discrimination as "any distinction, exclusion or preference that has the effect of nullifying or impairing equal enjoyment of rights."[150] These principles, therefore, may support the claim that an individual who is institutionalized has been discriminated against because he or she has been deprived of the right to live and work in the community, and to be "treated with humanity and respect for the inherent dignity of the human person."[151]

---

145 *Supra* note 101, at ¶¶ 63–64; *see also id.* at ¶ 22.

146 *See supra* note 96, and accompanying text.

147 *Id.* at Principle 3.

148 *Id.* at Principle 7(1).

149 *Id.* at Principle 9(1). This principle states that "every patient shall have the right to be treated in the least restrictive environment and with the least restrictive or intrusive treatment appropriate to the patients' health needs and the need to protect the physical safety of others." This right to treatment in the least restrictive environment is also reinforced by Principle 9(4) that requires treatment of every patient to be "directed towards preserving and enhancing personal autonomy."

150 *Id.* at Principle 1(4).

151 *Id.* at Principle 1(2).

Further, the MI Principles are of particular importance because in many countries, long-term mental health facilities often serve as repositories for people who have no history of mental illness, or no current mental illness, but who remain in the institutions due to the lack of alternative facilities or services in their communities. Thus the MI Principles may have major implications for the future design of mental health systems. Indeed, they already have been used by international oversight and enforcement bodies as an authoritative interpretation of the requirements of the ICESCR.[152] No doubt, the MI Principles are one of the international community's strongest statements promoting community integration and prohibiting institutionalization as a form of discrimination against people with disabilities.[153]

In addition to the MI Principles and the Declarations discussed above, the 1993 Standard Rules on Equalization of Opportunities for Persons with Disabilities also recognize the right to community integration. As the Preamble to the Standard Rules states, "intensified efforts are needed to achieve the full and equal enjoyment of human rights and participation in society by persons with disabilities."[154] The Standard

---

[152] UN Committee on Economic, Social, and Cultural Rights, General Comment 5, *supra* note 7, at ¶ 21 (use of MI Principle 13(3) to interpret Articles 6–8 of the ICESCR on rights relating to work). The importance of the MI Principles are noted more generally at ¶ 7 of General Comment 5.

[153] The MI Principles, *supra* note 96, have also served as model mental health legislation. According to Mental Disability Rights International, Mexico, Hungary, Portugal, and Australia have incorporated the MI Principles in whole or in part into their own domestic laws. Other countries such as Nicaragua and Costa Rica have used the MI Principles as a guide in the redesign of their mental health policies. *See* Rosenthal & Sundram, *supra* note 69. The MI Principles 15–18 establish standards for treatment and living conditions within psychiatric institutions, and they create protections against arbitrary detention in such facilities. These principles apply broadly to persons with mental illness, whether or not they are in psychiatric facilities, and they apply to all persons admitted to a mental health facility, whether or not they are diagnosed as mentally ill. *See* "Definitions," and Principle 24.

[154] Further, Rule 3 of the Standard Rules states that "[a]ll rehabilitation services should be available in the local community where the person with disabilities lives. However, in some instances, in order to attain a certain training objective, special time-limited rehabilitation courses may be organized, where appropriate, in residential form." *Supra* note 2.

Rules apply to all people with mental or physical disabilities, and establishes the right to community-based services to make such integration possible. Significantly, the Standard Rules also recognize the right of people with disabilities to participate in all decision making relating to plans and programs that concern them, instead of having others speak on their behalf, and calls specifically for the inclusion of people with disabilities in the public process of drafting legislation that affects their rights and social and economic status.[155]

Another more recent example of an international instrument recognizing a right to community integration is the Inter-American Convention on the Elimination of All Forms of Discrimination Against Persons with Disabilities, adopted by the Organization of American States (OAS).[156] This Convention contains many important provisions, including the explicit recognition of a right to community integration. However, unlike other general human rights conventions, the OAS Convention does not create an immediate obligation on states to enforce the rights it establishes.

Concern over the segregation of persons with mental disabilities was officially expressed in the Americas over a decade ago. At a 1990 Regional Conference held in Caracas, Venezuela, the Pan American Health Organization adopted the Declaration of Caracas, which calls for a major restructuring of mental health services, including banning exclusive reliance on inpatient treatment in a psychiatric hospital which "isolates patients from their natural environment. . . ."[157] The Declaration also establishes a link between mental health services and the right to community integration by concluding that such outmoded mental health services "imperil the human and civil rights of patients."[158]

---

[155] *Id.* at Rules 14(2) and 15(1).

[156] *Supra* note 49.

[157] 42(2) *International Digest of Health Legislation* 336338 (1991); the full text of the Declaration is also reprinted in Itzhak Levav, Helena Restrepo & Caryl Guerra de Macedo, "The Restructuring of Psychiatric Care in Latin America: A New Policy for Mental Health Services," 15 *J. Pub. Health & Pol'y* 71, preamble at 83 (1994).

[158] *Id.* at preamble.

The Council of Europe renewed its commitment to the right of people with disabilities to live in the community in 1992 when it recommended that states should "guarantee the right of people with disabilities to an independent life and full integration into society, and recognize society's duty to make this possible."[159] The recommendation also states that services should be provided to people with disabilities to enable persons to "be as free as possible from institutional settings and constraints" except where "unavoidable," and calls on countries to adopt policies "guaranteeing full and active participation in community life."[160] This 1992 policy reaffirmed the Council of Europe's original 1973 Resolution on the Social Services for Physically or Mentally Handicapped Persons, which states that "the general objective of this policy should be to give handicapped persons every opportunity to be as much integrated as possible into society. Whatever the cause, type and degree of their handicap may be, the handicapped should be given all opportunities for their personal development and for maximum participation in the activities of the community."[161]

Similarly, General Comment 5 to the ICESCR recognizes the right to community integration, including the right to receive medical and social services that will enable people to participate fully in the community, as an integral part of the ICESCR's protection against discrimination for people with disabilities. While there is no such specific language about community living in the General Comments of the ICCPR, the identification of segregated services as a form of discrimination under the ICESCR may indicate that the ICCPR provides similar protections.[162]

---

159 Committee of Ministers, Recommendation (92)6 *On a Coherent Policy for People with Disabilities*, adopted Apr. 9, 1992 at the 474th meeting of the Ministers' Deputies, § I.4.

160 *Id.* at §§ I.1 and I.2.

161 Committee of Ministers, Resolution (73)1 on the Social Services for Physically or Mentally Handicapped Persons, adopted Jan. 19, 1973 at the 217th Meeting of the Ministers' Deputies, *reprinted in* Council of Europe, *The Rights of the Child: A European Perspective* § I.A.1 (Strasbourg: Council of Europe, 1996).

162 *See* Gerard Quinn, "The International Covenant on Civil and Political Rights and Disability: A Conceptual Framework," *in* Degener & Koster-Dreese, *supra* note 8, 70.

Further, General Comment 5 makes clear that such rights are core principles under the ICESCR. For example, Comment 5 interprets the right to health as part of the general requirement to promote individual independence and social integration. As General Comment 5 states, "[t]he right to physical and mental health . . . implies the right to have access to, and to benefit from, those medical and social services . . . which enable persons with disabilities to become independent, prevent further disabilities and support their social integration."[163] Thus, in providing for rehabilitation, General Comment 5 quotes the Standard Rules to state that rehabilitation services should be designed to enable individuals "to reach and sustain their optimum level of independence and functioning."[164]

General Comment 14 also recognizes that states can address in their planning and budget development processes the need for a range of community services needed to serve people with mental disabilities. "Such steps must be deliberate, concrete and targeted towards the full realization of the right to health."[165]

These General Comments to the ICESCR, together with the other international laws and statements discussed above, provide standards against which the treatment of people with mental disabilities may be judged. But they do more as well. They establish a right to community integration for people with disabilities and support the claim that the institutional placement itself, as well as the continued confinement of people in institutions who are capable of living in the community, is prohibited by the anti-discrimination provisions of existing human rights laws and interpretations.

2. International Human Rights Protections For People with Disabilities in Institutions

In addition to the right of people with disabilities to live in the community under international law, international law and policies may also rec-

---

163 General Comment No. 5, *supra* note 7, at ¶ 34.

164 *Id., citing* Standard Rules, *supra* note 2, at Rule 3.

165 CESCR General Comment 14, *supra* note 112, at ¶ 30.

ognize the right to be free from improper institutionalization as unlawful discrimination.

In many countries in the world today, the absence of adequate community programs and services for people with disabilities, and people with mental illness in particular, leads to unnecessary reliance on institutions to provide treatment. Within these institutions, individuals may then be subject to abuse and neglect. A worldwide effort to document such patterns of abuses in institutions is underway. For example, Mental Disability Rights International (MDRI), an advocacy organization dedicated to using international human rights law to protect the rights of people with mental disabilities, has begun to investigate human rights violations against people with disabilities in 16 countries, primarily in Latin America and Central and Eastern Europe.[166] Over the last eight years, MDRI has published four major reports documenting widespread abuses in four countries.[167]

MDRI's findings in the countries in which they have investigated are remarkably similar.[168] People with mental and physical disabilities are commonly detained in closed, segregated institutions—out of public view and often in parts of a country that are remote from population centers. People may remain in these custodial facilities for life, living cut off from family, friends and community. In some cases, they are detained without any legal process to protect them against arbitrary detention. Even when legal procedures for civil commitment exist, these are often circumvented or ignored. For example, people with mental dis-

---

[166] For more information, *see* http://www.mdri.org/ or write: Mental Disability Rights International, 1156 15th Street NW, Suite 1001, Washington, D.C., U.S.A. 20005.

[167] MDRI has observed conditions in institutions in: Argentina, Armenia, Azerbaijan, Costa Rica, the Czech Republic, Hong Kong (China), Hungary, Kosovo (Yugoslavia), Lithuania, Macedonia, Mexico, Romania, Russia, Slovakia, Ukraine, and Uruguay. MDRI has published four reports: *See Mental Disability Rights International, Human Rights and Mental Health: Mexico* (2000); *Children in Russia's Institutions: Human Rights and Opportunities for Reform* (1999); *Mental Disability Rights International, Human Rights and Mental Health: Hungary* (1997); *Mental Disability Rights International, Human Rights and Mental Health: Uruguay* (1995).

[168] *See id.*

abilities are often placed under the "guardianship" of a mental health administrator, and then "voluntarily" committed to an institution. Many people are declared mentally incompetent without legal representation or due process protections, and their placement under guardianship functionally strips them of any legal right to make the most basic decisions about their own lives.

In many of the countries MDRI has visited, authorities report that the majority of people who are currently institutionalized could live in the community if appropriate services were available. A small percentage of institutionalized populations are made up of individuals who present a danger to themselves or others, or who are in need of treatment that must be provided in an institution. Many people without disabilities are placed in institutions simply because they are marginalized in society and have no community support network, but they become increasingly socially isolated and acquire mental disabilities because of living in an institution. This is particularly true for the large numbers of children placed in orphanages or residential schools.[169]

Behind the closed doors of institutions, people with disabilities are subject to inhuman and degrading treatment. In Mexico, Hungary, Armenia, and Kosovo, for example, MDRI found people detained in squalid conditions—in some cases left naked and covered in their own feces.[170] People are routinely strapped to benches, beds or wheelchairs—largely due to the lack of staff to provide basic care or nominal supervision. In Uruguay, MDRI found electro-convulsive therapy (ECT) used on people with mental retardation as a form of behavior control.[171] In Uruguay, Hungary and Romania, overdose, poly-pharmacy and the failure to monitor the side effects of medications expose hundreds of people to unnecessary and life-threatening dangers.[172] Children with

---

169 *Children in Russia's Institutions: Human Rights and Opportunities for Reform* (1999).

170 *Mental Disability Rights International, Human Rights and Mental Health: Mexico* (2000).

171 *Mental Disability Rights International, Human Rights and Mental Health: Uruguay* (1995).

172 *Id.*

disabilities are often denied medical care and are left to die in their institutions. Both children and adults with multiple disabilities are often relegated to the back wards of institutions, where they are "triaged" and left with the least care and attention. The entire population of some institutions is literally left to starve or freeze to death, with only the strongest individuals capable of surviving. In Armenia, for example, MDRI visited an institution that reported an annual mortality rate of 30 percent. MDRI has received reports—which they have not yet been able to document—of institutions with annual mortality rates upward of 80 percent.[173]

Women are particularly vulnerable to abuse in mental health systems. Women subjected to trauma—such as childhood sexual abuse, domestic violence or war-related traumas—are commonly misdiagnosed with major mental health disorders. They are often improperly institutionalized and then re-traumatized by the coercive treatment they receive in institutions. Women in institutions are particularly vulnerable to further abuse by staff or other patients. Non-consensual sterilization, forced abortions, and the arbitrary denial of parental rights are unfortunately all too common.

International covenants may provide important protections for institutionalized people with disabilities, including the subjects of MDRI's Reports. The arbitrary detention of individuals in institutions, as described above, violates their right to "liberty and security of the person" under Article 9 of the ICCPR. Similarly, "inhuman and degrading treatment" (inside state-run institutions) is prohibited by Article 7 of the ICCPR.[174] Subjecting individuals, including individuals with disabili-

---

173 Notes of Eric Rosenthal, *see* http://www.mdri.org/ or write: Mental Disability Rights International, 1156 15th Street NW, Suite 1001, Washington, D.C., U.S.A. 20005.

174 In recent years, the UN Human Rights Committee has taken a strong stand on the application of Article 7 of the ICCPR to all people in detention, including people in psychiatric facilities. *See* CCPR *General Comment 20: Replaces General Comment 7 Concerning Prohibition of Torture and Cruel Treatment or Punishment (Art. 7)* (1992) [hereinafter General Comment 20]. General Comment 20 states that Article 7 "is complemented by the positive requirements of article 10, paragraph 1 of the Covenant, which stipulates that 'All persons deprived of their liberty shall be treated with humanity and with respect for the inherent dignity of the human person.'" *Id.* at ¶ 2. In addition, the Human Rights Committee has stated that "[i]t

ties, to high risks of medical illness or death also violates their right to life under Article 6 of the ICCPR. As such, institutionalization may violate the right to the highest attainable standard of physical and mental health, as recognized by Article 12 of the ICESCR. Even clean, safe, well-administered institutions may result in the deterioration of psychological and social functioning as individuals lose their social ties with the community and adapt to the dependency of life in a closed environment.

The international standard that is most relevant to conditions in institutions, particularly for people with mental illness, is the MI Principles. The MI Principles include a broad array of rights within institutions, and a set of substantive standards and procedural protections for involuntary hospital admission, such as protections against "harm, including unjustified medication, abuse by other patients, staff or others."[175] These Principles require the establishment of monitoring and inspection of facilities to ensure compliance with the MI Principles.[176] They also require treatment that is "based on an individually prescribed plan"[177] and "directed towards preserving and enhancing personal autonomy."[178] The MI Principles provide to individuals detained in psychiatric institutions the right to a hearing before a judicial or other independent review body, the right to representation and independent experts, the right to attend one's own hearing, and the right to be given the reasons for any decision.[179] The Principles state that a person may

---

is appropriate to emphasize . . . that Article 7 protects, in particular, children, pupils and patients in teaching and medical institutions." *Id.* at ¶ 5. The UN Manual on reporting points out that "Article 7 protects not only detainees from ill-treatment by public authorities or by persons acting outside or without any official authority but also in general any person. This point is of particular relevance in situations concerning . . . patients in . . . medical institutions, whether public or private." UN Manual, *supra* note 115, at 197.

[175] *Supra* note 96, at Principle 8(2).

[176] *Id.* at Principle 22.

[177] *Id.* at Principle 9(1).

[178] *Id.* at Principle 9(4).

[179] *Id.* at Principles 17 & 18.

be involuntarily admitted only if the person has a mental illness diagnosed under accepted medical standards, and presents either a serious likelihood of immediate harm to him or herself or others, or that the person is severely mentally ill and his or her condition will substantially deteriorate, resulting in impaired judgment.[180] However, the Principles do not prohibit all involuntary institutionalization, which, in itself is a controversial human rights issue.

While these general arguments about the application of international human rights law are intuitively powerful, human rights covenants have not been used historically to protect against human rights abuses in psychiatric institutions. The major limitation on the use of existing covenants to enforce the rights of institutionalized people with disabilities is their failure to include specific provisions regarding people with disabilities.

Perhaps the most highly developed jurisprudence on the rights of people in institutions is in the European system of human rights. However, the case law in this area is mixed. In fact, the jurisprudence in the European human rights system reveals the difficulties of applying general human rights conventions in the context of institutional care, particularly in areas that have traditionally been left to medical discretion or domestic social policy.

The European and American conventions on human rights provide approximately parallel protections. Regional human rights systems in Europe and the Americas have the most effective enforcement mechanisms, and present the greatest opportunities for individual and systemic rights enforcement. The European and American courts of human rights can hear cases on the application of human rights to individual circumstances, presenting not only an opportunity for individual enforcement but also for the authoritative interpretation of international human rights protections under general conventions.

But while the European Court has been open to the possibility of finding inhuman and degrading treatment in institutions, there is also a long line of cases in which the Court has found that the amount of suf-

---

[180] *Id.* at Principle 16.

fering caused by poor conditions did not meet the standard required by the Convention.[181]

a. The European System

The European Commission of Human Rights and the European Court of Human Rights have heard numerous cases on the rights of institutionalized people.[182] In fact, the European Court has contributed greatly to the interpretation of Article 5 of the European Convention on Human Rights and Fundamental Freedoms (ECHR) protecting the right to liberty and security of the person. Further, the Court has required state parties to the ECHR to follow procedures set forth in their own domestic laws, and to provide individuals with a right to review by a court or other independent authority.

While the European Court has stated that special scrutiny is required to protect especially vulnerable people in institutions,[183] both the European Court and the European Commission have, in practice, been extremely deferential to institutions when reviewing allegations of inhuman and degrading treatment under Article 3 of the ECHR.[184] For example, in the case of *B. v. United Kingdom* the European Commission found a case inadmissible under Article 3 because the facts alleged did

---

181 One scholar who reviewed the European Court's decisions in 2000, before the *Price* case was decided, observed that "[t]he Strasbourg authorities have been so deferential in their Article 3 jurisprudence that the Commission or Court has never found that the conditions in a mental hospital were so inhuman and degrading as to breach Article 3. Yet, severe maltreatment, neglect, or humiliation of patients, or placing them in punitive or unsafe environments should give rise to an Article 3 claim." Gostin, *supra* note 77, at 152.

182 *See* Gostin, *id.*

183 The Court in *Herczegfalvy v. Austria* stated that, "[t]he position of inferiority and powerlessness which is typical of patients confined in psychiatric hospitals calls for increased vigilance in reviewing whether the Convention has been complied with." Judgment of 24 Sept. 1992, 244 Eur. Ct. H.R. (Ser. A) at ¶ 82; 15 E.H.R.R. 437, 484 (1993).

184 Article 3 of the ECHR on "Prohibition of Torture" states that "No one shall be subjected to torture or to inhuman or degrading treatment or punishment." *Supra* note 74.

not amount to inhuman and degrading treatment.[185] In the case, the applicant, a patient at a psychiatric hospital in the United Kingdom, claimed that he was "detained in grossly overcrowded conditions, lacking in adequate sanitary (e.g. toilet and washing) facilities, and in a constant atmosphere of violence. He alleged that dormitory beds were only 6–12 inches apart, and there was no privacy, and little fresh air or exercise. The applicant claimed he had received no treatment whatsoever and almost never saw a doctor."[186] The European Commission held that although the physical conditions at the hospital were "admittedly unsatisfactory and have been criticized by different official bodies over a number of years . . . [and while] the hospital staff may . . . do their best to cope with these inadequacies, this does not itself exclude the possibility that the physical conditions of detention could in themselves give rise to a question under Art. 3 which requires investigation and examination on the merits."[187]

In the case of *B. v. United Kingdom*, the Commission determined that despite the enormity of the suffering induced by the poor conditions, it did not rise to the level of a violation of the ECHR. Other cases have alleged similar inhuman and degrading treatment in psychiatric institutions in Europe, including the detention of individuals in prolonged physical restraints.[188] But the European Commission and Court of Human Rights have consistently found that such practices are not sufficiently extreme to constitute a human rights violation.[189]

---

[185] App. No. 6870/75, Second Partial Decision of the Commission as to Admissibility, 10 Eur. Comm. H.R. Dec. & Rep. 37 (1977), cited in Gostin, *supra* note 77, at 151.

[186] Gostin, *supra* note 77, at 151.

[187] App. No. 6870/75 at 66–67, as quoted in Gostin, *id.*

[188] Gostin, *supra* note 77, at 151.

[189] Gostin, *id.* at 152. In the case of *A v. United Kingdom*, App. No. 6840/74, Eur. Comm. H. R. Dec. & Rep. (1977), the Commission did accept a friendly settlement of a claim of inhuman treatment. It accepted that the requirements of the convention were met by the establishment of minimum standards for institutional conditions, including the provision of clothing, mattresses, latrines, and toilet paper, as well as safeguards against the improper use of seclusion and restraint.

It is significant, however, that the European Commission in *B. v. United Kingdom* recognized that conditions in institutions may violate the rights protected under the ECHR even if staff "do their best" to assist patients. In many circumstances, people with mental disabilities are not abused through the intentional infliction of pain and suffering, but because they receive inappropriate care due to a lack of resources or the administrative convenience of the institution. Unlike "torture," which is usually understood to be limited to cases where pain is inflicted on purpose,[190] "inhuman and degrading treatment" has no intent requirement.[191]

With the more recent case of *Herzcegfalvy v. Austria*, the European Court showed that it was becoming more aware of the particular vulnerability of psychiatric patients, and perhaps increasingly willing to find the presence of human rights abuse in institutions.[192] Most recently, in July 2001, the European Court of Human Rights decided the case of *Price v. United Kingdom*,[193] which establishes new rights for individuals with disabilities, particularly those detained in institutions. In the *Price* decision, the European Court found that a woman detained in jail for seven days had been subject to degrading treatment after she was forced to sleep in a wheelchair and left without an accessible bathroom.

---

[190] The Convention against Torture and Other Cruel, Inhuman or Degrading Treatment or Punishment defines torture as "any act by which severe pain or suffering, whether physical or mental, is intentionally inflicted on a person for such purposes as obtaining from him or a third person information or a confession, punishing him for an act he or a third person has committed or is suspected of having committed, or intimidating or coercing him or a third person, or for any reason based on discrimination of any kind . . . . It does not include pain or suffering arising only from, inherent in or incidental to lawful sanctions." *Supra* note 62, at art. 1, ¶ 1.

[191] Rosenthal & Rubenstein, *supra* note 97, at 273. The European Commission of Human Rights has held that "the word 'torture' is often used to describe inhuman treatment which has a purpose, such as the obtaining of information or confession, or the infliction of punishment, and it is generally an aggravated form of inhuman treatment." 12 *Y.B. Eur. Conv. on H.R.* 186 (1969) (Eur. Comm'n on H.R.).

[192] *See supra* note 183.

[193] Judgement of 10 July 2001, Application No. 00033394/96, HUDOC REF00002640, available *at* http://hudoc.echr.coe.int/Eng/Judgements.htm.

The *Price* decision suggests that international tribunals, such as the European Court, will now recognize that extra vigilance is required to ensure that governments protect against inhuman and degrading treatment of people with mental disabilities, particularly those detained in institutions.[194]

b. The Inter-American System

Jurisprudence in the Inter-American system of human rights has also become more active recently with respect to the rights of people with disabilities detained in institutions. In March 1999, the Inter-American Commission of Human Rights issued its first decision on the rights of an individual with a mental disability.[195] *The Case of Victor Rosario Congo* involved Mr. Congo, a man with a mental disability from Ecuador, who died of "dehydration" in pre-trial detention after he was beaten by a guard, placed in isolation, and denied adequate medical and psychiatric care.[196] The Commission found that Mr. Congo's mental state degenerated as a result of being held in isolation, and that holding him in seclusion under these circumstances constituted inhuman and degrading treatment in violation of Article 5 of the American Convention.[197] The Commission did not find that Congo was deliberately deprived of food and water, but that state authorities failed to take appropriate measures, given his mental health condition, to ensure that he received adequate food and water and was protected. The Commission found that Ecuador's failure to provide appropriate care for Mr. Congo

---

[194] The Human Rights Committee has followed a similar line of analysis in its explication of Article 7 of the ICCPR, acknowledging that there is no specific definition of "torture, inhuman or degrading treatment" in the Covenant, and no "sharp distinctions between the different kinds of punishment or treatment; the distinctions depend on the nature, purpose, and severity of the treatment applied." General Comment 20, *supra* note 174, at ¶ 4.

[195] *The Case of Victor Rosario Congo, supra* note 79.

[196] *Id.*

[197] *Id.* at ¶ 101. Article 5 of the American Convention on Human Rights states: "No one shall be subjected to torture or to cruel, inhuman, or degrading punishment or treatment. All persons deprived of their liberty shall be treated with respect for the inherent dignity of the human person." *Supra* note 71, at ¶ 5(2).

violated its duty to protect his life under Article 4(1) of the American Convention.[198]

In reaching its decision, the Commission applied special standards to the determination of whether the provisions of the American Convention on Human Rights "ha[d] been complied with in cases involving persons suffering from mental illnesses."[199] The Commission stated that protection against inhuman and degrading treatment under the American Convention "must be interpreted in light of the *Principles for the Protection of Persons with Mental Illness and for the Improvement of Mental Health Care*."[200] Although the Commission observed that detention of a person in a small, isolated cell "can in itself constitute inhumane treatment . . . when the person kept in isolation in a penitentiary institution has a mental disability, this could involve an even more serious violation of the State's obligation to protect the physical, mental and moral integrity of persons held under its custody."[201] The Commission found, therefore, that placement in isolation itself constituted inhuman and degrading treatment and that "[t]his violation is aggravated by the fact that he was left in isolation unable to satisfy his basic needs."[202] The Commission also noted that the European Commission had already established that detention "under deplorable conditions and without medical treatment" constituted an additional form of inhuman and degrading treatment.[203] As the Commission noted, "the right to physical integrity is even more serious in the case of a person

---

[198] Article 4(1) states: "Every person has the right to have his life respected. This right shall be protected by law and, in general, from the moment of conception. No one shall be arbitrarily deprived of his life." *Id.* at ¶ 4(1).

[199] *The Case of Victor Rosario Congo, supra* note 79, at ¶ 53. The Commission cites the European Court of Human Rights' decision in *Herczegfalvy v. Austria*, in support of this proposition. *Id.* at ¶ 54, *citing Herczegfalvy v. Austria, supra* note 183, at ¶ 82.

[200] *Id.* at ¶ 54.

[201] *Id.* at ¶ 58.

[202] *Id.* at ¶ 59.

[203] *Id.* at ¶ 66, *citing* the decision of *Ashingdane v. United Kingdom*, App. No. 8225/78, Series A No. 93; 6 E.H.R.R. 50 (1984).

held in preventative detention, suffering a mental disease, and therefore in the custody of the State in a particularly vulnerable position."[204]

The *Congo* decision is important because the Inter-American Commission indicated, for the first time, that it will adopt "special standards to the determination of whether the provisions of the Convention have been complied with in cases involving persons suffering from mental illnesses."[205] In addition, the case also marks the first time the Inter-American Commission relied on the Principles for the Protection of Persons with Mental Illness (MI Principles) as a guide to the interpretation of the American Convention.

The recognition of the MI Principles as an authoritative guide to the interpretation of the American Convention is important within the Inter-American system and in the development of international human rights law as well. The Inter-American Commission's recognition that the MI Principles constitute state practice consequently raises their value as a matter of customary international law. In the future, therefore, human rights bodies may be more likely to follow the precedent established by the Inter-American Commission in using the MI Principles as a guide to the interpretation of the American and other conventions.

Since its decision in *The Case of Victor Rosario Congo*, the Inter-American Commission has been willing to hear additional cases involving the rights of people with mental disabilities detained in psychiatric institutions. For example, in March 2000, the Commission granted a request from Mental Disability Rights International for a hearing on the findings of MDRI's February 2000 report, entitled *Human Rights & Mental Health: Mexico*, which documents a broad pattern of abuses in Mexico's psychiatric facilities. This hearing was the Inter-American Commission's first hearing on the protection of human rights in a mental health system as a whole, and prompted the Commission to raise concerns about human rights abuses in Mexico's psychiatric hospitals in the OAS's annual report on Mexico's human rights record.[206] This

---

204 *Id.* at ¶ 67.

205 *Id.* at ¶ 53.

206 Inter-American Commission on Human Rights, Annual Report of the Inter-American Commission on Human Rights 1999, III, para. 20, Doc. 6 Rev, OEA/

hearing also demonstrates the value of regional human rights systems as tools for human rights monitoring and public education about the conditions of people with disabilities in closed institutions.

Thus, the situation with respect to the effect of international conventions on state practices may be changing. The Inter-American Commission on Human Rights' precedent-setting decision in *The Case of Victor Rosario Congo* builds on the approach adopted by the European Court in *Herzcegfalvy v. Austria*,[207] and recognizes that the MI Principles can be used as a guide to the interpretation of the American Convention on Human Rights in regard to the rights of people with mental disabilities.[208]

Further, new interpretations of human rights conventions by international tribunals and bodies may create a window of opportunity for NGOs working for the rights of people with disabilities. By documenting abuses and submitting findings to international oversight bodies, activists, such as MDRI, can inform international bodies about the importance of increased monitoring and rights enforcement for people with disabilities. Activists can also provide the foundation of factual evidence necessary to demonstrate that, around the world today, the placement of people with disabilities in institutions inherently violates their rights, and subjects them to the increased risk of inhuman and degrading treatment, arbitrary detention, deprivation of the right to the highest attainable standards of physical and mental health, and a broad range of other rights violations. As such, NGOs now have an opportunity to help foster explicit recognition that the detention of people with disabilities in institutions and their segregation from society inherently constitutes discrimination under international law.

Ser.L.V/II.106 (Apr. 13, 1999). The report is available *at* www.cidh.oas.org/annualrep/99eng/Chapter5b.htm.

[207] *Supra* note 183.

[208] *The Case of Victor Rosario Congo, supra* note 79, at ¶ 54. The Inter-American Commission also cited the analysis in Rosenthal & Rubenstein, *supra* note 97 (describing the use of the MI Principles as a guide to the interpretation of international human rights conventions).

E. CONCLUSION

In *Olmstead v. L.C.*, the United States Supreme Court held that states may not detain individuals with disabilities in institutions if such individuals are capable of living in the community.[209] While the *Olmstead* decision includes significant limitations on the right of people with disabilities to live in the community and to receive any necessary medical treatment there, the Court establishes that improper institutionalization is discrimination under the anti-discrimination prohibition of Title II of the Americans with Disabilities Act. This decision, therefore, may provide guidance to international bodies interpreting international human rights covenants and declarations with similar anti-discrimination language. In international law, there is now a strikingly similar interpretation of the protection against discrimination. The Committee on Economic, Social and Cultural Rights' General Comment 5,[210] which interprets the anti-discrimination provision of the ICESCR to provide a right to community integration, opens the door to a broad new protection of this right under international law. General Comment 5 has not, as of yet, been widely interpreted or applied. U.S. jurisprudence under *Olmstead v. L.C.* provides an example of how the right to community integration can be understood and developed in international law.

Thus, an historic opportunity now exists for the broader application of the United States Supreme Court's community integration mandate, together with rights recognized in various international human rights conventions and interpretations. Although general international human rights documents may be applied to people with disabilities, the full promise of the Universal Declaration on Human Rights, that *all people* are equal in rights, has yet to be fulfilled. Specialized international conventions have been established to protect particular groups considered especially vulnerable, such as women, children, workers, and racial minorities.[211] But no such international convention yet exists to protect

---

209 527 U.S. 581 (1999).

210 *Supra* note 7.

211 *See supra* notes 59 to 65 and accompanying text, as well as the International Convention on the Elimination of All Forms of Racial Discrimination, G.A. Res.

the rights of people with disabilities.[212] Perhaps the time has come.

On December 19, 2001, the United Nations General Assembly adopted a resolution calling for the creation of an Ad Hoc Committee "to consider proposals for a comprehensive and integral international convention to promote and protect the rights and dignity of persons with disabilities."[213] "Encouraged by the increasing interest of the international community in the promotion and protection of the rights and dignity of persons with disabilities," the United Nations General Assembly is now on record acknowledging "the disadvantaged and vulnerable situation faced by six hundred million persons with disabilities around the world."[214] The adoption of a new specialized UN convention on the rights of people with disabilities could contribute significantly to the right of people with disabilities to equality and dignity, including those confined in institutions. As the drafters of new international law attempt to codify the minimum protections of existing international law in any new draft convention, they should be sure to include a recognition of the right to community integration as established in General Comment 5 and as developed in *Olmstead.*

It is not yet certain if the United Nations will adopt an international convention on the rights of people with disabilities. Even if such a convention is adopted by the United Nations, it would have to be ratified by governments throughout the world in order be legally binding. Such a process could take years to accomplish. In the meantime, governments remain obligated to abide by the requirements of existing international human rights conventions and customary international law. The adoption of domestic legislation that conforms to the requirements of international

---

2106 (XX), U.N. GAOR Sess. 20, Supp. No. 14 at 47, U.N. Doc. A/6014 (1965); *opened for signature* Mar. 7, 1966, *entered into force* Jan. 4, 1966, 660 U.N.T.S. 195. For text and details, see the official United Nations' web site http://www.un.org (visited Jan. 19, 2002).

212 In the past, efforts to adopt a specialized convention on the rights of people with disabilities has not garnered sufficient political support within the United Nations. *See supra* note 83.

213 *Supra* note 130, at ¶ 1.

214 *Id.* at preamble.

standards is one of the most important ways in which governments may meet their existing obligations to people with disabilities under international human rights law.[215] Thus, until such time as a strong, enforceable, international human rights convention protecting the rights of people with disabilities is drafted, adopted and ratified, advocates worldwide will, and must, develop new strategies and theories, such as those proposed here, to make better use of existing international human rights conventions and interpretations to advance the rights of people with disabilities throughout the world.

---

215 Approximately 40 countries have enacted legislation or constitutional provisions prohibiting discrimination against people with disabilities since 1993. *Disability Rights Education and Defense Fund, Inc., http://www.DREDF.org* (list of country laws compiled by Theresia Degener, with assistance from Susan Dennehy, Arlene Kanter Jenny Kern, Yoshiko Osawa, and Silvia Yee); *see also* Theresia Degener & Gerald Quinn, "A Survey Of International, Comparative And Regional Disability Law Reform," *supra* at Part I in this volume and *at* http://www.dredf.org.

Part IV:
Real Life—Needing, Getting and Living with Disability Anti-Discrimination Law

What Is Prejudice as It Relates to Disability Anti-Discrimination Law?

*David Ruebain**

A. INTRODUCTION

My background and interest in disabled people's rights stems from the fact that I was born with an impairment that affects my mobility and dexterity. Like all of us, I have a number of characteristics and identities, but overwhelmingly my identity as a disabled person has defined my relationship with the world and its relationship with me. From the anxiety and terror that my family experienced shortly before my birth upon being told by doctors that I was disabled, to my own experience of being sent to "special" segregated schools, to growing up as different and experiencing the fear and loathing (forgive my frank description) directed towards disabled people, my status as a disabled person has defined, informed and ultimately motivated my life. I currently work in a large law firm as head of a department of education & disability law, a specialist practice that provides legal services to disabled people, children and students. I am also involved with a number of disability advocacy organisations, including Rights Now, a U.K. coalition of which I am Vice-Chairperson that campaigns for comprehensive and enforceable civil rights legislation for disabled people.

In my exploration of the subject of prejudice and the extent to which laws can overcome discrimination, I will begin by considering the nature of discrimination and the extent to which laws can deal with its subtleties. I will then look at discrimination as manifested within a legal system, using a case study from Great Britain. Finally, I will give some thought to new gene technology and disability discrimination.[1]

* Head of Education & Disability Law, Levenes Solicitors, U.K.

[1] In my discussion of these topics, I will generally assume that the reader is familiar with the social model of disability and its implications for identifying and responding to disability discrimination.

B. THE NATURE OF DISCRIMINATION: EXAMPLES OF MARGINALISATION

Disabled people face explicit, implicit, visceral and systemic or institutional discrimination. Much has been written to illustrate this but it bears repeating; particularly because discrimination is rarely obvious, either because it forms part of the fabric of our institutions or because it is rooted in misconception and fear. By way of illustration, I would like to paraphrase from a seminal book: *Pride Against Prejudice: Transforming Attitudes to Disability* by Jenny Morris.[2] Dr. Morris quotes another disabled writer, Pam Evans, who lists the assumptions that she found non-disabled people in the U.K. have about the "real" lives and attitudes of disabled people. I imagine that at least some of them are held throughout the world. I emphasise that these are attitudes and assumptions and not truths:

1. That we feel ugly, inadequate and ashamed of our disability.
2. That our lives are a burden to us, barely worth living.
3. That we crave to be "normal and whole."
4. That whatever we choose to do or think, any work or pursuit that we undertake, is done so as "therapy" with the sole intention of taking our mind off our condition.
5. That we are naive and live sheltered lives.
6. That we can't ever really accept our condition, and if we appear to be leading a full and contented life, or are simply cheerful, we are "just putting a good face on it."
7. That we feel envy and resentment at the able-bodied.
8. That we feel our condition is an unjust punishment.
9. That any emotional distress that we show can only be due to our disability and not to the same things that hurt and upset them.
10. That our disability has affected us physiologically, making us bitter and neurotic.
11. That it is quite amazing if we laugh, are cheerful and pleasant and take pleasure in other people's happiness.
12. That we are ashamed of our inabilities, our "abnormalities" and loathe our wheelchairs, crutches or other aids.

---

2 19–22 (London: Women's Press, 1991).

13. That we never "give up hope" of a cure.
14. That when we affirm that we cannot, or do not wish to do something, our judgement and preferences are overridden and contradicted as inferior to theirs.
15. That we are asexual or at best sexually inadequate.
16. That if we have a partner who is disabled, we choose each other for no other reasons, and not for any other qualities that we might possess. When we choose "our own kind" in this way the able-bodied world feels relieved, until of course we wish to have children; then we are seen as irresponsible.
17. That we have not got a right to an able-bodied partner; and that if they happen to be very obviously "attractive," it is even more of a "waste."
18. That any able-bodied partner that we have is doing us a favour and that we bring nothing to the relationship.
19. That if we were particularly gifted, successful or attractive before the onset of disability, our fate is infinitely more tragic than if we were none of these things.
20. That our only true scale of merit and success is to judge ourselves by the standards of their world.
21. That we are sweet, deprived little souls who need to be compensated with treats, presents and praise.

And so the list goes on. These assumptions are born not of actual interactions with disabled people, but rather of fears that have been engendered as a result of the systematic exclusion of disabled people from society.

This exclusion is illustrated in studies undertaken by a number of bodies in the U.K. that established, beyond doubt, that discrimination against disabled people permeates society. For example, during the 1997 British general election, the charity SCOPE found that 94 percent of the polling stations it surveyed were inaccessible to disabled people voting independently. In employment studies into hiring practices in the private sector, two fictitious applications differing only in one respect were sent out in response to publicly advertised jobs—one was from a disabled person and the other was not. The studies revealed virtually identical evidence: the "non-disabled" candidate was one and one-half times more likely to receive a positive reply, whilst the "disabled" candidate was six times more likely to receive a negative response. Meanwhile, MIND, the U.K. mental health charity, found that out of 778 people with past or present mental health impairments, 47 percent had been harassed or abused in public, 49 percent had been abused at home, 14 percent had been physically attacked, and 25 percent had been rejected by insurance or finance companies. Within the U.K. in the mid-1990s, the average income of disabled people under retirement age was estimated as being 72 percent of the average for all people within this age group, and disabled adults were twice as likely to be unemployed as non-disabled adults.

This exclusion is reflected in various aspects of our culture—film, television, literature, and the media. Colin Barnes[3] identifies at least 11 stereotypes of disabled people, some of which are:

- The disabled person as pitiable and pathetic, e.g., Tiny Tim in Charles Dickens' *A Christmas Carol* and Porgy in George Gershwin's *Porgy & Bess*.
- The disabled person as an object of violence, e.g., Joan Crawford in *Whatever Happened to Baby Jane?* and Audrey Hepburn in *Wait until Dark*.
- The disabled person as sinister and evil, e.g., Shakespeare's Richard III, and also Black Dog, Blind Pew and Long John Silver in Stephenson's *Treasure Island*.
- The disabled person as atmosphere or curio, e.g., the characters of Merrick in *The Elephant Man* and Half Soldier in *The Good, the Bad, and the Ugly*.
- The disabled person as supercripple, e.g., the central characters in *My Left Foot* and *Reach for the Sky*.
- The disabled person as an object of ridicule, e.g., the cartoon *Mr. Magoo* and Harpo Marx of the Marx Brothers.
- The disabled person as his or her own worst and only enemy, e.g., the central characters in *Coming Home* and *Born on the Fourth of July*.

---

[3] *See Disabling Imagery and the Media: An Exploration of the Principles for Media Representations of Disabled People* (Ryburn Pub. and British Council of Organisations of Disabled People, 1992).

— The disabled person as a burden, e.g., in the recent British television drama *Keeping Tom Nice*.
— The disabled person as sexually abnormal, e.g., Hephaestus in Homer's *The Odyssey* and Lady Chatterley's husband in D.H. Lawrence's novel.

In other words, the disabled person as incapable of participating fully in community life, which is reflected in virtually all art and literature!

What is particularly invidious is that these prejudices are internalised by disabled people as well. As a consequence, a necessary part of any remedy is to bring disabled people to the heart of society. Only then can disabled and non-disabled people really reconsider and re-evaluate the misinformation arising from the history of oppression of disabled people that blights everyone's lives. For this reason, I contend that anti-discrimination laws are a necessary part of the ending of oppression—an enforceable mandate that will require the end of exclusion. The ending of exclusion is only the start, but nevertheless a critical one. Accordingly, I believe that without anti-discrimination laws, the process of re-evaluation, of transforming peoples' hearts and minds, cannot begin. Anti-discrimination laws are therefore not the sole solution, but a necessary part of the fabric of transformation. Still, we must ask ourselves: what is the extent to which laws can end exclusion?

C. THE EXTENT TO WHICH LAWS CAN REDRESS DISCRIMINATION

It seems straightforward to me that laws can regulate personal behaviour, so I would like to focus instead on the presence of systemic or institutionalised discrimination. It may be useful to begin with an explanation of what this means.

In his study of disability discrimination in Britain, Colin Barnes looks at the nature of institutional discrimination.[4] He argues that the

---

4 *Disabled People in Britain and Discrimination: A Case for Anti-Discrimination Legislation* (London: C. Hurst & Co; Calgary, Alberta: University of Calgary Press in Association with the British Council of Organisations of Disabled People, 1991), also discussed in Colin Barnes, "Institutional Discrimination Against

phenomenon is evident when the policies and activities of all types of modern organisation result in inequality between disabled people and non-disabled people. It is, he states, "embedded in the excessive paternalism of contemporary welfare systems and is apparent when they are ignoring or meeting inadequately the needs of disabled people."[5] It is also evident when these agencies regularly interfere in the lives of disabled people as a means of social control, in ways and/or to an extent not experienced by non-disabled people. Institutional discrimination incorporates the extreme forms of prejudice and intolerance usually associated with individual or direct discrimination, as well as those more covert and unconscious attitudes that contribute to and maintain indirect and/or passive discriminatory practices.

More recently, Barnes and Mike Oliver[6] argue that even comprehensive and fully enforceable civil rights legislation will not, by itself, solve the problem of discrimination against disabled people. This is because discrimination against disabled people, like racism, sexism, homophobia, and other forms of institutional prejudices, is institutionalised in the very fabric of British (and no doubt any other) society. It encompasses direct, indirect and passive discrimination. It lies rooted in the very foundations of western culture. In the U.K., it is evident in our abortion laws, education systems, labour market, benefit systems, health and social support services, built environment—housing, transport and public buildings, leisure industry, media, and political system.

The critical question then, is given the entrenched nature of this form of discrimination, to what extent is it susceptible to legal remedy?

Barnes and Oliver argue that institutional discrimination will only end with the existence of both a strong anti-discrimination policy based on the social model of disability, and a well-funded disabled people's movement to enforce it. They also argue for a meaningful freedom of information act to ensure that medical records and other information

---

Disabled People and the Campaign for Anti-discrimination Legislation," 12 *Critical Soc. Pol'y* 34 (1992).

5 Barnes, *Disabled People in Britain and Discrimination, id.* at 3.

6 "Disability Rights—Rhetoric and Reality in the U.K." in 10 *Disability and Soc'y* 111 (1995).

cannot be used to legitimate prejudice and ignorance. They state that what is needed is a comprehensive legislative programme, which will establish a suitable framework for the enforcement of policies that will ensure the integration of disabled people into the mainstream economic and social life of the community, and also provide public confirmation that discrimination against disabled people, for whatever reason, is no longer acceptable. In other words, we need legislation that emphasises civil rights rather than individual needs, and focuses on the shortcomings of the disabling society in which we live, and not on individual impairment.

Barnes and Oliver propose that civil rights cannot be achieved by legislation alone, but rather requires decisive political action, which itself is dependent on the presence of an adequately funded national network of organisations controlled and run by disabled people. It is these organisations that can place the issue of institutional discrimination onto the political agenda, and that are best suited to ensure the eventual eradication of disability discrimination.

In discussing how far laws can redress discrimination, it is of course useful to consider the experience of ten years of the Americans with Disabilities Act (ADA). Marca Bristow, Chairperson of the United States National Council on Disability, wrote to the U.S. President and summarised the enforcement of the law as follows:

> while the administration has consistently asserted its strong support for the civil rights of people with disabilities, the federal agencies charged with enforcement and policy development under ADA have, to varying degrees, been underfunded, overly cautious, reactive, and lacking any coherent and unifying national strategy. In addition, enforcement agencies have not consistently taken leadership roles in clarifying "frontier" or emergent issues.[7]

---

[7] Letter of Transmittal of June 27, 2000, accompanying a report of the National Council on Disability, *Promises to Keep: A Decade of Federal Enforcement of the Americans with Disabilities Act* (Washington, DC: U.S. Government Printing Office, 2000) [Also available online *at* http://www.ncd.gov/newsroom/publications/promises_1.html.]

Amongst other things, the report recorded that disabled people found dealing with government agencies frustrating: they felt that they received little information with regard to their complaints, that their complaints took excessive amounts of time to process, and that their cases were not seen as "big enough."[8] Interestingly, the report concludes that "[s]ince the passage of ADA in 1990, the nation has made a respectable, though far from flawless, start toward eliminating discrimination on the basis of disability."[9]

From a global perspective, Tom Shakespeare and Nick Watson analyze the development of global disability politics and its effects on the planets estimated 450 million disabled people.[10] The authors quote James Charlton, who states that what makes the Disability Rights Movement subversive is paradoxically the extraordinary world-wide oppression of disabled people: "[t]he oppression is systematic. The principles, demands and goals of the Disability Rights Movements cannot be accommodated by the present world system."[11] The implication is that the liberal ambition of civil rights is doomed by broader systems of power and established capitalist social relations. As the global market becomes more and more dominant, the scope for national social investment and egalitarian reform becomes more limited. On the other hand, the authors argue for "realpolitik"— *de facto* advances and success in achieving equality will occur regardless of "official" positions—and I agree; disability politics "is a continuing project and will involve reversals as well as success."[12]

Useful perspectives can also be gleaned from the experience of those who are engaged in fighting other forms of discrimination, such as sexism. The feminist advocate Sandra Fredman argues:

---

8 *Id.* at 385–88.

9 *Id.* at 392.

10 "Making the Difference: Disability, Politics, Recognition," *in The Handbook of Disability Studies* 546 (Gary L. Albrecht et al. eds., Thousand Oaks, CA: Sage Pub., 2001).

11 *Nothing About Us Without Us: Disability, Oppression and Empowerment* 149 (Berkeley: University of California Press, 1998).

12 Shakespeare & Watson, *supra* note 10.

> law must have a role in effecting change, if only because if it is not harnessed in support of progress, it frequently actively obstructs attempts to address patriarchy. But this is not the only reason: ultimately, it is a counsel of despair to conclude that law is intrinsically and unavoidably patriarchal. Instead, it can well be empowering. However, the programme of utilising law in support of change is a complex and risky one; and in the final analysis, it is only one element of a necessarily multi-faceted approach.[13]

With regards to the situation in Australia, Hauritz, Sampford and Blencowe remind us that laws can provide broad principles and institutional arrangements that further the rights of disabled people, establish criminal and civil sanctions to deter those who would deny the rights of disabled people, and can appropriate funds for either of these purposes.[14] However, they state that, as often as not, laws cannot provide the whole of the answer, and moreover, are often part of the problem. Legal responses lack coherence, partly because of the range of government policies (economic, econo-social and political) that they reflect. For example, the option of civil litigation in common law countries responds to disabled people in two fundamentally different ways, depending on the source of impairment and the assignability of blame. First, there is the "total compensation model," which seeks to restore the individual to his or her previous position, and second there is the "limited assistance model," which provides inadequate or no provision for persons whose impairment arises from a birth defect, an illness, or any accident not caused by a solvent perpetrator.[15] (There is in addition a third option in the civil rights approach.)

In their analysis of Australia's *Disability Discrimination Act 1992*, Jones and Basser Marks discuss what they see as general limits on the

---

[13] *Women and the Law* 367–68 (Oxford: Clarendon; New York: Oxford University Press, 1997).

[14] "Introduction," *in Justice for People with Disabilities* i, xv (Marge Hauritz, Charles Sampford & Sophie Blencowe eds., Sydney: Federation Press, 1998).

[15] *See* discussion *id*. at xvii.

use of law to promote rights.[16] The authors report that lawyers have a tendency to believe that laws will provide solutions to complex social and political problems. In contrast to this, they assert the view that at best, law can achieve only part of the larger strategy required to achieve rights for disabled people. They argue that successful redress of the systemic and institutional biases that undermine substantial equality for all members of society requires more than adherence to law. In particular, they support the development of "Disability Standards and Action Plans," which are designed to initiate and supplement the process of value formation through which attitudes and assumptions about disability become secondary to an idea of intrinsic human worth, independent of ability. Jones and Basser Marks assert that this foundational process of value formation cannot be achieved by law on its own, but they recognise that law no doubt has a role to play. For example, the *Disability Discrimination Act 1992* actually implements the use of Disability Standards and Action Plans, and thereby takes seriously the "normative and educative function of law."[17] Furthermore, a law proclaiming the rights of disabled people conveys the message that they are valued members of a community, whose dignity is protected. It also conveys a message to perpetrators of discrimination, fear and hatred that their behaviour is unacceptable. Accordingly, they conclude that the law can play a significant role in empowering disabled people.

Finally, Colin Barnes concludes that:

> [Cynics] might argue that institutional discrimination [against disabled people] is so entrenched within our [British] society that any serious thoughts of its eradication by whatever means are both utopian and unrealistic. Such people need to be reminded that contemporary society is neither utopia nor the real world, it is a socially created world. Institutional discrimination, in common with everything else in our world, is little more than a social creation, and as such can be socially eradi-

---

16 M. Jones & L. A. Basser Marks, "The Limitations on the Use of Law to Promote Rights: An Assessment of the *Disability Discrimination Act 1992* (Cth)," *in Justice for People with Disabilities, supra* note 14, at 60–84.

17 *Id.* at 78.

> cated. While the policies outlined above might not eradicate it overnight, they will certainly make a significant contribution to its demise.[18]

I also hold the view that laws alone cannot redress discrimination but are a necessary step to doing so. However, in addition to comprehensive anti-discrimination legislation, we require some means of achieving the educational process and personal and social catharsis which will ultimately allow people's worldviews to be reconfigured.

D. DISCRIMINATION WITHIN THE LEGAL SYSTEM

Since I propose the use of law as an important tool for the redress of discrimination, it becomes all the more necessary to be conscious of, and guard against, discrimination as it operates within a legal system itself. By way of illustration, I will look at the extent to which the law of England and Wales—as written and as enforced—affords rights to disabled children not to be excluded from their communities and peer groups, focussing particularly on the right of disabled children to attend ordinary schools.

The law currently governing this area is set out in Section 316 of the *Education Act 1996*.[19] This provides that where a parent wishes their (disabled) child to attend an ordinary school (i.e., not a special education school), that wish must be acceded to as long as:

- The needs of the disabled child can be met in an ordinary school;
- Other children would not be adversely affected by the presence of the disabled child in the school; and
- It would constitute an efficient use of resources for the disabled child to attend an ordinary school.

---

[18] Barnes, *Disabled People in Britain and Discrimination, supra* note 4, at 109.

[19] 1996, ch. 56 (Eng.).

The British government has announced proposals to amend s. 316 to remove the first criterion but nevertheless, the remaining two substantive conditions will have to be met before a disabled child will be entitled to attend at an ordinary school. The first of these, concerning the absence of any adverse effect on other children, is particularly invidious as, so far as I am aware, there is no other category of children whose rights to remain within their community are dependent on whether anyone else would be allegedly adversely affected. Even more disturbing, however, is the fact that even when both hurdles are successfully met and the law supports inclusion, it does not always follow through to enforce a disabled child's rights.

I would like to illustrate this by reference to a case study involving a disabled child and her attempts to progress through primary (ages 4–11) and secondary (ages 11–16+) education in mainstream schools.[20] Within England and Wales, the law requires most disabled children to be provided with a legal document, known as a Statement of Special Educational Needs, that records the child's needs, how these will be met, and the school that the child should attend. These Statements are prepared and maintained by the Local Education Authority (LEA) for the area in which the child lives. A key legal point for our purposes is that if a child has a Statement naming a particular maintained (i.e., state-funded) school, then pursuant to Section 324(5)(b) of the *Education Act 1996*, that school MUST admit the child.

Zahrah Manuel is a 13-year-old with cerebral palsy. She is of small stature, uses a wheelchair, and communicates non-verbally. After a four-year battle with her LEA, the London Borough of Camden, her mother, Preethi, succeeded in obtaining a place for her in an ordinary primary school within her area of Camden in North London. By all accounts, the placement was hugely successful for both Zahrah and the other children at the school. When Zahrah reached the age of 11, consideration ordinarily would have been given for her transfer from primary school to secondary school.

---

20 R. v. The Governors of Whitefield School ex parte Manuel, No. CO/4510/1999 (Crown Office, High Court, Royal Courts of Justice); settled.

Camden LEA agreed that Zahrah should transfer to a mainstream secondary school. The nearest accessible mainstream school happened to be just over the borough boundary, in the area of a neighboring LEA, the London Borough of Barnet. Nevertheless, Camden LEA accepted that, having regard to Section 316 of the *Education Act 1996*, Zahrah could attend a mainstream school, and agreed to amend Zahrah's Statement to name the secondary school in neighboring Barnet; that school was thereby legally required to admit her, as noted above. Equally importantly, Camden LEA agreed to fund the cost of two learning support assistants, as well an any additional therapy support and equipment needed at the school.

On September 3, 1999, Preethi took Zahrah to the secondary school named in her daughter's Statement, but the school, in effect, refused to permit Zahrah to attend. Instead, it insisted that Preethi, Zahrah, Camden LEA, and many others familiar with Zahrah were all mistaken, and Zahrah should attend a special, segregated school for disabled children. Even more astonishing, the Barnet school was already designated as (and equipped to be) wheelchair accessible.

A six-month court battle ensued, eventually resulting in the school agreeing to admit Zahrah in March 2000. Throughout this battle, the law was clearly on Zahrah's side: she had a Statement of Special Educational Needs that named an ordinary secondary school, and consequently the school was required to admit her. However, through a process of obfuscation, confusion and fear mongering, the school managed for six months to dissuade the British Secretary of State for Education & Employment, as well as two High Court Judges, from ordering the school to admit her, and they did so on a basis not more substantive than the claim that there is no smoke without fire: surely no school would object to a child attending unless they had good cause to do so. The school raised all manner of argument: that Zahrah would threaten hitherto harmonious relations within the school; that staff could not cope with Zahrah (despite the high level of additional resourcing agreed to and funded by Camden LEA); that there were no facilities for Zahrah to have a bath (even though no-one had suggested the need for such a thing); and so on. The consequence was that a marginalised child was effectively excluded for six months.

There is a postscript. In the midst of the battle for Zahrah to go to an ordinary secondary school, Preethi enquired of another local mainstream secondary school as to whether they would accept Zahrah. Although that school was not designated as accessible for disabled children, they readily agreed. Adaptations were made, and Zahrah commenced there in September 2000. The difference between the responses and attitudes of the two secondary schools is astonishing. Whereas the school in Barnet (supposedly designated for disabled children) eventually admitted her, they did so with extreme reluctance. Meanwhile the school in Camden, hitherto inaccessible, welcomed Zahrah with open arms, efficiently making whatever modifications were necessary to ensure that she is truly included.

In *Disability and the Law*, the authors quote Caroline Gooding, who contends that "the law is not an impartial arbitrator, but colludes with, and indeed itself perpetrates, discrimination."[21] The essence of this argument is based on the assertion that the law, in short, reflects the values and judgments of society, and if these are of themselves discriminatory, so will laws be. Furthermore, traditional legal systems frequently are based on a formal equality model, and consequently do not recognise or seek to redress structural inequalities. As Gooding states "this model cannot succeed in redressing inequality, and risks compounding the problem by legitimating inequality through its false account of equality."[22] In Zahrah's case, the law was clearly on her side. And yet, its application failed her for six months.

E. NEW GENE TECHNOLOGY AND DISABILITY DISCRIMINATION

I now turn from an area that has traditionally concerned disability advocates to consider the relatively recent and rapidly developing areas of genetics, bioethics and biotechnology. Disabled people and disability organizations are growing increasingly fearful that the moral and ethi-

---

21 Gooding, *Disabling Laws, Enabling Acts* xvii (London: Pluto Press, 1994) as quoted in Jeremy Cooper & Stuart Vernon, *Disability and the Law* 10 (London: Bristol; Pa: Jessica Kingsley Pub., 1996).

22 Gooding, *id.* at 32 [as quoted in Cooper & Stuart, *id.* at 21].

cal issues surrounding biotechnology and medicine are lagging behind scientific advances; history provides ample evidence of the risks involved in such a situation. Genetic counselling, pre-natal diagnosis, selective abortion, in-vitro fertilisation, embryo research, genetic engineering, gene therapy, voluntary euthanasia, "mercy killings"—these options are part of our lives and shape the societies in which we live, whether or not we understand them. Disabled children and adults have always been at risk of early death from either deliberate action or intentional inaction, such as the failure to be fed adequately. However, recent medical and scientific advances have "upped the ante" in this regard, and there are three main areas of contemporary concern for disabled people and their allies: pre-natal diagnosis and selective termination of pregnancy, withholding treatment and "mercy killing," and genetic engineering.

Pre-natal screening refers to a variety of tests that pregnant women undergo to gain information about the fetus that they are carrying. These include blood tests, amniocentesis and ultrasound scans. Anti-natal screening is also done on embryos conceived "in-vitro"—outside the womb. Only those embryos considered free of "defects" are implanted. This screening out of "negative" characteristics has already been joined by the screening in of "positive" ones—a couple can choose to buy another couple's embryos based on their "desirable" characteristics. The inescapable consequence of this is that disabled people, as a distinct group, are specifically targeted before they can even be born. Access to pre-natal diagnosis has for many years been driven by the goal of getting rid of certain groups of disabled people, for example, those with Downs Syndrome or Spina Bifida.

Selective abortion refers to choices about the termination of pregnancy made on the basis of the fetus possessing known or suspected characteristics that make it less desirable to its parents and to society in general. Such characteristics include race, sex, impairment, behaviour, and appearance. In the richer countries of the world, but increasingly in the poorer countries as well, there is enormous pressure on parents to undergo pre-natal screening, and to terminate a pregnancy where the foetus is possibly or probably affected by impairment.

Infanticide refers to the intentional killing of an infant shortly after birth. It is also often done because the newborn displays a particular characteristic—race, sex or impairment—that is seen as undesirable. The ethical justification of such killing is found in particular interpretations of terms such as "quality of life" and "personhood." In particular, philosophers such as Peter Singer have expressed views that support infanticide, on the basis of decisions about quality of life and values. These developments threaten all of us: the disabled and the not-yet disabled.

Up to 100 different inherited conditions can be detected through screening. Within the U.K., the number of babies born with Spina Bifida has dropped by 75 percent in ten years—partly as a result of folic acid supplements but also because of screening and abortions. The number of babies born with Downs Syndrome has only dipped slightly—perhaps due to the fact that many women are having children later in life and this is a factor associated with Downs Syndrome. Many of those foetuses aborted after screening have no evidence of impairment. A few years ago, a report in the British Medical Journal claimed that while it cost up to £38,000 to screen for and "avoid a Downs Syndrome child" (through abortion), the lifetime healthcare costs for a person living with Downs Syndrome are £120,000—clearly revealing the economic incentives behind screening and abortion.[23]

Disabled people generally are not consulted in policy making on pre-birth diagnosis and counselling, even though we could provide valuable information to counterbalance the often depressing input of the medical profession. Many parents want more information about particular impairments before deciding whether or not to terminate their pregnancy. Even when those foetuses screened for an impairment are not aborted, disabled people's rights to existence and development remain threatened throughout their lives. They and their families already face enormous pressure, both economic and social, as they struggle to get the support that they require. The very existence of these pressures inevitably is used to rationalise family decisions about pregnancy termination and the killing of disabled infants. I argue that selective abortion fundamentally devalues the lives of disabled people by assessing their lives as not worth living, and this devaluation in its turn further

---

[23] N. J. Wald *et al.*, "Antenatal Maternal Serum Screening for Downs's Syndrome: Results of a Demonstration Project," 305 *Brit. Med. J.* 391 (1992).

exacerbates medical and social pressure to avoid giving birth to disabled infants.

With regard to genetic testing, disabled people's concerns are rooted in the fear that society may come to consider appearance, behaviour and health or impairment status as entirely dependent on genetics, so that the impact of social, economic and cultural factors is ignored. This attitude could lead to a reduction in benefits and equalisation of opportunities programmes, as well as an increased interest in eugenics. In addition, genetic testing may actually enhance fears that disabled people are "deviant," thereby justifying the continuing disadvantage endured by disabled people.

Illness prevention may simply come to mean the routine selective abortion of foetuses with certain genetic markers, including those who have some risk of developing conditions such as Alzheimer's, heart disease or cancer in later life. Sterilization may be actively promoted as a "voluntary" sacrifice to be made by those whose characteristics are seen as undesirable and genetic in origin. Manipulation to remove "disease" may quickly become manipulation that defines "normal" variations in the population. Abortion and genetic manipulation may increasingly be used to guarantee what society regards as the most desirable height, colouring and sex. Apparently "made to order" embryos can already be bought in the United States—supposedly screened for "good" and "bad" characteristics.

In addition, people are already starting to suffer employment or insurance discrimination on the basis of a future predicted by genetic information as the practice of "genetic discrimination" spreads. Society may decide to withdraw resources from those with genetic disorders because these conditions—and the people who carry these conditions—are seen as preventable. Our whole view of what it means to be human and to be part of society—our value as individuals—may change because of extraordinary developments in this area.

All of this is frightening. Powerful eugenic assumptions about the kinds of lives that are worth living, linked with a utilitarian principle of benefit, appear to underpin much current human genetic research and clinical practice. A 1994/95 study by Dorothy Wertz and John Fletcher found that outside of Northern Europe, the vast majority of genetic counsellors hold overt eugenic views, and advise their patients on conception or pregnancy termination accordingly.[24]

These issues are an archetypal reflection of what Jennifer Fitzgerald has called "the commodification of the self," whereby we now value and commodify humans according to the value of their genes, so that persons with so called "bad" genes are defined out of humanity, and therefore potentially fall outside the boundaries of our collective moral responsibility. The "geneticisation" of the self compounds the oppression which disabled people currently experience in our society. Fitzgerald makes powerful comparisons between the illusory "earthly paradise" previously inhabited by Prince Siddhartha, who became the Buddha after seeing pain and suffering, and the modern western dream of beauty, control and perfection that forms the implicit basis for current developments in bioethics.[25]

These are complex moral, ethical, legal, political, and medical issues. Most disabled people do not oppose medical research or genetic testing if it is part of ameliorative therapy or the treatment of illness or genetic conditions. What we oppose is eugenic cleansing carried out in the name of treatment. Recently, an eminent researcher was quoted as having said "soon it will be a sin for parents to have a child which carries the heavy burden of genetic disease."[26] Marshall Nirenberg, Nobel Laureate said, in 1967:

> My guess is that cells will be programmed with synthetic messages within 25 years. . . . The point that deserves special emphasis is that man may be able to program his own cells long before he will be able to assess adequately the long-term consequences of such alterations, long before he will be able to for-

---

[24] D. C. Wertz & J. C. Fletcher, "Ethical and Social Issues in Prenatal Sex Selection: A Survey of Geneticists in 37 Nations," 46 *Social Science and Medicine* 255 (1998).

[25] Paper delivered at Rehabilitation International Conference in Auckland, New Zealand attended by author (1996).

[26] Bob Edwards, Embryologist and In-vitro Fertilisation Specialist, as reported in *Sunday Times of England*, July 4, 1999.

mulate goals, and long before he can resolve the ethical and moral problems which will be raised.[27]

And as Irving K. Zola said in 1972:

medicine is becoming a major institution of social control, nudging aside, if not incorporating, the more traditional institutions of religion and law. It is becoming the new repository of truth, the place where absolute and often final judgements are made by supposedly neutral and objective experts. And these judgements are made, not in the name of virtue or legitimacy, but in the name of health.[28]

We all are now living with the risks foreseen by these prescient scientists and authors, and new gene technologies can potentially determine every aspect of the lives of disabled people—from their very birth to their opportunities for health care and employment. We need laws drafted in consultation with disabled people. These laws should ban employers from using genetic information in any aspect of employment decision making, including but not limited to decisions about hiring and firing, promotions or demotions, pay rates, or any other employment rights or benefits. In addition, laws are required to ban life, disability and health insurers from using genetic information to deny insurance, increase insurance rates, or deny any insurance benefits. At a conference on bioethics held in Solihull, U.K., on February 12–13, 2000, disabled people and activists in attendance agreed to a declaration that demanded:

— the prohibition of compulsory genetic testing;
— the provision of full, accessible and balanced information so as to enable informed personal decision making;

---

[27] As quoted in *Disabled People Speak on the New Genetics* [Disabled Peoples' International (DPI) Europe Position Statement on Bioethics and Human Rights], available online *at* http://www.dpieurope.org/htm/bioethics/dpsngfullreport.htm.

[28] "Medicine as an Institution of Social Control," 20 *Sociological Review* 487 (1972).

— the right to assistance to live rather than assistance to die.[29]

In essence, the declaration tries to contain the very real threat that genetic information poses to the ideal expressed in the insight of Dr. Oscar Arias, Nobel Peace Prize winner and ex-President of Costa Rica:

> The most beautiful and enriching trait of human life is diversity—a diversity that can never be used to justify inequality. Repressing diversity will impoverish the human race. We must facilitate and strengthen diversity in order to reach a more equitable world for us all. For equality to exist, we must avoid standards that define what a normal human life should be or the normal way of achieving success and happiness. The only normal quality that can exist among human beings is life itself.[30]

Paul Miller, a Commissioner with the U.S. Equal Employment Opportunity Commission reports that "[t]he surge in genetic research and technology, fuelled in large part by the Human Genome Project (HGP), has resulted in the continuing expansion of the range of genetic tests and other genetic information available to physicians, insurance companies, employers, and the general public."[31] From the perspective of employment rights, Miller reports that if employers are permitted to base personal decisions on genetic information, an emerging and complex form of disability discrimination will develop. Miller reports that, as of August 1997, the U.S. Council for Responsible Genetics, a national bioethics advocacy organization, had documented over 200 cases of genetic discrimination by insurance companies, employers and others against asymptomatic individuals with genetic pre-dispositions to cer-

---

[29] Conference sponsored by DPI entitled *Disabled People, Bioethics and Human Rights*; the declaration that emerged from the conference is available on the DPI Europe website *at* http://www.dpieurope.org/htm/bioethics/biodeclaration.htm.

[30] "Introduction," *in From Exclusion to Inclusion: A Report of the Disability Rights Task Force on Civil Rights for Disabled People* 3 (London: Department for Education and Employment, 1999); the report is available online *at* http://www.disability.gov.uk.drtf/index2.html.

[31] Paul Steven Miller, "Is there a Pink Slip in my Genes? Genetic Discrimination in the Workplace," 3 *J. of Health Care L. & Pol'y* 225, at 226 (2000).

tain diseases. These numbers are bound to increase as greater information and diagnostic techniques become available.

Partly as a response to these and similar concerns, President Clinton issued the Genetic Executive Order on February 8, 2000 to prohibit discrimination in federal employment based on genetic information.[32] This order prohibits discrimination on the basis of protected genetic information in all aspects of civilian federal government employment, and limits federal departments and agencies' access to, and use of, genetic information. As the President stated at the time "[b]y signing this executive order, my goal is to set an example and pose a challenge for every employer in America, because I believe no employer should ever review your genetic records along with your resume."[33] This constitutes a clear recognition at the highest political circles of the risks for genetic information and new gene technology to be misapplied.

But have we really come to terms with this "genie" and are the issues really that clear cut?

Tom Shakespeare and Nick Watson present a dialogue between two hypothetical characters, in order to rehearse some of the main arguments used against pre-natal screening and highlight some of the flaws that they see in these arguments.[34] On the one hand, the opponent of pre-natal screening argues that selected termination: (i) is the same as eugenics; (ii) is discriminatory; (iii) takes advantage of the fact that women do not have free choice in a oppressive society and are pressured to consider disabled lives "unworthy"; (iv) is the thin end of the wedge (i.e., selected termination on the basis of impairment will result in termination choices made on the basis of increasingly superficial physical characteristics, such as hair colour, gender, etc.); (v) reduces diversity; and (vi) reduces choices for, and devalues, disabled people once they are born. On the other hand, the advocate of pre-natal screening argues

---

32 Executive Order 13,145, 65 Fed. Reg. 6877 (Feb. 10, 2000).

33 Bill Clinton, Speech to the American Association for the Advancement of Science (Feb. 8, 2000), in Extracts from the Office of the Press Secretary, The White House, Mar. 2000. Available online *at* http://clinton6.nara.gov/2000-02-08-remarks-of-president-on-genetic-discrimination.html.

34 *Supra* note 10.

that: (i) early 20th century eugenics policies are distinguishable because they were enforced by the state and involved coercion; (ii) it is hypocritical to voice support for a woman's right to control her own body while opposing her choice to terminate a foetus with a disability simply because one does not agree with the decision; (iii) increasing choices for and information about disabled people, and working to end their present oppression, is a separate issue from pre-natal screening; (iv) there is a difference between seeking to prevent impairment and oppressing disabled people; (v) moral absolutes are not helpful; and (vi) it is illogical to extrapolate the argument that "born" disabled people would (or should) not exist from the mere fact of pre-natal testing.

Meanwhile, in another approach to the issues, Patrick Bateson, Provost of King's College, Cambridge, and Paul Martin, an author, warn us that the presence of genetic determinists like Charles Murray of Bell Curve infamy:

> reminds us that the corpse of social Darwinism is still warm. . . . Those who are uncritically enthusiastic about the human genome project like to think of the genome as a blueprint. According to this view, if all the genetic information is fed into a sufficiently powerful computer equipped with the right software, the fully functioning adult will magically unfold before our eyes like a Japanese flower put into water. This view is deeply misguided. Genes make proteins, not people.[35]

People, on the other hand, are created through a complex continuous process of exchange between individuals and their environments.

The issues are complex. Genetic discrimination is, in one sense, no different than any other kind of discrimination. But I have wanted to conclude with an examination of this area because, if for no other reason, it emphasises that a society which marginalises disabled people will discriminate against them anew, as new structures and forums for discrimination evolve. One necessary approach is to combat the discrimination with laws, but fundamental change in society remains necessary.

---

[35] "Recipe for Humans: For All Our Genetic Triumphs, We Still Don't Understand Individuals say Patrick Bateson and Paul Martin," *The Guardian* (U.K.), Sept. 6, 2000.

F. CONCLUSION

I hope that I have illustrated three things—that discrimination against disabled people remains entrenched and widespread, that the law is a necessary and valuable component in combating discrimination, and that law itself will not succeed without a wider re-evaluation of our understanding of disability in society. I am optimistic. It is, I believe, not in our inherent nature to discriminate or oppress. Oppression arises through attitudes based on and cultivated by existing social structures and organisations, and these can be changed. Each of us has a part to play—individually and collectively—in achieving this change.

When to Hold 'Em and When to Fold 'Em: Lessons Learned from Enacting the Americans with Disabilities Act

Patrisha Wright as told to Jane West***

A. INTRODUCTION

The Americans with Disabilities Act (ADA), enacted in 1990, is considered to be the high water mark of disability legislation by the disability community in the United States. It is often looked to by other countries as a model, both for its progressive far-reaching policies and the political process that occurred to ensure its adoption. This article examines the political process that surrounded the enactment of the ADA in terms of the human dynamics that enabled the legislation to prevail. We hope that these lessons learned from the ADA will be useful to other countries as they design their own disability rights policies and utilize their systems of government to ensure the full participation of people with disabilities.

In any country with a legislative process, a law can only be enacted with the involvement of multiple parties playing different roles. Every role is critical. There must be people outside of the policy-making process—persons from the grassroots throughout the country who are willing to push the envelope, take direct actions, and even get arrested if necessary. There must be people with direct access to influential government leaders, who can then speak for and negotiate on behalf of the disability community. There must be attorneys connected to the dis-

---

* DREDF Governmental Affairs Director.

** Consultant in disability policy in Washington, DC. She served as Staff Director for the U.S. Senate Subcommittee on Disability Policy in the early 1980's and Senior Policy Analyst on the Presidential Commission on the HIV Epidemic. She has written extensively on the Americans with Disabilities Act and holds a doctorate in Special Education from the University of Maryland.

ability community who know how to draft disability laws, understand the legal implications of legislative language, and are willing to work with the grassroots to translate their concerns into legislative language. There must be people inside the policy making system, who are willing to advocate within the legislative process and work "off the record" with the disability community.

Many people take credit for the enactment of the ADA. And there is plenty of credit to go around. All of the parties noted above were critical to the enactment of the law. It is simply not possible for a small group of people to succeed in enacting a law as far-reaching and significant as the ADA. So when you hear hundreds of Americans claim credit for enacting the ADA, rest assured that the credit is well-deserved and there is plenty to go around!

B. EMPOWER AND ACTIVATE THE GRASSROOTS

Most oppressed groups of people believe that they are powerless. The notion that they could effectively influence government or change public policy is a foreign concept and one not easily believed. One of the great hallmarks of the passage of the ADA is that the grassroots came to "own" the legislation. They were mobilized and activated to vociferously fight for the legislation and tell their stories of why the legislation was needed. People came to Washington from all over the country to communicate with their representatives and press for passage of the law.

One key activity that generated grassroots participation was the writing of diaries of discrimination. Organizations and leaders of the disability community asked people with disabilities across the country to write diaries of their personal encounters with discrimination. Major Owens, a member of the House of Representatives and a disability ally, appointed Justin Dart, often considered the national leader of the disability rights movement, to head a Task Force. Under the auspices of this Task Force, Justin went to every state in the nation and held town hall meetings. People throughout the states came and presented testimony concerning the discrimination they were facing. They also held local "diary parties" in their communities where they would come together to support each other in writing about their experiences with discrimination.

Not only were these diaries presented to Members of Congress and the Committees that had jurisdiction over the ADA, they were submitted as part of the official record of information used by Congress during legislative deliberations. Every Member of Congress heard directly from his or her constituents about the discrimination the latter experienced in their district. The diaries educated Members of Congress about the nature and the breadth of the problem. They provided documentation on the need for a law like the ADA. Furthermore, they galvanized people with disabilities to take action to end their status as second class citizens.[1]

C. BUILD A COALITION OF DISABILITY ORGANIZATIONS

Coalitions are messy. The differing missions and motivations of organizations that represent people with disabilities challenged the development of a cohesive coalition. In the United States, the blind lobby and the lobby of war veterans historically have been the most effective in securing provisions in legislation. For example, in our Social Security legislation, blind individuals are singled out from those with other disabilities and treated more generously. Disabled veterans receive more generous pensions than people with disabilities on Social Security, are entitled to additional supports, and can keep their government provided health insurance indefinitely, whether they are employed or not.

Groups representing people with disabilities in Washington have tended to pursue services, research and benefits that are specific to the needs of their particular group. In other words, groups representing people with developmental disabilities sought services for people with developmental disabilities, etc. Lobbyists often viewed their jobs as increasing funding for the particular service providers that they represented. While there had been some activity around the enactment of disability rights laws, this was not the focus of the disability agenda prior to the ADA.

---

1 These diaries also were used during the disability community's October, 2000 argument before the Supreme Court in the Board of Trustees of the University of Alabama and the Alabama Dept. of Youth Services v. Garrett and Ash (531 U.S. 356 (2001)) to confirm the breadth and depth of disability discrimination throughout the United States.

In addition, there is potential tension between those representing people with disabilities and those representing service providers to people with disabilities. What may be good for a service provider, e.g., ease in administrative functioning, may yield a detrimental result for the intended beneficiary of the services, e.g., a lack of individualized programming. The lobbyists in Washington, DC tend to be dominated by service providers rather than people with disabilities themselves.

So how does one build a coalition out of so many groups with differing goals? One of the first prerequisites is the empowerment of the grassroots community. Since the provider community serves the grassroots, they are likely to listen to strong messages from their constituents. Provider groups are critical to the effort since they generally have greater financial resources than people with disabilities and can support the cost of organizing a coalition. Further, the provider community was well organized in Washington, DC as the Coalition for Citizens with Disabilities (CCD). CCD is made up of almost 100 organizations that provide services and support to people with disabilities.

Another vital component involves recognizing the reality of discrimination, which operates across the board no matter what type of disability is at issue. People who are blind, deaf, mentally impaired, physically impaired, learning disabled, and emotionally impaired have all experienced discrimination. Unlike the different types of services that people with different disabilities may seek or require, discrimination itself is a commonality. It is an experience that unites people with many different types of disabilities.

D. BUILD COALITIONS WITH BROADER HUMAN RIGHTS GROUPS

It would not have been possible to get the ADA enacted without the active support of other groups and coalitions concerned with civil rights. The Civil Rights Leadership Coalition (LCCR) is a well-established Washington based coalition of 180 groups that is concerned about civil rights in relation to race, religion and gender. Many race-specific groups belong to this coalition, as well as women's groups, union groups, religious groups, and groups representing the gay and lesbian community.

These well-established organizations, with their long history of civil rights activism, were brought into the disability fold. They were educated about how disability is another area in which individual civil rights needed protection. They were further reminded that their constituents—be they women, older people, racial minorities or religious minorities—also comprised people with disabilities. If they were not protecting the rights of people with disabilities, they were failing their own constituents as well.

These organizations were able to reach out to those Members of Congress who had been their champions previously and bring them on board behind the ADA. Various Congressional groups such as the Black Caucus, the Hispanic Caucus and the Women's Caucus became involved. When they threw their strength and power behind the ADA the campaign advanced to a much bigger playing field.

E. ESTABLISH THE RULES OF ENGAGEMENT

Organizations that banded together to promote the ADA met regularly as a coalition during the two and a half years of Congressional consideration of the bills. One of the first orders of business was to advance and agree on principles that the coalition would use in working on the ADA. This crucial step enabled the coalition to stay on track and maintain a clear final destination while staying flexible, since there are many ways to meet the terms of a principle. Without principles, people can attach themselves to a particular means of achieving a policy goal, and thus unnecessarily engender significant opposition. If a coalition unites around principles, it can keep numerous options open and negotiable as long as the principle is not violated. Principles also can be used to measure different proposals as they are put foreword, and more people can participate by developing various options for arriving at the same goal.

As a group, we agreed to the following inviolate principles:

1. One for All and All for One

Many groups of people with particular disabilities were often targeted for elimination from coverage under the ADA. For instance, amendments were proposed that would have excluded people with mental illness and people with HIV/AIDS. We were convinced that if single groups were picked off for exclusion, those opposing the bill would succeed in dividing the community and weakening its advocacy efforts. Consequently, people with developmental disabilities were just as committed to ensuring the inclusion of people with HIV/AIDS as to their own constituency.

Those who opposed the ADA wanted the coalition to believe that they would support the bill once a particular group was not included. This is a seductive argument when a bill is moving slowly and faces a lot of obstacles; there is a strong temptation to eliminate a single group for the sake of saving the bill as a whole. While the coalition's commitment to this primary principle was tested many times, we held tight in the end and no group was excluded from coverage.

2. Do Not Give Up on a Policy Position; Rather Extend the Timeline for Implementation of the Policy

Frequently our opponents would argue that particular provisions were too burdensome or too onerous and should be weakened. In one case, they asserted that it would be prohibitively expensive to make all buses accessible. It would bankrupt the nation's bus system and drive some companies out of business, thereby causing many citizens to lose their jobs. Our response to this sort of argument was to offer a phase-in period during which bus fleets could steadily work towards becoming entirely accessible in accordance with established timelines. For example, working buses did not have to be retrofitted with lifts; instead, whenever a bus company bought a new bus, it had to be equipped with a lift.

The ADA contains many similar kinds of timelines for implementing full compliance with its standards. These timelines are the result of our willingness to negotiate on the timing, but not the ultimate achievement, of our policy goals.

3. Always Consider the Policy Issue From the Point of View of a Person With a Disability Who Is Intended to be Protected by This Law

Whenever an issue would come up for debate, we would ask ourselves "What would the effect be on the individual with a disability?" This was our measuring stick. We were not primarily concerned with administrative expediency, cost or the burden on the covered entity. While these things matter, they were not our key consideration.

F. IDENTIFY A TRUSTED AND RESPECTED DISABILITY LEADER

Members of Congress and leaders in the White House and the executive agencies need one person they can communicate with who speaks for the entire coalition. They need to know that there is one person they can call and negotiate with, and, at the end of the negotiation, the agreement will hold. This person is the link between all of the stakeholders involved, and must therefore be acknowledged by the various interested parties as their leader.

Policy makers do not have the time to interact separately with many individuals over the multitude of issues that can come up during the course of enacting a law. They need to have the disability community speak with a united voice, and not several voices. If the community cannot resolve its differences of opinion internally, policy makers will be reluctant to get involved. They will not want to take sides in what will be seen as an internal debate, or be made to appear as a supporter of one faction's position over another. They must be able to assert confidently that "the disability community's position is X," so that they can deal with the larger forces opposing the enactment of the law.

The leader must be a person with great political savvy and awareness as well as entrée at the highest levels of government. This person must understand the broadest political contexts of the legislative process, as the bill may ground to a halt in the middle of negotiations over a matter that is not really even relevant to the bill. The coalition leader needs to be able to manage such entanglements while maintaining balance and cooperation within the community.

The leader for the disability community on the ADA was Pat Wright of the Disability Rights Education and Defense Fund (DREDF).

G. IDENTIFY AND CULTIVATE CHAMPIONS IN GOVERNMENT

The National Council on Disability (NCD), a small independent organization that is part of the executive branch of government, originally drafted the Americans with Disabilities Act and sent it to the Congress and the President for consideration. Bob Burgdorf, an attorney at the Council, drafted the original legislation. President Reagan, a conservative Republican, first appointed the members of the NCD.

When the original bill went to the Congress, members of the NCD and the disability community pursued Senator Lowell Weicker, a liberal Republican from Connecticut, to introduce the bill. Senator Weicker was chosen because he was a senior Member of Congress, a Member of the Majority party in the Senate, the Congress's foremost advocate for people with disabilities, and the father of a child with mental retardation. In the House of Representatives, Tony Coelho, the House Whip (a high level leadership position) and a Democrat from California, was targeted to be the lead sponsor of the bill. Representative Coelho was chosen because he was a senior member of the House, a member of the Majority party in the House, a recognized disability advocate, and a person with a disability (epilepsy) himself, who had extensive and profound personal experience with disability discrimination.

These two Members of Congress introduced the original bills in April 1988 and championed them before their colleagues. They spent many hours with the disability community discussing the bill and strategically planning its passage. They were the heroes and the allies of the community—individuals who immediately understood the need for the bill because of their own personal experiences and convictions. They did not have to be motivated to consider the bill urgent or educated about what disability discrimination was. This was a critical factor in our choice, for if a champion does not consider the legislation a personal priority, it is likely to become just one more item on a very long list that needs attention.

A few months after the legislation was introduced and the first hearing was held, the United States held elections for the Congress and for the President. Things began to change dramatically. In the Senate, Senator Weicker was defeated. Some months later, in the House, Representative Coelho resigned. The disability community had to find new champions.

Before his resignation, Representative Coelho asked Representative Steny Hoyer, a Democrat from Maryland, to take the lead in promoting the ADA. Representative Hoyer's wife had a disability and he fully understood the experience of disability discrimination. Representative Hoyer gladly took the reins and promoted the bill with great passion. In the Senate, Senator Tom Harkin (D-Iowa) and Senator Edward Kennedy (D-Mass.) took the lead. Senator Harkin chaired the Subcommittee on Disability Policy, as Senator Weicker had when the Republicans had held the majority. Senator Harkin was quite knowledgeable about disability issues since he had the experience of growing up with a brother who was deaf, and had witnessed the discrimination regularly encountered by his brother. Senator Edward Kennedy chaired the full Committee on Education and Labor, of which the Disability Policy Subcommittee was a part. Senator Kennedy was a natural champion given his long history of civil rights advocacy, his high visibility and seniority in politics, and his personal experience with disability; Senator Kennedy's son lost a leg to cancer and his sister has mental retardation.

Once again, the disability community had champions who understood disability discrimination and held the passage of the Americans with Disabilities Act as a personal priority.

In November 1988, George Bush won the presidency. During the campaign, disability activists had secured his promise that he would support the enactment of a disability rights law if elected President. In January of 1989, President-elect Bush said that he would support an act similar to the proposed Americans with Disabilities Act. Several of the key figures appointed by President Bush to his Administration were from the disability community, including Evan Kemp as Chairman of the Equal Employment Opportunity Commission. His Attorney

General, Dick Thornburg, was a parent of a child with a disability and early on declared his support for the bill. President Bush's Legal Counsel, C. Boyden Gray, also became a great ally of the disability community over time.

The disability community cultivated champions in both the Democratic and Republican parties, as well as in both the legislative and executive branch. Our strategy was to seek out people who either had disabilities themselves or had family members with disabilities, or who otherwise possessed close personal experiences with disability. This approach was motivated by the fact that a personal experience with disability almost always brings with it the understanding that people with disabilities are not and should not be second-class citizens. No one wants a member of their family or a close friend to be treated in a less than equal manner.

With a Republican President committed to signing a disability rights law, the Democratic Congress was in essence, being challenged to pass the bill. They certainly did not want to look more conservative than the Republican Administration.

H. ORGANIZE, STRATEGIZE AND ACT

We knew that it would be a massive task to get the law enacted. Such an effort was unprecedented in the disability area. The most similar effort was the campaign for the enactment of the civil rights law of 1964, a law that represents a watershed in our nation's commitment to ensuring equal rights under law. So we knew this required all of our collective resources and determination. It was time to mobilize our forces.

The coalition met regularly, usually once a week early on Monday mornings. Anywhere from 80–100 people would attend. We met at the same place and at the same time. The group would review the status of the bill, examine problems that were on the horizon, and develop strategies to keep the bill moving forward. The coalition organized itself to carry out an effective strategy for ensuring enactment of the ADA.

1. The Legal Team

The coalition developed a team of lawyers to draft legislation and review the proposals that were put forward. This team was headed by Arlene Mayerson, directing attorney of DREDF, and Chai Feldblum, counsel at the American Civil Liberties Union. Arlene came with over 15 years of disability and civil rights experience, including participation in all of the Supreme Court cases in which existing disability rights laws had been challenged. Chai's area of expertise was HIV/AIDS discrimination, a very active area of law at the time. Other attorneys on the team included Bonnie Milstein of the Bazelon Center, whose expertise was in mental illness; Jim Weisman of Paralyzed Veterans of America, whose expertise was in transportation; Sy Dubow and Karen Peltz-Strauss of the National Center for Law and the Deaf, whose expertise was in deafness issues; Tim Cook, attorney for ADAPT (a national grassroots disability organization devoted to activism); and Bob Burgdorf, counsel to the National Council on Disability, who had drafted the original law. The legal team also had access to various experts around the country who they could tap for advice on different issues as they arose. For example, how much does it cost to make a bus accessible? They were able to get accurate and timely information so they could respond quickly to the many challenges that continually needed to be met.

2. The Lobbying Teams

Liz Savage, then of the Epilepsy Foundation of America, led the lobbying effort. Our lobbying forces were divided into teams, each with a team captain. The team captains were representatives from different segments of the disability community, e.g., the Veterans, deaf groups, mental illness groups, etc. Team captains met with their teams every morning. The teams were made up of people from the grassroots all over the country, as well as those from within the Washington, DC area. In the morning meetings they would receive briefings from Liz Savage and others about the issues of the day, the kind of information and data that they needed to collect, and how to report back what they learned.

The teams developed a rapid response system that allowed them to identify an issue, develop a strategy, and carry it out in 24 hours. For example, if a Member of Congress raised a concern about a particular issue, the lobbying team would coordinate a response. They would have the legal team put together a one-page statement on the issue and distribute it to Members of Congress. They would have the grassroots contact Members of Congress on the issue. They would gather information about how Members were responding to the grassroots and to lobbyists in Washington, and then further refine our efforts. These teams operated as "lean clean fighting machines." They became so efficient that they had answers to questions before the Members even realized they wanted to ask the questions.

The lobbying teams also had the job of educating Members of Congress about disability discrimination. Team members spent a lot of time researching Members to determine if they had family members or friends with disabilities. Sometimes the community engaged the family member or friend to help in educating the member.

3. The Press

Most civil rights movements include use of the press (electronic and print) as an integral part of their legislative strategy. This was not the case with the ADA. At the beginning of the process, the bill received a lot of unfavorable one-sided attention from the press. A member would raise a concern about the bill and the press would write an entire story based on a single negative impression, i.e., how the proposed legislation would cost too much or was going to be too onerous for businesses. Other members of Congress would read these articles and their concerns would also grow.

The disability community's response to this negative spiral was to call for a press blackout. We were able to secure an agreement among everyone we were negotiating with to not talk to the press. Every party simply would tell the press that we were "in negotiations" and could not discuss the bill. Of course, members and organizations who were not party to the negotiations would make comments to the press. Nevertheless, we effectively stopped the press from getting verification of what was occurring in the development of the bill, since no one who was in on the negotiating would comment. This strategy was effective at containing the negative stories from the press. It also allowed us to put our own spin on relevant issues and release information according to timing that was beneficial to us.

4. Direct Actions: A Necessary Part of Strategy

Any successful strategy must involve those willing to engage in direct action. We recruited the activist arm of the disability community, led by ADAPT, to work with us during the course of the bill's consideration by carrying out strategic, targeted direct actions that involved members of the community in demonstrations and rallies. Members of Congress must be made to see their own constituents and answer to them. It is harder for members to say "no" to people with disabilities from their own districts than it is to say "no" to a Washington lobbyist in a suit.

When we needed to make a point to Congress or the White House, we called on ADAPT to help. When negotiations bogged down, we asked ADAPT to organize a direct action such as picketing at the White House. We tried to organize the timing of direct actions to coincide with key legislative moments. For instance, we went so far as to hold up Congressional consideration of the transportation part of the bill until ADAPT could organize their troops to get to the capital. We were concerned about losing the transportation section of the bill so we wanted a strong show of force for Congress during its consideration of the relevant provisions. We called the press to ensure coverage of ADAPT events.

Approximately 400 disabled people would typically participate in an ADAPT event. One direct action consisted of participants holding a sit-in in the Rotunda of the U.S. Capitol, some chaining themselves to the building and refusing to leave, to demand that Members of Congress move the bill forward. They crawled up the steps of the Capitol building, many leaving their wheelchairs at ground level to make the journey. The National Council on Independent Living (NCIL), another organization run by people with disabilities, organized a march on the White House to demand the passage of the Americans with Disabilities Act. People came to Washington by the trainloads for these events, flooding the Halls of Congress and the streets around the White House.

These activities galvanized the community and served to build a tremendous sense of common identity and support for the bill. Considered as a whole, these shows of force in Washington by people with disabilities from around the country demonstrated to Members of Congress that this was a bill that people cared about and would raise discussion on back in their own districts. The direct actions heightened the visibility and public profile of the legislation and created pressure on Congress to act.

I. TARGET MESSAGES FOR DIFFERENT AUDIENCES

Messages have to be targeted to specific audiences, taking into consideration the different perspectives and mission of the group/person you are trying to reach. Members of Congress have very different perspectives and motivations from either grassroots advocates or business owners. Too often people think that one slogan works for everyone. But it does not. A message that would empower the grassroots could be a message that would scare a business owner.

For the grassroots, the message was empowerment. The message was: "You have the right to be a part of society. Not having this law means that your country is treating you as a second-class citizen."

For the Republican and rather conservative federal Administration, the message was: "People with disabilities want to work so they can be tax generating citizens. When they don't work, they are dependent on tax dollars for subsidies. This is good economic policy for the country."

For Congress, the message was one of equality. Congress had already enacted many laws to ensure that no group is treated in a discriminatory manner. A large part of their responsibility as legislators was to ensure that all citizens are treated equally. The message to Congress was: "All citizens should be treated equally. People with disabilities deserve the same protection against discrimination as that given to other protected groups such as women and racial minorities."

For the business community and those from the private sector who would be responsible for complying with the law, the message was one of calming fears. We argued that for the last 15 years they had been complying with Section 504 of the Rehabilitation Act, which prevents discrimination on the basis of disability by any company that receives federal funds. No business had ever gone bankrupt or experienced financial difficulties in this time because of the burden of implementing Section 504. Since the requirements of the Americans with Disabilities Act were essentially the same as those of the Rehabilitation Act, it was unlikely that such business losses would occur under the ADA. The ADA simply extended Section 504 into the private sector, even in the absence of federal funds. We explained that we would protect them from bankruptcy by guaranteeing them "undue burden" protection—a clause that excused businesses from performing any accommodation which became prohibitively expensive for a business to undertake. We assured them that we did not want to close businesses; rather, we wanted to open the doors of opportunity for potential employees with disabilities. Unless this happened, the tax burden placed on businesses would continue to rise because of the expense of paying for Social Security benefits. We informed businesses that the law meant more customers for them. If a supermarket is accessible, customers with disabilities will use it. The economy was weak in the United States at that time, and we argued that the disability community offered an entire untapped market of consumers eager to gain access to all kinds of goods and services. We also told the transportation sector that it was in their interest to ensure accessible transportation as the number of people who are elderly and disabled are increasing, and this growing market would be lost if the industry did not work now to ensure accessibility.

For the broader civil rights groups, we argued that this was the continuing and latest aspect of ensuring civil rights for all. There are people with disabilities who are woman, who are of different ethnicities, and who hold different religious beliefs we argued. Our cause is your cause.

J. DEALING WITH OPPOSITION

The most significant opposition to the ADA was mounted by the transit industry. Their contention was that the law would cost too much to implement. The disability community had a few working models from various districts that we could use to demonstrate costs and make the point that ensuring the accessibility of fixed-route buses and generic transportation systems would ultimately be less expensive than providing for separate, door-to-door paratransit systems. The lack of extensive cost data was problematic, but we were able to find enough information to make our case.

Specifically, over-the-road coaches—most notably Greyhound—fought hard against the requirement to become accessible. Ten years after the ADA was enacted, they are still fighting the applicable provisions. The only transportation available to many people with disabilities in rural areas is the Greyhound bus. Knowing this and knowing that many minorities live in rural areas, we enlisted race civil rights groups to help us. Many lower-income African Americans would be stuck with no transportation at all if these buses were not made accessible. Greyhound recruited constituents of key Members of Congress to tell the latter that this provision would put constituents out of business. In the end, we reached a compromise: over-the-road coaches would be covered under the ADA, but subject to a study to be undertaken that would determine the extent of accessibility which would be required of them.

A second significant area of opposition was related to health insurance. As drafted by the NCD, the original bill prohibited discrimination in the provision of health insurance. The original Senate sponsor of the bill, Lowell Weicker, was from the state of Connecticut, the insurance capital of the United States. His constituents would have generated tremendous opposition to this bill had the health insurance provision remained part of it. One of his conditions for introducing the bill was that the health insurance provision be dropped. It was too big an issue and its inclusion would have ensured the defeat of the bill. Although the disability community believed passionately that discrimination in the provision of health insurance was a tremendous obstacle to employment and integration, they knew that Senator Weicker was correct on the politics of this issue. The inclusion of health insurance would have sunk the entire bill. We therefore accepted the hard assessment that it was better to leave health insurance out in exchange for gaining accessibility in so many other areas.

The small business community raised a number of issues. They were afraid that the bill would send them into bankruptcy. They complained that key concepts in the bill, such as the definition of disability, were too undefined and vague; they would have preferred a finite list of disabilities that would be covered under the law. They wanted a provision in the law that would set a clear dollar cap on the amount of money that any business was required to spend on an accommodation. They also sought a specific dollar figure for determining what would constitute an undue burden for a business. The disability community preferred having broad principles, rather than a specific dollar figure, for determining what constitutes an undue burden under the law. The flexibility of having principles in place would mean that a small grocery store would not be held to the same level of expenditure as a large corporation.

There was opposition from multiple other sectors. The motion picture industry was concerned that it would have to caption all films; the entertainment industry did not want interpreters on stage with performers; the religious community stated that they should not be covered by the bill at all, arguing separation of church and state. Increasingly narrow issues were raised. Owners of sports teams were concerned that they would not be able to expel drug users from their teams. Employers didn't want to be told that they had to hire certain applicants or that they could not fire certain employees. People who were blind did not want to be forced to accept an accommodation. Businesses did not want people with mental illness covered by the bill. Smokers raised the issue of whether or not smoking could be considered a disability.

At the very end of the process, in the closing moments of the bill's final passage into law, the National Restaurant Association launched a frontal attack that truly tested the primary "one for all and all for one" principle of the disability community. This proved to be the ultimate test for the coalition. The National Restaurant Association contended that the law should not cover people with HIV/AIDS, specifically because restaurant owners should not have to hire people with HIV/AIDS for food handling jobs due to the risk of transmitting the virus to customers via the food that was handled. Of course, this argument was completely unsupported by any scientific evidence to indicate that such an alleged mode of transmission could occur.

The disability community rose to the occasion with flying colors. We took the position that we would let the bill die before allowing one group to be excluded from its coverage. Bob Williams, a leader in the disability rights community who has cerebral palsy summed up the disability community's feeling about the amendment proposed by the National Restaurant Association: "It ain't civil and it ain't right." The disability community was never really put to the final test of pulling the bill down, as an agreement was worked out finally that turned the amendment into a study that was then accepted as part of the bill.

K. KNOW WHEN TO HOLD 'EM AND WHEN TO FOLD 'EM

The most important aspect of successfully enacting a piece of legislation is knowing when to compromise and when to hold out for a better deal. As the leader of negotiations for the disability rights community, Pat Wright had to know "when to hold 'em and when to fold 'em." Her method for determining this comes partially from art and partially from science. Her remarkable skill at sizing up a given situation comes from years of experience and tremendous political insight.

Pat always did her homework, and this allowed her to rapidly assess the various forces that could arise and how they would align themselves in relation to a controversial issue. She constantly gathered background information that could be used whenever needed. She counted votes. She developed strategies with numerous layers and back-up positions. She had several routes of access to top decision-makers and persons of influence in Congress, the White House, and outside of government. Given her knowledge of both the overall political landscape and the many ongoing agendas that operated within it, she knew how to maneuver the disability community into a winning position.

In the final analysis, the ability to determine when to hold out and when to compromise is the magic of a good negotiator and a good politician. It defies logical description, but when you see it in action, you know you have found it.

L. CONCLUSION

Making a law is a messy, complex and time-consuming process that involves many players from many sectors. There is no "one way" or single "recipe" to ensure that a law will reach enactment. However, there is considerable experience that can inform the many efforts to enact disability anti-discrimination laws currently taking place around the world. We hope that the lessons learned in the United States through the enactment of the Americans with Disabilities Act will be helpful to those in other countries who are seeking policy and legal reform to promote the inclusion and economic independence of people with disabilities.

Achieving Accessibility: How the Americans with Disabilities Act Is Changing the Face and Mind of a Nation

Silvia Yee[1] *and Marilyn Golden*[2]

A. INTRODUCTION

With the signing into law of the Americans with Disabilities Act of 1990 (ADA) on July 26, 1990, America unambiguously acknowledged that "the continuing existence of unfair and unnecessary discrimination and prejudice denies people with disabilities the opportunity to compete on an equal basis and to pursue those opportunities for which our free society is justifiably famous."[3] Disability activists celebrated the ADA as "the most comprehensive civil rights advancement for people with dis-

[1] Silvia Yee received her LL.B., B.Mus. and M.A. at the University of Alberta in Canada, and moved to the United States to pursue further graduate studies in Musicology at the University of California, Berkeley. She has previously worked in the area of health law, and is currently International Law and Policy Fellew at the Disability Rights Education and Defense Fund, Inc.

[2] Marilyn Golden is Policy Analyst for the Disability Rights Education and Defense Fund (DREDF), the foremost national law and policy center on disability civil rights in the United States. She has been closely involved with the Americans with Disabilities Act throughout all the stages of its proposal and passage and now during its implementation. Golden has led innumerable ADA training workshops. Before coming to DREDF, she served as Director of Access California, a resource center on architectural accessibility for people with disabilities, and as Co-Coordinator of the Disabled International Support Effort, an organization that provided material aid and technical assistance to disability groups in developing countries. Today she continues work in ADA policy and also consults internationally on the development of disability equal rights law.

[3] 42 U.S.C. § 12101(a)(9).

abilities ever to be enacted by the United States Congress."[4] More recent pronouncements on the law continue to echo the language of civil rights. John Wodatch, Chief of the Civil Rights Division of the U.S. Department of Justice (the primary federal agency responsible for enforcement of Titles II and III of the ADA), states succinctly that "[a] primary goal of the ADA is to open up everyday American life to persons with disabilities."[5] Policy analysts characterize the ADA's mandate as "broad and sweeping—to protect the civil rights of the nation's 49 million people with disabilities in virtually all aspects of public life."[6] In a recent survey of the ADA's implementation in municipalities, the authors begin by stating that the ADA "has been heralded as the most comprehensive piece of federal [rights] legislation since the Civil Rights Act of 1964."[7]

The statute is organized into five titles that deal with employment (Title I); state and local governments (Title II); privately operated accommodations, goods and services available to the public (Title III); telecommunications (Title IV); and miscellaneous provisions (Title V). Distinct compliance requirements, deadlines, enforcement procedures and remedies are specified in each section. A number of different federal agencies and departments are responsible for giving technical assistance and ensuring compliance within each area. Nonetheless, the overall language and goals of the ADA coalesce into a whole that is much greater than the sum of its parts. This article focuses on the oper-

---

[4] Marilyn Golden, Linda Kilb & Arlene Mayerson, *Americans with Disabilities Act: An Implementation Guide* 1 (Berkeley: Disability Rights Education and Defense Fund, Inc., 1993).

[5] DOJ presentation sponsored by the Pacific Disability and Business Technical Assistance Center in San Francisco, CA, Sept. 22, 2000.

[6] Jane West, "Introduction," *in Implementing the Americans with Disabilities Act* xiv, at xv (Jane West ed., Cambridge, MA. & Oxford, U.K.: Blackwell Publishers and Millbank Memorial Fund, 1996).

[7] Stephen E. Condrey & Jeffrey L. Brudney, "The Americans with Disabilities Act of 1990: Assessing Its Implementation in America's Largest Cities," 28 *American Review of Public Administration* 26 (1998). The article primarily concerns implementation of the ADA's Title I provisions, which are not a focus of this paper, but also makes some reference to the act's public access provisions.

ation of Titles II, III and IV of the ADA, but is not strictly organized according to those titles. Instead, after Part A's introduction to the overall social and civil rights goals of the ADA, we move into examining aspects of contemporary life as it is lived by people with disabilities in the United States in the year 2000. Through discussing "Getting Around" (Part B), "Places to Go" (Part C) and "People to Call" (Part D), we show how the technical language of infrastructure and the equality promise of civil rights are inextricably entwined for people with disabilities. "Just Like Everyone Else" (Part E) explores how the ADA is addressing systemic structural and social barriers that are preventing people with disabilities from participating in the everyday life of the community that others in the United States can take for granted. "A Civil Rights Tool" (Part F) concludes by giving an overview of legislative forerunners to the ADA, and analyzes the integral part that both federal enforcement and a private right of action (the right of a private individual to bring a lawsuit) play in the effectiveness of the ADA as a tool for social change.

Jane West noted in 1995 that "the greatest impact of the ADA to date is in two areas: the empowerment claimed by people with disabilities and changes in how our nation's institutions conduct routine business: in stores, on buses, in the office, and in our use of telecommunications."[8] The fact is, these two aspects—self-perception and the accessibility of everyday life—are deeply interrelated, and both are vital to the ADA as a civil rights law. As is evident from both the testimony of people with disabilities and professionals in the field, dramatic changes have taken place over the last ten years, and would not have occurred to the same extent or as quickly without the ADA. This article relates some of those testimonials "from the trenches," as well as an idea of how the ADA continues to function through litigation, settlements and voluntary compliance as an effective tool in the ongoing battle against disability discrimination. Now that the ADA has been in place for a decade, we have begun to see the kinds of structural and social changes for which it was enacted. True equality may not yet have been achieved, but the turning of a millennium is nonetheless a good time to assess the battle to change the face and mind of America.

---

8 West, "Introduction," *supra* note 6, at xiv.

B. GETTING AROUND

Regardless of the potential for a "virtual community" in our electronic age, real mobility is still integral to virtually all aspects of contemporary life. Most Americans take reliable, ubiquitous and relatively inexpensive transport for granted in their lives—especially in urban settings—and schedule school and work meetings, social appointments, entertainment events, and travel plans accordingly. For many people with disabilities faced with inaccessible public transportation, the making of business and personal plans have always been subject to complex logistical concerns about how to get from point A to B. The transportation industry as a whole has historically resisted spending funds on making public transportation accessible to people with disabilities, and federal policy had tried to juggle cost concerns with achieving legal equality. As transportation consultant Rosalyn Simon notes, "the provision of accessible transportation in the United States was always varied and uneven. Uniform accessible transportation did not exist until it was required by the passage of the Americans with Disabilities Act of 1990."[9]

The ADA requires accessibility in transportation provided to the public,[10] whether publicly funded (Title II) or privately funded (Title III). The importance of the act's comprehensiveness and its coverage of all modes of public and private transportation cannot be overemphasized. Some individual cities and states had accessible vehicles before 1990, as well as paratransit[11] services that specifically served the dis-

---

9 Rosalyn M. Simon, "Status of Transportation Accessibility in the United States: Impact of the Americans with Disabilities Act," *in Proceedings of Seminar L Held at the Planning and Transportation Research and Computation European Transport Forum*, Brunel University, England § 1.2 (Sept. 2–6, 1996).

10 Most modes of transportation are covered under the ADA, but transportation that is specifically covered through other laws are excluded (e.g., discrimination in air travel is prohibited by the Air Carrier Access Act of 1986). A small percentage of school transportation is also excluded because of the ADA's exemptions for religious organizations and some private schools (in certain narrow circumstances—*see* 42 U.S.C. §§ 12182(b)(2)(B), (C), (D)).

11 "Paratransit" refers generally to transit services that are intended specifically for use by people with disabilities, are available on demand (either through prior reservation, or possibly through real-time scheduling), and provide origin-to-

ability community, but a reliable full range of transportation—one that would allow an individual with disabilities to reach a fixed route bus stop, transfer to light rail transit, and then catch a cross-country train—rarely occurred. On this point, Marilyn Golden, Policy Analyst with the Disability Rights Education and Defense Fund (DREDF),[12] and a wheelchair user herself, recounts the following:

> I recall people at the ADA hearings in Washington, held prior to the passage of the act, speaking about what it can be like when transit is accessible. One gentleman who testified, a significantly disabled man using a wheelchair, said that he boarded an accessible transit in New York and rode to an Amtrak station, then caught an Amtrak train from New York to DC. In his sleeper car, he slept until the next morning, and transferred at Washington DC's Amtrak station to an accessible subway. He got to the hearing and testified that he would do the whole thing in reverse to get home *on his own*. While others could take such mobility for granted, this was the first time in his life he was able to do such a thing, and all the transportation systems had to be accessible for it to work. To him this was an amazing experience.[13]

Golden points out that the man's experience was fortuitous: he was traveling in the densely populated East where Amtrak is heavily used,

---

destination service (whether door-to-door or curb-to-curb). There are variations that involve providing an individual with transportation to accessible fixed-route transportation, or scheduling an accessible bus upon request when a fixed route's vehicles are not yet all accessible. Paratransit is often discussed in contrast to "fixed route transit," in which vehicles travel pre-arranged routes and pick up/drop off members of the general public at marked stops, according to a set schedule. The relationship between these two types of transit under the ADA will be discussed later in Part B.

12 DREDF is the foremost national law and policy center on disability civil rights in the United States. Founded in 1979, DREDF is directed by people with disabilities and parents of people with disabilities. It is dedicated to furthering the rights of people with disabilities, and was closely involved with the proposal, passage and implementation of the ADA. For Golden biography, *see supra* note 2.

13 Personal interview (Sept. 20, 2000).

and managed to catch a number of accessible vehicles in a row. One of the ADA's goals is to make such independent travel possible without reliance on location, sheer good fortune or the scheduling availability of accessible vehicles on a given day. Golden states:

> There is far more accessible mainline transit in this country now, in fixed route buses, and to some extent, in rail transit as well, such as subways, and commuter and light rail. There is also more paratransit. . . . More and more people with disabilities are getting places on public transportation than they were before the ADA. It is true that there are still problems in transportation, and that there is a gap between where we are and full compliance. It would be impossible for there not to be. I don't know of any significant social policy advance, whether in the area of civil rights, the environment, or any other, where there isn't a gap between where we are and full compliance . . . but there is a huge gap between where we would be if there was no ADA and what the ADA has provided.[14]

Another strong feature of the ADA is that it emphasizes accessibility from the viewpoint of people with disabilities. That is, the ADA sets a functional standard that requires public transportation to be "readily accessible to and usable by" people with disabilities, and not a financial standard that would allow transit authorities to spend varying real dollar amounts on accessibility improvements. The significance of this is highlighted by John Gaffney,[15] who discusses the "local option" accessibility policy that had been favored under Section 504 of the Rehabilitation Act of 1973:

> It was decided eventually by FTA [the Federal Transit Administration] that as long as the transit authority . . . was spending

[14] *Id.*

[15] Gaffney, now retired, worked in civil rights law enforcement in the 1970s and 1980s before serving in the Governor's Office of Handicapped Affairs in Boston, and as assistant to the manager of the Massachusetts Bay Transit Authority. He spent the last decade as a consultant on ADA transit issues. Gaffney has a disability himself, and uses a wheelchair.

> 3% of its total budget on accessible service—pretty much however defined—that they were doing what they had to do under Section 504, whether they were meeting needs or not. What was curious about that, of course, is that it became known not as the "3% minimum" but as the "3% cap," in the tradition of government that floors become ceilings. . . . ADA eliminated the whole idea of a cap, and said that we simply have to spend whatever it takes to provide the minimum level of service as defined by federal law for service for people with disabilities. That change was the most profound one under the ADA, I think.[16]

The requirements established by the ADA are also noteworthy for both their scope and their depth. The Department of Transportation's (DOT) technical standards[17] address a broad range of disabilities by calling for numerous accessibility features including "priority seating signs, interior handrails and stanchions, appropriate floor and step surfaces, lighting, fare collection, and destination and route signs."[18] Similarly, the depth of the ADA is shown by the fact that its requirements extend "beyond vehicles and system infrastructure to cover maintenance, personnel training, information services, and communication systems."[19] This comprehensiveness allows the ADA to bypass the problems of "local option" so vividly described by Gaffney:

> [Before the ADA] everyone had a different idea of how access would be achieved. Transit authorities set up different standards. Some used the accessibility of all or part of their fixed-route [fleet], while others decided that they would meet accessibility requirements entirely through paratransit. . . . The transit industry generally, I think, was successful at deferring any real significant change to the services they provided. In contrast, the ADA gave a very clear definition of what constituted access in

---

16 Personal telephone interview (Oct. 6, 2000).

17 49 CFR, pts. 27 & 38; first issued Sept. 6, 1991.

18 Golden *et al., Implementation Guide, supra* note 4, at 150.

19 Rosalyn M. Simon, "Toward Accessible Transportation" in *Implementing the ADA*, ed. West, *supra* note 6, 299 at 304.

mass transit. It meant that *every* vehicle had to be accessible over time as older vehicles were replaced.[20]

Gaffney's last point shows how the legislation gives realistic consideration to the sheer magnitude of change required of transit authorities by the mandate to offer transportation to people with disabilities "in the same vehicles and facilities as everyone else."[21] Transit authorities were not forced to offer instant 100 percent accessibility, but rather faced various statutory and regulatory requirements that were phased in over different deadlines. For example, the act required all new vehicles ordered by fixed route operators after August 26, 1990 (30 days after the ADA's enactment) to be equipped with accessibility features.[22] Transit agencies had to file their plans for providing paratransit services and begin implementing such services by January 26, 1992, though the final deadline for full compliance with the ADA's paratransit service requirements was July 26, 1997.[23] The dates set for full implementation of the ADA's accessibility requirements for private over-the-road bus operators[24]

---

20 Interview, *supra* note 16.

21 Simon, "Status of Transportation Accessibility," *supra* note 9, at § 2.

22 49 C.F.R. §§ 37.7, 37.9, 37.71.

23 49 C.F.R. §§ 37.135–37.147.

24 Over-the-road buses are high-floor buses with baggage compartments underneath, and are used mainly for intercity and tour purposes. Initially, compliance for over-the-road buses (OTRB's) was scheduled for 1997. However, privately operated OTRB companies—which are the vast majority—have been notorious for resisting implementation of ADA requirements. In 1998, DOT updated its ADA requirements by issuing a regulation that comprehensively details the accessibility rules and non-discrimination policies required of all private companies providing public transportation using OTRB's (49 C.F.R. §§ 37.181–37.215). The U.S. Department of Justice (DOJ) has taken further action against individual companies against whom complaints have been lodged. For example, in 1999 DOJ finally signed an out-of-court agreement with Greyhound Lines, Inc., the country's largest OTRB bus firm, in which the company "agreed to improve services for passengers with disabilities, resolving 14 complaints filed by riders who claim that the company's drivers and other employees violated ADA. The action brings to closure nearly eight years of negotiation related to over the road bus (OTRB) accessibility": "Greyhound Settles 14 Complaints; Vows OTRB Improvements," *7:18 TD Access and Safety Report* (Oct. 6, 1999).

and extraordinarily expensive structural changes to rapid, commuter and light rail key stations are even later.[25]

One of the earliest deadlines, involving the purchase or lease of new fixed route vehicles after August 26, 1990, has its own phase-in feature since public transit operators will reach full accessibility as they naturally turn over their fleet. An additional benefit of this approach is that it provides a strong incentive for the testing and steady development of new transit technologies. For example, fixed route transit authorities are increasingly purchasing low-floor buses with ramps rather than buses with lifts, since the earlier technology of the lifts generally requires more maintenance. Technological innovation is also supported by the concept of "equivalent facilitation," which is permitted under DOT's technical standards, "meaning that the literal requirements of the Guidelines need not be complied with, if an equal or greater degree of accessibility can be provided by other means."[26] Equivalent facilitation allows for the integration of such new technologies as the Cleveland Securement System, for example, which involves a docking latch instead of a four-point tie-down and can generally be used to secure a mobility device on a transit vehicle in under 90 seconds.[27]

Even with a phased-in approach, fixed route transit has changed remarkably over the last decade from the situation in 1987, when a national American Public Transit Association survey found that only 18 percent of 174 public transit systems operated accessible fixed route service. As Simon reports:

---

[25] 49 C.F.R. §§ 37.47, 37.53. 37.59.

[26] Golden *et al., supra* note 4, at 150; note that the equivalent facilitation provision requires formal approval by DOT in every specific case, and does not refer to service requirements.

[27] Trends in mobility aid lift and securement technology are covered in Rodger Koppa, Becky Davies, & Katherine Rodriguez, *Barriers to Use of Transportation Alternatives by People with Disabilities* (College Station, TX: Texas Transportation Institute, 1998). An entire 1999 issue of the *Journal of the Transportation Research Board* (Transportation Research Record 1671) is devoted to some of the very latest developments in bus accessibility for people with cognitive, sensory and mobility disabilities.

> In 1989, one-third (36%) of the national bus fleet was accessible. Post-ADA fixed route bus accessibility increased to 39 percent in 1990, 46 percent in 1991, and 52 percent in 1992. Using data reported in transit system 1994 ADA plans, the federal government reported the national bus fleet as 55 percent accessible with 29, 000 lift/ramp-equipped buses in 1994 and 60 percent accessible with 32,000 lift/ramp-equipped buses in 1995. Their projections indicate that by 2002, the national bus fleet will be 100 percent lift/ramp-equipped. In addition, by 2005, all fixed route buses will also be equipped with ADA-compliant communication systems. Currently fixed route bus service is available in 324 out of 360 urbanized areas (UZAs) in the country. More than 100 public transit systems are now providing 100 percent accessible fixed route bus service during peak hours.[28]

The above figures are impressive, painting a picture of sleek, shining, accessible buses ready to be boarded, but the availability of vehicles only tells part of the story. There is still the question of whether people with disabilities can actually reach the vehicles, and the issue of whether people with disabilities actually use fixed route transit once it becomes available. We focus on the mid-sized city of Austin, Texas to look at these aspects of transportation under the ADA, and let two workers on the front lines of implementation speak for themselves: Delores Gonzales, the city's ADA Compliance Officer, and Nancy Crowther, the ADA Coordinator for Capital Metro Transit Authority (Cap-Metro).

Gonzales has been in her current position with the city of Austin for about nine years, and humorously notes that "everyone is my customer,"[29] including every city department and every aspect of ADA

---

[28] Simon, "Status of Transportation Accessibility," *supra* note 9, at § 3.1. It should be noted that there is still considerable variation in the quality of transportation service for people with disabilities under the ADA. While the ADA has unquestionably caused a huge gain in quality overall, that gain has not been realized evenly in every city, and some, perhaps many, systems are not in compliance with the ADA's requirements.

[29] Delores Gonzales, "Urban Transportation Symposium Presentation" (1999), Texas [sent via personal communication].

implementation, from providing sensitivity training for city employees to procuring accessibility equipment such as Braille printers. She points out that Austin actually had started to work with the disability community before the ADA's effective date, and that she was first employed by the city to be a liaison with the disability community in the late 1980s. Gonzales credits the city's awareness of people with disabilities and their needs to the presence in the city of "a very vocal and active disability community" (including the country's second largest chapter of ADAPT—an important and effective national grassroots disability rights organization that utilizes extensive direct action, as well as litigation and other advocacy tools), and states that she is "proud to be one of 54 million Americans with Disabilities."[30]

When called at her Austin office, Gonzales mentions Austin's "Curb Ramp Program" as a highlight in her career with the city. The public works program was cited as "visionary" by DOT when it was given an award on the ADA's Tenth Anniversary, and consists of the well-planned and systematic construction of both sidewalk curb ramps for city walkways and accessible routes to facilities. After Austin surveyed one-third of its roadways, the city's estimate of the number of curb ramps required increased from 1,500 to 6,000; 4,500 of those have now been constructed. City representatives worked with members of the disability community, other levels of government with transportation jurisdiction, and Cap-Metro to set design standards for the curb ramps that would be acceptable to both those with mobility and visual impairments. Since Austin's major roadways are also public bus routes, those curb ramps would be implemented by Cap-Metro as part of its ADA obligation. In addition to the curb ramps, Gonzales describes other steps that the city is taking at pedestrian walkways to increase accessibility, such as installing directional beeps, audio "walk" signals, and vibrating tactile push buttons onto clearly located roadway poles to assist people with visual and hearing impairments.

Since Austin's work with the disability community had begun in the 1980s with obligations placed upon local governments under Section 504 of the Rehabilitation Act of 1973, we asked Gonzales if the curb ramp program would have been implemented even without the ADA.

---

30 *Id.*

Her decisive answer is that the ADA "was the tool we needed."[31] The ADA specifically sets prioritized requirements for curb ramps or other sloped areas at existing, as well as newly constructed, pedestrian walkways.[32] As well, the ADA's increased comprehensiveness prompted many state and local governments to submit an updated transition plan,[33] because the transition plans previously required under Section 504 were incomplete or otherwise insufficient in light of ADA requirements. Gonzales takes the ADA's inclusiveness mandate very seriously, and saw it as an opportunity to form a core group of representatives from different disability groups to review and comment on the transition plans that Gonzales asked every city department for. As she reflected on what having the ADA in place meant, she concluded with a practical insight into the benefits of having a private right of action:

> I received authority and a blank check from the city because they took to heart what the law said. We try to do the right thing because it is the law, and because it is a civil right, but also, to protect ourselves. We have been sued, we are not immune from being sued, but when we are, plaintiffs will not find negligence in my program—it is a win-win situation for the city. And if someone does sue, we work together to solve the problem.[34]

Nancy Crowther, a fellow member on Austin's Mayor's Committee for People with Disabilities, shares Gonzales's positive attitude. Crowther was diagnosed with spinal muscular atrophy at the age of two, and as a wheelchair user cites considerable personal familiarity with inaccessible transportation, having experienced it until the end of her college days. She recalls attending the University of Texas and becom-

---

31 Personal telephone interview (Oct. 5, 2000).

32 28 C.F.R. § 35.150(d)(2).

33 If structural changes are needed for program accessibility, and a state or local government has 50 or more employees, then the government entity must identify physical obstacles that limit accessibility and provide a detailed plan for their removal, as well as an implementation schedule (the deadline for structural changes was January 26, 1995, three years after the effective date of Title II): 28 C.F.R. §§ 35.150(d)(1), 35.150(d)(3).

34 *Supra* note 31.

ing involved with a lawsuit against the University because of its inaccessible campus shuttle service. The action was heard and lost in 1983 because the court found that the shuttle service didn't receive sufficient federal funding to come under Section 504, and was therefore not required to retrofit its fleet to provide accessible service or any kind of special service. Today, Crowther looks back with satisfaction and states "we lost that battle, but won the war when the ADA went into effect."[35]

Crowther first became involved with Cap-Metro in 1985, as a representative on the transit authority's Advisory Committee for People with Disabilities. In 1989, she actually joined the organization as an employee, in a new position designed to ensure that accessibility progress would continue. She initiated programs in driver sensitivity and lift training, and after the ADA was passed, she was placed in charge of Cap-Metro's paratransit plan as well. With the city of Austin and Cap-Metro's early start on addressing transit accessibility issues, fixed route transit became 100 percent lift equipped and accessible by 1993. Cap-Metro has put in over 18 miles of sidewalk and curb ramps along their bus routes to date, and instituted numerous education programs within the disability community as well, giving people with various disabilities lessons in taking public fixed route transit. When Crowther states that "people with disabilities really did want to ride" she has the numbers to back her up. In 1993, the year when full fleet accessibility was reached and people with disabilities no longer had to worry about whether or not a specific scheduled bus on a particular route would happen to have a lift, the number of boardings by passengers with wheelchairs on Cap-Metro's fixed route service jumped over 300 percent, from 12,625 to 38,582. Every succeeding year has seen a steady increase (the exception being 1995, when Austin suffered torrential rainfalls and the first lifts installed needed retrofitting), with the number of boardings reaching 83,574 in 1999.

Crowther is justly proud of Austin's fixed route service. When asked whether the passage into law of the ADA contributed to the move towards accessibility that Austin had already started in the late 1980s, Crowther replies "it helped tremendously, and gave a kind of credence

---

35 Personal telephone interview (Oct. 13, 2000).

to what we were doing. It was fully embraced here, and I was pleased to see that." She points out how Cap-Metro could only gain by having had an early start on accessibility:

> I know for a fact that the industry as a whole didn't grasp the law well. It screamed at all the hearings prior to the signing of the ADA. Within the industry, many transit authorities went ahead and bought buses in 1990, just prior to the coming into effect of the requirement for buying new buses with lifts. An entire fleet would then be inaccessible, and a bus's life is twelve years. I spoke with the Secretary of Transit at a recent conference in Virginia, and he confirmed that 83% of the nation's fleet is currently accessible, and in 2002 we will have 100% accessibility. . . . Now I *see* the impact on those transit authorities that refused to comply or tried to get under the wire of having lifts on their buses. They feel the impact in their paratransit, which is a much more costly service. For ourselves, there is no way in the world that we could have accommodated an additional 83,000 rides on our paratransit [referring to the 1999 boarding figure for Austin's fixed route service by people who use wheelchairs].[36]

Crowther has recently been promoted to the position of ADA Coordinator for Cap-Metro, and describes a number of innovative programs undertaken by the transit authority. Bus stop poles provide tactile clues for people with visual impairments: they are the only square poles in the city, with raised route numbers placed on the poles themselves. There is a toll-free number that gives route information. Bright yellow hailing guides have been issued so that people with disabilities can get a driver's attention, and drivers have been instructed to stop for pick ups and drop offs at safe sites between regular stops, since there are still a few inaccessible stops. Crowther agrees that the ADA has definitely been helpful in adding "teeth" to her programs: she knows that she can say "You *will* take care of this" to a Cap-Metro employee or department, and have the backing of the act and the federal Department of Transportation.

---

36 *Id.*

Crowther's last statement about fixed route and paratransit hints at the relationship between these two forms of transportation under the ADA. Before 1990, under Section 504 of the Rehabilitation Act of 1973, public transit services for people with disabilities could be provided *either* through fixed route service or paratransit. The ADA (which also amended Section 504) clearly advocates the use of fixed route by requiring full accessibility on buses, and on commuter, rapid and light rail transport. Nonetheless, the act recognizes that there are people with disabilities who are unable, for various reasons, to take fixed route transit, and therefore transit authorities that provide fixed route service to the general public must also provide complementary paratransit service to members of the general public who cannot use the fixed route service.[37] Paratransit is a more expensive service than fixed route, and the ADA's service criteria made it clear that the frequently inferior standards of many pre-ADA paratransit services would no longer be tolerated. Paratransit service must now be comparable to fixed route service in its service area, response time, fares, hours and days of service, and in a lack of restrictions on trip purpose or on capacity.[38]

While many disability advocates and transit authorities are concerned by the fact that increases in paratransit demand outpace the use of accessible fixed route systems by people with disabilities in many parts of the country, others make the point that paratransit is still the only feasible means of transportation for some people with disabilities. It is possible that the ADA is finally enabling these and other members of the public who need paratransit to travel for the first time.[39]

Russell Thatcher worked as a Section 504 Coordinator for the State of Massachusetts, and then moved into consulting work after passage

---

[37] 42 U.S.C.A. § 12143. For a summary of paratransit eligibility requirements, *see* Golden *et al., supra* note 4, at 157–59.

[38] For a more detailed look at the service criteria, *see* Golden *et al., supra* note 4, at 160–62.

[39] Nonetheless, considerable variation in quality of paratransit service for people with disabilities remains an issue under the ADA. While the ADA has prompted a tremendous improvement in overall quality, that improvement has not occurred consistently in every city, and some paratransit systems are still far from full compliance with the ADA's requirements.

of the ADA. He developed a handbook for the Federal Transit Authority (FTA) on implementing the ADA's paratransit provisions, and became involved in the FTA's reviews of paratransit plans and updates from 1992–97. Thatcher currently works with Multisystems, a private consulting firm, and runs a National Transit Institute course that trains transit staff to establish and conduct paratransit eligibility determinations. He makes the following observations:

> Paratransit back in the '70s and '80s was never really taken seriously by the transit industry. A female colleague of mine puts it this way: "It was always seen as human service, and it was run mainly by women—they were the managers. The *guys* did the 'big bus' stuff." Now paratransit is growing, both in number of trips and as a percentage of the budget. It's starting to get attention and be taken seriously as *part* of each system's program. This is really positive, and until it happened, I don't think we could even get to a point where we could provide mobility, let alone equality. I think the *specificity* of the ADA has greatly helped.[40]

When Thatcher states that "between 1992 and 1997, the number of paratransit rides more than doubled," it is just one of numerous observations about fixed route and rail service accessibility that together lead him to conclude "we've moved an awful long way in 10 years." Thatcher also makes the point that even though "it used to be the feeling in the industry that no matter how many vehicles were put into paratransit, there would always be an unending growth in demand, there are some systems now that are seeing growth in demand level off. It isn't because they have serious problems or strengths, but because they are beginning to achieve full service to eligible riders."[41]

The ADA's success in changing the face of mass transit for people with disabilities, especially in the areas of fixed route accessibility and paratransit, is due in part to how the transit industry has evolved in this country. Golden observes that transportation is unique among areas cov-

---

40 Personal telephone interview (Oct. 13, 2000).

41 *Id.*

ered by the ADA in not having to apply to literally thousands of potential establishments. "Each big city has one (or just a handful of) public transit agencies. Even though they carry many passengers, they are still only one target. People with disabilities across the country had been largely organized to pressure their transit authorities for inclusion even before the ADA was passed. Since many of the transit agencies knew they were being watched, many complied with the ADA, whereas a public accommodation such as a small restaurant might not even know about its obligations."[42]

Thatcher also takes a broad view of the ADA when he addresses how the act's civil rights approach has been necessitated by the structure of the transit industry in this country, but may also fall short of achieving full mobility for people with disabilities:

> In this country, only 5% of the population uses public transportation; 95% of our trips are made in private vehicles. Equality is going to get people mobility in those areas where that 5% of the population has access to good public transportation. A civil rights law does not mean that you are going to have the best mobility to support independence, only equal access to public transportation. It is a good baseline, but as you get into suburban areas, rural areas and even urban areas that lack good public service, *equal* transportation is not going to ensure that people with disabilities can get a job, keep a job, get to school, travel and do other things equally.[43]

The same idea is expressed succinctly, if less formally, by DREDF's Director of Government Affairs, Patrisha Wright, when she says "people with disabilities discovered that what the ADA entitled them to was the same lousy mass transit available to everyone else."[44]

Thatcher notes that a number of European states address mobility issues for people with disabilities through public policy programs, but

---

42 Golden interview, *supra* note 13.

43 Thatcher interview, *supra* note 40.

44 Related in Golden interview, *supra* note 13.

invariably those are countries that have strong nation-wide public transportation programs as well as high per capita transportation budgets. He continues:

> The U.S. does not have a strong national public transportation program. Everything is local. The federal government passes out money, and the local authorities decide what to do with it. The state of accessible transportation back in the '80s was pretty dismal. . . . I really question whether or not we could come as far as we have without something like a civil rights law. It made sense for us. The other thing, unfortunately, is that if you rely on national programs and policies, it ultimately comes down to who is in power and who is running the programs.[45]

An equality, integration-oriented approach offers additional benefits besides those mentioned by Thatcher. Within the disability community, the chance to get on and ride the same buses as the general public has often been viewed as a mark of independence and pride. A lead advocate in Topeka, Kansas [Mike Oxford], demonstrated this when he spoke of his organization's outreach plans once accessibility was achieved in Topeka:

> We'll do things like being real public and campaign for integration as the way to go; [we'll] encourage people to ride the big bus because it's cool, make it "disability cool" and "disability pride" to get on the mainline bus; "don't be a weenie and ride the bus."[46]

When people with disabilities and the general public have equal and shared mass transportation, then they also have an equal stake in maintaining and improving that transportation. The possibility of building real communities, in which people with disabilities can work in tandem with the rest of the public for better services that will be made available to all, can only be achieved with real integration. Clearly the goal of full

---

45 *Id.*

46 DREDF, Inc. and Crain & Associates, Inc., *ADA Paratransit Compliance Study Final Report* 2–14 (prepared for Project ACTION, Oct. 1996).

mobility for people with disabilities—whether in the cause of work, recreation, community involvement, or personal interactions—is an ideal which has not yet been achieved, but the ADA's transit requirements have succeeded in bringing people with disabilities that much closer to the ideal.

C. PLACES TO GO

Now that the ADA has enabled people with disabilities to move about in their communities and in the country, the inevitable question is: where will they go? The answer: more places than they could ten years ago. The ADA's accessibility requirements flow from the equality provisions of Title II and Title III, and generally came into effect on January 26, 1992 (18 months after the ADA's enactment date). Title II prohibits discrimination against people with disabilities in all services, programs and activities operated or provided by state or local governments.[47] Title III is the sister prohibition placed on private businesses, since it prohibits discrimination by privately operated public accommodations,[48] commercial facilities, and private entities that offer certain courses and examinations (e.g., courses and exams leading to a professional license). While the precise language used in each title differs slightly, the prohibitions on discrimination in the two titles are very similar,[49] and are

---

47 Title II of the ADA extended the protection previously afforded under Section 504 of the Rehabilitation Act of 1973, which barred discrimination on the basis of handicap in all state and local government programs and activities that receive federal funds. The receipt of federal financial assistance is irrelevant to the applicability of the ADA's Title II.

48 A place of public accommodation is any facility that is owned, leased or operated by a private entity, and whose operations fall within one of a number of twelve specified categories (examples of the kinds of establishments included would be restaurants, shopping malls, dry cleaners, museums, day care facilities, health clubs, etc.). In general, all such facilities are covered by Title III, regardless of their size, though there are particular exceptions, such as an owner-occupied place of lodging renting fewer than six rooms. An exemption is also given to certain private clubs and religious organizations. For a more detailed examination of the provisions of both Title II and Title III, *see* Golden *et al., supra* note 4, at 77–117 (Title III) and 119–48 (Title II).

49 The one major difference is that the two titles take different approaches to

intended to ensure that no individual or class of individuals is denied, on the basis of disability, the right to participate in and benefit from the goods, services, programs, activities, or other advantages offered by any place of public accommodation or any local or state government.[50] State and local governments, and private entities that own, lease or operate places of public accommodation, cannot avoid the act through contracting out their activities. Nor will the prohibition against discrimination be satisfied by providing opportunities to participate that are unequal to those given to the general public or unnecessarily separate, since goods, programs and services must be provided in the most integrated setting appropriate to the needs of the individual(s) in question.[51] Places of public accommodation and state and local governments must also provide reasonable modifications to their policies, practices or procedures when needed to avoid discrimination on the basis of disability, though any modification that fundamentally alters the nature of the goods or services provided need not be made.[52]

Discrimination under Titles II and III includes a failure to make provision for structural accessibility for people with disabilities. The ADA requires the removal or avoidance of architectural and other structural barriers in existing facilities, newly built facilities and facilities that are altered, but it does not impose these requirements without regard for such balancing factors as expense or the difficulty of accomplishing the changes given the resources of the covered entity. For example, places of public accommodation are required to remove architectural, communication and transportation barriers[53] in existing facilities only to the

---

the removal of architectural barriers in existing facilities. Those titles' approaches are discussed further *infra*, note 55 and accompanying text.

50 42 U.S.C.A. § 12182 (Title III) and § 12132 (Title II).

51 42 U.S.C.A. §§ 12182(b)(1), 12201(d); 28 C.F.R. § 36.203 (Title III), 28 C.F.R. §§ 35.130(b)(1)(iv), 35.130(c), 35.130(d) (Title II).

52 42 U.S.C.A § 12182(b)(2)(A)(ii) (Title III); 28 C.F.R. § 35.130(b)(7) (Title II).

53 An example of a communication barrier would be a lack of accessible signage. A transportation barrier could be the unavailability of a car with hand- or foot-only controls for a test drive, even when a potential buyer has given the car dealership advance notice: *see* Golden *et al., supra* note 4, at 97–98.

extent that such removal is readily achievable, which is defined as "easily accomplishable and able to be carried out without much difficulty or expense."[54] Such readily achievable barrier removal may include, for example, the installation of entrance ramps or grab bars in restrooms, rearranging restaurant tables or display aisles, adding Braille/raised letters to elevators, or installing flashing alarm lights in hotel rooms. The flexibility of the "readily achievable" standard is designed to allow consideration of many factors, including the business's size (large, prosperous businesses are expected to do more than "mom and pop" stores) and the economic realities faced by the public accommodation in question. The published ADA Accessibility Guidelines provide further guidance for compliance.

The obligation placed upon state and local governments to make their existing programs, services and benefits accessible to people with disabilities is generally higher than the "readily achievable" standard to which private entities are held. For example, government programs offered in existing facilities must, when viewed in their entirety, be readily accessible and usable by people with disabilities, up to the point at which such access would fundamentally alter the program or impose an undue financial or administrative burden.[55] The requirement for the government program to be viewed in its entirety means that providing accessibility does not always come down to the need for architectural modifications. For example, if a city currently centralizes all its utility payment services in one inaccessible building the decision to collect payment to an equivalent service level at an accessible building in an equally convenient location in the city, avoids the need to structurally modify the original building. However, if the original building is the city hall, which is the site of many other vital community and government operations, then the local government must also make those services accessible when viewed in their entirety.

After only a decade of operation, the ADA has not made every building in America accessible. Just as full transit mobility is still an unrealized ideal in the area of transportation, fully accessible design is

---

[54] 42 U.S.C.A. § 12182(b)(2)(A)(iv), (v).

[55] 28 C.F.R. §§ 35.149, 35.150.

an ideal in the construction and alteration of spaces in the built environment. Bill Hecker, an architect who has done consulting work on the ADA and is the founder of Hecker Design, Ltd. in Alabama, describes "universal design" as a concept in which design and the dynamic accessibility needs of all people are considered together right from the very beginning of the architectural process. Unfortunately, he finds that universal design still seems to be given a relatively low priority in the architect's general scheme of design, with ADA compliance and disability issues addressed as an afterthought only after a plan is essentially completed. Still, he is encouraged by the fact that the Architectural Registration Exam has added an entire section dealing with accessibility since the ADA passed, and that ADA issues have even been included on the National Council of Architecture Registration Board's Model Exam.[56]

One of the reasons that accessible design remains an unrealized ideal at this point is because its adoption still requires conscious and deliberate intent from architects and designers.[57] The fact that an intellectual understanding of accessibility issues is officially required from the current generation of architects is a very important first step, but accessibility issues will not become integral to the design process until people with disabilities begin to be seen and characterized as members of the general public and as clients themselves. This is precisely what the public accommodations and program provisions of the ADA are designed to encourage. Underlying all the technical requirements and the balancing concepts is the fact that the act gives people with disabil-

---

56 Personal telephone interview (Oct. 17, 2000).

57 This is evident in the fact that so many of the compliance agreements won under the ADA against public accommodations continue to include new construction. For example, DREDF's successful lawsuits against Shell and Chevron over the inaccessibility of gas stations resulted in comprehensive consent decrees in which both corporations are required not only to bring older, existing facilities into compliance, but also to modify newly constructed facilities which continued to fall short of the ADA requirements, even though the new facilities had been designed and built in a post-ADA environment. These cases involve the removal of architectural barriers at thousands of gas stations nationwide. Greener v. Shell, Civ. No. C-98-2425-CAL (N.D. Cal.), (Consent Decree Entered Sept. 11, 1998), Lawson v. Chevron, Civ. No. C99-0529CAL (N.D. Cal.) (Consent Decree Entered Apr. 23, 1999).

ities the opportunity to assume an active presence in every aspect of American life, whether eating out, assuming civic duties, shopping, traveling, or just relaxing at a movie. The benefits of this are felt not only by people with disabilities, but by family members and friends, and even by businesses that may see returns on their ADA "investment." The following interviews and testimonies bear witness to the ADA's effectiveness as a tool for changing accessibility in American business.

On the fifth anniversary of the ADA, the National Council on Disability (NCD) held town meetings and interviewed people with disabilities and their families in all 50 states, the District of Columbia and the U.S. Virgin Islands to gain an idea of the ADA's impact in everyday life. One of the report's major findings is that "in every State of the Union, consumers testified that the Americans with Disabilities Act (ADA) has created greater access to the physical environment over the past five years. Consumers spoke in great detail about the important changes that have occurred in virtually every type of environment. Some spoke of entire jurisdictions that had voluntarily embraced the ADA."[58] The personal testimonies in the Report cover such varied government facilities as community centers, public libraries, courthouses, and public schools, as well as voting sites and universities. Public accommodations that are cited included large retail chains like Wal-Mart, hotel chains, restaurants, and outdoor sports and recreation facilities. The ADA's "ripple" effect on the families of people with disabilities can clearly be seen in numerous comments on accessibility.[59] Shelley Peterman Schwarz of Wisconsin explains "[b]efore the ADA, I couldn't even shop with my daughter for her first prom dress. But things have changed, and I recently did shop with my daughter to buy clothes: for her job interview!" Kristopher Hazard of Tennessee similarly states "[b]efore the ADA was passed, my family couldn't go any place together because of my Mom's wheelchair. But now many places are accessible, and we can go on outings as a family." Linda Hawkins, the parent of a boy with disabilities, says that her son "wanted to participate in weight training, but he couldn't get to the field house because it was located

---

58 NCD, *Voices of Freedom: America Speaks Out on the ADA* (July 26, 1995), located *at* http://www.ncd.gov/newsroom/publications/voices.html (Oct. 16, 2000).

59 Following three quotations from *Voices of Freedom*, *id.*

down a steep gravel hill, inaccessible to wheelchairs. I couldn't get the school to make accommodations until I had ADA behind me."

For these individuals, the changes they and their families experienced in their physical environment were clearly attributable to the legislation. Title III's applicability to privately owned public accommodations (and even such non-public commercial facilities as warehouses and factories in some instances[60]) is groundbreaking. Has Title II made as much difference to people with disabilities? In the opinion of Michael Muehe, who worked as the Director of Disability Discrimination for the City of Cambridge in Massachusetts pre-ADA, and who has been that city's ADA Coordinator for the last six and a half years, the ADA did not drastically alter the city's pre-existing obligations under Section 504 from a purely technical point of view. As Cambridge had always received considerable amounts of federal funding, and was also generally advanced in its political consciousness, the city had taken its Section 504 requirements seriously. But he admits that disability awareness had stagnated somewhat by the mid 1980s. For city and state officials, enactment of the ADA served to revitalize their sense of a need to work on accessibility, and sharpened their awareness of disability discrimination as a civil rights issue. Accessibility became a "social imperative." He adds:

> The ADA really propelled disability issues into the public consciousness. The ADA is recognized by the typical Joe in the street. I don't know how many times a contractor will say to me "I've put the ADA ramp here" or "the ADA accessible route is there." The ADA has become a synonym for disability consciousness and accessibility, and in that sense, the ADA has been very successful. . . . Also, it has made a tremendous difference in the lives of people with disabilities and in [the accessibility] of everyday life. People with disabilities have a much keener sense of their civil rights and disability exclusion, and they want an equal opportunity.[61]

---

60 Commercial facilities which may be potential places of employment must comply with ADA regulations in both new construction and alterations to existing facilities: 42 U.S.C.A. § 12183.

61 Personal telephone interview (Oct. 5, 2000).

Muehe remembers meeting a woman using a wheelchair on the sidewalk in 1986, the year he became disabled himself, and recalls that she didn't know about Section 504. He finds it difficult to imagine that being the case with the ADA today.

Enforcement of the law has played a large role in the ADA's success in raising public awareness of disability rights. The Disability Rights Section of the Civil Rights Division of the U.S. Department of Justic (DOJ) is given the lead federal role for enforcing Title III.[62] In doing so, the agency may (i) investigate complaints lodged by the public alleging Title III violations; (ii) undertake periodic compliance reviews; and (iii) bring a civil enforcement action.[63] In the summer of 2000, DOJ issued a special commemorative report that reviewed the past decade of ADA enforcement.[64] The Report highlights a number of the informal agreements, formal settlements, and judgments that have been won by DOJ since 1990, as well as the fact that the act gives DOJ the right to initiate an action in cases in which there is a pattern or practice of discrimination, or where there are issues of general public importance.

Under this mandate, DOJ has entered into ADA enforcement actions in many spheres of life, including government services and public accommodations of all kinds. One important area that has been addressed strategically is recreational travel destinations. Given the huge popularity of Disneyland and Hawaii as domestic American vacation destinations, DOJ came to realize that addressing the inaccessibility of both locations would serve to raise awareness of people with disabilities as travelers.

---

62 42 U.S.C.A. § 12188(b)(1)(A)(i).

63 *Id.* DOJ may also choose to intervene as a plaintiff in a civil action that has been initiated by a private litigant alleging a violation of Title III, not because of any explicit ADA provision, but because of the normal application of the Federal Rules of Civil Procedure, Rule 24(b)(2): *see* Richard Landfield, "Enforcement of Rights Under the ADA," *in Accessibility Under the Americans with Disabilities Act and Other Laws* 118, at 129 (Earl B. Slavitt & Donna J. Pugh eds., Chicago: American Bar Association, 2000).

64 DOJ, *Enforcing the ADA: Looking Back on a Decade of Progress* (July 2000).

At Disney World and Disneyland, the issue did not concern architectural barriers as much as the communications inaccessibility engendered by Disney's failure to provide auxiliary aids to people who are deaf or hard of hearing.[65] Under the comprehensive agreement reached by DOJ and Disney, Disney agreed to numerous measures to ensure that hearing impaired people could enjoy the various attractions and shows available at Disney World and Disneyland. These accommodations include the provision of such things as oral and sign language interpreters at various specified attractions when given advance notice of a planned visit; written transcripts and assistive listening systems at most attractions; closed captioning on video monitors placed near queues throughout the park; interpreter schedules from Guest Services; employee training to improve service to hard of hearing or deaf guests, and advertisement of these services to guests who are deaf or hard of hearing.[66] For John Wodatch, the Disney agreement is a success story not only because DOJ managed to reach an agreement, but because once Disney got past its initial resistance, the company finally began to turn all their renowned originality and innovation towards meeting the needs of people with disabilities. Wodatch reports that at this point, Disney is serving a much larger clientele of people with disabilities.[67]

In Hawaii, accessibility for blind and visually impaired people was limited by the state's policy of requiring all dogs to be quarantined in a state facility for 120 days. For people with disabilities who have guide dogs, the choice was between visiting Hawaii without the capacity for independence provided by their dogs or not going at all. DOJ intervened in a lawsuit and eventually reached an agreement with the State "which allows individuals with vision impairments to travel to Hawaii with their

---

65 A place of public accommodation is guilty of discrimination if it fails to provide auxiliary aids and services (measures to ensure communication accessibility) to persons with impaired vision, speech or hearing, and as a result, such persons are excluded, segregated, or denied goods or services; the auxiliary aid or service need not be provided if doing so would fundamentally alter the nature of the service being provided or be an undue burden: 42 U.S.C.A. § 12182(B)(2)(A)(III).

66 *Supra* note 64, at 16–17.

67 DOJ presentation, *supra* note 5.

guide dogs without having to undergo the quarantine, as long as they are able to demonstrate that the dog is free from rabies through documentation of rabies vaccination and serological testing."[68] Jenine Stanley and her husband are both blind and each has a guide dog. She speaks of her husband's longstanding desire to live in Hawaii: "now, we can do that freely and travel back to the mainland as often as we want. We have choices. Choice is not always as available to people with disabilities as to others in our society. From raised character and Braille signage on hotel room doors to being able to work my guide dog in Hawaii, the ADA has given me the tools and supports to feel included in society, rather than cared for by it."[69]

Hawaii's tropical climate is helpful for many people with disabilities who have problems with circulation or mobility, and it is estimated that 12–20 percent of Hawaii's total population falls under the disability provisions of the ADA. This fact, along with the state's popularity as a tourist spot, may have prompted the increasing level of accessibility in Hawaii. In a recent in-depth article assessing the impact of the ADA in Hawaii, journalist Andrew Gomes spoke with many Islanders such as Paul Sheriff, a person with disabilities and an ADA consultant, who "says that of all the cities he has visited recently—Los Angeles, San Francisco, Seattle, Denver, New Orleans, Minneapolis, Chicago, Washington and New York—Honolulu is the most accessible."[70] Bob Peterson, the president of Peterson Sign Co., also in Hawaii, admits that he initially questioned the helpfulness of the law, even though he himself has made ADA-compliant signs. But today he notices an increasing number of people who are blind or in wheelchairs out in the community. "I think that says something about the ADA law. I think it allows people to get out and do more things, he said."[71]

---

68 DOJ, "Faces of the ADA" *at* http://www.usdoj.gov/crt/ada/fhawaii2.htm (Sept. 19, 2000).

69 *Id.*

70 Andrew Gomes, "Hawai'i Makes Headway in Conforming to Disability Act," *Honolulu Advertiser* (Sept. 17, 2000), available *at* wysiwyg://17/http://the.honoluluad . . . com/2000/Sep/17/917business1.html (Sept. 21, 2000).

71 *Id.*

Another popular vacation state is Alaska, where the possibility of litigation under the ADA has played a critical part in achieving increased accessibility. Janel Wright is a staff attorney with the Disability Law Center of Alaska, one of the state's protection and advocacy agencies. The very ambitious "ramp project" was run in two stages by herself and a fellow staff attorney in 1995. Each stage began with the identification of public accommodations that had failed to meet their ADA obligation to ensure architectural accessibility, and in particular, had failed to remove barriers caused by having steps. The next step involved sending a letter to each public accommodation, informing it of its ADA obligation and asking for some indication of how the business planned to meet this obligation. If a business failed to reply in a responsible manner, a second letter would be sent, after which Wright would make the decision to file an administrative complaint or lawsuit if the business still refused to take action. To date, the project has resulted in approximately 140 ramps being built in business establishments across the state.

In Phase One of the project, 62 letters were sent out, resulting in a total of 38 ramps being built. Not all of these were achieved through voluntary compliance with the initial letter. Wright had to file administrative complaints against 12 of those 38 businesses, two of which then promised to build ramps and eventually did. Of the remainder that had been sent a letter, five provided alternative service, 12 already had access but no visible signage indicating this to be the case, and seven were determined to be in compliance for other reasons. In Phase Two, 271 letters were sent out. 85 of the establishments responded with voluntary compliance, 19 provided alternative service, six posted signage about existing accessibility, and 33 were determined to be in compliance for other reasons. Wright filed lawsuits against 19 of the businesses (a number of the cases are still open), and most of these were resolved through a consent decree in which the businesses agreed not only to provide a ramp, but also to pay attorney's fees.

The initiative for the ramp project came from Jesse Owens, a professor at the University of Alaska who has used a wheelchair since a snowmobile accident some years ago, and has remained very active outdoors. Wright explains:

> He would be so frustrated because he would be traveling on the highway system in Alaska, and go through a town like Glen Allen, between Anchorage and Valdez, and he would not be able to get in anywhere to go to the restroom or get a bite to eat. He came to our office, where we shared his interest in pursuing compliance from businesses on the highway systems. From there, it grew, and he has been our plaintiff in 15 of the 19 law suits. . . . He is not doing this to cause any kind of financial hardship to a business, he just wants access.[72]

Wright realizes the important place that litigation has in the scheme of the ADA. While some of the letters prompted awareness and swift compliance on the part of the public accommodation, a number of others "fought everything every step of the way." Phase Two of the project received a lot of media coverage, tracking lawsuits as they were each filed about two weeks apart. Wright reports that two of the recalcitrant businesses targeted for a lawsuit eventually called and said that they were looking into building a ramp, but only after *15* other lawsuits had already been filed. Furthermore, lawsuits—or at least their potential—seem to do more to publicize the fact of the law than any number of technical assistance publications. Wright notes that "a lot of businesses [which] might not have received a letter, but were next door to a business that did receive a letter, built a ramp as well." She adds that Alaska's "state statutes have protection for people with disabilities, but that is not something that people look to for enforcement. It's great to have the ADA to supplement and complement that [state] law." Wright also believes that the project "changed some attitudes in this state, which is a huge accomplishment."[73]

Jim Beck, a resident of Alaska who has done considerable work in developing state-wide ADA training and technical assistance, and who also played a part in the ramp project, describes it in these terms:

> It didn't necessarily generate a lot of good will, but it wasn't about good will. We wanted to get ramps built. We were not try-

---

72 Personal telephone interview (Oct. 17, 2000).

73 *Id.*

> ing to get businesses to feel good about what they had not done. . . . When I drive around in the area where I live, which is an hour north of Anchorage and much more rural, I see businesses building ramps, and they are doing it because they have heard of this project and because they don't want to get sued. We would rather have them doing it because they want to, but the result is that these places are becoming accessible. I'm seeing new ramps built on old buildings. It's amazing.[74]

Beck has an equally clear opinion about the benefit of having a law like the ADA: "We can write a letter now, and know that we have some backup. Without that, it's a charity case. The issues don't get approached with the seriousness that they deserve when it's a charity case. Now it's a civil rights issue, and we wouldn't have that without the law behind us." Beck sums up the law in an apt metaphor that also acknowledges those businesses that readily complied with the ramp project letters: "It's nice to have the tool, and the tool is not always a club. . . ."[75]

James Terry, a partner in the architecture firm of Evan Terry and Associates in Birmingham, Alabama, provides a contrast to many of the advocates and attorneys profiled above. Having worked as a facilities and program accessibility consultant all over the country, both for DOJ and for private corporations, Terry is fully aware and supportive of the ADA as a civil rights law, but what really fires his enthusiasm for the ADA is the still little-known fact that accessibility compliance can be a good business investment. He has seen numerous clients come to understand this fact, but only after making the changes required by the ADA. He explains:

> Most people don't know the demographics. The number of people with disabilities is increasing every year. Most people just haven't thought through the benefits of accommodating people with disabilities. They haven't thought of the ripple effect to others who also benefit. . . . For example, people eat in restaurants in groups of 2 to 4. The person in the group with a dis-

---

[74] Personal telephone interview (Oct. 13, 2000).

[75] *Id.*

> ability will likely get to choose the place where they will eat because everyone wants everyone else to be comfortable. For the establishment that can accommodate the disability, the result is not one additional customer with a disability, but any number of additional customers.[76]

Terry also talks about the unexpected benefits of barrier removal. One client installed automatic doors at a cost of $10,000.00 per door. By the time six months had passed, the doors were receiving steadily increasing traffic—people leaving with multiple packages, people with strollers, people with disabilities, elderly people and their families. As a result, the client decided to install automatic doors in other stores in their retail chain. Another large well-known retailer decided to lower portions of all its counters as an ADA accommodation. It received numerous appreciative comments from customers about the increased comfort and experience of the lowered counters, but most of these comments came not from people with disabilities, but from non-disabled customers who happened to be short. Yet another client, a bank, made the decision to offer Braille bank statements, both as an ADA accommodation and as an incentive for blind people to switch banks. The unanticipated result was that they gained customers drawn not only from among blind people who no longer had to rely on someone else to read them their bank statement, but among those family members and friends who had once had to do the reading, and were appreciative of the newfound independence that Braille statements afforded blind people.

When asked if he thought businesses had become more aware of the investment possibilities of accommodation over the last ten years, Terry replied:

> Yes. What we are finding is that companies, particularly companies who complied early, are discovering that it was money well spent. The return on their money often did not come from where they thought it was going to come from, and they didn't see the ADA as an investment to start with—they thought of it as an expense—but it turned out to be a [good] investment with

---

76 Personal telephone interview (Oct. 6, 2000).

> far wider and more beneficial ramifications than they had expected. The fact is, everyone needed the stick, the carrot, the incentive [to make accommodations].[77]

Another area of significant activity under Title III is access to sports facilities. Before the ADA, people with disabilities encountered many barriers that inhibited their equal enjoyment of sports events: a lack of seating, poor sight lines, and difficulty sitting next to the friends they came with. Even when seating was available, it was frequently isolated, so that wheelchair or mobility aid users could not share the feeling of being part of the crowd as it roots for a particular team or shares admiration for a favorite athlete. Lee Page, a wheelchair user from Virginia, recalls a personal experience from attending ball games in stadiums built before the ADA came into effect:

> All the accessible seating was located in the end zone part of the stadium. Wheelchair users sat up on a cement slab with a railing in front. Your companion, the person you came to the event with, would sit in a fixed seat in front of you and the railing, but at a much lower level. I didn't really feel part of the crowd and it was difficult to interact with my friend.[78]

Even such newly constructed sporting facilities as the venues planned for the 1996 Olympic and Paralympic Games in Atlanta failed to provide integrated seating and full accessibility. However, the ADA gave DOJ the capacity to redress the situation in Atlanta. After investigating complaints filed by people with disabilities, DOJ entered into agreements concerning five newly constructed venues. Under the agreements, the venues were required to (i) designate a least one percent of their total seats for wheelchair users and ensure that these seats were dispersed throughout the stadium; (ii) ensure that accessible seats provided lines of sight comparable to those given other spectators, even if the spectators in front of those seats stood; and (iii) provide a companion seat adjacent to each wheelchair space, so that people with disabil-

---

[77] *Id.*

[78] DOJ, "Faces of the ADA" *at* http://www.usdoj.gov/crt/ada/fpage.htm (Sept. 19, 2000).

ities could watch events next to family and friends. For Page, attending the opening ceremonies of the Paralympics in Atlanta "was a very emotional and fulfilling night. I finally felt like a part of the crowd."[79]

In movie theaters, the ADA has also been interpreted to require adjacent companion seats in addition to accessible seats. The formal consent decree entered between DOJ and United Artists Theater Circuit, Inc., one of the country's largest theater chains, addressed barrier removal at existing theaters as well as the barrier-free construction of new theaters at over 400 locations. In existing theaters, United Artists was required to provide the same number of wheelchair seating spaces that would be required in newly constructed auditoriums of a comparable size, with companion seating beside these spaces. Also, at least 1 percent of the total number of aisle seats was required to have folding or removable aisle-side armrests, thereby offering another integrated seating choice. All newly constructed theaters that had been designed for first occupancy after January 26, 1993, were to be fully ADA compliant no later than June 30, 1997, and future construction had to fully comply.[80]

D. PEOPLE TO CALL

One of the biggest limitations placed on the social, economic and physical well-being of people with disabilities has been telephone inaccessibility. The two primary requirements set by Title IV of the ADA for telecommunications accessibility for individuals with hearing impairments are the provision of telecommunications relay services, and the closed captioning of all federally-funded TV public service announcements.[81] The Act requires all common carriers (telephone companies) to provide intra- and interstate telecommunications relay services (TRSs) by July 26, 1993. These services enable people with teletypewriters (TTY's) to initiate or receive telephone calls even when the other party does not have TTY equipment. Use of the TTY (a device that functions like a typewriter with a message display) enables a person with

---

79 *Id.*

80 DOJ, *Enforcing the ADA, supra* note 64, at 19–20.

81 47 U.S.C.A. § 225; *see also* Golden *et al., supra* note 4, at 189–93.

a speech or hearing impairment to send and receive coded signals over telephone lines. The TRS provides trained operators who act as intermediaries between a caller who is using a TTY and one who is not. The operator can receive a TTY message and relay it by voice, and then relay the response back via TTY to a deaf person, or simply let a speech-impaired person listen to the voice of the other party. Alternatively, a deaf person may choose to speak directly to someone, and only require relay services to receive responses. TRSs are subject to strict service requirements regarding availability. No restrictions are allowed on the length, type or number of calls made by any relay user. The overarching goal of the service is "functional equivalence" with voice telecommunication, and relay users must have the same choice of long distance carriers that voice telephone users have, at rates that are comparable to any direct dialed call of the same length and dialing origin/destination.

The TRS requirement established by the ADA has made the phone system in the United States truly accessible for the first time to speech and hearing-impaired people throughout the country. Given the fact that Alexander Graham Bell first invented the telephone in 1876,[82] and considering the absolutely critical role that has been held by the telephone in all aspects of contemporary society ever since, the TRS amounts to nothing short of a revolution for deaf and speech-impaired people. Karen Peltz Strauss, the Deputy Bureau Chief of the Federal Communication Commission's (FCC) Consumer Information Bureau, speaks of the tremendous difference that access to the telephone made when deaf people could use the telephone to order pizza, gather and compare insurance prices, and set up employment interviews. "It created freedom, independence, autonomy, and all kinds of new worlds in employment, education and entertainment. [People with hearing and speech impairments] became an economic force, both by removing themselves

---

82 Bell's first work in the United States consisted of lecturing and demonstrating in Boston a method for teaching speech to the deaf that was first developed by his father. Apart from Bell's lifelong association with the hearing impaired, he never remained with any single project for long, so it is singularly ironic that the invention with which he is most associated has functioned to the exclusion of the deaf for over a century: 1999–2000 Britannica.comInc (Nov. 28, 2000).

from being a drain on the system, and by becoming consumers themselves through ordering and buying."[83]

Peltz Strauss describes the pre-ADA situation as one in which perhaps 20 states had initiated relay systems, most of which were inadequate, underfunded and severely limited. For example, calls could only be made at certain times for certain purposes and for limited periods, and even so, there were "no guarantees." In such a situation, a deaf person's ability to call friends or family members who lived in other parts of the country, let alone within the same state, was severely restricted. Peltz Srauss applauds the open-ended "functional equivalence" criterion for the TRS, since it not only guarantees a baseline standard of service and availability, it also means that telecommunications for deaf people will continue to improve technologically in an effort to reach the efficiency of voice-based technologies. As an example, she cites the latest order issued by the FCC regarding new relay services, in which such new technologies as video relays (featuring sign-language interpreters at remote locations) and Speech-to-Speech relay (featuring operators trained to comprehend individuals with speech impairments, so that both the operator and the third party can hear the actual voice of a speech impaired caller) have been approved. Peltz Strauss is also realistic about the fact that relay services attained their pinnacle of use for only the three or four years that followed full implementation on July 26, 1993, the ADA's effective date for relay services. After that, more affluent and educated hearing-impaired people increasingly moved to the use of e-mail. She believes that "technology and education is the future," and warns that we need to ensure that the initially accessible technology of computers does not become *in*accessible to individuals with hearing and vision impairment as computers increasingly incorporate the extensive use of graphics and audio.

Shelley Bergum, Executive Director of the Deaf and Disabled Telecommunications Program of the California Relay Service (one of the few state relay services recognized by Peltz Strauss as functional even before the ADA), agrees with Peltz Strauss' assessment of the impact of TRSs:

---

[83] Personal interview (Oct. 22, 2000).

> Telecommunications Relay Services (TRS) have made a *huge* difference in the lives, both personally and professionally, of deaf people and people with speech disabilities. The California Relay Service (CRS), which began in 1987, was the first statewide 24 hour, 7 day a week relay service in the country. Before CRS, deaf people had to rely on friends, family members, or interpreters to make telephone calls for them to anyone who did not have a TTY. With CRS, deaf people can now be completely independent in their use of the telephone. . . . We have heard many stories from consumers who say that they had never used the phone independently before, and now they can call anyone they want. One user told us that because of Speech-to-Speech service, she now plans to attend law school.[84]

Bergum also praises the standard of "functional equivalence" imbedded in the ADA's telecommunications requirements. She believes that the FCC has established a positive standard for interpreting and enforcing the ADA as a civil rights statute, and endorses their effort:

> to provide telecommunications services to people with disabilities that are functionally equivalent to those provided to all other telecommunications service consumers, and not just to provide the ability to use the telephone or make a phone call. In this area, technology truly is driving how functional equivalence can be provided, and the FCC's regulations have to keep up with that.[85]

TRSs indisputably need to keep up with technology, but for people with hearing and speech impairments and members of their family, the simple ability to pick up a phone and make a call remains a miracle. The National Council on Disability describes a woman at the Arkansas town meeting who reported that she had never used a telephone in her life. She was excited about the relay system: 'Now I can talk on the phone all I want.'" In another town meeting, Mark Palmer,

---

[84] E-mail communication sent in response to authors' questions (Oct. 19, 2000).

[85] *Id.*

the son of deaf parents:

> described the pressure he felt growing up having to hear and speak for his parents. In medical situations, with merchants, with the police, on the phone, even when he was sick, he was continually thrust into the adult role of having to take care of his parents' needs. Palmer recounted how difficult it was to make phone calls for his parents: "People often wouldn't respond to me because they knew I was a kid." But today the situation is much improved. Palmer's parents use the relay services, and they watch captioned TV: "I am no longer required to make sure my parents' needs are met because they can do it themselves!"[86]

E. JUST LIKE EVERYONE ELSE

Most people in America take for granted the ability to accomplish their many daily and weekly errands. Yet people with disabilities are often prevented from performing these common activities, and must therefore forego a great deal of community interaction, because of thoughtless or needlessly restrictive structural or systemic barriers. Grocery stores frequently place cart corral rails at every entrance that are less than 32 inches apart, and as a result, wheelchair users cannot do their own grocery shopping.[87] Businesses often refuse to accept payment by personal check unless the customer can corroborate his or her identity with a driver's license, so some individuals whose seizure disorders are such that they are prevented from getting a driver's license can not pay for purchases with their personal checks.[88] People with disabilities are not asking for anything extraordinary when they want to shop for groceries, watch their children play with their peers, move into a neighborhood, or go to college. They merely want to live their lives like everyone else, and just as the ADA prohibits structural and communications barriers, it also operates to dismantle the social discrimination that prevents people with disabilities from achieving this simple goal. This section looks

---

86 *Voices of Freedom, supra* note 58.

87 DOJ, *Enforcing the ADA, supra* note 64, at 16.

88 *Id.* at 13.

at how the benefits of the ADA extend beyond the tangible realms of transportation, architecture, and communication.

Jeremy Orr, a nine year old with multiple disabilities, attended an after school program at a California KinderCare center, where "he was treated like other children. . . . Jeremy attended the field trips and participated in other children's parties at the center, and even got invited to a few parties outside of the center."[89] After several months, Jeremy's parents were told that his disabilities prevented him from participating in KinderCare activities in the same manner as other children in the program. KinderCare would neither let Jeremy attend their program nor make any kind of modification for an aide (provided by Jeremy's parents and paid for through State funds).[90] Jeremy's parents filed a lawsuit under the ADA, supported by a DOJ amicus brief. The case was eventually settled and KinderCare changed its policy and admitted Jeremy back into its program, with his aide. His mother, Sherry Johnson, describes the kinds of interaction with his peers that any loving parent would desire for his or her child:

> As a parent, the biggest benefit I received was in the day to day observation of his inclusion and acceptance by other children during the time he attended the center. Whether it was the time he came to the table to join some younger children in a coloring project and one girl remarked "Where is his walking chair?" or whether it was sitting behind the boys playing computer games and their suggestion that it was his turn to play. Jeremy was their friend and part of their day to day activities.[91]

---

[89] DOJ, "Faces of the ADA" *at* http://www.usdoj.gov/crt/ada/fjerorr.htm (Sept. 19, 2000).

[90] A daycare's refusal to allow its staff to perform even the simplest of medical therapeutic procedures required by children with disabilities (such as the finger-prick test for diabetes) is a closely related example of the kind of discriminatory acts which prevent children with disabilities from entering daycare programs. *See* DREDF's settlement agreement with KinderCare Learning Centers, Inc., in which Kindercare agreed to admit children with diabetes and monitor their blood glucose levels when asked to do so: Stuthard v. Kindercare, Civ. No. C2-96-0185 (N.D. Ohio) (Dismissal Based on Settlement Agreement 8/22/96).

[91] DOJ, "Faces of the ADA," *supra* note 89.

The U.S. Supreme Court heard *Olmstead v. L.C. Zimring*[92] in its 1998–99 term, and issued an opinion that finally addressed the issue of discrimination raised by the placement of individuals with mental disabilities in institutions rather than community settings. The NCD describes the decision as:

> the most significant ADA decision acknowledging that unjustified isolation is a form of discrimination under the ADA's integration mandate. The *L.C.* decision expands options for individuals who are currently in state mental institutions because it affirms a right for an individual to receive community-based services. As the Court noted: "Institutional placement of people who can handle and benefit from community settings perpetuates unwarranted assumptions that people so isolated are incapable or unworthy of participating in community life and cultural enrichment."[93]

The Supreme Court's endorsement of community integration does carry conditions, however. The professional health staff must agree that community placements are appropriate, the affected individual must not oppose community placement, and State defendants may raise a cost-based defense against the immediate community placement of the affected individual. More positively, the decision also clearly indicated that the waiting lists for people to move from institutions into the community must move at a reasonable pace, and the reasonableness of the pace could not be dictated by the State's endeavors to keep its institutions fully populated.

In Arlington, Virginia, the EndDependence Center of Northern Virginia is a part of the Independent Living Movement, which provides

---

[92] 527 U.S. 581, 119 S. Ct. 2176.

[93] NCD, *National Disability Policy: A Progress Report* (Nov. 1, 1998—Nov. 19, 1999) *at* http://www.NCDprogrep_11-19–00.html (Oct. 16, 2000), quoting from 527 U.S. 581, 600. In finding discrimination, a majority of the Supreme Court specified that "confinement in an institution severely diminishes the everyday life activities of individuals, including family relations, social contacts, work options, economic independence, educational advancement, and cultural enrichment." *Id.* at 600.

resources for and empowers people with disabilities to live independently. Michael Cooper, the first volunteer on the President's Task Force on Disability and a person with a mental disability himself, has been the Executive Director of the Center since 1995. He tells of the Center's search for a rental location in the summer of 1998. The Center had been having difficulty finding a site for its offices after a search of some length, and attempted to lease office space in a Rosslyn, Virginia building owned by TrizecHahn Corporation, a Canadian-based commercial real estate corporation with holdings in every continent. Initially, the leasing agent was very enthusiastic about the Center, which was an established non-profit organization with an excellent tenant record, good credit, and long-standing support sources; the Center was even asked to consider "moving in on short notice." This situation changed abruptly after two Board members arrived in power wheelchairs to look at the prospective property. TrizecHahn's leasing agent "refused to enter into any negotiations with the [C]enter, and instead, simply refused to lease the space to the [C]enter solely because the [C]enter serves people with disabilities"[94]; Cooper was told the company wanted "a more standard lessee." The Center filed a complaint with DOJ in 1998, and won an out of court agreement on April 7, 1999, whereby TrizecHahn agreed to pay $560,000 in damages ($550,000 to the Center and $10,000 in civil penalties to the federal government). Cooper is certain that "the only way we were successful in addressing our concerns was because of DOJ's intervention." TrizecHahn is a multinational corporation, and even though its actions also violated a local human rights ordinance and state law, Cooper believes the real authority came from the federal legislation:

> The ADA is a profoundly important piece of civil rights legislation. It was the first time Congress recognized that there was a persistent, longstanding pattern of discrimination against [people with disabilities as] a segment of the American people. Everything that we've accomplished since then is because of the ADA.[95]

---

[94] DOJ Press Release, "Corporate Leasing Agency to No Longer Discriminate Against People with Disabilities, under Justice Department Agreement" (Apr. 7, 1999) at 1–2.

[95] Personal interview (Oct. 26, 2000).

The Center moved into its present location in January 1999, after taking out a loan to ensure that the Center would be completely accessible. The monthly investment income from the TrizecHahn settlement award is being used to pay off the loan. When Cooper describes the Center's technical and structural innovations, its ability to serve a clientele with disabilities that vary from Downs Syndrome to environmental disorders, and its present location right on the accessible Metro, he speaks with the conviction of someone who knows the urgent need for building communities that are free from barriers of any kind.

Jackie Okin, a student at the American University School of Law, had her first direct encounter with the ADA as a high school student. Since Okin has cerebral palsy, she needed an accommodation to take the SAT exams that are a prerequisite for entrance into college. When Okin discovered that the SAT exams were offered on several dates for students who did not require an accommodation, but only once for her, she filed a complaint with DOJ. After a federal investigation, the Educational Testing Service and the College Entrance Examination Board agreed to increase the availability of the SAT exam to students with disabilities. Okin's words reveal how much she is the product of a world that has already been altered by the ADA:

> I often take the ADA for granted and forget that my life would be completely different if the law did not exist. There is no question that, without the ADA, I would not have been able to get a college education and pursue my dream of being an attorney. Yet, the idea of not being able to accomplish these goals because of discrimination is a foreign concept to me because of the ADA. I was only thirteen when the law was passed. I have been extremely fortunate to grow up in a society where my rights have been protected. . . . Despite the tremendous strides that have been made in this country as a result of the ADA, there is still a great deal that needs to be done. I plan to be a disability rights attorney. Not only because I believe there is no reason for discrimination, but also because I feel a responsibility to ensure that others have the same opportunities that I had. I may never be able to personally thank all the people who are responsible for the passage of the ADA; perhaps if I am able to

ensure that their legacy is maintained, then my gratitude will be sufficiently expressed.[96]

F. A CIVIL RIGHTS TOOL

When Jackie Okin expresses her intention of becoming a disability rights lawyer so that she can help preserve and fortify the gains that have been made against disability discrimination, she implicitly pays tribute to the role that civil rights law has played in the battle for equality in this country. The ADA was only achieved after decades of tireless advocacy, and the ADA's enactment can clearly be traced to numerous pivotal anti-discrimination laws enacted over the last 36 years. The Civil Rights Act of 1964 did not include people with disabilities within its ambit, but it did provide a legislative and regulatory model for all subsequent federal civil rights laws, including the ADA. The Rehabilitation Act of 1973[97] was the first federal act to take the civil rights/anti-discrimination approach developed in racial and gender laws into the area of disability, and prohibited discrimination against people with disabilities in federally funded programs and activities.[98] By the mid-1970s, the civil rights emphasis on equal treatment and insistence on integration was even more firmly entrenched in disability legislation with the passage of the Education for All Handicapped Children Act in 1975,[99] now known as the Individuals with Disabilities Education Act. The late 1980s saw a further wave of civil rights legislation relating to people

---

[96] DOJ, "Faces of the ADA" *at* http://www.usdoj.gov/crt/ada/fokin.htm (Sept. 19, 2000).

[97] Title V of the Rehabilitation Act of 1973, 29 U.S.C.A. §§ 701–97.

[98] Part of the ADA can be considered a direct extension of Section 504 of the Rehabilitation Act of 1973, since the later statute's Title II extends the ban on discrimination "to all programs, activities, and services provided or made available by state or local governments or instrumentalities or agencies thereof, regardless of whether or not such entities receive federal financial assistance": Richard Landfield, "Enforcement of Rights Under the ADA," *in Accessibility Under the Americans with Disabilities Act and Other Laws, supra* note 63, 118 at 137. *See also* Chris Palames, "Accessibility Codes and Statutes in the United States from WW II to the ADA," *in* Slavitt & Pugh, *id.* at 5–18.

[99] 20 U.S.C. §§ 1232, 1401, 1405–1420, 1453.

with disabilities, beginning with the enactment of the 1986 Air Carriers Access Act, and the Fair Housing Amendments Act of 1988,[100] which amended the 1968 Fair Housing Act by adding people with disabilities to the classes of people protected against discrimination in the rental or purchase of private housing. The enactment of the ADA in 1990 was the federal government's response to an increasingly vocal and empowered disability community, and "is as much a capstone to earlier disability rights policies as it is a bold venture to place the federal government at the forefront of the 'last civil rights movement'."[101]

The private right of action lies at the heart of civil rights enforcement, and this fact has been recognized in relation to the ADA both negatively and positively. When the ADA was first enacted, the private business community frequently warned of expensive, abundant and unnecessary lawsuits—presumably brought by over-litigious members of the disability community.[102] As of 1995, these fears proved to have been unwarranted; "less than 1/100th of a percent of cases in federal court were ADA cases."[103] More recently, a summary of federal ADA enforcement cites numerous examples of inaccurate print and electronic media coverage of ADA litigation: questionable actions are reported without mention of their dismissal, and controversial claims are

---

[100] 42 U.S.C. §§ 3601–3619.

[101] S. Percy, "ADA, Disability Rights, and Evolving Regulatory Federalism," 23 *Publius: The Journal of Federalism* 87 (1993).

[102] Under Titles II and III of the ADA, people with disabilities have a private right of action if they experience (or believe they will or could experience) discrimination prohibited by the ADA. For Title III, *see* 42 U.S.C.A. § 12188(a), *see also* 28 C.F.R. § 36.501(a) and § 36.201(a). For Title II, a private right of action is inferred from the ADA's incorporation by reference (in 42 U.S.C.A. § 12133) of the procedures and remedies available under Section 504 of the Rehabilitation Act, 29 U.S.C. § 794(a). Section 504, in its turn, refers to the remedies and procedures originally set forth in Title VI of the Civil Rights Act of 1964, 42 U.S.C. §§ 2000 *et seq.*, the first federal statute to prohibit discrimination on the basis of race, color or national origin in federally funded programs. Note: some aspects of a private right of action under Title II have been ruled unconstitutional by the U.S. Supreme Court in a decision heard in the fall of 2000—*see* Board of Trustees of the University of Alabama v. Garrett, 531 U.S. 356 (2001).

[103] West, "Editor's Note," *in Implementing the ADA, supra* note 6, at 30.

presented without any context or comparison with the complaints and results achieved under civil rights laws for racial minorities or women.[104] On the other hand, litigation is undoubtedly critical to the effectiveness of the ADA, and some authors have acknowledged this without sensationalism. "ADA litigation shows the fundamental impact of disability law on American law and society. The litigation effectuates the two primary purposes of the act: prohibiting discrimination in civil society and dismantling barriers to full participation. It also has the potential to do much more. . . ."[105] Disability advocates also recognize the need for litigation as a tool. John Gaffney, for example, singled out the creation of national standards and "the ability of individuals to sue" as the most valuable theoretical achievements of the ADA in transportation.[106]

One critical distinction between litigation under the ADA and litigation undertaken under the auspices of more traditional welfare-oriented legislation is that under the ADA, the focus should not be on who "deserves" benefits,[107] but on requiring states, institutions and businesses to face real consequences for their own discriminatory conduct. The fact is, the bringing of lawsuits is not the central point of the ADA, any more than the enactment of laws is the ultimate goal of the disability movement. For centuries people with disabilities all over the world have been left economically powerless, physically and socially isolated, and bereft of the most common opportunities of daily life because of discrimination arising from false assumptions about their needs, desires and worth, as well as the persistent presence of structural, communication and other

---

[104] National Council on Disability, *Promises to Keep: A Decade of Federal Enforcement of the Americans with Disabilities Act* (Washington: National Council on Disability, June 27, 2000), 379–83.

[105] Lawrence O Gostin, "Litigation Review" in *Implementing the ADA, supra* note 6, 29 at 63.

[106] Gaffney interview, *supra* note 16.

[107] Unfortunately, the role that courts have traditionally played as "gatekeepers" to welfare benefits for people with disabilities has seeped into judicial interpretation of the ADA. The Supreme Court has insisted that anyone claiming rights under the ADA must first establish that he or she is a "person with a disability," but has simultaneously narrowed and strictly interpreted what constitutes a disability under the ADA, *see* Sutton v. United Airlines, Inc., 119 S. Ct. 2139 (1999); Toyota Motor Mfg., Inc., v. Williams, 122 S. Ct. 681 (2002).

barriers. The ADA was enacted to redress this situation in the United States, and the abolishment of discrimination in all of our human interactions and personal decisions is the broader purpose for which the law remains a tool. Furthermore, since the ADA is directed specifically towards the urgent need to prohibit discriminatory effects, the attitude *behind* discrimination—whether one of conscious ill will, negligence, or mere benign ignorance—is not particularly relevant to the law's operation.[108] This does not mean, however, that the act's supporters are unconcerned with such attitudes, or that the legislation will not ultimately have an effect upon society's understanding of disability. Disability advocates merely reject the contention that lasting or substantial change can be initiated only changing attitudes. Nor do they believe that attitudes will ever change if people with disabilities cannot get out of their homes, and are limited to the tools of charitable appeal or civil disobedience.

Arthur Lopez, who heads the Federal Transit Administration's Office of Civil Rights, makes an analogy between the symbolic importance of achieving visible transportation accessibility under the ADA and the racial desegregation of buses in the 1960s. Lopez asserts that the "bad people" in the racial segregation cases—those who resisted serving racial minorities or fought against legal change—did not all simply "go away" when desegregation became law. He says: "First off, they weren't 'bad' [in the sense of being personally evil], and second, those same people went on to make it possible for desegregation to occur."[109] ADA compliance means that people who have not made up their minds to be either heroes or villains must at least act without discrimination; in the process, equality stops being an abstract duty with no reward, and assumes form and substance in the person with a disability who is now your passenger, classmate or neighbor. This process does not happen quickly or easily, but it can at least begin with a law.

---

[108] This very fact has raised constitutional issues concerning the extent to which Title II may be applied to states; *see* Board of Trustees of the University of Alabama v. Garrett, 531 U.S. 356 (2001); *see also* discussion in Part B (The U.S. Model of Equality) of "The ADA and Models of Equality," *infra*, Part III.

[109] Personal telephone interview (Oct. 6, 2000).

Janel Wright makes a similar point when asked whether she sensed any lingering resentment from the business community over the ramp program lawsuits:

> I think there are always going to be individuals out there who own businesses and have the attitude that I'm a "filthy, scum-sucking lawyer" because I'm trying to protect someone's civil rights, and make businesses do something as a result. But even beyond that, I think there is a lot of resentment and misunderstanding in society. I have discussions with people all the time about why access is necessary. They'll say "Well, they [people with disabilities] don't need to get there, they can go somewhere else." I'll answer "That's like saying you don't need to go in there because you're black, or you don't need to go in there because you're a woman." When I make that comparison, it gets through to them quicker than trying to explain: "This person has a disability and uses a wheelchair, so steps are not acceptable. They need to get into this business. To deny them access is like putting a sign up [saying 'disabled not allowed']." For some reason, it doesn't click until I make the comparison to denying access to an individual because they're black or a woman or another minority group who has "been there." . . . The other minority groups have been in the public consciousness since 1964 [the enactment of the Civil Rights Act], over 30 years ago. The ADA is just 10 years old, so we have a long way to go.[110]

The fact that people can relate to the ADA better through a comparison to older civil rights movements rather than hearing a rational explanation reveals something about both how long it takes for non-discrimination to *feel* like the right thing to do, and how difficult it is for the benefits of integration to be understood until personally experienced.

Marilyn Golden saw this firsthand when, in the capacity of a transportation accessibility advisor, she met with two individuals in Capetown, South Africa who were among South Africa's planning committee for the country's bid for the Olympic Games. The two South Africans

---

[110] Wright interview, *supra* note 72.

had visited the 1996 Games in Atlanta where, among other things, they had attended an event held in a remote location. A fully accessible shuttle provided transportation to the event, and when they boarded, they noticed that one of their fellow passengers was a person with a disability who rode with them to the event, enjoyed it with everyone else, and then came back on the shuttle. They told Golden: "We have never seen this happen on public transportation in any country we have been in." For Golden,

> [i]t was truly amazing to hear people from a country halfway around the world comment on how impressive it was to see what it means when things are accessible. They saw that a person who was not an organizer or an advocate or someone with any special status, could go to see the Olympics like everyone else—just because he wanted to. . . . It's hard for people to understand what integration really means, not in a theoretical sense but in a real sense. It should be easy to conceive of it by hearing about it but the full human impact can't be understood, sometimes, until it is actually witnessed.[111]

The vivid impact of a personal experience with integration is inestimable, but it still takes time to change attitudes, and the slow process is only exacerbated by the fact that full compliance also takes time. As advocates, people with disabilities, and professionals who work with the act every day, every one of the individuals interviewed for this paper could tell of places and occasions where compliance has fallen short: segments of the transportation system that are not yet accessible, telephones without TTY capability, property owners looking for a "more standard lessee," or a blind person rejected for jury duty. At the same time, no one interviewed had any difficulty with discussing or remembering particular instances where the ADA had a beneficial effect. Change has not occurred uniformly across the country, but it has undoubtedly occurred and continues to do so. One of the most encouraging observations was made by Jim Beck, who said of accessibility in Alaska: "I've seen more change in the last 3 years than in the previous 7."[112]

---

110 Golden interview, *supra* note 13.

112 Beck interview, *supra* note 74.

As people with disabilities gain increased visibility, interaction and integration in all aspects of American society, the very face and nature of that society is changing. This, in turn, can lead to better laws and further opportunities to achieve equality for all. Michael Cooper mentions Section 508 of the Rehabilitation Act of 1973, a new provision according to which the federal government will not acquire telecommunications equipment unless it is accessible. In Cooper's opinion, it would never have been added without the ADA's strong mandate against disability discrimination.[113] Russell Thatcher believes that as America's "baby boomer" population ages, demographics are eventually going to force the transportation industry to provide transportation for seniors that goes well beyond the service limits currently established by public transportation. He states:

> It's fortunate that the ADA was passed and put into place, because it has placed transit authorities into the position that they need to be in. . . . Without the ADA, they would have been taken totally by surprise. They would still have poor paratransit and inaccessible services, and a huge population, many of whom will be frail and have mobility problems, would not have been served.[114]

Perhaps the most lasting achievement of the ADA is the very fact of its dual identity: it speaks directly to the particulars of barrier removal, accessibility and lawsuits, while simultaneously fostering hope for a much deeper awareness of all the diverse and constituent parts of American society. This is something that it brings to the general public, as well as people with disabilities themselves. Or as Mark Obatake, Executive Director of Hawaii Centers for Independent Living, says:

> This is not a law about disabilities. . . . This is a law—like every other piece of civil rights legislation—about how, as a nation, a state, a community, we can embrace our differences.[115]

---

113 Cooper interview, *supra* note 95.

114 Thatcher interview, *supra* note 40.

115 Gomes, *supra* note 70.

Afterword

Strange as it may seem I am going to begin this afterword with a post-script. As I always do, I sent a draft of this afterward to Mary Lou Breslin for advice. Her comment to me prompts my departure from form. She said, "I have never heard you sound so pessimistic." Mary Lou's comment made me realize how much I have been shaken by negative decisions in the U.S. Supreme Court. I am, indeed, pessimistic about the Court. But I remain wide-eyed and bushy-tailed about the power of the international disability rights movement to make profound changes in not only the way society is structured but in the hearts and minds of people everywhere. The Court's regressive rulings are a big bump in the road to realization of the ADA's promise, but the dedication and power of the movement will not be halted. That said, let me begin.

At the end of my article for this book, *The ADA and Models of Equality*, I wrote that the world was awaiting the U.S. Supreme Court's decision in *Board of Trustees of Univ. of Alabama v. Garrett*, 531 U.S. 356 (2001), the first pronouncement about the Americans with Disabilities Act's (ADA) constitutional underpinnings. Would the Court recognize that the ADA was enacted to give people with disabilities the equal protection of the law, a protection that our country touts as fundamental to our values as a nation? Could people with disabilities successfully build on the civil rights paradigms established for minorities and women? I regret to inform the world that our Supreme Court just does not understand or accept that people with disabilities have a sordid history of state-sponsored persecution, segregation and discrimination in every aspect of civil society, or that Congress had the right to remedy this history in the ADA by applying the law's mandate to states. (*Garrett* only addressed the constitutionality of applying the ADA to State governments. All other applications are intact). It is true that the "state's rights" agenda of the conservative majority of the court is far reaching and goes beyond its decisions on disability. If the *Garrett* case was simply one more decision in this regressive trend, it would not say much about our struggle to have the segregation and exclusion of people with disabilities seen through the civil rights lens. But the Court's decision exposes a much more sinister outlook. The Court's failure to recognize the basic premises of the ADA is revealed throughout the decision. For example, the decision explains that the ADA goes far beyond the equal protection guarantee with this example: "whereas it would be entirely rational (and therefore constitutional) for a state employer to conserve scarce financial resources by hiring employees who are able to use existing facilities, the ADA requires employers to 'mak[e] existing facilities used by employees readily accessible to and usable by individuals with disabilities.'" *Garrett* at 372. There really is no way to put a good interpretive spin on the *Garrett* case. It is deeply troublesome because it rejects the central underpinning of the disability rights as civil rights argument—that equal treatment is not equality. *Garrett* reveals a "let them eat cake" mentality not only in its dismissal of real life experience but also in its callousness.

I wish I could report that *Garrett* is the only bad news from the U.S. Supreme Court, but it is not. It seems that every month there is a new blow. As recently as June, 2002, the Court held in *Chevron U.S.A. Inc. v. Echazabal*, 122 S.Ct. 2045 (2002), that the ADA does not prohibit an employer from firing or refusing to hire a disabled person "for his own good." An employer can decide that the work environment is too risky even if the disabled person can do the job and wants to take the risk. This decision ignores the ADA's legislative history, which emphasized both the importance of self-determination and the invidiousness of paternalism. Those of us that were involved in the drafting and negotiating of the ADA have been shell shocked by these decisions. How could the Court get it so wrong? Or what could we have done to foresee and prevent these decisions that ignore the social-civil rights model of disability which we were confident that we were creating? The Court lags far behind this new consciousness, still seeing disability in medical-charity terms.

So why speak at length about the U.S. Supreme Court when there is so much else happening around the world? When we started to conceive the amazing symposium that generated the papers in this book, we were just starting to get bad decisions on the definition of disability in the ADA. At the same time we were getting visitors from around the world who were using the ADA as a model, a beacon of progressive thinking. We felt an urgency to communicate to our compatriots from around the word what we had learned from our experience with the courts. We wanted to avert, as best we could, the development of new laws that may have the same implementation problems that we have had to face. We thought a symposium was the best way to get the word out to a lot of people from many countries at once. As the planning progressed, it was clear that there were many lessons learned around the world that needed to be shared. During the symposium it became vividly clear that through sharing our experiences, both triumphant and disappointing, we can learn more about how to advance our common cause. The questions are deep and perplexing. Can you have a social safety net and civil rights simultaneously? Can you argue that everyone can work if given the chance and maintain financial benefits for those that are jobless because of disability? Can you keep a protected class concept and still have an expansive definition of disability? Is there a workable definition of disability that does not carry the limiting connotations of the medical model? Are new words necessary? How do we communicate that disability is a social construct having little to do with the impairment of the individual? Should we be pragmatic or idealistic about demands for accommodations? I know that U.S. activists and advocates are asking all of these questions. We learned a lot from our colleagues from around the world at the symposium and continue to thrive on those interactions.

The image of the world that we are trying to create is not fully developed but tremendous headway has been made. At the same time that we see interpretive erosion by the courts, there has been a burgeoning awareness of, and change in attitude about, people with disabilities. Being disabled now is a different experience than before the ADA. Ask any person who uses a wheelchair if the ADA has made a difference in their lives and I think you will hear "yes." As my friends and colleagues who use wheelchairs will be the first to tell you, the ability to use a restroom should never be underestimated. Ask a deaf person what it is like to have a national telecommunications relay system. Ask any school child, employer or owner of a public accommodation if they are aware that people with disabilities are part of our communities, and the answer now is far more likely to be "yes" than before the ADA was enacted . People with highly stigmatized disabilities like mental illness are starting to discuss their disabilities and organize more openly.

The executive director of the American Association of People with Disabilities is a person with bi-polar disorder, representing a new awareness of psychiatric illnesses among people with disabilities as well. The ADA has helped spring a revolution in technology with talking Automated Teller Machines, accessible voting equipment and low floor buses as just a few examples. I also think that the growing recognition of disability as a legitimate area of study in the academy is nurtured by this new awareness, and with that comes a new intellectual environment which will elevate disability issues that were at best marginal before the ADA.

I can not even explain the exhilaration that I felt at the international symposium when I heard about the 48 disability rights laws enacted around the word since the passage of the ADA. The ADA *is* an international word, and disability rights is an international force. As is evident from this book and the many knowledgeable, dedicated, dynamic participants at the conference, our momentum is unstoppable. Societies have and will continue to be transformed. But to build the future and beat the set backs we need each other. Thank you all for being part of this future.

Arlene Mayerson
Berkeley, California
June 2002

Table of International Laws and Instruments

- This table lists international agreements cited by the articles in this book. It includes non-binding documents such as United Nations Declarations and conference agendas, but it does not include interpretive documents such as Comments issued by specific UN bodies or Council of Europe Policy Recommendations. Such additional documents can be important, particularly for people with disabilities who often lack explicit inclusion under general human rights instruments; many key Comments and Recommendations are addressed by individual articles within this volume.
- Laws and instruments are listed alphabetically within each sponsoring organization, beginning with the United Nations, through regional affiliations such as the Council of Europe and the Organization of American States, to topic-specific international non-governmental organizations like the International Labour Organization.
- For an index of selected domestic national laws concerning disability anti-discrimination, see chapters one (Theresia Degener and Gerard Quinn), and two (Aart Hendriks).
- The designation "not published" after a document generally only refers to the lack of official publication in English.

UNITED NATIONS <http://www.unorg>

Convention Against Torture and Other Cruel , Inhuman or Degrading Treatment or Punishment, G.A. Res. 39/46, U.N. GAOR, 39th Sess., Supp. No. 51, Annex, at 197, U.N. Doc. A/39/51 (1984); *opened for signature* 10 December 1984, *entered into force* 26 June 1987; *at* http://www.unhchr.ch/html/menu3/ b/h_cat39.htm.

Convention on the Elimination of All Forms of Discrimination Against Women, G.A. Res. 34/180, U.N. GAOR, 34th Sess., Supp. No. 46, at 193, U.N. Doc. A/34/46 (1979); *opened for signature* 18 December 1979, *entered into force* 3 September 1981; *at* http://www.unhchr.ch/html/menu3/b/e1cedaw.htm.

Convention on the Prevention and Punishment of the Crime of Genocide, G.A. Res. 260A(III), *opened for signature* 9 December 1948, *entered into force* 12 January 1951, 78 U.N.T.S. 277; *at* http://www.unhchr.ch/html/menu3/b/p_genoci.htm.

Convention on the Rights of the Child, G.A. Res. 44/25, U.N. GAOR, 44th Sess., Supp. No. 49, Annex, at 167, U.N. Doc. A/44/49 (1989); *opened for signature* 20 November 1989, *entered into force* 2 September 1990; *at* http://www.unhchr.ch/html/menu3/b/k2crc.htm.

Convention Relating to the Status of Refugees, U.N. Conference of Plenopotentiaries on the Status of Refugees and Stateless Persons convened under G.A. Res. 429(V), *opened for signature* 28 July 1951, *entered into force* 22 April 1954, 189 U.N.T.S. 150; *at* http://www.unhchr.ch/html/menu3/b/o_c_ref.htm.

Declaration on the Rights of Disabled Persons, G.A. Res. 3447 (XXX), U.N. GAOR , 30th Sess., Supp. No. 34, at 88, U.N. Doc. A/10034 (1975); *at* http://www.unhchr.ch/html/menu3/b/72.htm.

Declaration on The Rights of Mentally Retarded Persons, G.A. Res. 2856 (XXVI), U.N. GAOR, 26th Sess., Supp. No. 29, ¶¶ 1,7 at 93, U.N. Doc. A/8429 (1971); *at* http://www.unhchr.ch/html/menu3/b/m_mental.htm.

International Convention on the Elimination of All Forms of Racial Discrimination, G.A. Res. 2106 (XX), U.N. GAOR Sess. 20, Supp. No. 14, at 47, U.N. Doc. A/6014 (1965); *opened for signature* 7 March1966, *entered into force* 4 January 1969, 660 U.N.T.S. 195; *at* http:// www.unhchr.ch/html/menu3/b/d_icerd.htm.

International Covenant on Civil and Political Rights, G.A. Res. 2200A (XXI), U.N. GAOR, 21st Sess., Supp. No. 16, at 52, U.N. Doc. A/6316 (1966); *opened for signature* 16 December 1966; *entered into force* 23 March 1976, 999 & 1057 U.N.T.S. 171 & 407 respectively; *at* http:// www.unhchr.ch/html/menu3/b/a_ccpr.htm.

International Covenant on Economic, Social and Cultural Rights, G.A. Res. 2200A (XXI), U.N. GAOR, 21st Sess., Supp. No. 16, at 49, U.N. Doc. A/6316 (1966); *opened for signature* 16 December 1966, *entered into force* 3 January 1976, 993 U.N.T.S. 3; *at* http:// www.unhchr.ch/html/menu3/b/d_cescr.htm.

Principles for the Protection of Persons with Mental Illness and for the Improvement of Mental Health Care, G.A. Res. 119, U.N. GAOR, 46th Sess., Supp. No. 49, Annex, at 188, U.N. Doc. A/46/49 (1992).

Standard Rules on the Equalization of Opportunities for Persons with Disabilities, G.A. Res. 48/96, U.N. GAOR., 48th Sess., Supp. No. 48, Annex, at 202–11, U.N. Doc. A/Res/48/49 (1993).

Tallinn Guidelines for Action on Human Resources Development in the Field of Disability, G.A. Res. 44/70, U.N. GAOR, 44th Sess., Supp. No. 49, Annex, at 196, U.N. Doc. A/44/49 (1990).

U.N. Charter, 59 Stat. 1031; *opened for signature* 26 June 1945, *entered into force* 24 October 1945; *at* http://www.un.org/aboutun/charter/index.html.

Universal Declaration of Human Rights, G.A. Res. 217 A(III), U.N. Doc. A/810, at 71 (1948); *at* http://www.unhcrh.ch/udhr/index.htm.

Vienna Convention on the Law of Treaties, *opened for signature* 23 May 1969, *entered into force* 27 January 1980, 1155 U.N.T.S. 331; *at* http://www.un.org/law/ilc/texts/treatfra.htm.

Vienna Declaration and Programme of Action, U.N. Doc. A/CONF. 157/23, ¶ 63 (1993).

World Programme of Action Concerning Disabled Persons, U.N. Doc. A/37/351/Add.1, Annex, pp. 19–58; adopted by the U.N. General Assembly at its 37th sess., 9th mtg., U.N. Doc. A/RES/37/52 (3 December 1982).

Proposed Convention on People with Disabilities:
Comprehensive and integral international convention to promote and protect the rights and dignity of persons with disabilities, G.A. Res. 56/119b, U.N. GAOR 3rd Comm., 56 Sess., ¶ 1, U.N. Doc. A/C.3/ 56/L67/Rev.1 (2001).

Resolution to create an Ad Hoc Committee "to consider proposals for a comprehensive and integral international convention to protect and promote the rights and dignity of persons with disabilities," G.A. Res., 56th Sess. [on the report of the 3rd Committee on the draft resolution concerning a comprehensive and integral international convention to promote and protect the rights and dignity of persons with disabilities (A/56/583/Add.2)], U.N. Doc. A/RES/ 56/168 (2001).

Resolution on a comprehensive and integral international Convention to promote and protect the rights and dignity of persons with disabilities, Agenda item 3(b)(ii), adopted at the 40th Sess. of the Committee for Social Development (11–27 February, 2002) available *at* (B).htm.

COUNCIL OF EUROPE <http://www.coe.int>

Convention for the Prevention of Torture and Inhuman or Degrading Treatment or Punishment (1987), *opened for signature* 26 November 1987, *entered into force* 1 February 1989; E.T.S. No. 126.

Convention for the Protection of Human Rights and Dignity of the Human Being with Regard to the Application of Biology and Medicine: Convention on Human Rights and Biomedicine (1997), *opened for signature* 4 April 1997, *entered into force* 1 December 1989; E.T.S. No. 164.

Convention for the Protection of Human Rights and Fundamental Freedoms (1950), *opened for signature* 4 November 1950, *entered into force* 3 September1953; E.T.S. No. 005.

Protocol to the Convention for the Protection of Human Rights and Fundamental Freedoms, *opened for signature* 20 March 1952, *entered into force* 18 May 1954; E.T.S. No. 009.

Convention on Insider Trading, *opened for signature* 20 April 1989, *entered in force* 10 January 1991; E.T.S. No. 130.

Convention on Transfrontier Television, *opened for signature* 5 May 1989, *entered into force* 5 January 1993; E.T.S. No. 132.

European Social Charter, *opened for signature* 18 October 1961, *entered into force* 26 February 1965, E.T.S. No. 035, 529 U.N.T.S. 89.

Additional Protocol to the European Social Charter Providing for a System of Collective Complaints (1995), *opened for signature* 9 November 9, 1995, *entered into force* 7 January 1998; E.T.S. No. 158.

Framework Convention for the Protection of National Minorities, *opened for signature* 1 February 1995, *entered into force* 2 January 1998; E.T.S. No. 157.

Revised European Social Charter (1996), *opened for signature* 3 May 1996, *entered into* *force* 7 January 1999; E.T.S. No. 163.

Statute of the Council of Europe, *opened for signature* 5 May 1949, *entered into force* 3 August, 1949; E.T.S. No. 001.

EUROPEAN UNION/COMMISSION <http://www.europa.eu.int>

Council Directive 76/207/EEC of 9 February 1976 on the implementation of the principle of equal treatment for men and women as regards access to employment, vocational training and promotion, and working conditions, O.J. L39/40 (1976).

Council Directive 2000/43/EC of 29 June 2000 implementing the principle of equal treatment between persons irrespective of racial or ethnic origin, O.J. L180/22 (2000).

Council Directive 2000/78/EC of 27 November 2000 establishing a general framework for equal treatment in employment and occupation [including on the grounds of disability], O.J. L303/16 (2000).

Draft Charter of Fundamental Rights of the European Union, *proposed* 7 December 2000; O.J. C364/1 (2000); *at* .

Treaty of Amsterdam, *opened for signature* 7 October 1997, *entered into force* 1 May 1999; O.J. 1997, C 340.

Treaty on European Union (as amended by the Treaty of Amsterdam), *opened for signature* 7 February 1992, *entered into force* 1 November 1993; O.J. 1997, C 340, 145–72.

Treaty of Nice, *opened for signature* 26 February 2001; O.J. 2001, C 80.

ORGANIZATION OF AFRICAN UNITY

African [Banjul] Charter on Human and Peoples' Rights, OAU Doc. CAB/LEG/67/3 rev. 5; *opened for signature* 27 June 1981, *entered into force* 21 October 1986; 21 I.L.M. 58 (1982).

ORGANIZATION OF AMERICAN STATES <http://www.cidh.org>

American Convention on Human Rights (1969), *opened for signature* 22 November 1969, *entered into force* 18 July 1978; O.A.S. Treaty Series No. 36, 1144 U.N.T.S. 123; *reprinted in* Basic Documents Pertaining to Human Rights in the Inter-American System, OEA/Ser.L.V/II.82 doc. 6 rev.1, at 25 (1992).

Inter-American Convention on the Elimination of Discrimination Against Persons with Disabilities, A.G. Res. 1608 (XXIX–0/99), 29th Sess. of the General Assembly, O.E.A. Doc. OEA/Ser. P AG/doc .3826/99 (1999); *opened for signature* 7 June 1999, *entered into force* 14 September 2001 [not published].

Inter-American Convention on the Prevention, Punishment and Eradication of Violence Against Women, *opened for signature* 9 June 1994, *entered into force* 5 March 1995 [not published].

Inter-American Convention to Prevent and Punish Torture, *opened for signature* 9 December 1985, *entered into force* 28 February 1987; O.A.S. Treaty Series No. 67.

INTERNATIONAL LABOUR ORGANIZATION <http://www.ilo.org/>

Convention Concerning Discrimination in Respect of Employment and Occupation, Convention No. 111 (1958), *opened for signature* 25 June 1958 by the General Conference of the International Labour Organization at its 42nd Session, *entered into force* 25 June 1960; *at* http://www.unhchr.ch/html/menu3/b/d_ilo111.htm.

Convention Concerning Employment Policy, Convention No. 122 (1964), *opened for signature* 9 July 1964 by the General Conference of the ILO at its 48th Session, *entered into force* 15 July 1966; *at* http://www.ilolex.ilo.ch:1567/cgi-lex/convde.pl?query=C122&query0=122 .

Convention Concerning Indigenous and Tribal Peoples in Independent Countries, ILO Convention No. 169, *opened for signature* 27 June 1989, *entered into force* 5 September 1991 (1989); *reprinted* in 28 *Int'l Legal Materials* 1382 (1989); *at* http://www.ilolex.ilo.ch:1567/english/convdisp1.htm.

Convention Concerning Vocational Guidance and Vocational Training in the Development of Human Resources, Convention No. 142 (1975), *opened for signature* 23 June 1975 by the General Conference of the ILO at its 60th Session, *entered into force* 19 July 1977.

Convention Concerning Vocational Rehabilitation and Employment (Disabled Persons), Convention No 159 (1983), *opened for signature* 20 June 1983 by the General Conference of the ILO at its 69th Session, *entered into force* 20 June 1985.

PAN-AMERICAN HEALTH ORGANIZATION

Declaration of Caracas, 42(2) *International Digest of Health Legislation* 336338 (1991); the full text of the Declaration is also reprinted in Itzhak Levav, Helena Restrepo & Caryl Guerra de Macedo, *The Restructuring of Psychiatric Care in Latin America: A New Policy for Mental Health Services* 15 J. PUB. HEALTH AND POLICY 71 (1994).

About the Authors

Mary Lou Breslin co-founded the Disability Rights Education and Defense Fund (DREDF), and currently serves as its Senior Policy Advisor, directing special projects and international law and policy initiatives. She is a lecturer at the University of California, Berkeley, and serves as editor and researcher with the Disabled Persons Independence Project of the Regional Oral History Office of the Bancroft Library, University of California, Berkeley. She has also taught graduate courses at the University of San Francisco, McLaren School of Business. Breslin spearheaded DREDF's leadership in the enactment of such landmark legislation as the 1990 Americans with Disabilities Act (ADA), the Fair Housing Amendments Act, and the Civil Rights Restoration Act. In 1993 she founded the DREDF Development Partnership, a corporation dedicated to supporting and securing DREDF's programs. She has trained, lectured and provided consultation on diverse disability and related civil rights topics to disability rights leaders throughout Europe and Asia. Breslin received the prestigious Henry B. Betts award in 2002 for improving the lives of people with disabilities, the Paul A. Hearne Award from the Physical and Mental Disability Rights Committee of the American Bar Association in 2000, and a Mary E. Switzer Merit Fellowship in 1995.

Theresia Degener is a Professor of Law, Administration and Organization at the University of Applied Sciences in Bochum, Germany. She serves as an expert on the German Parliament's Commission on Law and Ethics of Modern Medicine, and represents Disabled Peoples' International (an international non-governmental organization) on the United Nations Human Rights Commission and Sub-Commission. In addition to lecturing at a number of German universities, and at the University of California, Berkeley (Boalt Hall School of Law) in 1999/2000, Professor Degener has worked for the UN Center for Human Rights in Geneva and trained people with disabilities all over the world in international human rights. She has published on sexual violence against disabled women, feminist ethics and biotechnology, disabled women and human rights, and is the co-editor of *Human Rights and Disabled Persons* (Dordrecht: M. Nijhoff, 1995). Degener studied law at the Wolfgang Goethe University in Frankfurt, Germany, from which she also received her doctor's degree in law, and earned her LL.M. from Boalt Hall.

Matthew Diller is a Professor of Law at Fordham University in New York City. His articles on issues relating to disability, welfare and social security have appeared in major law journals and in other publications. Diller is also Co-Director of the Louis Stein Center for Law and Ethics, Fordham Law School. Before joining the faculty at Fordham, he served as an attorney in the Civil Appeals and Law Reform Unit of the Legal Aid Society in New York City from 1986 to 1993. At Legal Aid, he litigated class action lawsuits concerning government benefit programs, including social security and public assistance. Diller is a graduate of Harvard College (1981) and Harvard Law School (1985), where he was an editor of *The Harvard Law Review*. He served as law clerk to the Late Judge Walter R. Mansfield of the United States Court of Appeals for the Second Circuit.

Marilyn Golden is a Policy Analyst at DREDF with particular expertise in the areas of transportation, architectural barriers and civil rights advocacy, and serves on the U.S. Architectural and Transportation Barriers Compliance Board, to which she was appointed by the President in 1996. She is a highly lauded ADA trainer and the principal author of DREDF's ADA curriculum, *The ADA, an Implementation Guide* (the "Bluebook"). She served for nine years as Director of Access California, a resource center on architectural accessibility for people with disabilities, and also as Co-Coordinator of the Disabled International Support Effort, which provided material aid and technical assistance to disability organizations in developing countries. Her involvement in international disability rights has continued with trainings in Europe, Africa and Central America, as well as at the UN Fourth World Conference on Women in Beijing, China. Golden attended Brandeis University (Magna Cum Laude and Phi Beta Kappa), and has authored many articles and received a number of awards for her efforts toward of the integration of people with disabilities into all aspects of society.

Aart Hendriks is Commissioner of the Dutch Equal Opportunities Commission (CGB) and secretary of the programme on health law evaluation of the Health Research and Development Council of the Netherlands (ZON). He serves as an Advisory Board member of the Dutch Council of People with Chronic Illnesses and Disabilities, the Foundation for the Tracing of Individuals with Hereditary Hyper-cholesterolaemia, and the Clara Wichmann Instituut (institute for women and law), is a Board member of the Dutch Association of Health Law, and is Secretary of the Board of Directors of the Centre on Housing Rights and Evictions. Hendriks is editor of the *European Journal of Health Law* (The Hague: Kluwer) and the *NJCM-Bulletin/Journal of the Dutch Section of the International Commission of Jurists* (Leiden: NJCM), and a member of the editorial board of *Medicine and Law* (University of Haifa) and *Health and Human Rights* (Boston: Harvard). He has published extensively on issues related to equality/non-discrimination in relation to health, disability and employment. He holds LL.M. and M.Pol.Sc. degrees from Leiden University, and a Ph.D. degree from the University of Amsterdam where his dissertation focused on equal access to employment for people with disabilities.

Arlene Kanter is a Professor in the areas of disability law and policy at the Syracuse University College of Law in the United States, and director of the College of Law's nationally recognized Office of Clinical Legal Education. Prior to joining the law faculty, she served as an attorney on behalf of people with disabilities at the Bazelon Center for Mental Health Law, formerly the Mental Health Law Project, and represented people with mental disabilities before the U.S. Supreme Court, Congress, federal and state courts, and state and local legislatures. Kanter has also lectured at the Hebrew University in Jerusalem, where she taught the school's first comparative clinical course on disability law, and at Charles University in Prague where she presented a series of lectures on advocacy on behalf of people with disabilities. She has published widely in the area of international and comparative disability law and policy, and her most recent publications include "The Right to Asylum for People with Disabilities" (with Kristen Dadey), "The Need for Representation of People with Disabilities in Immigration Proceedings" (with Chris Nugent and C. Blake Chisam), and a series of articles on involuntary outpatient commitment based on her research on Israel's mental health laws.

Arlene B. Mayerson has been the Directing Attorney of DREDF since 1981. One of the nation's leading experts in disability rights law, she has been a key advisor to both Congress and the disability community on the major disability rights legislation of the past two decades, including the ADA and the Handicapped Children's Protection Act. Mayerson has devoted her career exclusively to disability rights practice, representing clients in a wide array of issues. She has provided representation, consultation to counsel, and coordination of amicus briefs on key disability rights cases before the U.S. Supreme Court, and was appointed by the Secretary of the U.S. Department of Education to the Civil Rights Reviewing Authority, responsible for reviewing civil rights decisions of the Department. Mayerson also lectures in disability law at the University of California, Berkeley (Boalt Hall). She has published many articles on disability rights and is the author of a comprehensive three-volume treatise on the ADA: *Americans with Disabilities Act Annotated-Legislative History, Regulations & Commentary* (Deerfield, IL: Clark Boardman Callaghan, 1994), which sets forth the legislative history and regulations for each provision of the ADA.

Gerard Quinn holds the main statutory Chair in Law at the National University of Ireland (Galway Campus), is a member of Ireland's Department of Foreign Affairs Joint/NGO Standing Committee on Human Rights, and a board member of AHEAD (Association for Higher Education Access and Disability, Dublin) and EC-OC (European Children-Our Children, Brussels). He is also a member of the Research Advisory Board of the Landmine Survivors Network (Washington, D.C.), and is academic co-ordinator of a European Commission Network of European Legal Experts on Discrimination Law in the field of Disability. Quinn was recently elected to serve on the Committee of Independent Experts under the European Social Charter (Council of Europe), and has worked with the European Commission on general human rights issues as well as on the preparation of European Union (EU) policy instruments in the field of disability rights. He has published widely on economic, social and cultural rights, on the rights of persons with disabilities, and on the EU and human rights, and recently finished a large research project on disability rights for the Office of the UN High Commission on Human Rights. Professor Quinn holds a Harvard Doctorate in Juridical Science (S.J.D.).

Eric Rosenthal is the founder, and Executive Director since 1993, of Mental Disability Rights International (MDRI), a U.S.-based advocacy organization dedicated to the international recognition and enforcement of the rights of people with mental disabilities. He has trained disability activists, advised governments on legislative reform, and conducted monitoring and evaluation missions in psychiatric institutions, mental retardation facilities, prisons, jails, and orphanages in fourteen countries. Rosenthal is the primary author of four major reports on international disability rights: *Human Rights & Mental Health: Mexico* (2000); *Children in Russia's Institutions: Human Rights and Opportunities for Reform* (1999); *Human Rights and Mental Health: Hungary* (1997); *Human Rights and Mental Health: Uruguay* (1995). His work has been profiled in the Washington Post and in the New York Times Magazine, and he has been interviewed on National Public Radio, ABC News 20/20, CNN International, BBC, UNIVISION, and Voice of America. He has also published op-ed pieces in the New York Times, the Washington Post and the Minneapolis Star-Tribune. Rosenthal graduated from the University of Chicago in 1985 and received his law degree (Magna Cum Laude) from the Georgetown University Law Center in 1992.

David Ruebain heads the department of Education and Disability Law with Levenes Solicitors in the United Kingdom, which specializes in all aspects of public law and human rights law including education law, community care and health law, and disability discrimination law. Ruebain is a trustee of the Disability Discrimination Act Representation and Advice Project, Vice-Chair of the Rights Now Campaign (a national umbrella organization of over 80 individual organizations campaigning for full and enforceable civil rights for disabled people), an editorial board member of *Disability and Society*, a council member of the Alliance for Inclusive Education, Vice-Chair of Disability Equality in Education (a charitable training organization), a member of the Disability Discrimination Act Advisers Group, and an Honorary Legal Advisor to the Independent Panel for Special Education Advice (a national charity providing assistance to parents of children with special educational needs). He also serves in other disability and education-related legal organizations. Ruebain has taught and published extensively on education and disability law, and is co-author of *Notes on the Disability Discrimination Act* (now in its 9th edition) and *Education Law and Practice*.

Lisa Waddington is an Associate Professor in European Union Law at Maastricht University in the Netherlands. She has written and lectured widely and is the author of *Disability, Employment and the European Community* (London: Blackstone,1995) as well as a wide variety of articles on disability policy, European social policy and equality law. She is the Chair of the European Disability Forum's Legal Rights Group (a non-governmental organization representing the interest of 37 million disabled EU citizens and residents), a member of the European Commission Group of Experts on Combating Discrimination on Grounds of Disability, and a member of the Advisory Committee of the Dutch Disability and Chronically Ill Council (an umbrella non-governmental organization in the Netherlands). She completed her undergraduate degree at Birmingham University (UK) and her Ph.D. on European Community disability policy, at the European University Institute in Florence (Italy).

Jane West is a consultant on disability policy in Washington, DC. She has served as staff director of the U.S. Senate Subcommittee on Disability Policy, Senior Policy Analyst on the Presidential Task Force on the HIV Epidemic, and faculty at the Johns Hopkins University and the University of San Francisco. She has edited two books on the ADA and written numerous articles on disability policy. She provides government relations consulting for several national organizations and serves on the Board of the DREDF Development Partnership, the Consortium for Citizens with Disabilities, and the Committee for Education Funding. She earned her Ph.D. From the University of Maryland in Special Education.

Pat Wright has served as Director of Government Affairs for DREDF in Washington, DC since 1979. Widely acknowledged as "the General" who coordinated the campaign to enact the ADA, Wright fought to establish acceptance of disability as a legitimate civil rights cause within the broad civil rights community as well as within traditional disability services organizations. She has been the primary legislative and policy strategist for the disability civil rights community through both Democratic and Republican Administrations, and was a driving force in the campaign to halt the deregulation of Section 504 of the 1973 Rehabilitation Act (the legislative precursor to the ADA). Wright has also worked to secure enactment of the Handicapped Children's Protection Act of 1986, represented disability concerns in a civil rights coalition working for the passage of the Civil Rights Restoration Act of 1987, and fought for groundbreaking amendments to the Fair Housing Act that banned discrimination against people with disabilities by landlords and established accessibility and adaptability principles for multifamily dwellings. Wright has received numerous honors for her contribution to the disability rights movement, including the Presidential Citizen's Medal in 2001. She speaks and consults on disability policy issues internationally.

Silvia Yee is DREDF's first International Law Fellow and is also active in DREDF's domestic national litigation and policy work. She has previously worked with the Health Law Institute at the University of Alberta in Canada, where she published in the areas of Canadian Health Care Standards and the extent of the nursing profession's legal authority. Yee received her LL.B. from the University of Alberta and clerked with the Honorable Justice William Stevenson at the Alberta Court of Appeal.

Table of Cases

Index